IB DIPLOMA PROGRAMME

Theory of Knowledge

Course Companion

Eileen Dombrowski
Lena Rotenberg
Mimi Bick

OXFORD
UNIVERSITY PRESS

IBO

OXFORD
UNIVERSITY PRESS

Great Clarendon Street, Oxford OX2 6DP

Oxford University Press is a department of the University of Oxford.
It furthers the University's objective of excellence in research, scholarship,
and education by publishing worldwide in

Oxford   New York

Auckland   Cape Town   Dar es Salaam   Hong Kong   Karachi
Kuala Lumpur   Madrid   Melbourne   Mexico City   Nairobi
New Delhi   Shanghai   Taipei   Toronto

With offices in

Argentina   Austria   Brazil   Chile   Czech Republic   France   Greece
Guatemala   Hungary   Italy   Japan   Poland   Portugal   Singapore
South Korea   Switzerland   Thailand   Turkey   Ukraine   Vietnam

© Eileen Dombrowski, Lena Rotenberg, Mimi Bick

The moral rights of the authors have been asserted

Database right Oxford University Press (maker)

First published 2007

British Library Cataloguing in Publication Data

Data available

ISBN: 978-019-915122-6

10 9 8 7 6

Printed in Great Britain by Bell & Bain Ltd., Glasgow

Acknowledgments
We are grateful for permission to reprint the following copyright texts:
Extracts from the *Theory of Knowledge Subject Guide*, reprinted by permission of the
International Baccalaureate Organization; Dictionary definition of 'Rainbow' from
Merriam-Webster's Collegiate® Dictionary (11th edition, 2003), copyright © 2003
by Merriam-Webster Inc. (www.Merriam-Webster.com), reprinted by permission of
the publisher; Kofi Annan: from press release SG/SM/6782, 3 November 1998,
reprinted by permission of the United Nations Publications Office; The Dalai Lama
and Alexander Norman: from 'No Magic, No Mystery' in *Ethics for the New Millennium*
(Riverhead, 1999), copyright © 1999 by His Holiness The Dalai Lama, reprinted by
permission of Riverhead Books, an imprint of Penguin Group (USA) Inc, and of The
Wylie Agency, Inc; Arthur Eddington: from *The Philosophy of Physical Science*
(Cambridge University Press, 1949), reprinted by permission of the publishers; A C
Grayling: from *The Meaning of Things: Applying Philosophy to Life* (Phoenix Press, 2002),
reprinted by permission of the publisher, a division of The Orion Publishing
Group; E Y Harburg: from the lyrics for 'Over the Rainbow', music by Harold
Arlen, words by E Y Harburg, copyright © 1938 EMI Feist Catalog Inc, EMI
Catalogue Partnership and EMI United Partnership Ltd. USA Worldwide print
rights controlled by Alfred Publishing Co, Inc, USA, administered in Europe by
Faber Music Ltd, and reproduced with their permission. All rights reserved; Chris
Hedges: from War is a Force that Gives Us Meaning (Public Affairs, 2002),
copyright © Chris Hedges 2002, reprinted by permission of Public Affairs, a
member of the Perseus Books Group; Tim Kirk: figure from *Physics for the IB
Diploma* by Tim Kirk (OUP, 2003), reprinted by permission of Oxford University
Press; George Lakoff: from *Women, Fire and Dangerous Things* (University of Chicago
Press, 1987), copyright © George Lakoff 1987, reprinted by permission of the
publisher; Raymond Lee and Alistair Fraser: from *The Rainbow Bridge* (Pennsylvania
State University Press, 2001), copyright © 2001 by the Pennsylvania State
University, reprinted by permission of the publisher; Denise Levertov: 'Talking to
Grief' from *Poems 1972-1982* (New Directions, 1987) copyright © Denise Levertov

1987, reprinted by permission of New Directions Publishing Corp and Pollinger
Ltd for the proprietor; Louis MacNeice: 'The Sunlight in the Garden' from *Collected
Poems* (Faber, 1979), reprinted by permission of David Higham Associates; Peter
Medawar: from *Pluto's Republic* (OUP, 1982), reprinted by permission of Oxford
University Press; Martha Nussbaum: from 'Non Relative Virtues: An Aristotelian
Approach', first published in *Midwest Studies in Philosophy*, XIII, 32 (1988), reprinted
in M Nussbaum & A Sen (eds.): *The Quality of Life* (Clarendon Press, 1993), including
quote from Gopalan (1992) 'Under Nutrition: Measurement and Implications',
reprinted by permission of the author; T Roszak: from *The Cult of Information: The
Folklore of Computers and the True Art of Thinking* (Lutterworths, 1986), reprinted by
permission of James Clarke & Co Ltd, The Lutterworth Press; Susan Sontag: from
On Photography (Allen Lane 1978/FSG, 1977), copyright © Susan Sontag 1973, 1974,
1977, reprinted by permission of Penguin Books Ltd and Farrar Straus & Giroux,
LLC; Derek Walcott: 'Parades, Parades' from *Sea Grapes* (Jonathan Cape/FSG, 1976),
reprinted by permission of Farrar, Straus & Giroux, LLC; Keith M Woods: 'Take
back the Language. Words tell a story of their own', 20.3.03 from
www.poynter.org, reprinted by permission of The Poynter Institute and Poynter
Online; Virginia Woolf: from *Flush: A Biography* (Hogarth Press/Harcourt, 1933),
copyright © by Harcourt Inc and renewed 1961 by Leonard Woolf, reprinted by
permission of The Society of Authors as the Literary Representative of the Estate
of Virginia Woolf and of Harcourt, Inc .

and to the following for use of images:
p 13 Oxford Cartographers; **pp 22, 48** Bridgeman Art Library/Sebastian Stoskopff
(1596/99-1657): 'The Five Senses, or Summer' 1833 (oil on canvas), Musee de
L'Oeuvre de Notre Dame, Strasbourg, France/Giraudon/The Bridgeman Art Library;
p 51 Edgar Degas (1834-1917): 'In a Cafe, or The Absinthe', c1875-76 (oil on
canvas), The Musee D'Orsay, Paris, France/Giraoudon/The Bridgeman Art Library;
p 209 Emile Prisse d'Avennes (1807-79) (after): Wall tiles from the mihrab of the
Mosque of Cheykhoun, in *Arab Art as Seen Through the Monuments of Cairo in the 7th
Century to the End of the 18th Century*, engraved by Marchand, published in 1877
(colour litho), Private Collection, The Stapleton Collection/The Bridgeman Art
Library; Simone Martini (1284-1344): 'The Annunciation with St Margaret and St
Asano', 1333 (tempera on panel), Galleria degli Uffizi, Florence, Italy/Giraudon/The
Bridgeman Art Library; Pahari School (19th Century): 'Vishnu the Preserver', c1840
(paint on paper), Private Collection/Ann & Bury Peerless Picture Library/The
Bridgeman Art Library; Terracotta Army (Qin Dynasty, 210 BC: Warriors (detail),
Tomb of Qin shi Huang Di, Xianyang, China/The Bridgeman Art Library; **pp 209,
214, 222** Pablo Picasso (1981-1973): 'Guernica', 1937 (oil on canvas), Museo
Nacional Centro de Arte Reina Sofia, Madrid, Spain/The Bridgeman Art Library,
copyright © Succession Picasso/DACS 2006. Oxford University Press has paid DACS'
visual creators for the use of their artistic works. ; **p 29** Creators Syndicate/
Dave Coverley, Speed Bump: 'Black or White' 6.26.02, © 2002 Creators Syndicate,
Inc; **p 100** Speed Bump: 'Information v Nonsense 1.12.98, © 1998 Creators
Syndicate, Inc.; **p 56** Universal Press Syndicate/Bill Watterson: Calvin & Hobbes:
'Fear' 7.12.92, © 1992 Bill Watterson; **p 149** Calvin & Hobbes: 'The Whys' 4.1.88,
© 1988 Bill Watterson; **p 180** Calvin & Hobbes: 'Average Households' 1.8.88, ©
1988 Bill Watterson; **p 103** Wiley Miller: Non Sequitur: 'The Opening and Closing
Ceremony of the Dogma Day Parade' 2.3.98, © 1998 Wiley Miller; All distributed
by Universal Press Syndicate, and reprinted by permission. All rights reserved;
p 106 Knight Features for United Media/Charles M Schulz: Peanuts: 'True or False'
12.9.73, © 1973 United Features Syndicate Inc; **p 108** Bob Thaves: Frank and
Ernest: 'Gullibility' 9.18.97, © 1997 Bob Thaves; **p 138** Frank and Ernest:
'Multiplication Table' 7.27.02, © 2002 Bob Thaves; **p 189** Frank and Ernest: 'Flat
World' 10.13.97, © 1997 Newspaper Enterprise Association, Inc; **p 166** Pat Brady:
Rose is Rose: 'Axioms' 9.13.97, © 1997 United Features Syndicate Inc; **p 176** Dave
Whammond: Reality Check: 'Hawthorne Effect' 9.9.97, © 1997 United Features
Syndicate Inc.; **p 126** Randall Bytwerk/Nazi Propaganda Poster image and front
cover of *Der Ewige Jude* (1937); **p 197** International Institute for Social History/
Mao Zedong poster, IISH Stefan R Landsberger Collection (http://www.iisg.nl/
~landsberger); **p 208** Vancouver International Airport Authority/Bill Reid: 'The
Spirit of Haida Gwaii:The Jade Canoe' 1993/second and final bronze cast, in the
collection of the Vancouver International Airport Authority; **p 252**: Aspect Photo
Library/Mike Wells: 'Starving boy and missionary', Karamoja district, Uganda, April
1980.

We have tried to trace and contact all copyright holders before publication. If
notified the publishers will be pleased to rectify any errors or omissions at the
earliest opportunity.

—Dedication
Eileen, Mimi, and Lena thank Theo, Alberto, and Harvey for their loving support,
without which no book would have been possible.

Mixed Sources
Product group from well-managed
forests and other controlled sources
www.fsc.org Cert no. TT-COC-002769
© 1996 Forest Stewardship Council
FSC

Course Companion definition

The IB Diploma Programme Course Companions are resource materials designed to provide students with extra support through their two-year course of study. These books will help students gain an understanding of what is expected from the study of an IB Diploma Programme subject.

The Course Companions reflect the philosophy and approach of the IB Diploma Programme and present content in a way that illustrates the purpose and aims of the IBO. They encourage a deep understanding of each subject by making connections to wider issues and providing opportunities for critical thinking.

These Course Companions, therefore, may or may not contain all of the curriculum content required in each IB Diploma Programme subject, and so are not designed to be complete and prescriptive textbooks. Each book will try to ensure that areas of curriculum that are unique to the IB or to a new course revision are thoroughly covered. These books mirror the IB philosophy of viewing the curriculum in terms of a whole-course approach; the use of a wide range of resources; international-mindedness; the IB learner profile and the IB Diploma Programme core requirements; theory of knowledge; the extended essay; and creativity, action, service (CAS).

In addition, the Course Companions provide advice and guidance on the specific course assessment requirements and also on academic honesty protocol.

The Course Companions are not designed to be:

- study/revision guides or a one-stop solution for students to pass the subjects
- prescriptive or essential subject textbooks.

IBO Mission Statement

The International Baccalaureate Organization aims to develop inquiring, knowledgable and caring young people who help to create a better and more peaceful world through intercultural understanding and respect.

To this end the IBO works with schools, governments and international organizations to develop challenging programmes of international education and rigorous assessment.

These programmes encourage students across the world to become active, compassionate, and lifelong learners who understand that other people, with their differences, can also be right.

The IB learner profile

The aim of all IB programmes is to develop internationally minded people who, recognizing their common humanity and shared guardianship of the planet, help to create a better and more peaceful world. IB learners strive to be:

Inquirers They develop their natural curiosity. They acquire the skills necessary to conduct inquiry and research and show independence in learning. They actively enjoy learning and this love of learning will be sustained throughout their lives.

Knowledgable They explore concepts, ideas, and issues that have local and global significance. In so doing, they acquire in-depth knowledge and develop understanding across a broad and balanced range of disciplines.

Thinkers They exercise initiative in applying thinking skills critically and creatively to recognize and approach complex problems, and make reasoned, ethical decisions.

Communicators They understand and express ideas and information confidently and creatively in more than one language and in a variety of modes of communication. They work effectively and willingly in collaboration with others.

Principled They act with integrity and honesty, with a strong sense of fairness, justice, and respect for the dignity of the individual, groups, and communities. They take responsibility for their own actions and the consequences that accompany them.

Open-minded They understand and appreciate their own cultures and personal histories, and are open to the perspectives, values, and traditions of other individuals and communities. They are accustomed to seeking and evaluating a range of points of view, and are willing to grow from the experience.

Caring They show empathy, compassion, and respect towards the needs and feelings of others. They have a personal commitment to service, and act to make a positive difference to the lives of others and to the environment.

Risk-takers They approach unfamiliar situations and uncertainty with courage and forethought, and have the independence of spirit to explore new roles, ideas, and strategies. They are brave and articulate in defending their beliefs.

Balanced They understand the importance of intellectual, physical, and emotional balance to achieve personal well-being for themselves and others.

Reflective They give thoughtful consideration to their own learning and experience. They are able to assess and understand their strengths and limitations in order to support their learning and personal development.

A note on academic honesty

It is of vital importance to acknowledge and appropriately credit the owners of information when that information is used in your work. After all, owners of ideas (intellectual property) have property rights. To have an authentic piece of work, it must be based on your individual and original ideas with the work of others fully acknowledged. Therefore, all assignments, written or oral, completed for assessment must use your own language and expression. Where sources are used or referred to, whether in the form of direct quotation or paraphrase, such sources must be appropriately acknowledged.

How do I acknowledge the work of others?

The way that you acknowledge that you have used the ideas of other people is through the use of footnotes and bibliographies.

Footnotes (placed at the bottom of a page) or endnotes (placed at the end of a document) are to be provided when you quote or paraphrase from another document, or closely summarize the information provided in another document. You do not need to provide a footnote for information that is part of a 'body of knowledge'. That is, definitions do not need to be footnoted as they are part of the assumed knowledge.

Bibliographies should include a formal list of the resources that you used in your work. 'Formal' means that you should use one of the several accepted forms of presentation. This usually involves separating the resources that you use into different categories (e.g. books, magazines, newspaper articles, Internet-based resources, CDs and works of art) and providing full information as to how a reader or viewer of your work can find the same information. A bibliography is compulsory in the extended essay.

What constitutes malpractice?

Malpractice is behaviour that results in, or may result in, you or any student gaining an unfair advantage in one or more assessment component. Malpractice includes plagiarism and collusion.

Plagiarism is defined as the representation of the ideas or work of another person as your own. The following are some of the ways to avoid plagiarism:

- Words and ideas of another person used to support one's arguments must be acknowledged.
- Passages that are quoted verbatim must be enclosed within quotation marks and acknowledged.
- CD-ROMs, email messages, web sites on the Internet, and any other electronic media must be treated in the same way as books and journals.
- The sources of all photographs, maps, illustrations, computer programs, data, graphs, audio-visual, and similar material must be acknowledged if they are not your own work.
- Works of art, whether music, film, dance, theatre arts, or visual arts, and where the creative use of a part of a work takes place, must be acknowledged.

Collusion is defined as supporting malpractice by another student. This includes:

- allowing your work to be copied or submitted for assessment by another student
- duplicating work for different assessment components and/or diploma requirements.

Other forms of malpractice include any action that gives you an unfair advantage or affects the results of another student. Examples include, taking unauthorized material into an examination room, misconduct during an examination, and falsifying a CAS record.

Contents

Foreword 6
Meet the authors 7

Chapter 1 Knowing 9

Chapter 2 How do we know? 20
1 Sense perception 21
2 Language 32
3 Emotion 49
4 Reasoning 64
5 Classification 83

Chapter 3 Knowledge and the search for truth 90

Chapter 4 Persuasion and propaganda 115

Chapter 5 Areas of knowledge 130
1 Mathematics 134
2 The natural sciences, human sciences and history 148

3 The natural sciences 152
4 The human sciences 171
5 History 187
6 The arts 205
7 Ethics 221

Chapter 6 Knowledge in the world 241

Chapter 7 Course assessment 266
1 Knowledge issues 269
2 The TOK presentation 276
3 The TOK essay 281

Chapter 8 References 297

Twenty-one thematic links 306

Foreword

Surely theory of knowledge (TOK) is one of the boldest courses ever to figure in any school's curriculum. How can any course deal with all knowledge – and open discussion potentially to any knowledge from any culture in any historical time? The scope is vast.

Offering a book to accompany such a course must be done with humility. It is impossible for any book to "cover" TOK, and to try to do so would be to confine the living exploration of the course ideas that belongs with students and their teachers. In offering this book, we aim not to close the discussion but to open it. We are giving one path through the labyrinth of knowledge issues with appreciative recognition of the many other trails that lie just off to the side, intersecting and beckoning. We would never want to impose a prescriptive textbook with its sense of closure and finality. Instead, we seek to give students a course companion — a supportive guide. We invite students to reflect on their own experiences, to open themselves to experiences and attitudes beyond their own, and to think critically and

creatively. It is for the students themselves, though, to take up the invitation and make the thinking their own within the context of a course guided by their teachers.

This course companion is the combined work of TOK teachers and examiners, with the shared contribution that has been so much a hallmark of this International Baccalaureate course. The seven contributors have all offered specific ideas and broad encouragement, and the three authors have worked together intensively to build on each other's ideas toward a common goal. The fact that the book exists at all is a bit of a miracle, as it was written cooperatively across continents entirely through electronic communication and completed in less than a year. In extensive exchanges of working plans, materials, and critiques, we authors have also shared wry moments and touching ones, and a lot of mutual support. We welcome others reading this book to continue to build this course cooperatively, as has been the tradition, and to supplement what we offer here.

Eileen Dombrowski, Lena Rotenberg and Mimi Bick

Meet the authors

Eileen Dombrowski

While still a university student, Eileen Dombrowski rejected journalism for English literature, drawn by its resonant treatment of eternal themes. After teaching literature at university and in the IB for some years, though, she discovered theory of knowledge and promptly fell in love with it as an ideal home subject for someone who really enjoys ideas. She has taught TOK since 1988, became an assessor in 1990, served as deputy chief assessor between 1997 and 2002, and has been involved in curriculum review and leading TOK workshops. She has taken the enrichment of these IB experiences back home to the role dearest to her – the role of a teacher. Having lived with international students on a small college campus for some 28 years, she has long been part of discussions inside and outside the classroom, multicultural student life, and many CAS activities that involve forms of journalism, service, and activism. Although she has taught at United World Colleges in Italy and Norway, she has been rooted at Lester B Pearson College, the United World College that has given her simultaneously her home as a Canadian on Vancouver Island and an international horizon. With their two children now adult, she and her husband Theo have just retired and are looking toward that horizon with a curiosity that has not been satisfied by their travel so far. Eileen hikes (moderately), kayaks (moderately), skis (moderately), and gains pleasure (extremely) from just watching the waves. She loves laughter and hopes one day for wisdom.

Lena Rotenberg

Lena Rotenberg was born in Brazil, where she lived her first 33 years. Her intellectual path, as she successively focused on different elements of the TOK diagram, has increasingly led her to appreciate the complexity of everyday things. Believing the most challenging endeavor to be to discover the laws of nature, she initially pursued physics and earned an M.S. Partially through her Ph.D. program she taught at Universidade de São Paulo, and was reminded that she missed people. Thus she went to law school to explore the laws of humans—which she considered far more intricate than physics—while teaching at IB School 0353. There, in 1985, Lena fell in love with TOK immediately upon seeing its syllabus, and since 1990 has served as a TOK assessor, workshop facilitator, member of the curriculum review team, deputy chief assessor (1995-2000), and editor of Forum. After completing a M.Ed. in instructional technology at the University of Texas, she concluded that teaching, being a blend of cognitive psychology, language, art, and intuition, is even thornier than law. More recently, Lena co-founded Simplicity Matters Earth Institute, an educational environmental organization, and now believes that changing people's opinions and behaviours is the second most complicated thing anyone can do. The most difficult is to nurture healthy human relationships, which she is learning along with her life partner Harvey and his two teenage daughters in Maryland. To Lin-Chi's "When hungry, eat your rice; when tired, close your eyes" Lena adds, "and laugh and hug as much as possible."

Mimi Bick

Mimi Bick grew up in the city of Montréal where she completed a BA at McGill University. She won a Domus Scholarship to study at Balliol College, Oxford, which allowed her to earn M.Phil and D.Phil degrees in Politics. She spent many happy moments at Holywell Manor, Balliol's graduate residence, in discussion (and on tennis and squash courts amongst other places) with fellow students whose nationalities and cultural backgrounds spanned the globe, and who were conducting research in subjects ranging from computer science to French poetry. On hindsight, this was undoubtedly Mimi's first TOK experience. At the end of the Pinochet régime Mimi moved to Santiago, Chile, and has attentively observed and participated in the many changes that have taken place in democracy since then. After working for fifteen years in IB schools in Santiago where she taught Philosophy and TOK, she is currently employed at the Ministry of Education's Curriculum and Evaluation Unit, from where she hopes to help improve the state educational system. Working with the International Baccalaureate has been professionally and personally rewarding for Mimi, especially as a member of two TOK curriculum review teams, as a workshop leader, and as chief assessor (1999-2005). It has allowed her to learn from TOK educators around the world who, like her, believe in the value of the habits of the mind and heart that underlie TOK, and in their ability to empower young people in their personal lives, as citizens and as agents who will command the future.

Meet the contributors

Vivek Bammi

Vivek Bammi was born close to nature, amidst the tea plantations of Assam in Eastern India, and "learned everything from the close contact with the wild." Later additions to knowledge were sought at Carnegie-Mellon University in Pittsburgh, USA (doctorate in history) and at the University of London (MA in social anthropology). Theory of knowledge is the icing on his inter-disciplinary cake. He has taught TOK for 3 years in Manila and since 1990 teaches TOK in Jakarta. He has been an assessor and senior assessor/team leader since 1988, and was appointed deputy chief assessor in 2006. He has recently published two books combining photographs and text: *Golden Buddhism*, based on travels in Burma, Thailand, and Cambodia; and *Indonesia, a Feast for the Senses*, a celebration of the natural and cultural richness of this incredible archipelago. He subscribes to a motto shared by Assam and Java: 'Lahe, lahe' or 'pelan, pelan' ('slowly, slowly').

Sue Bastian

Sue Bastian, whose service to the IB spans three decades, has been an all round drum-thumper for TOK, "the best educational invention of the 20th century." In June 2005, The IBO's regional office in the US presented her with the Inspiration Award honouring those who were crucial to the IB in its formative stages. She has served as a member of the IBNA Board of Directors, deputy and chief assessor of TOK, chair of the curriculum review team, speaker, writer, and workshop leader. She began her teaching career in 1975 at Makati International School in Manila followed by twelve years at the UN School in New York City. She was President of Teaching Matters from 1994 to 2002, and is now the founder and President of Wisdom Writers, where, fittingly, she is filming a video history of IBNA. "Teaching TOK has always brought out the best in me, and I am grateful. It is wonderful to have a passion of worth."

Charles Freeman

Charles Freeman is a recognized freelance academic author of *Egypt, Greece and Rome, Civilizations of the Ancient Mediterranean* (Oxford University Press, second edition, 2004), *The Closing of the Western Mind* (2002), and several other books about the ancient world. In between terms studying law at Cambridge, he excavated Roman villas, Hellenistic cities and the site of ancient Meroe in the Sudan. He worked for ten years at St Clare's, Oxford, teaching and serving as head of history, director of the Diploma Programme history, and teaching TOK, which entered his life in 1978. As senior assessor of TOK he has regularly attended most grade award meetings in Cardiff since 1990. He has found the camaraderie of the TOK world an immense stimulus to his own academic work in the history of ideas.

Anita Holt

Anita Bjelke Holt was raised in Lima, Peru, of Danish and Bolivian parents. Upon finishing school she went off to study in England, where she ended up teaching and marrying one of the natives. After being head of modern languages for many years, she now works at Markham College, Lima, where she is head of TOK and head of the upper school. She has taught TOK since 1992, became an assessor in 2001, and led several workshops for teachers in South America. In 2005 she was appointed deputy chief assessor of TOK. Her pastimes include going to the theatre, reading (but driving her family mad with "this could be really useful for my TOK classes"), playing squash, walking in the mountains, and cooking (i.e. eating, drinking, and talking).

Julian Kitching

Julian Kitching grew up and was educated in Scotland, and has spent the last twenty years in international education, divided into two spells each in Germany and Ghana. His most satisfying professional experience has been his role in the introduction of the IB Diploma Programme into schools in West Africa, in particular the SOS Hermann Gmeiner International College in the Ghanaian port of Tema, where he is Diploma Programme coordinator and teacher of TOK and biology. Having taught TOK for the last sixteen consecutive years, he hopes that others are able to see the course in terms of Antonio Gramsci's challenge to "live without illusions and without becoming disillusioned." In 2005, he assumed the role of deputy chief assessor for the Africa/Europe/Middle East region.

Susana Leventhal

Susana Leventhal Tachna holds a M.Ed. with specialization in cognitive development from the Instituto Tecnológico y de Estudios Superiores de Monterrey, Mexico (ITESM). At Preparatoria Eugenio Garza Sada, for twenty years she taught English, thinking skills, entrepreneurship, philosophy, human relations, ethics, and TOK, as well as developed curricula and evaluation methods for several of these subjects. Susana facilitatates TOK workshops for IB Latin American regional office and IB North American and Caribbean regional office in Spanish and English, and as a senior assessor has participated in grade award meetings in Cardiff since 2000. Co-author of the book *Aprender cómo Aprender*, at ITESM Susana trains teachers in microteaching and thinking skills, and is now working in the Humanities and Citizenship Development programme (and teaching one TOK class, which she loves doing). She often quotes Amos Bronson Alcott, "The true teacher defends his pupils against his own personal influence."

Manjula Salomon

Dr. Manjula Salomon was born in South India, and has been involved with the IB since 1973. "I'm a Hindu with a Christian and secular education in Britain and the United States, married to a Jew, living in Muslim countries for 25 years—that's my most important TOK training." She taught Applied Philosophy at the University of Madras, TOK at the UN School in New York and Teheran International School, and since 1985 has been part of the TOK team in Jakarta International School, Indonesia. She has served on two TOK curriculum review teams, and also as TOK deputy chief assessor (2000-2005). She has written two ESOL textbooks for Orient Longmans, but mostly she "fills her rice bowl by teaching IB Diploma Programme history, anthropology, and TOK, advising students, and marking papers." She is grateful to the many TOK students and teachers who have lit her learning lamp over the years.

Students of Theory of Knowledge

Many thanks to the students and graduates of Lester B Pearson College of the Pacific who have contributed directly to this book, adding their own voices to TOK discussions to encourage current students to join them. We also have reason to thank all of the students with whom we authors and contributors have shared TOK over many years for the stimulation and sense of purpose they have given us.

1 Knowing

Welcome to theory of knowledge

For many years already, you have lived in the world with your own range of experiences. Already, you believe many things about yourself, the way the world works, and the values that should guide life. But why do you hold these beliefs? And why do others often hold different ones?

Welcome to a journey into thinking which, we hope, will intrigue you. If you bring to it a mind that is alive to questions and open to exploring possible answers, this course has the potential to give you a way of approaching issues of knowledge that will benefit your thinking for the rest of your life.

Theory of knowledge, binding together the classroom education of your Diploma Programme subjects and the experiential education of creativity, action, and service, offers you a chance to reflect with others on the whole of your International Baccalaureate Diploma, its approach to learning and knowing, and its place in your more complete life as a "knower". It offers you a chance to look at how beliefs and knowledge fit together not just for you but for others. Take hold of this chance you've been given. Prepare yourself to think critically but not disrespectfully, to share your thoughts and listen well to others, and to consider with your class group the ways we come to know things in all areas of our lives.

Who's in the centre?

Being "critical" is sometimes interpreted as passing negative judgments. In TOK as in thoughtful public discussion, however, engaging your mind to ask questions does not presuppose rejection of the answers, and being critical does not imply looking only for faults. Examining and evaluating are thoughtful, reflective activities which recognize uncertainties and differing points of view while at the same time appreciating knowledge as an achievement. Examining and evaluating allow us to sift the ideas we have been given in order to affirm the ones with the best claim on our belief, by considering the reasons that support different claims.

Before this course is over, we will invite you to apply critical thinking to how we know anything at all, with particular attention to sense perception, emotion, language, and reasoning. We will ask you to assess what we consider knowledge to be and how we approach finding truth and recognizing deception. We will ask you to examine major areas of knowledge to see their bases, to compare them for a more holistic picture of knowing, and to consider the responsibilities that knowledge may bring in the world. Finally, we will give you support toward demonstrating your TOK skills most effectively for assessment for the course. Questioning and thinking critically, with appreciation of variability and complexity, will carry you through theory of knowledge and, we hope, beyond.

If you are to gain tools in this course for effective critical reflection on the claims of others, however, you need also to develop your awareness of yourself. Our own backgrounds affect how we do the sifting and examining, often without our being aware of their influence—to the point that it may be much easier to question new ideas given to us than to be aware of those we already have and the way that they interact with the new. Let us start, then, with the place where you stand, and your viewpoint on the world.

Who is the "international student"? Isn't it *you*?

Consider for a moment what it means to be an "international student". Does it mean that you come from a particular part of the world, or do not come from a particular part of the world? Or does it mean that you are taking courses in a diploma such as the IB Diploma Programme, which encourages intercultural understanding? Or does it suggest something about your own attitude, your own interest in learning about the viewpoints of others who differ from yourself in any number of ways?

Each one of us has a way of living and a worldview that is familiar to ourselves but possibly strange to someone else. If you live and go to school with others much like yourself, you may not have the incentive to put your own worldview in the context of others. Yet, no less than others from faraway places, you carry a perspective you may wish to try to identify and understand, and to frame with awareness of other cultural possibilities.

Take a few minutes now to write quietly, trying to pick out from your own background features that probably affect what you know, how you know it, and what your attitude is toward knowledge. You may wish to keep your thoughts private for further reflection and expansion during the course. If you are comfortable in sharing some of your "profile" with the rest of your group, however, it could act as an introduction of yourself as a knower.

Tomas Jagelka,
Slovak Republic

Claire Boychuk,
Canada

Personal profile as a knower

1 How old are you? How might your age affect both what you know and your attitude toward gaining knowledge?

2 What is your mother tongue? What other languages do you speak? How might your particular languages affect your knowledge?

3 What sex are you? Does your gender role affect how you see the world and what expectations you have about your knowledge and education?

4 Are you urban or rural? How might living in a city or living in the countryside affect how you have learned and what you know?

5 What is your spiritual worldview? How do you think that your following a particular religion, or not doing so, affects your knowledge?

6 What other aspects of your background belong here? The questions so far have just been guides, opening thoughts to which you can readily add.

Shaterra Redd, USA

Ahmad Sahray, Afghanistan

Clare Ogilvy, New Zealand

Leo Anzagira, Ghana

Mohamed Sehwail, Palestine

Lkhagvajargal Yondonjamts, Mongolia

The students here have completed their own theory of knowledge course. They and their classmates will be adding their "international" voices to your own in discussions throughout the book to contribute an extra perspective or to stir further ideas.

PLEASE DO NOT READ THE BOX BELOW. NOT YET.

First, please make sure you have a sheet of blank paper and a pen or dark pencil. Write your name and nationality clearly at the top of the paper. When your whole class is ready, read and follow the instructions. May your journey begin!

> You have seven minutes in which to draw, as accurately and completely as you can, a map of the world.
>
> Don't waste time telling yourself that you can't. Just do your best and discover what you carry (or don't carry) in your mind as your picture of the world. You will not be marked or otherwise judged on the accuracy of the results.
>
> When you have finished, be prepared to show the results to others in your class.

Your own maps

Look at your own map and the drawings of your classmates. If they are quite different from each other, can you suggest reasons? If they are quite similar to each other, can you suggest reasons? As an international student, with other international students in your class, you show in your drawing some of your own perspective on the world.

- What part of the world is in the centre of your map?
- What parts of the world have you drawn in greatest detail? What parts of the world have you drawn in little detail or even left out?

- The maps on this page were drawn by students from: Japan, Greenland, Italy, Costa Rica, and Canada. Can you match the most likely map with each student?

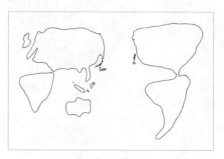
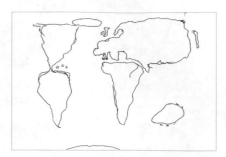

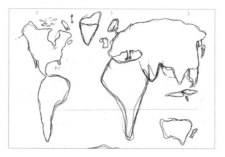
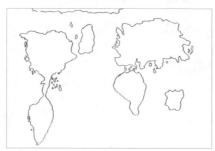

The maps of cartographers

It is understandable that student maps sketched from memory will vary. However, shouldn't the maps made by professional cartographers give a correct version of the world?

There's a problem. It is impossible to make an entirely accurate map of the world. Shrinking the whole world to a page means that so much is left out and so much is made tiny at such a large scale that the map represents the ground at a very, very high level of overall generalization.

It is also impossible to show a sphere on a flat surface without warping and distorting it. Imagine peeling an orange or other globular fruit. The peel removed simply does not lie flat. What solutions do cartographers find to this problem? They use different projections to peel the earth in different ways, each way stretching and warping the "peel" differently. Look at the results on the next page. Which world map is most familiar to you? Does the familiar one seem "right"? Do any of the maps seem "wrong"?

So, what choices have the mapmakers made in each of the versions opposite? Supplement these small images, if you can, with full-sized wall maps or images on the Internet.

- *What is selected to be shown?* Do human beings have a greater interest, in general, in the land or in the water? Do our maps show the bias of our species? Do the maps represent the physical geography of the world or its human political divisions?
- *What is emphasized in each case?* What is in the centre—or both in the centre and at the top? What is artificially enlarged by the particular projection chosen? Compare the other maps to the Peters equal area projection, which chooses to distort shapes in order to preserve correct relative size.

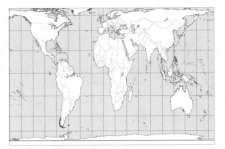
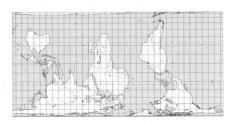

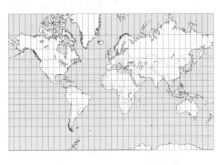

- *Which map features are found in the world and which ones are humanly created?* Do lines of latitude and longitude "really" exist? Do national borders exist in the world if seen from space? Do north, south, east, and west exist in nature? How do north and south differ in this way from east and west? Does north have to be at the top? How do we separate west from east, since all points are west of something and east of something else? What political and economic ideas come with "north" and "south", "east" and "west"?

- *In what context and how are the map images used?* Maps are made, in general, for a practical purpose, whether to show relative position, to navigate, or to represent a connection between the physical world and an idea (population growth, spread of AIDS, incidence of hunger, distribution of the world's languages or religions, and so forth). But how is the map used?

For example, the Mercator map, devised originally by Mercator in Germany in 1569 as a mariner's map, has become almost an icon of Eurocentric thinking because of the ways that it was adopted by colonial powers and spread by them. South America is actually almost double the size of Europe, but Europe appears larger. India is roughly three times the size of Scandinavia, but Scandinavia appears larger. The southern hemisphere is squashed into one third of the map's surface, while the northern hemisphere takes up two thirds. It is a view of Europe top, centre, dominant. Most Europeans would have been, and perhaps still are, unaware of the bias in their familiar image of their world.

What's in the middle when west and east are just relative directions on a spinning globe?

Toi Yam Karyn Wong, China

In Chinese the name for China is "Middle Kingdom." Historically we thought of ourselves in the centre of the world. We didn't actually need anyone else. You can see the idea of "middle" in the first character of the name.

中国

How many continents are there?

Adam Spooner, England

There are seven continents – Antarctica, North America, South America, Europe, Asia, Africa, and Australasia (or Oceania). This is what I learned in school and all continent maps colour these seven differently.

The division of North and South America is just common sense. They have completely different histories as they were colonized differently. The Panama Canal divides them, though it does leave Central America in a rather grey zone.

Europe and Asia are different continents, divided along the Ural Mountains and the Black and Bosphorus Seas. I learned that Istanbul (or Constantinople) was seen historically as the gateway to Asia and the last step of what was known. This vision was tied to the idea of the Roman Empire as the civilized world.

I can see now the inconsistencies in division of continents, in that some have a geographical justification and some have a political or historical justification.

Giorgina Alfonso Rodriguez, Uruguay

North America, Central America, and South America – they are all one continent. They are naturally joined together. The Panama Canal was man-made. If it's more than one, it has to be three if you are dividing geographically, to recognize Central America. How can some Europeans say that it's two continents and call Europe, which is joined to Asia, a continent?

I think that when some people divide America, they are thinking about culture and not the land at all. When they talk about North America, they're really talking only about Canada and the United States.

Does north have to be at the top? What is "up" on a globe in space?

Ruakiri Fairhill, New Zealand

Our Maori map always puts the south at the top because the map is actually a picture of the creation of the islands of New Zealand. The name of the south island, *Te waka-a-Maui*, means "Maui's canoe" and the name of the north island, *Te ika-a-Maui*, means "Maui's fish." In the story, Maui, our god ancestor, had travelled from faraway islands with his four brothers. His canoe hit a rock (Rakiura, Stewart Island) and got stuck. It never moved again and became the south island. There the brothers decided to go fishing, sensing that there was something big under the sea. Maui hooked a giant fish and dragged it to the surface. His brothers jumped on it and killed it with their oars. It turned to stone and became the north island. You can see the fish in the shape of the island. It's a stingray. The map has to put the fish's mouth at the top because that's how Maui pulled it out of the water. Besides, the head has to be at the top because it's the most significant part of the body – it's the first part the sun sees, it's the first part that you see when someone appears over a hill, and it's the part that holds all knowledge. Our picture of the islands as the canoe and the fish is part of our everyday speech in Maori. I live on the north island, and my region is referred to as "the fish's stomach." If I go to the south island, I'd say, "I'm going up to the canoe." And we refer to Wellington as "the fish's mouth."

Some reflections on maps as knowledge, and knowledge as a map

"Oops, I forgot that bit that sticks down in the Far East!" remarked a student from Europe (from which the East is Far) as she examined the map she had just drawn. As we dredge up from memory our pictures of the world and attempt to draw them, we are obviously doing so as individuals with differing past attention to geography, differing memories, and differing drawing skills. At the same time as we are individuals, though, we are also members of our own social groups in our own home spot on the planet. The students who call the Far East "home" are not likely to forget, accidentally, the Southeast Asian peninsula—though they might not remember all the bumps of Europe. Our pictures of the world, and our knowledge of the world, are learned within our own contexts and our own cultural worldviews.

Our maps, often beautiful and enticing, are images not just of our planet but the way that we think about it. As we flatten planet Earth for viewing, we choose a particular projection (with its influence on shape and size), up/down orientation, and centring. We overlay the image with conceptual schemes that cannot be seen in nature: the grid lines, borders, colours, and names. These precious images, which pack so much knowledge onto a small surface, are a product of our history, our technological skill, and our politics. It is strange to think that, aside from recent astronauts, none of us through all of history has ever seen the whole Earth with our own eyes. It is stranger still that the astronauts could not see what is so often most important to us about the surface of our planet—the ideas that we tie to it. We link the Earth with ideas of time (zones), economics (developed/developing world), and culture (for example, the west/the east). We link ourselves to it with ideas of belonging to certain places and not to others. And, sometimes with grim consequences, we link it with ownership (borders and names).

Knowledge is power, it has often been said, and map knowledge stands as a graphic example. As an idea-tool, maps have long been used for controlling empire; map knowledge was once the knowledge of rulers. With a map, colonizing nations have laid claim to territory, dispossessing or killing indigenous people who had no concept of "ownership" of their homeland, no deeds of possession, no flags. With a map, colonial powers carved up their territorial possessions from a distance, imposing borders and ownership that created on the ground a reality with vast consequences. With a map, technologically advanced nations drop bombs on targets without their people ever having to see the faces of the people exploded by the blast. Maps are at the heart of many of the fierce conflicts of the world, representations not only of the land but of all the ideas tied to it; maps represent not what we see but what we believe.

Yet a map is an idea-tool that, in itself, is neutral. Although it can be used for conquest, it can also be used for learning and appreciation. Is it wrong to put ourselves in the centre of our own maps of the world? Surely not. Surely we learn in part by reaching out from our own centres of self and family and society and job and religion and political affiliation, to meet others reaching out from theirs. Imaginatively entering a different vision of the world that is "off centre" or "upside down" according to our own conventions and beliefs can bring an exciting jolt of realization of other possibilities. Familiarity with other centres can refresh us as we come to place

Follow-up activity

Can you find your own part of the world on maps using different projections, such as conical, cylindrical, and single-centred?

our own "centre" within a larger context of many centres, with the new multi-centred version illuminating things we never noticed about our own. "I never knew Africa was so big," commented an African student from a former European colony, realizing for the first time that the map on his classroom wall had exaggerated the size of Europe. "I didn't know that India's map of Kashmir wasn't everyone's," acknowledged a student from India, and painfully recognized at least the existence of alternative political claims.

Does appreciation of others' maps, though, mean that all maps are equally right? Yes, if all we ask the map to do is to represent our worldview or be useful for a practical purpose. However, as soon as we expect the map's picture of the world to correspond to how the world really is, we will have to recognize that some images are better than others—better, as a picture of the world outside our minds. If a version leaves out (or invents) an entire continent, it is faulty. If a version changes sizes of land masses in a way inconsistent with its projection, it is faulty. If a version imposes borders that are not accepted by the world community, it may be harder to declare it faulty but we still have political criteria for doing so. Our picture of the world needs to be checked against the world itself.

Here is one of the major challenges for all of us, human beings building our understanding of ourselves and our world. So many different representations surround us. How can we simultaneously appreciate the variability of worldviews, and at the same time insist on some standard of accurate representation with which to evaluate them all? How do we deal with worldviews that clash? In attempting to understand, evaluate, reject, or reconcile multiple views, we are taking on possibly the most interesting and significant challenge of living in an international, intercultural world.

Gaining our maps

We have numerous sources for our knowledge. Our families, friends, and classmates, books, television, and the Internet, sports coaches, political leaders, religious teachers—these are just some of the influences upon us, giving us information, skills, and views of the world and our place in it. From all the ideas we absorb, combined with all our personal experiences, we shape our own beliefs and our own knowledge.

One of the major influences on almost all of us is the educational systems within which we have been taught. Those systems have been created by people who were entrusted to decide what is most important for us to know and how best we can learn it. Each educational system reflects the values of the community of knowers who authored it, and is embedded in the values of the larger society. Hardly surprisingly, what is taught in schools today is rather different from the curriculum in schools two hundred years ago as knowledge changes and so do the priorities of societies.

Let us have a quick look at the educational systems you were exposed to before you started the Diploma Programme to try to identify not only what subjects you were taught but also some of the cultural values that accompanied your knowledge. The responses to these questions are quite variable from one part of the world to another.

Gaining knowledge in the context of values:

Your school system

1 What was included in your schooling? What subjects were you taught, and why do you think these ones were judged to be the important ones for you to know? Were any of the following included in your schooling: politics, religious instruction, military training, gardening, cooking, or sports?

2 What value seemed to be placed on the subjects in your school? Were some subjects considered to be superior, or to be the ones to which the best students should give their attention? If so, why do you think these subjects were most valued? How was the attitude toward them conveyed?

3 Compared with the six subjects of your Diploma Programme and their balance, did your school system encourage greater or less specialization in particular areas of knowledge?

4 What was considered by the school system to be proper behaviour toward teachers and other figures in authority? To what extent did it include appropriate dress, manner of speaking, and body language? What values lay behind the expectations?

5 What measures were used by school authorities to deal with behaviour considered inappropriate? What attitudes toward social regulation and punishment seem to lie behind these choices?

6 To what extent was your school system competitive to gain good marks? Were good marks important to students or their families? Were they made public and rewarded?

7 To what extent did the values of the teachers, students, and their families seem to be in harmony regarding education in general, subjects studied, marks, and appropriate behaviour?

8 In sum, how would you describe a "good student" in the context of your own school system? The students pictured here are speaking from their personal impressions of their cultural backgrounds and do not claim to be experts on culture or education. How would you, also not as an expert but as a student who has experienced years of education, express your impression of what it is to be a "good student"? What values emerge?

Halimatou Bachir Abdou, Niger

In Niger in rural societies (in the village, for example) most parents don't like to send their children to school because they want them to stay at home and work in the kitchen or on the farm. But in urban areas, people send their children to school because they want them to receive a good, modern education so that they will have more luck to have a job later.

Synnøve Paulen, Norway

In Norway, you are supposed to respect your teachers, even though you talk to them in a familiar way.

At one time teachers were big authorities, but now they are respected instead of maybe feared. A good teacher listens to the students and respects their points of view, even if they are different from his/her own.

The ability to work together is also highly valued, and we do a lot of projects in groups. I would also mention the appreciation of the independent individual, who can gain knowledge and understanding on his/her own.

Rie Endo, Japan

In Japan, the modest and obedient student is "good". Let me describe the behavior of a good student. Sit down on the chair, put the hands on the thigh (male way, female way), look at the teachers' faces and listen to them carefully with shining eyes.

And you should keep quiet during the classes until the teacher asks you a question.

The good student studies very hard after school and gets high scores in the exams. And the good student would hardly complain about anything especially about their teacher or school. They believe in respecting what their teachers say and try hard to understand more from the teachers.

Education in the context of values:

Your IB Diploma Programme

One of the contributors to your current knowledge is, of course, the International Baccalaureate Organization. As an educational organization with consciously developed and articulated goals, it publicly asserts its goal in education on its website and in its publications.

> The International Baccalaureate Organization aims to develop inquiring, knowledgable, and caring young people who help to create a better and more peaceful world through intercultural understanding and respect.

> To this end the IBO works with schools, governments, and international organizations to develop challenging programmes of international education and rigorous assessment. These programmes encourage students across the world to become active, compassionate, and lifelong learners who understand that other people, with their differences, can also be right.

Read the above mission statement closely. The IB, like other educational systems, has choices to make about what is taught and how it is taught. What is the important knowledge that students should gain? Why is it considered important?

We will be discussing "values" in detail later in the TOK course, but for now pick out what seem to you to be the major ideals of the International Baccalaureate. To what extent and in what ways do you think your Diploma Programme subjects and CAS contribute to the fulfilment of these ideals?

Your own growing knowledge

Pause for a moment to think about your changing, growing knowledge. What, for you, is the contribution of formal education? To what extent do others, in school or in other parts of your life, guide your learning? To what extent are you the one who guides the directions in which your knowledge will develop? Are you the one who is responsible for your own knowledge, as well as for the actions that you take based on what you know or don't know? Going a step further, to what extent is ignorance a good excuse for acting or not acting in a certain way? These are questions that will recur later in the TOK course.

International — or internationally minded?

Who is "domestic" and who is "international" is clearly as relative as east and west and as affected by where you are standing yourself. Your recognition of differing perspectives from different geographical centres is only the beginning in TOK and a step toward a larger goal of trying to become, if you choose, not just "international" (as is everyone, from someone else's point of view) but "internationally minded".

Yet where you stand and what perspective you take is not, evidently, simply a matter of geography. When you identified your own personal characteristics within your profile as a knower at the

Farhanaz Majedi, Afghanistan
If you are educated you can help your country develop. You can tell other people the value of education and teach them that girls are equal. When I was 11 my father took us out of Afghanistan because he wanted his daughters to get an education too, but in the refugee camp in Pakistan he couldn't work. To earn money my brothers and I worked at making carpets for 10 or 11 hours a day. We went to school for 3 hours and I studied a lot to learn English and French. That's why I was able to get into a good school when we went back to Afghanistan. There were 50 to 70 students in the class, but we had desks and books.

beginning of this chapter, you were giving a description of your own "centre", and acknowledging the different groups—the different communities of knowers—with whom you share elements of your vision. In growing more aware of your own perspective and understanding it as one possibility among many, you become more internationally minded without needing ever to travel from your home.

Developing in yourself a spirit of inquiry, an openness to views other than your own, and a capacity to think critically and communicate effectively is significant for your place in a world where people live in different ways and hold different beliefs. Being internationally minded may be equally enriching, however, for your place in your own community—including your own TOK class.

Who's in the centre?

In many ways, it is you who are at the centre of your knowledge—you who are shaping your understanding from all that you have experienced directly or been given by others. Yet you are not alone as you stand in one place on the planet and take your view of the world. Others have guided you, and others share many of your views.

In the diagram here of the TOK course, the traditional one in the IB subject guide, the knower(s) in the centre are both singular and plural. Take a close look at the diagram and think of what we have discussed so far. To how many communities of knowers do you consider yourself to belong? At the end of this course, please return to this page and ask yourself the same question.

If there are major figures in your life who have given you knowledge that you value—or have supportively helped you to gain it yourself—you might wish to send them an appreciative thought.

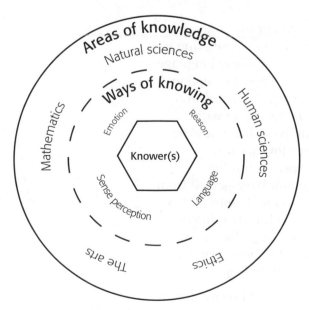

Traditional theory of knowledge diagram.

How do we know?

How have we come to know all that we do at this point in our lives? Regardless of where on the planet we live and regardless of all the influences upon us, we gain our knowledge as human beings in similar ways. In TOK we will look more closely at four particular ways: sense perception, language, emotion, and reasoning. Although these four may not be the only ones, and although we do not use them separately from each other, we will try to disentangle them to give each one some special attention for how it contributes to our knowledge.

Four ways of knowing

How do you know it's raining? Suppose that you hear a spattering start on the roof. You also hear a distant rumble, and as you step outdoors to bring your bicycle under shelter you see a bright flash against the dark sky. Suddenly you feel wet splashes against your skin and very quickly the sodden clinging of your shirt. In this case quite clearly your senses "told" you that it is raining as you felt and recognized sensations. Often we know through **sense perception**: by referring to information gained by using our five senses—sight, sound, smell, touch, and taste. Although our senses have many limitations, as you will see when you do some of the activities in this chapter, they are a "window on the world", because we gain so much knowledge through them. Some would add that they constitute an important part of our makeup as human creators, as chefs and food lovers, swimmers and sports fans would attest. Our senses and the technologies we have invented to extend them play a role in how we gain knowledge in all disciplines.

How else might we know that it is raining? From another room, you hear your father call, "It's starting to rain. Would you please bring in the bicycles and the patio chairs?" In that simple call, using **language**, he reported his own conclusion based on his own sense perception and he set you in motion to act in a particular way. Reporting and giving instructions are only two of the many things we do with language, to the point that it is hard to imagine what life would be like without it—without the conversations, the stories, the information archived for ready access. In one way or another, language is involved in most of the knowledge you have gained from others, from the cultural knowledge passed to you by family to the information you gathered from books, and it significantly influences your other ways of knowing. Like perception, language has its limitations and even deceptions, but is so crucial to knowledge that some consider it essential even to a definition of knowledge.

Just as perception and language both give us ways of knowing that it is raining, so **emotion**, too, can give us knowledge, sometimes so swiftly that we are unaware of the process. The lightning and thunder, perceived through our senses, may provoke fear and an instant search for shelter, in a way similar to the sight of a scorpion prompting us into a protective recoil. Emotion can be a way of knowing that is private and deeply personal, and which affects knowing other human beings. Through emotional sensitivity we may understand that something is wrong with a friend even though she has not said a word, or respond empathically to a photograph on the front page of a newspaper. More than any of the other ways of knowing, emotion has had its flaws emphasized by individuals, historical epochs, and cultures. However, emotions provide us with an avenue to knowing ideas, people, and situations, and modern scientific findings even indicate that emotions are essential to reasoning.[1]

Sometimes placed in opposition to emotion as a way of knowing is **reasoning**, though like the other ways it has its strengths and limitations. When the rain starts, why do you go outdoors to bring in the furniture and bicycles? From past experiences, you have generalized (and so has your father) that objects left out in the rain get wet. Through reasoning, you apply this general understanding to tonight's particular rainfall, and conclude that your own particular bicycle will get wet.

Reasoning comes so naturally to us that we may rarely stop to think about how we arrive at our conclusions. Yet reasoning is the way of knowing that allows us to reach sound conclusions, as well as convince others that our arguments are valid. As we will see, reasoning has limitations and can be applied carelessly, yet it interacts with the other ways to contribute powerfully to our knowledge.

Although for most of this chapter you will be invited to think about these four ways of knowing one at a time, in real life our experience is more complex and messy. Sense perception, language, reason, and emotion rarely operate on their own, and in part it is their combination and the sometimes conflicting information they provide that makes the pursuit of knowledge so fascinating.

Sense perception

Contact with the world around us

In the most general of definitions, sense perception is the physical response of our senses to stimuli. Our senses include hearing, taste, touch, smell, and sight, for which we have sense receptors in different parts of our bodies. We also have internal physical receptors for awareness of our own bodily sensations, such as hunger, pain, and arousal.

Today the study of sense perception is largely the domain of psychology. In a very simplified fashion, the process of sense perception is three-fold. First, our sense receptors are stimulated by sensory information. The brain then translates that sensory information into sensations such as sound, taste, temperature, pressure, smell, or sight, for example. Finally, higher centres in the brain either ignore or recognize the sensations and their meanings, based on neuronal networks of past association and expectation.

We do not sense all the stimuli that we're potentially able to sense. There's too much going on in our environment for us to handle, and we unconsciously ignore many stimuli. Close your eyes and listen carefully to all the sounds around you, for one full minute. Which sounds had you not been aware of, prior to this exercise? Do the same by focusing your attention for

Sense contact with the world: some questions for reflection

A man sits at a table on a terrace overlooking the sea. There is a light breeze in the air and he feels the warmth of the sun on his skin. He is drinking orange juice and savouring the smell of his coffee, as he prepares toast with creamy unsalted butter and homemade strawberry jam. You are at a table nearby, reading your newspaper. When you look up a few minutes later, you notice he isn't moving. You learn that he has had what we could call a "sensory breakdown". First the smoky taste of the coffee disappeared and he could not tell if the liquid in his mouth was hot or cold. Then the cup fell away from his fingers and crashed to the ground, burning him on his leg—though he didn't feel it nor did he hear the sound of the china breaking. Within seconds he was overcome by silence and darkness.

STOSKOPFF, Sébastien, *Summer or the Five Senses*, 1633. Oil on canvas, Musée de l'Oeuvre de Notre Dame, Strasbourg

Reading about the man's "sensory breakdown" often makes people feel uncomfortable or scared. Does it make you feel uncomfortable? If so, why?

Identify how each of the elements in the painting is connected to one or more of our senses. How do you think each of the elements might be appreciated to it fullest?

If you were forced to accept the loss of one of your five senses, which would you choose? Compare with other people's answers. Is there a general agreement over which sense people are willing to give up with the least resistance?

Choose one IB Diploma Programme subject, one sport and one job or profession. In what ways are your senses necessary for learning and becoming an expert in these domains?

one minute respectively on: (a) the smells around you, (b) the feelings your body is experiencing such as the pressure of your hands holding this book, and (c) the images in your environment. Which ones had you not been paying attention to before?

Now let's try to bring all our senses together. Imagine you're walking by yourself in a dark alley, and suddenly become aware that you have company. You feel a surge of adrenaline. What sensations might you have experienced that would have allowed you to recognize danger in that situation?

The word "perception" can be ambiguous, however, because its common use includes our entire understanding of something, including our opinions. We speak of "perceiving" an experience as being desirable or dangerous, even though we are not receiving a value such as "desirable" through our senses. Very often we use the word "perception" as roughly equivalent to our conception of (or idea about) something. It may be difficult in any case to separate physical perception from our whole understanding. However, attempting to restrict our attention to sense perception will be helpful. It will make us more aware of the interplay of perception and conception, and how they come together to shape the pursuit and justification of knowledge.

The painting and the scene described in the "Sense contact with the world" box might illustrate why it is said that our five senses are like threads that connect us to our inner selves and, crucially, to the world outside ourselves. Much of what we learn, remember, believe, and know depends on our senses. Many of us might even wonder to what extent the man who suffered the sensory breakdown is truly alive.

The range of human senses

By definition, every sentient creature has receptors that capture a certain kind and range of stimuli from the external environment. Other animals have senses we do not share: for example, bats and dolphins use sonar for navigation, and homing pigeons and sockeye salmon have deposits of magnetite in their bodies that enable them to detect the Earth's magnetic field to find their way home. Even the senses that we do share with other animals, we possess to different degrees: we don't smell as keenly as wolves, or see as well as eagles.

Knowing how other animals gain sensory information makes us aware of our own specifically human perception of the world, a world that most people assume to exist outside themselves. We are not perceiving the world as it is, in the only way it can be perceived. We are sensing in a human way, and building our knowledge from a limited range of all the sensory possibilities of all the species on this planet.

How does the world appear to be to him? How might he sense you?

With your class, do some research and use your imagination to explore beyond our human range

1 Find out, alone or in a small group, as much as you can about animal senses unlike our own. Some suggestions: the lateral line system of fish for sensing pressure, echolocation and barometric sensitivity of bats, use of tongue by snakes for smell and taste and their sensitivity to vibration, electrosensing of sharks, chemoreceptors on the entire bodies of earthworms, compound eyes of insects.[2]

2 Drawing on the information you gained about other species, choose any one and be prepared to enter imaginatively into the sensory world it

inhabits. Without revealing your choice to others in your group, take 15 to 20 minutes to write a description of your classroom as if you are this animal. (Imagine that your classroom is underwater if necessary!) When finished, volunteer to read your description if you feel comfortable doing so. While someone else is reading a description, take note of the number of times the description involves each of the senses. At the end, try to guess what animal's sensory world is being described.

These activities encourage awareness that we are at the centre of our own knowledge not only as people with different experiences and cultural backgrounds, but even more basically, all together as a species. We use perception as a way of knowing with all the strengths and restrictions specific to human beings.

Not only are our sense receptors and sensations particularly human, but our interpretation of sensations is likewise dependent on our brains. It seems to us, as we see the pink roses or taste the sweet honey, that the pinkness and sweetness are in the roses and honey rather than in their effect upon us. Yet our conscious experiences of honey are the product of the electrical and chemical organization of

Observe the descriptions of smells and textures in this extract from Virginia Woolf's *Flush: A Biography* (1933).[3] Often described as a biography of Elizabeth Barrett Browning from the point of view of her dog, some may think it is in fact the biography of this spaniel himself.

...it was in the world of smell that Flush mostly lived. Love was chiefly smell; form and colour were smell; music and architecture, law, politics and science were smell. To him religion itself was smell...Flush wandered off into the streets of Florence to enjoy the rapture of smell. He threaded his path through main streets and back streets, through squares and alleys, by smell. He nosed his way from smell to smell; the rough, the smooth, the dark, the golden. He went in and out, up and down, where they beat brass, where they bake bread, where the women sit combing their hair, where the bird-cages are piled high on the causeway, where the wine spills itself in dark red stains on the pavement, where leather smells and harness and garlic, where cloth is beaten, where vine leaves tremble, where men sit and drink and spit and dice—he ran in and out, always with his nose to the ground, drinking in the essence; or with his nose in the air vibrating with the aroma. He slept in this hot patch of sun—how sun made the stone reek! He sought that tunnel of shade—how acid shade made the stone smell! He devoured whole bunches of ripe grapes largely because of their purple smell; he chewed and spat out whatever tough relic of goat or macaroni the Italian housewife had thrown from the balcony—goat and macaroni were raucous smells, crimson smells. He followed the swooning sweetness of incense into the violet intricacies of dark cathedrals; and, sniffing, tried to lap the gold on the window-stained tomb. Nor was his sense of touch much less acute. He knew Florence in its marmoreal smoothness and in its gritty and cobbled roughness. Hoary folds of drapery, smooth fingers and feet of stone received the lick of his tongue, the quiver of his shivering snout. Upon the infinitely sensitive pads of his feet he took the clear stamp of proud Latin inscriptions. In short, he knew Florence as no human being has ever known it; as Ruskin never knew it or George Eliot either. He knew it as only the dumb know. Not a single one of his myriad sensations ever submitted itself to the deformity of words.

our brains. "Our conscious world," declares one biopsychologist, "is a grand illusion!"[4]

The table at the top of the following page summarizes how we translate external stimuli into sensations, and how we might describe them.

Some technological extensions

Technology gives us access to knowledge of the world beyond that which our senses allow us. Instruments such as telescopes and microscopes extend our senses by allowing us to see distant and small objects that reflect visible light. More recent technologies enable us to go beyond the range of what we can sense naturally,

Human sense perception			
Stimuli	Sense receptors	Sensation	Response (example of meaning attributed)
Electromagnetic energy (EM) between approximately 400 nm and 700 nm	Eyes, retina	Light and colour EM radiation shining on an object results in visual perception.	"That's my cat."
Vibrations or waves with a frequency between 20 and 20,000 Hz	Ear, auditory nerve	Sound The presence of certain frequencies results in auditory perception.	"That's our national anthem they're playing."
Odour molecules	Nose, olfactory receptor neurons	Smell The presence of a certain combination of molecules results in the perception of smell.	"Freshly baked oatmeal cookies!"
Chemical composition	Mouth, taste buds, chemoreceptor cells	Sweet, salty, sour, and bitter The presence of a certain composition results in taste.	"This dark chocolate is bittersweet."
Pressure, temperature	Skin, nerve endings	Hot, cold, textures, pressure, pain These stimuli result in touch.	"The coffee is very hot."

vastly extending the range of phenomena we can perceive. Consider the devices listed below, and the things they enable us to detect. On which of our five senses do they rely to enable us to use them? How many other technological extensions can you add to this table?

An interesting question, to be explored when we discuss the natural sciences, is how we can know that we are detecting, through these devices, what we think we are detecting. Our awareness of the limitations of human sense perception has acted as a spur toward trying to overcome them. Bats have a natural sonar. Many animals can see at night. Not so endowed, human beings have compensated by developing knowledge.

Technological extensions		
Device	What can be detected	Relies on which sense?
Night-sight detectors	Infrared radiation	Vision
Geiger counters	Radiation (alpha, beta, gamma)	Sound, vision
X-ray machines	X-rays	
Video cameras	Processes too fast or too slow for our eyes to perceive	
Radio telescopes	Radio waves	
Microphones	Sounds at very low volume	
Ultrasound devices	Sounds at very high frequencies	
Sonar equipment	Sounds at very low frequencies	
Smoke detectors	Tiny smoke particles produced during burning	
Litmus paper	Acidity	
Sensitive scales	Very small weights	
Compasses, magnetometers	Magnetic fields	
Electrometers	Electric fields	
Thermometers	Temperatures beyond the range humans can survive in	
Ammeters	Electric currents	

Individual variability of human senses

Sense perception varies not just from species to species, but also from person to person within our species. Some people suffer from a neurological condition called synesthesia, and can "smell" colours and "feel" tastes. Some people, such as acclaimed wine tasters and perfume makers, also have extraordinary capabilities to sense certain things. The story of Cristina Frías (see box) illustrates how other senses can be enhanced to compensate for one that is lacking.

Explore the following questions:

1   How can you tell if your ability to perceive is in the "normal" range? How is that norm defined?

2   How do you know that what you call "red" is what your classmate calls "red"? Assume that neither of you is colour blind.

3   Recall how, as a child, you learned the names of colours and tastes. If you and your classmate are not colour blind, does it really matter if you use the word "red" for slightly different sensations?

4   If you are interested, do some research on the language wine tasters use to describe different wines. How can you come to understand what they mean by those terms?

5   Does it seem to you that you perceive things other people cannot, such as details of plant leaves or insects, details of automobiles, or subtle elements of football play? Can others perceive things you cannot? How would you explain the differences? Can these be changed, say if you took an interest in a field that's currently not important to you?

Sensory information and interpretation

Taking in information through our senses is only part of sense perception, however. That information travels to our brain, which makes sense of the stimuli. Even when we are not consciously aware of interpreting our perceptions, our brains are actively engaged in doing so.

Look at the pictures on the right and first ask yourself the question "what do I see?" Once you have answered, ask yourself what is "really there" in the image.

Now, read the text below. Can you read it? Is it English?

I cdnoult blveiee taht I cluod aulaclty uesdnatnrd waht I was rdanieg. The phaonmneal pweor of the hmuan mnid! Aoccdrnig to a rscheearch at Cmabrigde Uinervitisy, it deosn't mttaer in waht oredr the ltteers in a wrod are, the olny iprmoatnt tihng is taht the frist and lsat ltteer be in the rghit pclae. The rset can be a taotl mses and you can sitll raed it wouthit a porbelm. Tihs is bcuseae the huamn mnid deos not raed ervey lteter by istlef, but the wrod as a wlohe. Amzanig huh? Yaeh and I awlyas thought slpeling was ipmorantt.

Our brains translate stimuli into sensations such as images, temperature, colours, and sounds, which are meaningless without a further step. Imagine that you didn't know English. Do you think you'd have been able to understand any part of the text above?

Cristina Frías worked as counsellor in a school in Santiago, Chile, attended by about 1800 students. Generations of alumni remember her well: she had a beautiful Labrador guide dog – clearly the only canine on the school premises and, rain or shine, Cristina walked to and from school to her house in the neighbourhood. But first and foremost Cristina is renowned to generations of teachers and students because despite being blind since childhood, she had an uncanny ability to identify individual people. She would cheerfully call out, "Good morning, so-and-so!" even if one tried to pass unnoticed. When asked how she accomplished what seemed to many of us to be quite a feat, she said she recognized individuals by how we walked up stairs and down corridors, by our unique odours and the ways we knocked (or didn't!) on her office door when it was shut.

The text can be understood by native English speakers because repeated encounters with the correctly spelled words generated neuronal networks in their brains. Stimuli are not being processed by your brain as if it were a blank slate. Rather, the resulting sensations are being integrated, compared, and contrasted with everything you've perceived before. This kind of seemingly simple and involuntary filling in of missing information to form a recognizable pattern or interpretation was what generated the lines and figures in the examples above.

According to the Gestalt theory of psychology, we tend to perceive objects visually as meaningful patterns or groups, rather than as collections of separate parts. When you look at your teacher, you recognize her face immediately without being aware of all its separate components. If your recollection of the first picture above is a square with concentric circles on each angle, you've followed the principles of Gestalt. The picture is actually constituted of four groups of four concentric 270 degree arcs, placed at 90 degrees to each other. There is no square there, and there are no circles there. We tend to simplify visual information, grouping it in patterns that are easier to process. It works quite well for us, except that sometimes we tend to recall what's not there.

Mirages and optical illusions, too, bring to our attention how quickly and unconsciously we interpret, and how easily our senses can be fooled. If you are interested in exploring optical illusions, many are available in books or on websites, circulated, like the misspelled sentence above, so widely that their original source becomes lost. Their popularity, like the popularity of magic shows, suggests that we often enjoy being tricked when we have consented to be so.

The fact that our brains interpret new stimuli based on past experiences is critical to our being able to use perception as a way of knowing. As you approach the door of your house, you recognize it, even if it is standing open at an unusual angle, one at which it has never exactly stood before. As you approach a door you have never seen before, you do not stop in confusion, but open it and go in. You have associated and grouped your experiences of doors of the past: you have learned. If we perceived every new sensation as a unique experience, without any associations from the past, we would not be able to act in the world, and probably not survive in it either.

We expect perception to provide quick recognition and to fill the gaps. As your friend passes quickly in the distance, you recognize him with very little sensory information: you have noted instantly the characteristic way of walking, caught a quick flash of a familiar coat, or heard his laugh. As your friend calls you on a telephone with a poor connection, you can still understand (up to a point) what she is saying, despite words being cut out by static or seconds of silence. In 2005, *New Scientist* published an article about Esref Armagan, a man who has never been able to see, yet who can paint sophisticated pictures that all can recognize. This suggests that we interpret stimuli and create mental images in very complex ways.[5]

Perception completely free of interpretation may appear to be an ideal as we gain our knowledge, but it is humanly impossible.

Moreover, is it truly an ideal? This question will recur in the TOK course as we consider the interaction of different ways of knowing, the creation of different areas of knowledge and, in all areas of knowledge, the interplay between the eye and the mind—between our perceptions and our conceptions.

Perception and selection

What we perceive out of all the "sense noise" of the environment depends on a host of factors about the object of perception, the person who is perceiving, and the context in which the perception is taking place. Many factors influence what we perceive and remember: out of all possible sense observations that we might make, we catch only a few, and out of all that we might remember, we recall even fewer. Perception is a selective process.

To give some attention to your own process of perception, try one or two class exercises, followed by discussion.

Group exercises

Perception in the present

Choose in advance someone to prepare an object for observation. It could be an object with considerable detail found anywhere in the school or at home, or it could be an object made by the appointed person. All members of the group should sit in a circle, eyes closed, while the person places the object in the centre. When told to do so, everyone should open their eyes, observe the object, and then make a record of their perceptions on a sheet of paper either in words or in drawing. When everyone is ready, place your papers around the object in the centre so that all of you can see all the different records.

- How can you check your own record to determine whether it is accurate?
- In what ways do your different records of perception vary, and why? Pin down as many reasons as you can.
- Is it possible to separate sense perception entirely from interpretation in the records that you have made?
- What are the recording methods used by different students? Is any method particularly effective, in the judgment of your group?
- If all the different records by all members of your group are combined, do you then have a better record of the object? Why or why not? If all are combined, is the record complete?

Perception in the past

Choose together something within your school that all students in the class could have had access to within the past day or two, even if they did not give it close attention. Choose something with abundant detail that could have been observed. It could be, for example, a school notice board or web page that regularly updates notices, or a school play, dance, or sports event.

- Impose a time limit of roughly 5 minutes, in which everyone is to write down, as swiftly as possible, as many observations as possible made with the senses. What were all the notices on the board? Or what were the key observations of the sports event?
- Compare your lists and descriptions. What influenced what each of you noticed and remembered?

- In spite of personal variability, are some observations simply wrong? How do you know?
- If your records are combined, do you have a better record? If your answer to this question is yes, explain what you mean by "a better record".

"Seeing," we often hear, "is believing." We tend to be convinced by our own first-hand observations (though perhaps with more awareness of possible selection or error if we have reflected on the limitations and interpretations of the senses). Outside a court of law, eyewitness reporting similarly carries a stamp of credibility. "I know someone who was actually there, and he told me…" However, even when their senses are functioning perfectly well, and even with the strongest of intentions to tell the truth, witnesses may vary considerably in their accounts of an event. Indeed, all may tell the truth, and still not give the same account because of all the factors which influenced what they selected, consciously or unconsciously.

Some striking stories are told of expectation as a particularly strong influence upon perception. A group of medical students, told to listen closely to the opening and closing sounds of a patient's heart valve, succeeded in hearing it. Their instructor then revealed that their stethoscopes were stuffed with cotton wool and inoperative. Their lesson was not on the valve of the heart, but on the need to be on guard against imagining hearing what they expected to hear, and against reporting what they thought the rest of the group heard and the instructor expected them to hear. This story may ring true to any student doing a lab who is helped considerably by knowing in advance what the results are supposed to be. It may also sound familiar to anyone knowing the story of the emperor's new clothes.

A similar account is made of the explorer Columbus, setting out from Spain in 1492, and expecting to encounter the humanoid monsters who were believed to live beyond the limits of the known world. The Native Americans he actually met clearly did not fit his expectations, so he gave their appearance considerable attention in his records. Yet he persisted in his inquiries about humanoid monsters, and recorded reports that seemed to fit, for example descriptions of human beings with tails. "The tales to which Columbus paid attention, and the manner in which he interpreted them, undoubtedly reflected both his expectations and his hopes. The poor communication between Columbus and the Indians…gave him considerable leeway in imposing his own meanings on the Indians' stories."[6] In listening for stories of monsters and even seeking them out, Columbus was not particularly foolish. He was merely responding in context of the beliefs of his culture and historical time.

What we perceive, ultimately, is much affected not just by what is there but by who were are, biologically, personally, and culturally. Perhaps, metaphorically, the zebra will always tend to see in black and white and the elephant will always tend to see in grey. Who, after all, is doing the perceiving? Who, once again, is in the centre?

Cultural conceptions of the cow

Shobha Lalwani, Barbados

As a Hindu, I've grown up seeing the cow as a mother. A cow gives us milk to nourish the population, and holds an honoured place in society. You would never do anything to hurt a cow any more than you would hurt your mother. If you see a cow roaming the streets alone, you wouldn't honk your horn or overtake it but drive behind it and be respectful. I wouldn't eat beef or any other meat either. I'm completely vegetarian.

Mading Ayuen Angeth, Sudan

The Dinka nation holds cows as an essential part of our daily life. They provide us with hides, leather, meat, and milk. A Dinka may wonder why Hindus regard cows as sacred animals that cannot be slaughtered. "Why would they keep cattle they wouldn't kill for meat? They obviously don't recognize the significance of cows!" A modern Sudanese living in a city, however, would think that "it is just a waste of time to spend so much time chasing after the beast day and night".

Christy Drever, Alberta, Canada

When I see a cow, I see meat first thing but I also immediately recognize several breeds. Some people think that Angus meat is the best, but others prefer Charolais. I would never become vegetarian because that would be a slap in the face of my family. Cows are our staple food and our income, but to me they also mean home and a whole lifestyle. We have about 1,000 cows of several breeds, and for me the cattle drives and calving are just part of normal life. I've sometimes come home from school to find a calf in our bathtub because if they're born when the temperature is −20 °C, they'll freeze if they're not put in a warm bath. It's amazing that people don't know how to chase cows. I thought it was a natural thing.

Timothy Hall, Yukon, Canada

At home, we consider beef a lower quality meat. Wild meat like caribou or moose is much higher quality. It's leaner. It's also got a more authentic feel because you didn't buy it in the store in a packet but you've earned it. You've camped for days and walked around in the mountains, and you've skinned it, cut it up, and packed it out yourself. I don't enjoy seeing an animal die, but hunting season is a special time with my Dad and my brothers, hiking in the mountains.

Tanaka Lesedi Mhambi, Zimbabwe

In traditional Shona culture, cows were often a measure of wealth. It was common for cows to be used as payment of the bride price. Cows were sometimes dedicated to ancestors, in which case they would not be killed. Cows are used for their milk and meat, and oxen are usually used to draw carts or plough the fields.

Alvaro Ballarin Cabrera, Spain

We have a great tradition of bullfighting and the running of the bulls. The bull is a symbol of strength and power, so a symbol of Spain. The Iberian Peninsula even looks like the hide of a bull. Along the roads, you see a lot of giant cut-outs of bulls, but that's just advertising for a kind of wine.

Perception, conception, and the influence of culture

Do all of the students pictured here perceive cows and bulls in a similar way? Yes, they all use their senses and believe they do so within the normal range. Their sense perceptions of the animals are similar, but their conceptions—shaped by prior learning including cultural practices and beliefs—differ considerably.

Likewise, a dog might be conceived as a beloved pet to be treated as a member of the family, a guard dog or a sled dog to be treated as a working animal, an unclean animal to be kept out of a Muslim home, a sign in the Chinese zodiac with a story behind it, or an ingredient in a delicious dish that your mother makes.

What cultural attitude do we take, more broadly, to other living things? Should the life of an animal be given any of the same respect that is commonly attributed to human life in ethical discussion? A Canadian IB graduate, Carla Brown, tells of living in accommodation shared with three other students from different cultures. One of her roommates was about to step on a spider that had invaded their room when another roommate screamed and insisted on not killing it. "As a Buddhist, she felt that killing a creature was a terrible thing to do. She picked up a cup, gently swept the spider into it, and released it outside. And so it continued for the rest of our time together. Angela would spot an insect and Palm would busily scoop it up and set it free."

If you are interested in learning more about cultural perspectives on animals, you might start by investigating the lion or the spider. Attitudes toward animals can highlight the way in which we stand in the centre of our knowledge, with others from our cultural group, even in the most everyday of our perceptions. At the same time, the attitudes we adopt toward other creatures can lead to much more complex issues, such as the nature of human responsibility toward other living things and the environment. We will return to ethical ideas of responsibility in a later chapter.

The enigma of sense perception

Though scientists know more about our senses now than at any time in the past, human perception continues to be something of an enigma. It is fascinating that as humans we convert physical stimuli in the form of electromagnetic or other kinds of energy into meaningful objects and events. You hear not just noise, but the song you danced to the night you first fell in love; you see not just the sensation of light, colour, and shade, but your father who is waving to you as you step onto the station platform and into his familiar embrace.

The world is not as we sense it, but we do not know how it "really is". As we learn more about our own brains and as we see deep into the subatomic world with senses extended by technology, we gain further understanding that tells us, in some ways, how little we still know. Indeed, some philosophers have argued that we cannot know that the world even exists outside ourselves at all, as all we know is our sense impressions of it, and not the world itself. How we deal with this questioning of sense perception depends upon our goals in knowing.

As we will return to examine in more detail, different areas of our knowledge use perception in different ways. But look briefly ahead now, to consider the following questions. Please realize that attempting to answer any one of them in detail could require a lifetime of discussion!

- The sciences use perception in gaining knowledge, gathering observations with great care in order to converge in a common understanding of what the world (assuming that it exists outside our sense information of it) is really like. How does science seek to overcome individual or group variability in pursuit of truth?

Follow-up summary

You might want to compare the factors you and your classmates identified as affecting perception with the following list.

- *Characteristics of the object or incident under observation*: size, colour, shape, loudness, composition, distance away, familiarity or unusualness, length of time it can be seen or heard.

- *Characteristics of the observing conditions or context*: angle of observation, frequency of observation, quality of light, amount of background noise or other distractions, reactions of others drawing attention to or shying away from the object or incident.

- *Characteristics of the observer*: normality of the person's senses at the time, person's emotions, degree of interest in what is being observed, expectations, background knowledge.

- The arts use perception as a source for their more divergent work. How do the arts (literature, for instance, or music) use individual or group variability of perception as a strength?

Perception does not function by itself as a way of knowing, but is intertwined with language, emotion, and reasoning. In each of the areas above—the sciences and the arts—what do you consider at this point to be the particular balance and blend of the four ways of knowing?

Language

Like sense perception, language is a fascinating study in itself. In TOK, we give our attention to some of its particularly intriguing characteristics in considering it as a way of knowing. Before we do so, though, please gather some of the ideas you already have on this topic.

- What would you say, right from the outset, is the role of language in knowing? How does it influence what we know and how we know it?

Symbolic representation

No matter where we go in the world, people possess the amazing ability to make noises to each other with their mouths and convey this thing we call meaning. In many places, they also make marks on paper or other surfaces and expect others to be able to understand meaning from the marks. This capacity for language is a human characteristic, with children everywhere learning the language passed on to them by their own speech community, joining not just in mouth noise and marks on paper but also in communication. Language is so much part of our lives that its power can escape us: many of us may never wonder how language serves to give us knowledge and affect our understanding of the world and ourselves.

Much of the power of language is rooted in its symbolic nature, the use of sounds to stand for things or ideas with which they have no necessary connection, within a grammatical system that enables the symbols to be combined to connect ideas. How exactly language creates meaning eludes full understanding, though different theories suggest different ways: through the way our symbols refer to things and ideas, through the way they stir associations of ideas, or through the way they create the stimulus and response of language behaviour.[7] Central, though, to all forms of symbolism is the use of one thing (an object, an image, a sound, a word, for example) to stand for something else.

How is this connection made? Some visual images may stand for very specific ideas and seem, to those familiar with them, quite clear and self-evident: the image of the man or woman on the door of the public toilet indicates who is expected to use the facilities; a road sign that pictures falling rocks indicates a form of danger. Even in such cases where the sign uses a picture, though, we are already removed from a self-evident or necessary connection between the picture and what it refers to. Placing an image of a woman on a door does not communicate anything in itself; all we have is a door with something on it that we interpret as a picture of a woman. It may be no more than a decorated door. The meaning comes from the connection we have learned between that image and a particular cultural practice of indicating toilets and separating the sexes in their toilet usage.

The sign for falling rock, even though the picture shows the tumbling objects, possibly demands even more background familiarity. Those of us familiar with road signs read the shapes as rocks and a slope, the static image as motion, the triangular shape of the sign as a warning, and the specific warning as applying to driving conditions on a road. The sign exists within a system of road signs agreed on so that we do not actually have to decipher its meaning; we learn it. The relationship is a matter of convention—of agreed, accepted connection.

Symbolic representation

1   Think now of the variety of different kinds of connections between symbols and things symbolized that surround us as we communicate daily and observe communication around us. What distinctions would you draw between elements in the following list?

   a   an animal danger sign, such as the flash of a deer's tail or the cry of a bird

   b   a human danger sign, such as the warning for falling rocks

   c   the word "danger"

   A distinction is sometimes drawn between signs and symbols: those which are genetically inherited as a characteristic of the species, fixed in their meaning, and anchored in the immediate place and time are called "signs" (seemingly almost all animal communication) while those which are created through convention are called "symbols". Human signs, invented and accepted by convention, are a subcategory of symbols. (In other usage, the way language works symbolically to create meaning is analysed as a system of signs in relationship with the objects or ideas to which they refer.)

2   What is the difference, in your view, between your sense perception of the bird we call a dove, an image of the dove with an olive branch in its beak, and the word "dove"? What characteristics of language do you note, in this context, as you read the sentence "He dove into the water"?

3   Consider these symbols associated with different religions or worldviews. How many of them are familiar to you? Is any of them significant to you in the context of your own

community? Could anyone outside your community, looking up or being told the meaning of the symbol, understand it as you do? If not, why not?

4   What does a flag symbolize? If, as we have said, the relationship between the flag and what it refers to is a matter of convention, which could easily be otherwise, why does waving a flag—or burning it—reflect and generate passion? In what ways is the action itself symbolic? Can you think of other examples of symbolic actions?

When the sign is not pictorial the connection becomes even more obviously a learned one. There is no necessary link between the tree of our sense perception and the word "tree", any more than between it and the word "arbre" in French, or any other sound we might generate. If we called that experience of sense perception a

It doesn't translate #1: influence of geography

As we look over the many different languages of the world, our attention may be drawn less to the similarities in the way all human beings use symbolic systems than to the differences. With words in one language not equating with words in another, the gulf at first may seem enormous.

Yet is it really very surprising that languages of the far north, with their vast horizon without a tree in sight, will not have words for mangoes and monkeys? Is it surprising that languages of the tropics will not abound in fine distinctions in snow conditions or types of bears? Such variations do not indicate that different groups of people use symbolism differently or are confined in their thought to a mango-free world; they do suggest that different groups open their eyes on very different geographical conditions.

The translation gulf grows with the effects of geography on the way people live in the world—their sources of food and shelter, for example, and all that follows in their cultures. A language may liken the ages of women to the stages of ripeness of a yam,

Mohamed Shakir, Maldives
In Dhivehi, which we speak in the Maldives, we have many words for coconuts or the coconut tree. There's a word for the coconut palm tree itself and another for its edible tip. There are several words for the stages of ripeness of the coconut, and others for the leaves, trunk, and roots. I think that's because we use the tree in so many different ways for food, building materials, fuel, or decoration.

or divide its society into eagle or wolf clans, since the natural environment influences particular categories and images. Yet, as long as we are willing to use many words in one language to translate one word in another, we possibly face a smaller gap in language than in our geographical and cultural experience. "Translation is always a shift," says writer and translator Umberto Eco, "not between two languages but between two cultures."[8]

"gooble" or a "fingfang" we would still communicate just as well as long as everyone in our speech community had learned the same convention. Unlike systematized road signs, though, very few words of our language have gained their link through any group meeting to decide the reference. No matter how the words came into the language, though, the conventional meaning is the usage we start to learn as babies when we babble our first sounds.

This capacity to move into symbolism, using our sounds meaningfully, opens to us as human beings vast possibilities for thinking and communicating: we can think and talk in abstractions removed from our immediate sense experiences; we can speak not just of what is here before us but of what has been, will be, might be, or could be only in the imagination. We are able to connect our own lives with the lives of others in our language community, giving words to categories of experiences that we seem to share and allowing us to create meaning socially. Words group the sensations that we associate in the neuronal networks of our sense perception—or possibly give us a grouping that influences our perception of them. This capacity for symbolism to group and classify our experiences, with its impact on thought and culture, is a topic to which we will return after considering all four ways of knowing, for it profoundly affects what and how we know.

Much of what is involved in human relationships, projects, and endeavours requires verbal and written language. But are there circumstances when words aren't enough, when gestures or other kinds of expression are necessary to get something done? With a classmate or friend, in pairs, try these exercises to consider this question.

Language and "body language": alternative or complementary?

1   For this exercise both partners need to be wearing shoes with laces. Imagine that you have been asked to help write a manual on practical matters and have been assigned the task of submitting the instructions for people who have never before tied shoe-laces (they have always used sandals or have gone barefoot).

Independently, both you and your partner should take up to 10 minutes to write the clearest instructions possible. One of you should then read out loud, step by step, your instructions while the other partner tries to carry them out. There is only one rule: **hands off!** Instructions must be verbal; you are NOT allowed to provide any help through gestures or body language. And definitely no touching the laces! Switch roles when the task is achieved (or someone gives up).

2   On a sheet of paper draw a series of lines to make a fairly simple geometrical figure (this usually works with 8–12 lines). Your task will be to describe your figure to your partner so he or she can reproduce it exactly. Here's an example of what such a figure might look like:

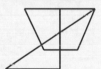

Take your drawing, some clean sheets of paper and a pencil. Sit back to back on chairs or on the floor so that neither of you can see the other's drawing. One rule: no turning round, stretching of necks or outright peeking is permitted! Clue: you might want to say things like "fold your paper in half", "divide your paper into quadrants" and the like.

3   You and your partner will work as a team on the next exercise, facing another pair as an opposing team. Both teams will write one simple sentence on a piece of paper, and give it to one person on the opposing team to act out for his partner, using no words, no props, but only body movements.

When both teams have done so, try another round. This second time, aim to make the sentence more difficult for the other pair.

Example

Round 1 sentence: "You have just received a letter from a friend saying that she is engaged to be married."

Round 2 sentence: "You have just received a message from a friend asking you whether you would be willing to make a speech at her wedding, which will be a small and modest ceremony next June."

What did you find easy to act out? What was difficult? Why? What can body language communicate more effectively than language can? What can language communicate more effectively than body language can?

In the first exercise, you probably found it was hard to transmit to your partner what you wanted him or her to do without the help of your body. It's likely that you moved your head or hands to indicate (or to represent the idea of) up, down, under or over. Body language, facial expressions and gestures often go together with the words we speak. Very naturally we speak with our hands, move our arms, raise our eyebrows. Together with the words we speak, our bodies help carry the message we want to communicate. You may have suspected that reading a manual with instructions for tying shoes wouldn't be nearly as successful as having an older brother or sister willing to show you patiently how to do it. If so, you were right.

As for the second exercise, ask yourself to what extent having a shared vocabulary helped you and your partner reproduce each other's drawings and what made it difficult to carry out precisely, nonetheless. If you and your partner hadn't had any vocabulary regarding length and angles, and other conventions to describe the parts of this figure, the task surely would have been even harder to accomplish than it was. Our vocabulary in general, and specialized vocabularies in particular, are central to getting things done and to seeing the world in a specific way.

In the third exercise, you may have many further reflections on the capacity of language to speak of what is not physical, or not physically there, and to make many kinds of connections between ideas.

Language as a symbolic system

Focusing on the words within language can give us a ready grasp of symbolism, with its abstraction from the world of sense perception and its learned, conventionalized references. Yet those words are not isolated. They gain their force in relationship to one another as we manipulate them within the operating rules of our language. We do not possess just independent word-symbols; the entire system is symbolic and gives us nearly infinite possibilities for meaningful combinations.

Each language has its own grammar, learned by every speaker from babyhood. Perhaps later, in school, we may be taught the rules consciously, but prior to any analysis we know how to use words in combination. In order to illustrate how readily we use our grammatical system, try this short exercise.

Work with one other person. If in class, divide up into pairs. Take a sheet of paper and write on it a single sentence of roughly 10 words, spacing the words far apart. Then cut it apart with scissors so that each word is by itself. Shuffle the words into a random order, and let your partner try to make your nonsense order into a meaningful sentence. He is free to make a new sentence rather than duplicating yours.

Sample sentences:
● The horse in the stable quickly ate its crunchy oats.
● The paramedics carefully carried the wounded patient into the hospital.

Now try in your group an exercise in placing ideas in relationship to each other. Look at the cartoon, and write one single sentence that puts into words what is illustrated visually in the two frames. Please do not read the follow-up instructions until you have written your sentence.

Now read the following questions and keep them in mind as each of your classmates in turn reads out his or her sentence.

What kinds of connections are being made?
● Is the emphasis on sequence ("and"), on consequence ("because", "causes"), on time relationship ("after", "before"), or on another form of relationship of ideas?
● Listen for what is placed in the main clause of the sentence, and what is placed in a subordinate position. Even if you do not know the terms for sentence analysis, with attention you are likely to hear the differences in pattern.

It is likely that, even given the same pictures of a simple sequence, no two people wrote exactly the same sentence. Although the grammar of the language does dictate that only certain word orders are possible, it also allows such flexibility we may possibly generate utterances that no previous speaker of the language has ever used.

But let us not, while concentrating on language, forget entirely about sense perception as providing the information about which we were writing. Consider the following questions.

● Did you or any of your classmates mention a ball? Can you see a ball?

- Did any of you say that the man had been hit? Does the cartoon show him being hit?
- Did any of you mention the emotional state of the girl or the man, or their intentions? How do you know what they are? In putting what you saw in the cartoon into a sentence, did you include things that you did not see at all, but inferred, making connections between the frames? If so, you have just given yourself a good example of seeing interpretively. In this book, the cartoon is framed with text in English. If the same cartoon were framed with Hebrew or Arabic text, read from right to left, how might you interpret it?

How do we learn language?

Words and grammar, together, give us the symbolic system of language, learned as part of our human heritage. But how do we learn this system?

> Many English speakers are concerned about gender bias in English, with the grammatically correct generic form for "he and she" being the male pronoun "he". Many now use the gender neutral "they" in the singular, overriding grammatical correctness in favour of inclusion. Do you think that the dominance of male forms in English (including words such as "chairman" which are now commonly modified to "chair") affects how you think yourself about gender roles?

It doesn't translate #2: gender

Sex, they say, is a biological concept. Gender, they say, is a social one—and a grammatical one. Some languages divide their words according to gender: nouns are either feminine or masculine, regardless of whether they refer to beings with sex or sexless objects or ideas. Does that gender division affect how people think or feel about the objects? Does a noun with a feminine gender bring to mind female characteristics?

Conclusions based on introspection and individual experience may not be as convincing as conclusions based on psychological testing and more general surveys, yet they certainly bring to life the question of whether our language affects how we think about the world. It is a question that has intrigued linguists and psychologists.

Kati Temonen, Finland
In Finnish we have no "he" or "she" even for people. We use "han" which is both and gives us a gender-neutral language. It's not confusing because we add extra words in a context where it's relevant to know whether someone is male or female.

Caroline Laroche, French Canada
A wall couldn't be feminine gender. It just couldn't! If I had to draw cartoons of the things in this room, they would all be male or female.

It doesn't translate #3: structure of politeness

Phiriyaphong Chaengchenwet, Thailand

In Thai the value we place on politeness is reflected in our language. There are several levels of formality that affect the structure of our language, so that we do not use the same forms in interactions between the common people as we would if we spoke to a monk. There is also a special language form for the Monarch.

We also greet very respectfully. The literal translation of "Hello, King" would be "May the power of the glow of the dust under your majesty's foot bless me." So it's quite obvious that we honour the monarch.

Also, as far as the monarch goes, I think that we have embedded Buddhism in our country quite strongly. The word for "I" used by the monarch would translate as "Buddha's servant". In the special relationship between the monks and the monarch, the monks will call the king "the great supporter", and he calls himself "Self" (after all, it's quite obvious that he's Buddha's servant).

Different possible views have been given within the past century. Behaviourist psychologists considered language acquisition to be a form of behaviour. They considered human beings to enter the world with no inborn capacity for language, but to learn through imitation, through stimulus and response, with correct sounds being reinforced by the positive reaction they received. However, the view of Noam Chomsky is that human beings are born already possessing the capacity for symbolic manipulation, a universal grammar of language that provides a kind of template for learning the particular language of the local speech community.

Although the behaviourist approach illuminated much about the process of imitation and reinforcement in learning generally, Chomsky's version explains more. For one thing, it accounts better for the tendency of young children to regularize the language. A child who says, "I goed there all by myself" rather than "went" has internalized the linguistic rules of the language, and has produced an utterance not by imitating what he has heard but by understanding what, if consistent, it ought to be. Chomsky's model also explains the way children absorb language at an amazing rate, generating meaningful utterances which they have never heard before by combining words using the underlying grammar. His theory seems to be in accord with our current understanding of brain centres for symbolic manipulation.

That symbolic manipulation, by the way, includes the sign language of the deaf, who communicate using a spatial grammar. Before sign language was developed, with the first schools for the deaf being established in France in the 18th century, the deaf had no language connection with those around them. They were often treated as imbeciles and even considered to lack minds. This topic, quite fascinating, might appeal to you for further investigation.[9]

Our theories about how we learn our mother tongues have also influenced how foreign languages have been taught over the past century or so. Two major approaches were based on the idea that we had to be taught explicitly every aspect of a foreign language. First, the grammar-translation method of the earlier 20th century, affected by the long European tradition of teaching the dead languages of ancient Greek and Latin, taught grammatical rules and vocabulary to enable the foreign language to be written. Then, the audio-lingual method, affected by behaviourist views, shifted the emphasis to oral language, training response to verbal cues. Based on the current view that we are naturally "programmed" to absorb language, the newer method of immersion soaks the student in language with the expectation that more will be learned than is explicitly taught. As you look back over your own learning of foreign languages, including your present IB classes in language B, you might see the influence of these differing approaches to language acquisition.

Words: precise or suggestive?

Significant as it is for understanding the way symbolism works, the idea of something standing for something else runs into problems when we try to pin down the reference. Perhaps it is useful to consider the idea that words gain their meaning not solely through their reference but through the associated ideas that come to our minds when we use them.

Even with words for which the reference seems obvious, we quickly encounter ambiguity, a lack of precision that allows differing interpretations. Try a simple exercise with others to recognize that language, although it allows us to match up our personal experiences with the general ones of our language group, still carries personal variability.

> Designate one person to choose a word for some familiar object or animal, preferably one with which most people in the group are likely to have had experience. The rest of you prepare to hear the word and catch what rises in your mind. Then go quickly from person to person and describe what the word stirred you to think of.

Though everyone might agree on the denotation of the word "chicken" (everyone who knows English would point to the picture of a chicken in a book as opposed to that of a tiger or horse), the connotations each person brings to the word differ. I may think of my pet Cornish hen, whereas you might think of yesterday's fried chicken dinner. So it is unlikely, even with a word that stands for a concrete thing, that we will all carry the same associations. How unlikely it is, then, that we will all carry the same associations with words that refer to abstract ideas such as "justice" and "international-mindedness".

Attempting to converge in our associations with words leads us to attempt precise definitions, as well as to use concrete examples for illustration. "Skinny" and "slender" both converge in the denotation of "thin", but diverge considerably in their connotative overtones of meaning, created in this case by the different values placed on being thin. These connotations of words can be extremely difficult to pin down, as most new speakers of a language are aware. How exactly is that word used, and why is the one in the dictionary just not right in that context? What is the "flavour" of the word or its "halo" of meaning?

Choosing the right word can be a struggle in all areas of knowledge, but the nature of that struggle—whether it is to try to pin down definitions more and more precisely in order to use language entirely denotatively, or whether it is to choose words deliberately for exactly the right aura of connotations—depends on the area. In one area we might complain that language is imprecise; in another we may praise its suggestive resonance. For an appreciation of the way that different goals affect our language use, respond to the following questions on sunlight, gold, and gardens.

The Sunlight on the Garden

The sunlight on the garden
Hardens and grows cold,
We cannot cage the minute
Within its nets of gold,
When all is told
We cannot beg for pardon.

Our freedom as free lances
Advances towards its end;
The Earth compels, upon it
Sonnets and birds descend;
And soon, my friend,
We shall have no time for
dances.

The sky was good for flying
Defying the church bells
And every evil iron
Siren and what it tells:
The Earth compels,
We are dying, Egypt, dying

And not expecting pardon,
Hardened in heart anew,
But glad to have sat under
Thunder and rain with you,
And grateful too
For sunlight on the garden.

Louis MacNeice

Photons on the ecosystem

Language in science

- Physics students, what is light? How would you describe it, using language appropriate to physics? How does it travel? What is its speed?

- Chemistry students, what is gold? How would you describe its properties, using language appropriate to chemistry? What is its symbol and position on the periodic table?

- Biology and environmental systems students, what is a garden? How would you describe an ecosystem, using language appropriate to biology? What is the reaction of plants to light? Can you give a formula?

What is the attitude in the sciences toward ambiguity of language? What kind of language do you expect in this area of knowledge and why? Why are numbers and other symbols used?

Denotations and connotations

Now take each of the words above not solely for their denotations but for their connotations, their shades or overtones of meaning.

- What are your associations with "sunlight"? Does "sunlight" mean something other than "light"? Do you have a personal response to the word?

- What are your associations with "gold"? What stories or legends do you know in which gold is important? What sports events or social practices?

- What are your associations with a "garden"? Do you have personal memories, or cultural (perhaps religious) associations?

Now read the poem by Louis MacNeice, and consider ways in which his use of language differs from what you would expect in your science course.

Language in poetry

- Does sunlight factually "harden and grow cold"? Would you try literally to cage a minute? What is a metaphor? Is MacNeice, in the poem as a whole, actually talking about a garden and sunlight, or is he saying something else?

- Does "beg for pardon" mean (a) to apologize, or (b) to petition to cancel a punishment such as execution? How can you tell? Is every interpretation in poetry equally valid?

- "We are dying, Egypt, dying" is a modification of "I am dying, Egypt, dying" in Shakespeare's Anthony and Cleopatra, IV, xv, 41. These are among Anthony's last words, addressed to his beloved Cleopatra of Egypt, as he dies. In their private love affair, the lovers have not been able to escape the forces of empire and their public roles. Why does MacNeice use Shakespeare's line here? Would borrowing someone else's work without acknowledgement be acceptable in science?

- Would you expect scientific language to use rhythm, rhyme, alliteration, assonance, and words seemingly selected for their sound? What is their effect in this poem?

- Why does MacNeice repeat himself in the final stanza? Was he not able to make his point the first time?

- Does the meaning of the poem change with the addition of the information that it was written in 1937, when MacNeice could see war in Europe on the horizon? Does it affect your interpretation of the poem as a whole to know that the "iron sirens" are air raid warnings?

- A poem, like a song, can gather personal associations which add to its meaning for you individually. Does it surprise you that many people have such associations with this poem? Does it surprise you that past IB students have written songs with this poem as the lyrics?[10] Would it surprise you if they had written songs using text from their chemistry textbooks?

A note on "symbols"

As you move from TOK class to your language A1, you may encounter confusion over usage of the word "symbol", as the word is placed in context of a different kind of discussion. Although in TOK we speak of all words as symbolic, the literary use of "symbol" involves a further level of suggestion. As we see in this poem, words or clusters of words can be used as images with suggestive power: the sunlight on the garden is a metaphor for the happy moments shared with a friend in a paradise threatened by the new circumstances of changing times. A symbol in literature has ambiguity and suggestive resonance beyond that of a metaphor. It can no longer be treated as a reference to something else specific, or as an "equation" with the parts, although equivalent, still separate. Instead, a symbol in literature is a fused unit resonant with meaning that cannot be rationally explained. Symbols may be drawn from culture (the cock crowing) or from psychological archetypes (the "man within"), or may be created within the work by the way in which the author treats an object, image, or action to make it gather associations.

It doesn't translate #4: sacred text

Isaac Sadaqah, Jordan
We can't translate the Koran to any other language. The Arabic is perfect, given by God—Allah—to Mohamed, and if we translated it, it would lose its perfection.

Mohamed Shakir, Maldives
If we translated the Koran, it wouldn't be a miracle anymore. I don't speak Arabic, but I read the Koran in Arabic. I do have a translation to understand the meaning, but I learn the Arabic to hear the beautiful rhythm and hear the words given by Allah to the Prophet.

It doesn't translate #5: your own examples

Can you add examples of your own? What, for instance, are "tones" in Chinese, Vietnamese, or Thai? How are family relationships named in different languages, and do the differences suggest anything about cultural attitudes toward family?

Hypothesis of linguistic relativity

It has been suggested that the particular language we speak causes us to think in a certain way (Sapir-Whorf's hypothesis of linguistic relativity, 1920s to 1930s), and that speakers of different languages consequently perceive the world quite differently. This hypothesis has not been supported: (a) it was based on too little research for the reach of its conclusions and may not even be testable because of the difficulty of separating language from culture to examine reciprocal causal influences; (b) it does not seem compatible with the differences in thinking of speakers of the same language, or similarity of those of different languages; and (c) it exaggerates the difficulty of translating from language to language, given that we are not restricted to finding single word equivalents. Yet the hypothesis has received considerable attention, perhaps because it seemed to illuminate differences between ourselves and others, or perhaps because the idea of being tricked by language into seeing the world in a particular way was intriguing. We now consider differences between languages to be the surface of a deeper symbolic capacity. The variation, however, is far from trivial for those seeking a window into the cultural worldviews of others.

Roles of language

Chemistry textbooks and poetry are only two of the forms in which we meet language in our daily lives. All day long, we use language for a huge variety of purposes, often fused together.

- We think, using the symbols of language as tools for thought.
- We interact socially, connecting with others through greeting and conversation.
- We give factual reports.
- We express our emotions.
- We create, using language for literature or for humour.
- We persuade others.
- We give instructions, make requests, or otherwise affect actions around us.
- We change our lives, for example by pronouncing marriage vows.

What other uses of language would you add to this list? For which ones are clarity and precision important, and for which is ambiguity either less of a problem or even an advantage?

In a chemistry textbook or a poem, we can recognize the role that language is playing and can identify the way that authors will treat connotative overtones of meaning. In many other contexts, though, it is far less evident what the writer is attempting to do, and it is by giving our attention to features of language that we can judge whether we are being given a factual report—or whether we are being given something closer to an expression of emotions or even an attempt to persuade us to think and act in a particular way.

Names and connotations

Shakespeare wrote, "What's in a name? That which we call a rose by any other name would smell as sweet." (Romeo & Juliet, Act II, Sc. II) Not everyone agrees.

- Would it have made a difference to the story had Romeo fallen in love with "Harriet" or "Susan", not "Juliet"?

- Does your name (first name, last name) mean anything? If it doesn't, is it easy to imagine exchanging it for any other name?

- In your society, are there more common and less common last names? Do certain names have certain socio-economic, political, religious, ethnic, or other connotations?

When you hear names like "Smith", "Goldstein" or "Gómez" do particular associations come to mind? Where do these come from? Are these assumptions or connotations true in the same way that saying triangles have three sides is true?

What would your view be of someone who you have casually spoken to whose business card you happened to find on the locker room floor and

whose name is accompanied by: MD, D.Phil, CEO, Mrs, Sir, III, Junior or Lady?

How might your preconceptions about names influence your perception of the people you meet? How might others' preconceptions of your name (or nationality, religion, skin colour, etc.) affect how they perceive you?

Language, emotion, and values

In trying to make this judgment on whether we are being given a factual report, we meet four points for attention similar to those we first encountered in Chapter 1, applied to maps.

- *Selection*: Out of all possible events or details that could have been reported, what has been chosen? Is it possible to compare the description with another by someone else? We can be grateful that a writer selects only the important things to tell us—whatever "important" might mean to him—rather than drowning us in detail. We can also expect that the purpose of the report and its intended audience affect what he picks out. Yet any selection is made according to criteria, and we need to be alert to what the criteria seem to be.

- *Emphasis*: Out of all the events or details reported, what has been stressed as most important, and, again, what do the guiding values or criteria seem to be for this emphasis? How has the emphasis been achieved: through placement of ideas in the main clause rather than the subordinate clause of the sentence? through placement in emphasized positions, such as the final words of a sentence or paragraph? through more detailed treatment of some details rather than others?

- *Word choice*: What kind of language has been used, and does it seem to be appropriate to the apparent purpose of the description? Is it denotative, factual language, or is it connotative and suggestive? What emotions are expressed? What values, positive or negative, are expressed or suggested? Is there evidence of bias? Is a person described as "courageous" or "reckless", as "relaxed" or "lazy", as "curious" or "nosy", as "assertive" or "pushy"? The choice of words in the description may tell you more about the writer's values than about the person being described.

- *Context*: In what context has the description been placed, and how might this framing affect the overall meaning of the passage? What does its purpose seem to be?

Creative writing activity

Choose one incident from your own life, possibly an event familiar also to others so that you can share your writing afterwards with a sense of recognition (and perhaps amusement). Write a list of five to ten pieces of information about your subject. Then write two descriptions of it which do not contradict each other factually but which communicate quite different

values and emotions through your selection of information, the emphasis
you place on some information, and your word choice. Examples follow.

Home in the Negev Desert 1

In the centre of the vast Negev desert lies a small spot of green. That miraculously green dot in the endless yellow is my home. It lies on the edge of a gorgeous valley where the view is breathtaking and the peace and quiet feel like divine magic. The air is so clear and pure, so different from the city. On most days the weather is very good: the sun is shining and the sky is blue. Everyone knows each other in my village, and smiles when they say hello. It is a wonderful place to grow up in—no commotion, traffic, drugs, or violence.

By Gal Pinshow

Home in the Negev Desert 2

In the centre of the dry and harsh Negev desert lies an almost unnoticeable spot of green. That small spot in the endless nothingness is where I reside. It is situated on the edge of an arid valley where everything is so quiet that one can almost hear the sound of death. The air is so clear that it has no special fragrance, maybe because there is nothing out there to smell of anything, apart from sand and half dead bushes. Most of the time the sun is shining full blast so that it gets so hot breathing becomes hard. Everyone in the village knows everything about each other because there is nothing better to do than gossip. Nothing ever happens in the village. Even thieves don't bother making the trip out into the middle of nowhere.

Arrival at an International College 1

It was the beginning of a wonderful adventure. As soon as I arrived on campus I could sense the anticipation in the warm air. I walked around the campus in search of my new home, which I had been told was called "East House" and wondered at the flowers and the landscaped scenery which the small path meandered through. As I walked past the cozy wooden buildings which nestled close to the sloping lawns I came upon a group of students lounging in the sunshine. Struck by the diversity of the group I stood for a moment in amazement; it was real, all the smiling pictures of a perfectly balanced "ethnic mosaic" which had graced the pages of my guidebook were in fact small glimpses of the cultural cross-section which I was to encounter here. As I stood there, one of the girls in the group noticed me and smiled in greeting. "Welcome! Do you need a hand with your luggage or anything?" she asked, and before I even answered she bounded to her feet and cheerily offered to carry some of my bags while accompanying me to East House. I followed her gratefully and only hoped that the other people I met would be as friendly.

by Snow Dowd

Arrival at an International College 2

It was the end of my wonderful summer and the start of untold troubles, struggles and academics. As I crawled out of the sweltering car I could feel the tension in the air. I struggled up the crooked, concrete path dragging my belongings and hoping desperately to find the obscure residence which I knew only as "East House". As I wandered hopelessly through the maze of brooding low-slung buildings and bedraggled rhododendron bushes I finally came upon what I hoped was a change of direction. A motley group of students lay sprawled on the yellowed grass in the merciless heat. As I stood there stunned by the strangeness of the faces, one of the girls in the group spotted me and instantly donned a plastic smile; it could have been photocopied from one of the many "happy ethnic" pictures which splattered the pages of my handbook. "Welcome!" she yelled as if a string had been pulled. "Do you need a hand with your luggage or anything?" she demanded, and before I could respond she charged to her feet and grabbed my bags while gleefully informing me that she would take me to my residence. I trudged after her and only hoped that the other people I met would be more amiable.

Take back the language: words tell a story of their own

by Keith M. Woods

March 20, 2003. The Iraq campaign has commenced. Embeds are sending in their dispatches. Now, journalists must be vigilant in protecting against collateral damage. Because in times of war, clarity is often the first casualty. And independence is usually not far behind.

The language of the military, like that of the local police department or civil court, can be muddled in obtuse, euphemistic jargon that has the seductive quality of making journalists sound like they're in the know.

Language has always had a power that tilts toward those who define the terms. Journalists interested in maintaining their independence—real and perceived—have to pay attention to the difference, say, between a war and a "campaign"; between "collateral damage" and the killing of innocent people.

The military isn't making it easy, layering atop its lingo a hefty supply of patriotism, nobility and machismo. The bombing and invasion of Iraq is called "Operation Iraqi Freedom". The concurrent assault on Afghanistan is called "Operation Valiant Strike". US soldiers in Kuwait fire "Patriot" missiles to bring down incoming Iraqi missiles.

When warships and bombers fired the first shots of this war, trying to kill Iraqi leader Saddam Hussein and other leaders, military analysts dubbed the goal a "decapitation", a gruesome euphemism that sidesteps another loaded term for killing a national leader: assassination. The 2,000-pound bomb used in that attack carries the flippant nom de guerre "bunker buster".

The argument here isn't that there should be a prohibition on using government—and military—speak...The trouble comes when journalists adopt the language, take it out of quotation marks, remove the modifiers that tell viewers and listeners that this is someone else's language. Then the patriotism, the nobility, the testosterone-infused terminology slip insidiously into the cracks of our independence and erode one of the profession's cornerstones.

So "shock and awe" becomes more than just the coined slogan of one military man. "Smart" bombs drop with their intelligence unchallenged by the media. In our prose, distant warriors launch surgical strikes without quotation marks, allowing one more military-slanted phrase to slip past numbed sensibilities. Chalk up another victim of friendly fire.

In times of war, clarity is often the first casualty. It's not so hard to avoid such a fate. First, recognize that what's at stake is more than a word here or there. Journalists are not beholden to the military or its choice of words. Nor should they appear to be. Next, take a clear-eyed look at why some of the language makes its way into your sentences. It's cool. It's edgy. It endears journalists to their military sources and an audience that, especially during these tense days, wants to know that we're all on the same side. You can't defend that journalistically. Not even with a Patriot missile.

Recapture the language with specifics and precision. "Smart" bombs are, more accurately, laser-guided or computer-guided bombs. Leave the IQ assessment to someone else. Reserve language declaring missions "surgical" for events witnessed by reporters or reliable sources. Otherwise, just describe what happened. Avoid repeated use of aggrandized mission names: Desert Shield, Desert Storm, Iraqi Freedom, Valiant Strike. They are not neutral terms.

As the war escalates, as people die and buildings fall and the unpredictable future unfolds, remember that the words you use to tell the story will tell a story of their own. Make it a story of journalistic independence. Clear. Accurate. Precise.

Anything but surgical.[11]

Metaphors of time and space: the case of the Aymara culture[12]

The metaphors that come naturally to speakers can be very different, a fact that probably contributes to the view, held by some, that people who speak different languages in some sense (a metaphorical sense) live in different worlds.

If someone asks you to point to the past, you will probably do something like lift your arm and point your thumb over your shoulder, indicating what is behind you. In most Indo-European languages, including English and Spanish, it is assumed that the past is behind while the future lies ahead, as a road or path as yet untravelled. These are our languages' spatial metaphors for time.

Roughly one million Aymara speakers live in Peru, Bolivia and northern Chile. According to anthropologists, in the Aymara culture and language a very different set of spatial metaphors operates. The Aymara situate themselves in time as if seated in a rowboat, travelling into the future (at their back) while facing the past from where they have come.

In Aymara *q'ipa nia marana* means next year; when literally translated the expression means "in the year behind" or "at our back".

In Aymara *ancha mayna pachan* means a long time ago; literally translated it means "a long time in front of you."

What are other metaphors you use to refer to time? To get started, think of some typical aphorisms like "time flies when you're having fun". What might these metaphors reveal about a culture's attitude to time? Compare your findings with how your language B treats time.

Metaphors as pervasive figures of thought

by Julian Kitching

Metaphor involves the application or use of a word or phrase as a form of comparison. If you said that someone is a snake, you would not mean it literally. When you make this comparison you imply that there is something about that person that reminds you of a snake. In other words, metaphor is mapping one concept onto another or comparing one with another. The source, what the concept or entity is compared to, the snake in this example, is often either more concrete or better understood than the target, the idea under consideration, the person you are talking about. The relationship between the two is focused through a selective treatment of their similarities and differences. The comparison often stretches systematically beyond the particular metaphor itself into other metaphors and assertions that extend the comparison.

Thinking a little more deeply, it is possible to identify certain systematic and pervasive metaphors that underlie our thinking: we often talk about organisms—our own bodies and those of other creatures, for example—as machines. Bodies "function" and "break down", the food we eat is "fuel" and we "burn energy" when we exercise.

Metaphors play different roles when we use them.

- They can have an explanatory role, for example your biology text might portray the nervous, immune, and endocrine systems as components in a telephone or communications network. As a result this metaphor helps you think immediately of connections and relations, not isolated parts.

- They can serve to challenge orthodox thinking, as Darwin's "natural selection" did in his day, and Richard Dawkins's "selfish gene" has done more recently.

- They can condition our thoughts and actions, such as in the case of the "war on terror", where a geopolitical situation has been portrayed in one particular manner. Perhaps even more pervasive is the way we associate environmental factors (e.g. light and dark) and basic orientations (up and down) with connotative words of values. Consider the values suggested by the Dark Ages as opposed to the Enlightenment, or "feeling high" as opposed to "feeling low".

A case has been made for metaphor being a basic mode of thought. If this is anywhere near the truth, it has far-reaching implications for our approaches to knowledge. It would support the contention that we function within systematic conceptual frameworks constructed largely through comparison, which guide our sense perception and thinking.

Knowledge itself has also been subject to extended metaphorical treatment, being regarded, for example, as a building or a ship at sea. Below are elaborations for these two metaphors.

Knowledge is a building

It is constructed and solid. It is built from the bottom up, and the foundations must be secure in order to support the rest. It can be added to, or renovated, and it could also be knocked down. It can be functional or it can be aesthetically pleasing. All the parts fit together.

It could be claimed that the building metaphor has affected attitudes to knowledge. You might be attracted to the idea of a unitary system of knowledge that considers simplicity as a virtue and has the most reliable knowledge at the base. But opinions differ as to what this most reliable knowledge might be. Do you think it might be mathematics? Logic? Knowledge of self, or of history?

Knowledge is a ship at sea

The ship must be maintained and repaired without returning to port. This means that it cannot be entirely disassembled; at least certain parts of it must be kept intact in order to prevent the entire vessel from sinking.

What would this metaphor imply about how knowledge evolves? Can you think of any examples that fit this metaphor?

Now, in small groups, take on one of the following metaphors, prepare a short presentation showing how you might develop it, and then defend it as the best of all the metaphors for knowledge: Knowledge is a web, Knowledge is a map, Knowledge is a collection of stories, Knowledge is a mirror, Knowledge is a crossword, Knowledge is a chain, Knowledge is a window into an aquarium.

On pervasive ideas and metaphors

Sometimes an idea becomes so commonplace, so much a part of the cultural consensus, that it sinks out of awareness, becoming an invisible thread in the fabric of thought. Then we ask and answer questions, collecting information without reflecting upon the underlying idea that makes this possible. The idea becomes as subliminal as the grammar that governs our language each time we speak.

Most of our master ideas about nature and human nature, logic and value eventually become so nearly subliminal that we rarely reflect upon them as human inventions, artefacts of the mind. We take them for granted as part of the cultural heritage. We live off the top of these ideas, harvesting facts from their surface.

Theodore Roszak (1986)[13]

Language and other forms of symbolic representation

Language is our dominant form of symbolism, but it is certainly not our only one. Compare language with other forms of symbolism such as maps, photographs, scientific models, paintings, mathematics, and music and consider the roles all of these play in our gaining and communicating knowledge. Feel free to bring in other forms beyond these six into class discussion, and to compare them on bases that go beyond the ones raised in the questions below.

1   Do any of the other forms of symbolism operate as a system, as the combination of words and grammar does in language to create meaning? What similarities and differences do you find?

2   Look back to the list of roles of language on page 42, to which you will have added your own ideas. Does any of the other symbolic forms function for as many purposes in our lives as language does? What, would you say, is the role that each of the others plays most effectively? Is any of the others, do you think, actually more effective than language to communicate certain things?

3   Place these forms of symbolism on a scale from:
    ● at one end, maximum precision of meaning and convergence of public understanding to
    ● at the other end, maximum ambiguity and divergence into individual understanding.

Compare within your class both your scales and your reasons for placing particular forms of symbolism in their positions.

4   With what other ways of knowing (sense perception, emotion, and reasoning) do you most closely associate each of these forms of symbolism?

5   With what areas of knowledge do you most closely associate each of these forms of symbolism?

Notice how you have been discussing symbolism and language: through language. Could any of the other forms of symbolism have been used in this way?

Notice how familiar it is for us to compare and contrast, group and make distinctions. We will return to a discussion of classification after considering two more ways of knowing: emotion and reasoning.

maps

music

$(73 \times 10) + 83 = 813$

mathematics

photographs

scientific models

paintings

Language: a tool for thinking and communicating

Expanding your vocabulary gives you better tools for drawing distinctions and understanding shades of meaning. As a result, you increase your potential for exploring ideas and communicating effectively with others. Use your own familiarity with usage or a dictionary to ensure that you understand the following words, useful in TOK and elsewhere.

Does a dictionary describe how words are used or prescribe how they ought to be used? Some languages (French and Spanish, for example) have language academies which decide regularly which new words to accept into the language and thus to add to their dictionary. Other languages have no such control over their change.

What arguments would you make for preserving a language? What arguments would you make for accepting change?

The words below are ones useful for you to know. Even if you do not add them to your active spoken vocabulary, they will increase your reading comprehension.

evaluate	concrete	cogent	dubious
assess	empirical	relevant/irrelevant	spurious
judge/judgment	objective	deplore	duplicitous
assume/ assumption	subjective	incite	fraudulent
presume/ presumption	rudimentary	denounce	bogus
premise	fundamental	vilify	alluring
axiom	subtle	coerce	dazzling
principle	flagrant	dogma/ dogmatize	unscrupulous
conception	blatant	declaim	insidious
preconception	implicit	pontificate	devious
stereotype	explicit	indoctrinate	deft
archetype	subliminal	allege	illusion
antithesis	arcane	insinuate	delusion
contradiction	esoteric	equivocate/ equivocal	ruse
cohere/ coherence	erudite	engender	ploy
correspond/ correspondence	covert	bypass	insight/insightful
pragmatic	credence/credible/ credulous	clutter	perceptive
expedient	susceptible	subvert	acute
infer/inference	naive	feign	obtuse
imply/implication	gullible	denotation	engage/ engagement
demonstrate/ demonstration	skeptical	connotation	inquiry
contend/contention	sagacious	resonance	balance
abstract	judicious	bias/biased	reflection
	compel/ compelling	distorted	self-awareness
	discerning		

As you learn in all of your IB Diploma Programme subjects, you will be challenged to increase the range of your thinking and your vocabulary.

● ●

Emotion

Our direct experience of the world has at its core our emotions. The words "emotion" and "motivation" both derive from the Latin *movere*, meaning "to move". "Emotions shape the landscape of our mental and social lives," says Martha Nussbaum, author of *Upheavals of Thought: the intelligence of emotions*.[14] Our emotions accompany us throughout our lives so thoroughly and profoundly that it may be difficult for us, in experiences and memories, to consider sense perceptions and ideas without their inter-threaded emotions.

We know that emotions can be activated by external causes (being chased by a famished lion causes fear) and internal causes (one may wake up feeling sad one morning but not know why). We also know that different cultures and languages catalogue the emotions in different ways. But there is still no exact, universally agreed upon definition and categorization of emotion, nor agreement about the boundaries between emotions on the one hand, and feelings and moods on the other. Moreover, the relationship between the emotions and our cognitive (intellectual) apparatus—that is, what we know, think, believe, desire, and value—is also the subject of academic discussion and debate amongst philosophers, psychologists, and neuroscientists. However, we can assert very broadly that emotions are reactions or responses related to sense perceptions, internal states, thoughts, or beliefs about things or people, real or imagined. For the purposes of this book, we will use the terms "emotions" and "feelings" interchangeably.

Knowing our emotions

It is likely that our emotions have prompted us to reflection more frequently than other ways of knowing. We may be more likely to ask ourselves, "Why am I feeling this way?" than "Why am I hearing this way?" or "Why am I speaking this way?" The perceptual sweetness of honey has provoked fewer songs than the emotional "sweetness" of love.

Yet how do we know our emotions? Before we go on, push your own reflection further by asking four questions, and giving as many answers as you can. Share your ideas with others in order to build up together the greatest range of possible responses.

1   How are you feeling right now, at this moment? How do you know?
2   Why do you think you're feeling this way?
3   Ask for a volunteer willing to share what he is feeling. Before he does that, try to guess what that person is feeling right now, at this moment. How do you know?
4   To what extent do you think knowing your own feelings depends on knowing the feelings of others, and knowing the feelings of others depends on knowing your own?

It is likely that by focusing on these few questions, you will have identified key topics that are being actively researched by psychologists and neuroscientists right now.

To an extent, though, one answer appears, at least at first, to be very straightforward. You know your emotions because you feel them. Your own personal introspection provides you with privileged access to your own feelings. Just as only you know your own sense experience of the world "from inside", only you know your own emotions directly, as something felt inside yourself. If you say, "Right now I know I am happy," (or bored, depressed, or in love) you mean that your direct experience and personal familiarity with yourself leads you to this conclusion.

But can you be wrong when you identify your own feelings? Might parents, friends, or teachers help you recognize what you are really feeling when you initially thought you were feeling something else? Those who know you well may give you, at times, some indication that you seem to be feeling something that you had not yet noticed yourself. You might realize through others, for example, that you are under stress, excited, jealous, or falling in love. Although attitudes toward counselling vary considerably with culture, many people have benefited from counselling which has helped them to recognize their feelings better and identify possible causes for them.

Emotional intelligence

In recent years emotions—others' and our own—have been a subject for research on the brain and learning. Understanding of our own emotions (intrapersonal intelligence) and the emotions of others (interpersonal intelligence) has been treated as "emotional intelligence". Howard Gardner put forward in his book *Frames of Mind* in 1983 a theory of seven intelligences: linguistic intelligence, logical-mathematical intelligence, spatial intelligence, musical intelligence, bodily-kinesthetic intelligence, interpersonal intelligence, and intrapersonal intelligence. These last two kinds of intelligences are related. Interpersonal intelligence means understanding other people and their motivations and implies being able to work well in cooperation and collaboration. All sorts of successful people from teachers to religious leaders and politicians probably display these skills to a high degree. Intrapersonal intelligence involves just the same abilities turned inwards onto oneself.[16] Identified as separate forms of intelligence, interpersonal and intrapersonal intelligence nevertheless involve us in similar ways of trying to answer the question, "How do I know?"

Perhaps it is not surprising that some of the ways of identifying our emotions include language, sense perception, and reasoning. All three provide highly interconnected ways of associating the emotions we experience with those that other people experience, and allow us to emerge from solitary introspective awareness into some degree of shared knowledge.

Knowing emotion through perception

Our senses allow us to gather sensations from outside and inside our bodies, and to observe both our own physical responses and the behaviour of others. Admittedly, observation does not allow us to see the emotions of others directly: we can perceive a rose's "redness" but cannot directly perceive someone else's "sadness". However, our senses give us clues about what the emotional state of others might be, and, if the inquiry is structured into systematic studies, our senses can tell us even more.

How is another person feeling? Can you read his "body language"? When people communicate, observers gain information from seeing

> " *One of the pitfalls of childhood is that one doesn't have to understand something to feel it. By the time the mind is able to comprehend what has happened, the wounds of the heart are already too deep.* "
> *Carlos Ruiz Zafón*[15]

Edgar Degas, *Absinthe*, c.1875–76

What do you "read" the woman's body language to be? How does the structural composition of the painting heighten the emotional impact? How does the title of the painting affect the interpretation?

their actions: how they move their hands, sigh, play with their hair, shuffle their feet. Listeners catch the tone of the voice and the pauses of silence. We can often catch very subtle cues, from the slight constriction of the lips or forehead, or the involuntary dilation of the pupils of the eyes. Highly acute observers, often not even conscious of their swift reading of tiny signals, are often considered intuitive in their capacity to "sense" how someone else is feeling.

In observing a particular pattern of actions or gestures, we come to associate it with a particular emotion (through the naming of language and generalizing of reasoning). Observation of others' actions can then give us a context for recognizing our own (and vice versa). You can realize that you are angry as you notice that you are sounding and acting like an angry person.

Activity: Ask for a volunteer or two to go out of the room and then re-enter, simulating the body language of a particular emotion. The rest of the group tries to guess what emotion has been acted. Is there general agreement?

Attempts to know an emotion based on such observation, though, do encounter some evident problems. Misinterpretation is a constant danger, especially when we do not know the person very well, or when the person is from an unfamiliar culture with possibly different codes for what emotions are acceptable to express and what physical gestures are appropriate. Moreover, people can often choose whether to hide or display their emotions.

More rigorous observation has taken the form of studies, such as those on facial expression of emotion. Researcher Paul Ekman, internationally testing recognition of emotional facial

---

THE MAN, HIS WIFE, AND THE OTHER WOMAN:
A VERY, VERY, VERY SHORT NOVEL

Chapter 1 ✍

"I'll be back soon, dear." With a quick squeeze of his hand, his wife was gone, and he was left an opportunity to sit down and rest his weary feet.

The fresh aroma of the famous house coffee filled his nostrils, and he decided upon a cappuccino with just a light dusting of cinnamon, and, of course, the chocolate torte. From the shade of the umbrella over his small table he soaked in the warmth of the summer and noticed the gentle breeze which stirred his hair and rustled his newspaper. He was aware of the glorious colour of blossoms among the greenery of the park across the street and the laughter of children at play.

He glanced at the clock. Still plenty of time to relax! He turned to the sports page.

What emotion do you think the character is experiencing? How can emotion affect our perception of our surroundings? How can our surroundings affect our emotions?

THE MAN, HIS WIFE, AND THE OTHER WOMAN

Chapter 2 ✍

"It's been a long time," she said.

"Yes. A long time."

"I saw her leave. Your wife."

"Yes, my wife. My wife."

Her dark eyes held his and neither spoke. A waiter approaching with a menu hesitated, and then retreated to leave them alone.

"I didn't think," he faltered, "that I would ever see you again."

This text doesn't give the feelings of the characters, just their dialogue. If you were the director of this film, what emotions would you tell the actors to play and how would you suggest them to the audience? Is there more than one interpretation of this scene?

expressions, concluded that four specific emotions were recognized everywhere: fear, anger, sadness, and enjoyment.[17]

Observation has also taken the form of biological study of the human body to tell us more closely what is going on "inside". Physiological changes in the body (heart rate, sweaty palms, and so forth) can be monitored as evidence of certain emotional states. In language we distinguish between the "physical" and the "emotional", but mounting medical findings indicate that this distinction cannot be made neatly. Emotions are affected by (or created by) our physical state, such as our biochemical balance; and our physical state, even our health, is affected by our emotions. Indeed, it has been argued that the biological condition is not just the cause of the emotion but is the emotion itself as we sense it.

Knowing emotion through language

Our ability to give names to emotions and speak of them with others indicates an emotional life shared with others and understood in terms of the classifications given by our own particular language. Language and perception together contribute to our understanding: we learn the word as it is applied to observable behaviour and use it to describe the invisible emotion.

However, applying words from external clues, we can't be sure that what we experience ourselves is exactly what someone else has experienced and means by the word. It is quite common to wonder if what one is feeling is really "love", or if you and your partner mean the same thing when you say "I love you".

Naming also faces the further difficulty of the shifting and blending of emotions. Naming sense perceptions is difficult enough as red gives way to orange on the way to yellow, or as a rock becomes an island on the way to a continent. Emotions are even more difficult to classify, not just because we cannot see them, but also because they may mix together in a way that our perceptions do not. An emotion can, metaphorically, be experienced as red and yellow simultaneously without being orange, in a way which reasoning would condemn as contradictory: it is possible to be sad and happy at the same time (at a wedding), or feel love and hatred mixed together (in jealousy), or feel joy at being reunited with your family at the same time as you feel sadness over leaving behind your friends. Words for emotion are thus extremely ambiguous.

The naming and classifying of these emotional responses and their combinations has not been without debate. Having done his studies of facial expressions, Ekman concluded that the four that his subjects had identified were the "core" emotions, rather like primary colours that could be the basis for shades and blends. Other psychologists have argued for different sets of basic emotions, from the simple opposition of happiness and sadness (Weiner and Graham) to Tomkins' set of nine: anger, interest, contempt, disgust, distress, fear, joy, shame, surprise.[18]

It would seem that, whether happiness is a basic emotion or not, the concept we have of it is not necessarily a human universal that applies across all cultures at all times, but is rather a concept that has

Nakhshab Farhikhtah
Once I was speaking Persian on the phone with my sister and I was trying to explain to her how frustrated I was about something. In Persian we don't have a specific word for frustration so by the time I had tried to explain my emotion the meaning of what I was saying had slightly changed from what I really meant. My knowledge (of language in this case) became a tool for distinguishing the difference in my emotions, but its limitation was that I could only express it properly in the very same language that I had learnt it in.

Kohei Noda

In Japan, we like to keep communication a little fuzzy. We prefer being able to understand from a hint and not being so precise. We have so many ways of suggesting and saying things indirectly that a foreigner couldn't catch.

Emotions are not shown as openly as in North America, though in our generation we do show more than our parents did. In terms of love, we're really shy. Parents don't say, "I love you" to their children and children don't say it to their parents. But we can still see it. The scale is just different.

We also have to be sensitive to relationships and circumstances as we speak politely, so that we choose a more respectful level of language when speaking to elders. In most schools in secondary education, we have to use the words giving respect to the older students, even if they are just a grade ahead.

But it's not as simple as having different levels of formality or politeness, because so many different factors are involved. There are more than ten ways of saying "you" depending on your respect for the person, a combination of your age and their age, and their sex. Some choices sound a bit feminine but they are still okay for men, depending on the situation and the relationship. We can sound more loving, more hostile, more formal, more casual. The right choice of words communicates feelings for them.

changed over time. According to Darrin McMahon, a historian at Florida State University, "In virtually every Indo-European language, the modern word for happiness is cognate with luck, fortune or fate." *Happ* was the Middle English word for "chance, fortune, what *happens* in the world" according to him, "giving us such words as 'happenstance, 'haphazard', 'hapless' and 'perhaps'".[19]

It is probably unsurprising, given the variability of ways of classifying and thinking about emotions, that different languages reflect, and possibly reinforce, particular feelings. The words that different cultures use to describe the emotional worlds of their members give us a clue about the way different structures may mould the emotional experiences of their people, according to David Matsumoto.[20] He reports, for example, that the German word *schadenfreude* has no equivalent in English, though roughly translated it means pleasure derived from someone else's misfortune. The Japanese words *itoshii, ijirashii,* and *amae* also have no exact English translations, though they describe longing for an absent loved one, a feeling associated with seeing someone praiseworthy overcoming an obstacle, and dependence, respectively. Similarly, the metaphors for emotion in different languages vary with the cultural background of the speakers, for example with black being associated with mourning in Europe and white with mourning in India.

Knowing emotion through reasoning

Reasoning, as we will soon be discussing, enables us to establish a relationship between particular experiences and more broadly general ones within the world we perceive. We watch the tide rise and fall not once but again and again, and then we draw a general conclusion. We thus arrive at a general understanding that allows us to fit today's tides into a pattern and to predict them. Even actions in the world that are less regular can be placed in the context of broad

> THE MAN, HIS WIFE, AND THE OTHER WOMAN
>
> Chapter 3 ✍
>
> "I'll be in the bookstore by the church at 10:00 tomorrow morning. If you joined me, we could go somewhere…and talk," she offered, her eyes shining. "Maybe we could even…even go back to my place. For…some lunch."
>
> "Oh yes!" he gasped. "But what if he found out? You mustn't put yourself at risk!"
>
> "I don't care! I can't bear being separated from you forever! I can't let him rule my life."
>
> "Even if it means your being thrown out—cast out without a penny?"
>
> "Yes! Yes!" she cried. "I am able now to take care of myself, and I must make my own choices."

You may have an opinion as to whether or not what is going on in this scene is moral or not. But stop now to concentrate on the emotions involved. If this scene is a plan for a romantic rendezvous, with both characters married to other people, what is your moral judgment not on their actions but on their feelings?

generalization—on patterns of consumerism, for example, or the need to be careful near snarling dogs. We are also able to reason toward connections between causes and effects, both in the natural world and in human actions.

This capacity to see the place of the particular within the general adds greatly to being able to understand how emotions can affect people. We might also gain a greater understanding of our own emotions as we recognize them to fall into patterns within human experience—experiences of grief, for example, or conflict. Psychologists, professional counsellors, and psychiatrists, who know the emotional experience through study, can guide us to recognize our individual experiences. It is not necessary to be a trained professional, though, to use past experience for a better understanding of the present.

Reasoning can also help us to project consequences and to judge whether a reaction "makes sense" in its context. We might conclude we need to seek help to manage anger, for example, or to combat phobias.

Yet the application of reasoning, considering what "makes sense" within a situation, draws heavily on our prior beliefs. At least some (and according to some authors all) emotions are cognitively dependent. For example, feeling indignation about something depends on your beliefs about what is and what is not a fair or just treatment of others. If two people's beliefs about what is fair in a certain situation are very different from each other—think of a slave owner and an abolitionist, for example—they will most certainly have very different emotional responses when confronted with the same situation, ranging from indifference to indignation. Other emotions much affected by beliefs include regret, remorse, and guilt.

Emotion and reasoning: opposition or balance?

Both at the individual and the collective level there is often an implicit but weighty assumption that emotion and reasoning are opposed to each other. In the western philosophical tradition the further assumption is that reasoning is far superior to emotion; emotion is not considered a way of knowing, but a problem to be overcome. From this point of view "emotional intelligence" appears to be nothing but an oxymoronic joke.

What does this cartoon suggest about the relationship between beliefs and emotions?

If you were Calvin, how would you go about overcoming your fear?

If you were Calvin's father, how could you go about helping him overcome it?

To what extent is it preferable to "overcome" negative emotions, and to what extent is it preferable to accept them? How would you decide?

To some extent, a suspicion of emotion seems well grounded. Emotions have a reputation for "clouding" our reasoning, preventing us from "clear" thinking when they "flood" over us. To reason clearly is to be able, potentially, to exercise control and restraint in our actions, in opposition to being "taken over" by the storm of uncontrolled emotions. Like laughter in the cinema, hatred and fear can spread to transform a crowd into a dangerous mob; anger can unleash violence and make a person a murderer; and even happy, uplifting emotions can be worked up to a crazed frenzy. Many group excesses of emotion are associated with language powerfully delivered by a demagogue, or the ideological manipulation of a leader who has "washed" people's minds.

THE MAN, HIS WIFE, AND THE OTHER WOMAN

Chapter 4 ✍

"You know that Papa really will disinherit and reject you if he finds out," he countered, "just as he did me! He said he never wanted to see me again!"

"I tell you, I don't care!" she retorted. "I've missed you so much these past four years. We all have. At times I'm sure Papa misses you terribly, too, but he doesn't know how to admit it or apologize."

"Not a day goes by that I don't think of you, miss you all. It's hard to hide my feelings from Marie. I don't ever want her to feel that I regret marrying her."

"You should never have had to choose between her and your family," responded Violet firmly. "It's not her fault or yours that Papa is so prejudiced and has such a temper."

What connotations does the title of this story encourage? Is the "romantic triangle" a generalization, a stereotype, or a cliché? What's the difference?

The story twists the conventions of the "other woman", as she turns out to be Paul's sister. The twist is also a convention of plot—the surprise reversal or revelation frequent in both comedy and tragedy. If you were fooled and then surprised, what is your reaction to being tricked? Are you amused? Irritated? If you were not surprised, why not?

The sheer speed of our emotional response, too, can place it in opposition to a slower, reasoned response. There are neuronal pathways to the brain that allow certain stimuli (e.g. those that are perceived as dangerous) to shortcut the parts of the brain that think and go directly to the evolutionarily much more primitive parts of the brain, triggering an immediate fear response. That instant reaction can save us as we leap back in fear from a threatening situation, but may also cause us to misjudge the danger of the stimulus and to lash out irrationally.

However, recent research indicates that reason and emotion are much more complementary than has often been thought, and that each keeps the other in balance. The classical case of Phineas Gage (who in 1848 suffered brain damage to his frontal lobes, which prevented him both from feeling any emotion and from making any decisions)[21] is often cited to demonstrate the close connection between our emotional and reasoning centres. Recent studies[22] also indicate that many of our decision-making capabilities—from choosing food to solving mathematical problems, from forming grammatical phrases to making ethical choices—are based on emotion, possibly on the desire to maximize pleasure.

Consider for yourself the interaction between emotion and reasoning in your own life experiences with the following questions.

Would you agree with the assertion that reasoning can guide emotion?

- Recall a few instances when you were really scared or really angry. In any one of these times, did your fear or anger subside when you got more information about what was happening? (Examples: you jumped back thinking you were about to step on a snake, but it turned out to be a piece of piping; you were angry because your friend did not show up for a meeting, then found out he had a car accident on his way to meet you.)
- Have you ever been madly in love with someone you were very attracted to, but upon spending more time with him and getting to know him, you concluded that you were better off without him?

Now, let's consider the converse, and examine the assertion that emotion can guide reasoning.

- What are the criteria you are applying to choose your path after you earn your IB diploma? You might face questions such as, "Which university should I attend?" or "How many years should I give to training/education before I start applying for jobs?" Are all of the criteria you use for making the decision rational or are you also bringing in concepts such as "like", "dislike", "passion", "interest", "motivation", or "enjoy"?
- Imagine that you're not pressed for time, and are working on a research paper, a painting, a letter to a friend, a musical composition, or a video…any of which you could tinker with indefinitely. At some point, however, you decide that what you've done is good enough. Is this always a rational conclusion, or is there a feeling that tells you when to stop working on something?

THE MAN, HIS WIFE, AND THE OTHER WOMAN

Chapter 5 ✍

They both looked up as a figure in blue approached swiftly.

"Marie!" he exclaimed joyfully, jumping up and scooping her into the curve of his arm. "Let me introduce my sister Violet."

"Violet! What a pleasure!", exclaimed Marie, smiling warmly at her. "You know, he misses you terribly—the whole family, but especially you."

"I didn't think you knew," stammered Paul.

"You never told me—in words," she smiled. "You didn't have to."

Marie says she does not have to be told how Paul feels in order to know. She understands without words. In your experience, are some people particularly gifted at understanding the feelings of others? Is empathy something you value in others, and in yourself? Is it a capacity you are born with or a skill that can be trained?

Examining the emotions behind certain collective beliefs

Some of our beliefs we can justify with a rational argument. Other beliefs we consider to be self-evident, so pervasive in our cultures that we never question them. Because within the IB we're aiming for international-mindedness, and because TOK is a course that encourages us to examine the bases for our beliefs, let us find out to what extent each of us is emotionally invested in the idea of patriotism (or more generally in the idea of loyalty for a particular group, be it national, ethnic, or religious).

The following questions are centred on identity and the characteristics you share with others in your community. They are formulated in terms of country, but should be adapted to match your own situation. If your identity is tied to a city, province, religion, ethnicity, or language, substitute one of these words for "country".

- What are your feelings about and towards your country? If you now live in a place where you were not born, how do you feel about your "new" country and about your parents' country or countries of origin?
- Do the words you used to describe these feelings have positive or negative connotations?
- Are these your feelings, which you developed independently? Or have you learned them (as you have learned the customs, manners, and language of your community)? If you say you've learned them, the implication is that feelings can be taught. Do you agree with that assertion? If not, can you resolve this contradiction?
- Do you think other people in your community have the same feelings as you do towards your country? How do you know whether they do or don't?
- If someone from another country asked you about your feelings, would you describe them in the same way as you would describe them to someone in your own country? Why or why not?
- To what extent do your beliefs and emotions depend on each other?

An interlude on happiness
by Julian Kitching

What does it mean to say you are happy? Perhaps when you say you are happy, you are talking about an emotion or feeling. Or maybe you have made a more rational assessment of the state of your life. If you say you are happy, this might be a selfish assessment insofar as you are thinking strictly about yourself; or your assessment might have taken others into account—your family, for example, or even someone you like very much. Whatever you do mean when you say you are happy, it seems justified to say that as humans we all want to be happy, and that there are certain things that we are willing to do to achieve that state. But what are those things? Consider two "thought experiments" on the importance you give happiness in your life. Your responses will be significant later in discussion of the human sciences and ethics.

The Happiness Machine

Imagine that you are presented with a special gift: a machine—the "Happiness Machine"—that can give you wonderfully positive emotions. All you have to do is hook yourself up, and switch it on. But there's a price: once the machine is switched on, you will not remember anything that happened prior to your switching on the machine.

The key question is: do you want to switch the machine on?

NB This machine will never break down or be switched off by someone else. (This is a thought experiment, so perfection is possible.)

What did you decide, and why? Compare with classmates your responses and reasons for them.

It seems that, in controlled studies, most people decide to say "no". Why? Apparently, as humans we believe that happiness should be a product of

commendable action—we should be happy because we have done something other than directly seek happiness itself.

Perhaps you decided not to switch on because you considered that your own happiness might not be the most important thing—you probably have friends and family who should be taken into account. So your own happiness might depend on the situation of others.

Better living through chemicals?

"I drank to drown my sorrows, but my sorrows learned to swim." (Anon.)

Imagine you have a supply of a happiness-inducing substance that can be ingested by anyone, and has no harmful side-effects. You could take it and give it to all your friends and family. Everyone would be happy. Are you prepared to do this?

In *Brave New World*, the novel by Aldous Huxley, a chemical called "soma" is legal and in common usage. Huxley describes this drug as having "all the advantages of Christianity and alcohol; none of their defects". Could administering pleasure be considered an effective way of managing society? If you were in charge of the public water supply where you live, and had on hand the perfect drug to make people happy, would you add it to the system? After discussing your answer and the reasons for it with your classmates, don't be too surprised to find yourself back where you started from, asking about the nature of happiness. And don't consider yourself too odd if you reach the conclusion, as many others have before you, that happiness cannot coherently be thought of as a direct goal of life.

Over the last few decades, experimentation on substances that affect brain chemistry have led to the creation of drugs that affect some emotions we might sometimes rather avoid—pain, depression, agitation, and anxiety, to name only a few. Independent of whether you think taking medically approved drugs to modify an emotional state is a good idea or not, the fact that these drugs can work adds to the evidence of the inseparability of the brain and the body.

Moreover, MRI and PET scanners have helped researchers to see where brain activity takes place in order to explain how our minds work the way they do. Recently the orbitofrontal cortex just behind the eyes has been identified as a part of the brain registering a lot of brain activity when we are seeking pleasure, feeling pain or generally reacting emotionally. When this part of the brain is damaged, people can lose their ability to experience emotion while still retaining their ability to reason. Ask yourself: shouldn't we want to hire people with this kind of crystal-clear logic unencumbered by emotion to work in our businesses, industries, schools, and government? Probably not. Confirming previous research, psychologist Jonathon Haidt claims that, lacking emotion, they have great difficulty functioning even in everyday life. For when people who have suffered this kind of brain damage think about what to do "they see dozens of choices but lack immediate internal feelings of like or dislike. They must examine the pros and cons of every choice with their reasoning, but in the absence of feeling they see little reason to pick one or the other."[23]

> THE MAN, HIS WIFE, AND THE OTHER WOMAN
>
> Chapter 6 ❧
>
> "I'm so sorry about the way my family has behaved," said Violet, "I was afraid to meet you because I thought you'd be hostile. But if you'll accept me, I'd like to welcome you as a sister."
>
> Marie glanced from her sister-in-law to her husband, and smiled. "Of course I always hoped that someday Paul would have his family back."
>
> Paul beamed at both of them, his wife and his sister standing together at last.
>
> "You've made me so happy, both of you," he exclaimed from the heart.
>
> "I'm so very happy, too," his sister cried. "I never want to be parted from you again."
>
> I'm very happy for both of you," said Marie softly, "but also for myself. Now I have a sister."

> And this is the end of our story. It's a happy, happy, happy ending.
>
> They're all so happy—so they say. You might wonder whether the fact that all three of them declare themselves to be "happy" necessarily means that they are having identical emotional experiences.

Emotional education

As we grow up in a society, shaped by different influences—family, sports organizations, school systems, community groups, and religions, to mention a few—we receive guidance about what emotions are acceptable to display, and which should be kept within us. In explicit learning situations or through experiential learning, our emotions are also directed toward the "right" attitudes and actions. (Some of the factors that govern whether attitudes and actions are "right" will be considered in our discussion of Ethics in a later chapter.)

However, exactly what we are trying to educate as we expose, teach, or train carries the uncertainty over whether emotional intelligence can be measured and taught[24] and the familiar ambiguity of language and interpretation of culture. The current Dalai Lama (spiritual leader of Tibetan Buddhists) teaches that humans should strive for happiness. According to him the route to happiness is through loving kindness to others. He adopts a concept of the mind that does not equate to that in the west:

> *I believe that happiness can be achieved through training the mind…*
> *When I say "training the mind" in this context I'm not referring to "mind"*
> *merely as one's cognitive ability or intellect. Rather, I'm using the term in the sense*
> *of the Tibetan word Sem, which has a much broader meaning, closer to "psyche" or*
> *"spirit"; it includes intellect and feeling, heart and mind. By bringing about a certain*
> *inner discipline, we can undergo a transformation of our attitude, or entire*
> *outlook and approach to living.*[25]

An interlude on grief

Talking to Grief

Ah, Grief, I should not treat you
like a homeless dog
who comes to the back door
for a crust, for a meatless bone.
I should trust you.

I should coax you
into the house and give you
your own corner,
a worn mat to lie on,
your own water dish.

You think I don't know you've been living
under my porch.
You long for your real place to be readied
before winter comes. You need your name,
your collar and tag. You need
the right to warn off intruders,
to consider
my house your own
and me your person
and yourself
my own dog.

Denise Levertov

The grief cycle

Response to death or other catastrophic news has been summed up in five stages of emotion. In 1969 Dr. Elisabeth Kübler-Ross identified these characteristic phases of grief in working with the dying, and the pattern she observed has been developed, debated, modified, and applied more broadly by others since that time.

1 Denial
2 Anger
3 Bargaining
4 Depression
5 Acceptance

The healer

Cultures differ in the emotions they consider to be negative (such as anger, pain, and grief), in their attitudes toward enduring them, and in the ways in which they attempt to modify or heal them. In some cultures the healer is a single figure, while in others the role may be split, for example between a spiritual healer, a physical healer (doctor) and a psychological healer.

Who knows grief better—the person who experiences it or the person who has observed and studied it? Your answer to this simple question has many implications for what knowledge is considered to be.

Are some emotions undesirable ones to be avoided, overcome, or healed, while other ones are desirable ones to be cultivated? If so, how do you determine the difference?

Both the poem by Denise Levertov and the model of the grief cycle involve, in the end, an acceptance. Is the same thing being accepted in each case? In what ways do the poem and the five-stage cycle illustrate the characteristics of literature and psychology respectively in treating emotion as (a) subject matter and (b) a way of knowing?

Find out about the medicine wheel of the Ojibway or Lakota native American cultures, with the four quarters: spiritual, emotional, physical, and mental. In attitudes toward health in either of these cultures, is it more important to be symptom-free or to be balanced? How might these two states differ?

The complexity of emotional education increases further as we consider what *empathy* involves. Gardner's interpersonal intelligence, the Dalai Lama's loving kindness to others, Jesus Christ's teaching to love thy neighbour as thyself, and the many similar teachings in other religious traditions all emphasize the relationship between oneself and other people. Yet one might encounter a number of difficulties in trying to be truly empathetic to others—in trying imaginatively to stand in their shoes, to see through their eyes, or to feel with their feelings. No one can be someone else and know an experience from the "inside". Working by analogy to ourselves, moreover, we are limited in the degree to which we can genuinely imagine the experiences of someone else based on our own.

When the emotional outreach crosses culture, it meets further layers of difficulty in gaps of assumptions, experiences, values, and communication. A first step in cross-cultural awareness, it has been said, is to realize that people elsewhere are really just like you. A second step, without denying the first, is to realize that they are not.

Outside the emotional comfort zone

Journalists, like other human beings, shy away from stories that make them feel uncomfortable emotions, argues journalist Susan M LoTempio. As a result, it is difficult for people in the media to cover stories of disability.

"We like to think of ourselves as consummate professionals, capable of rising above our biases and fears. But the fear of disability is so personal, so deeply ingrained, that we must first acknowledge it before we can write the real stories."

The result, she suggests, is that disability stories tend to focus on the pity that accompanies victimization or the inspirational uplift that accompanies heroic overcoming of obstacles.

"Yes, such stories can calm fears, but they also reinforce inaccurate stereotypes and prevent journalists from digging deeper and doing better."[26]

A third, it could be argued, is not to give up the attempt, but to watch, listen, think, and learn. When we realize the limitations of sense perception as a way of knowing, we are not likely to close our eyes and give up, but to accept those limitations and try to overcome them through further perception, possibly with the deliberate methods of an area of knowledge. Similarly, in recognizing the difficulties of empathy, if we wish to know, we do not turn away, but try to develop it further. Part of knowing through sense perception and emotion is learning how to learn.

In which of your IB subjects do you think emotion is most significant as a way of knowing—knowing your own emotions and those of others, and thereby knowing other things? To what extent is emotion part of the subject matter of your courses or the methods of the subject that lead to the content you are learning? Consider the following questions with your class group:

- What is the role of emotional response, imaginative engagement, and empathy in treating the literature of language A1? What is their role in learning a foreign language in language B?
- What role do emotions play in your group 3 subject? Are they part of the human subject matter being studied or part of the human method of study?
- In your group 4 science course and in the mathematics of group 5, to what extent have you entered an emotion-free zone? Consider the creation and communication of knowledge in addition to the subject matter.
- In your group 6 subject of art, music, theatre, film, or dance, what is the role of emotion as subject matter or method? Which of your other subjects is most like it, and most unlike it, in use of emotion as a way of knowing?

Creativity, Action, Service: reflection on emotions

In the CAS part of your IB Diploma Programme, what is the role of emotion in each of Creativity, Action, and Service?

Read the conclusions two students reached about a CAS activity that each remembered for its impact on their emotions and their ideas.

From "Chino" to "Uncle Pablo"

I went to teach children K-3rd grade in a poor area of Santiago, completely different from anything I had ever seen. One thing was to know that these areas exist, another is to be there. The first day the kids called me "Chino" [Chinese] and I felt bad that they did not respect me. Teaching them was chaotic and I did not feel that I was in a safe place. I felt insecure. After the second week the kids ended up calling me Tio Pablo [Uncle Pablo] and trusting me. They opened up to me and told me about their difficult lives. Everyone has an idea of what they think poverty is like but when you relate to poor people on this level you understand them in terms of what kind of people they are. They are just like us. There is no difference.

Pablo Lee, Korea

Walking a mile in bare feet

With a special sensitivity tightly knit to the front of my heart, I was a girl ready to embark on a mission to save the world. With this in mind I joined 79 other students to build primitive wooden homes for economically disadvantaged families who I felt needed my help. After leaving I realized that the world around them, including me, needed help. They deserved more respect and admiration than I arrived there with. I could help them through this home, but in turn, they helped me realize that life has much to offer even in the absence of material things. Walking a mile in their bare feet taught me where I wanted to head in life and the power within myself.

Nili Silverstein, Chile

With a friend or in small groups, choose one of the following questions and discuss it in the context of your school's CAS programme and your own personal experience to date. It is important that you answer the question bearing in mind specific CAS experiences, not CAS in general.

- In what ways have your emotions affected (positively and negatively) your ability to perform and to make decisions? Conversely, how have your decisions affected what you feel and think about what you are doing?
- Have your emotions changed during the time you have been involved in this activity? Have your ideas and beliefs about the people you are working with also changed, and if so, in what ways?
- In what ways can the emotions open or close avenues to understanding? In what ways can your beliefs—and the language you use to describe situations and people—do this too?

Who's in the centre?

In Chapter 1, we asked the question "Who's in the centre?" applied to your own worldview, reflecting on the terms "international" and "internationally minded". Pause now to revisit this same question, looking back on the three ways of knowing we have treated so far.

In the following questions, you may take your "centre" to be yourself as an individual, yourself in the context of a community of knowers (e.g. your school, church, nation), or yourself in the context of all human beings. Take about 10 minutes for brainstorming, then exchange your views with others in your group.

- In what ways are you in the centre of your knowledge as you use your sense perception as a way of knowing?
- In what ways are you in the centre as you use language as a way of knowing?
- In what ways are you in the centre as you use emotion as a way of knowing?

Profit from the ambiguity of this "centre" metaphor to explore ideas.

Reasoning

Like the other ways of knowing treated in this chapter, reasoning comes so naturally to us that we rarely pay close attention to the capabilities it offers us. Yet reasoning can scarcely be separated from the thinking that we do every day in our lives.

We consider abstract ideas and symbols, and manipulate them into poems, mathematical formulae, musical scores, plays, advertisements, and political speeches. We make decisions; we set goals, and then control our actions in order to see them through. We organize, research, and plan; we solve problems on many levels, from deciding when it's safe to cross the street to building an International Space Station.

When we decide that information which we have learned in the past is pertinent to our present, we purposefully choose to recall particular memories. We select, compile, include, exclude, compare, contrast, classify, name, count, estimate, and calculate. Children as well as scientists—though with different degrees of rigour— question, put forth hypotheses and test them, seek evidence and evaluate it, analyse the results, and reach conclusions. We associate causes and effects, make correlations, and predict. When we reason, we induce, deduce, infer, generalize, specify, recognize similarities, and draw analogies. Finally, we judge, and argue endlessly about what is true, good, right, beautiful, and just…and what is not.

Abstract thinking, planning, and imagination are cognitive capabilities that constitute our human make-up. They are believed to be associated with the prefrontal cortex, a part of the neocortex that is far more developed in humans than in other primates,[27] and which provides researchers with countless unanswered questions. Neuroscientists, armed with tools such as positron emission tomography (PET scanning) and functional magnetic resonance imaging (fMRI), investigate the human brain to better understand how we reason[28] and how cognition is connected with other ways of knowing. At the opposite end of the spectrum, researchers in cognitive computing, a new interdisciplinary field, build large-scale computer models of the brain to simulate huge numbers of neurons in the neocortex.[29]

Reasoning and the other ways of knowing

Reasoning is closely connected with emotion, sense perception, and language. We have already discussed the idea that decision-making relies on emotion, so that fictional characters who are "all logic and no emotion" would lack far more than the ability to feel love and anger. They would also be unable to decide what food to have for lunch, unless very specific, measurable criteria (perhaps involving number of calories, nutritional content, and time necessary to consume the meal) were pre-programmed into them.

When we discussed sense perception we mentioned the Gestalt theory of psychology (see page 27), and the fact that our brains perceive visual patterns of meaningful wholes rather than collections of separate parts. Our natural perceptual tendency to group things together and to recognize patterns also directly affects the way we reason, particularly when we use induction and analogy.

Language is at the very core of reasoning. To recognize how easily and naturally you combine the ways of knowing in the reasoning process, meet the IB Genie.

The IB Genie

In legends spread through IB Lands
We find the story told
Of a genie in a magic lamp
Who turns all marks to gold.

The seven friends had heard the tale
And wished that it were true.
"Just find the IB Knowledge Lamp!
Success will come to you."

"It can't be true, inductively,"
Paul morosely wailed,
"I've tested all the lamps in town
And all of them have failed."

"It takes just one," Christina cried,
"To overturn your doubt.
Extend the search beyond the town!
Find the genie! Let him out!"

The seven friends searched everywhere
Till each felt quite a fool.
Abandoning the quest, they met
In the library at school.

And there between the lofty shelves,
The seven puzzled sadly,
"But could there be another way
To knowledge we want badly?"

Then eerily behind the books
Suffused a golden glow,
And from it came the husky growl,
"What do you want to know?"

"I give you wishes for a week –
I'll grant you one each day.
So take your turns and wish before
I vanish far away!"

The seven friends by accident
Had found what they did seek.
So there amidst the books at school
They planned their magic week.

The first to wish chose "eloquence"
Upon a Sunday noon
"Let others understand my thoughts!
Oh, grant this language boon!"

On Wednesday eve another friend
Chose "rationality".
"I want to understand the math
That often eludes me."

"It's talents of the heart that count,"
Another day cried Lee.
"True understanding that I seek
Consists of empathy."

After Lee had made her wish,
The next turn went to Paul,
"Athletic prowess, give me please –
Hot shots in basketball."

"I want to sing amazingly,"
Said Saturday's friend, doing trills.
Another day Maimouna begged,
"Please give me essay skills."

On Friday in the setting sun
A friend (not Sally) said,
"I'd like to understand myself,
And the confusing life I've led."

Chiara one day took a turn
And later also Tim.
It wasn't Tim who wished to sing
Or know himself within.

The seven friends were jubilant
And eager now to learn,
With knowledge skills so granted them
As each had had a turn.

And off they went to practise scales
Or basketball or math—
Or introspection, kindness, or
Whatever was the path.

The genie snug behind the books
Dimmed down the lamplight's glow
And, smiling to himself, intoned,
"What do you what to know?

Questions

1   Why do you think stories that deal that deal with magic, which
    defies rationality, are so popular?

2   If your own school library had an IB genie, what form of
    knowledge would you wish for and why? (Should every IB library
    have a genie?)

3   What is the name given to the approach of testing many lamps
    and reaching a general conclusion about them? (Hint: the name
    you want was included in the poem.)

There is actually a puzzle embedded in "The IB Genie" poem. You will
not be able to solve it in your head, but will need paper. Your task is
to determine: which friend wished on which day, and for what?

Hint: Which day, according to you, is the first of the week? Which day
or days are "the weekend"? Unless you make the cultural assumption
that Sunday comes first, you will not be able to do the puzzle. (Being
aware what you are assuming has an important role in reasoning.)

Pay attention to your process, in order to answer the following
questions:

a   As you were solving the puzzle, how did you know that you'd
    made a mistake?

b   How did you know that you solved the puzzle successfully?

c   Concluding question: The solution of the puzzle[30] allowed you to
    know things you did not know before. How did you achieve that
    new knowledge? How did the approach differ from the one in
    question 3?

Language and reasoning

Toddlers will start using nouns such as "cookie" and "dog" as early as age one or one-and-a-half.[31] If you have contact with toddlers, this scene might seem familiar to you. The toddler sees a large black animal, and Mummy says, "doggie" as they look at it. The toddler then sees another animal, this one brown, and Mummy says, "doggie". The next time the toddler sees a similar animal, he says, "doggie". If he has generalized correctly, Mummy confirms. If he has generalized incorrectly, Mummy corrects, "No, that's a deer." The child continues to apply language by perceiving common features and generalizing them, and connecting them to words he's hearing.

Like language acquisition, reasoning involves a continual interplay between the particular and the general. We experience the world as particular instances of things (such as faces, raindrops, and cookies), but to be able to think effectively we generalize those instances into categories to which we give names. These names—these words—are associated with our concept of the category, as well as with the common features they share (think about cookies now—what characteristics do all cookies share?). After we have developed the concept we are able to reason in the opposite direction, applying the knowledge associated with the concept to particular cases.

Having mental concepts, for example of "dog" and "cookie", allows us to live in the world without having to treat every new encounter with a dog or a cookie as unique. Even if you have never seen this particular dog or that particular cookie, you have a good idea of how to respond to both—which to bite into and which to take for a walk on a leash.

Establishing categories, naming them, and classifying are part of the inductive reasoning process: it begins with the observations we make, with information we take in through sense perceptions, and it results in a generalization applicable to all the members of the class or category.

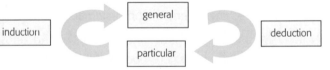

We'll revisit this interplay between the particular and the general later in this chapter, when we discuss inductive and deductive reasoning in more detail. Now let's focus on deductive reasoning, which begins with general statements.

Playing with all, none, and some

The way a generalization is expressed is significant in understanding its breadth and its limits. Who or what are we including?

Generalizations are expressed in language with sentences that start with the word "all", for example, "all cookies are sweet". Sometimes generalizations are also expressed in sentences that start with the word "no" or "none", such as "no dogs are five-legged" or "none of the dogs is five-legged". (Can you convert these two sentences into a sentence starting with "all"?)

Independently of whether or not these generalizations are true, each makes a statement about every single cookie and every single dog in the universe (all dogs in the universe are not five-legged). How many non-sweet cookies and five-legged dogs would we have to find in order to contradict these statements?

If you said in both cases "one", or "at least one", you were correct. One counter-example will demolish a whole generalization. Thus, sentences starting with "all", "no" and "none" are fragile statements, and should be used carefully. And watch out. The "all" doesn't need to be explicitly stated. So, if someone says, "Teenagers are self-centred", this statement refers to *all* teenagers in the world, whereas if someone says, "The teenagers in this room are self-centred" the statement includes only some of them. (Hint: you may wish to remember this when writing TOK essays.)

The words "always", "never", "everyone", "no one", "everywhere", and "nowhere" are used similarly; they also describe every single instance. What would you have to say, to contradict the following statements?

1   You never talk to me.
2   You can find this gadget everywhere.
3   Nobody loves me.
4   Everyone here is rude.
5   I have nothing to wear.

You might have given the following correct answers: "I talked to you *on Wednesday*", "I can't find this gadget at *the store* I like to shop at", "*Your mother* loves you", "*I'm* not rude", or "You have *that beautiful shirt*". You could also have said, "*Sometimes* I talk to you", "There are *some* stores in my town where I can't find this gadget", "*Some* people love you", "*Some* people here are not rude", and "You have *some* things to wear in that full closet of yours", and you would also have been correct.

Notice the pattern: all sentences in the second set of answers contain the word "some", which is another important word to be aware of. "Some" can stand for *any* number of cases between "all" and "none", and means "at least one". It expresses a very vague idea, as do "sometimes", "some people", and "somewhere". "Some" does not express a generalization; it refers to a particular case, or a number of particular cases.

Of course, "some" isn't the only word we use to describe the numerous possibilities between "none" and "all". For example, we could also use the expressions "a couple" or "a few" or "5.3%" or "$\frac{1}{3}$" or "14" or "many" or "nearly everyone" or "almost all". (How do the expressions with numbers affect you emotionally? Do you shy away from them, or do you enjoy their precision?)

Let's stick with the very imprecise "some" for now. What would you have to say to contradict the statement, "Some teenagers are lazy?"

If you answered "Some teenagers are not lazy", you were wrong: you'd have to say, "All teenagers are not lazy". That vague word "some" can stand for 99.999% of instances, but it can also stand for *one single* instance of teenager laziness. In order to prove that this one instance isn't the case, you'd have to prove that there are no instances whatsoever of teenage laziness. Impossible, you say?

Indeed, it is very difficult to demolish sentences that start with "some". Some teenagers may be lazy and some not, without any contradiction.

Can you *negate* (a more precise way of saying "contradict", which has a very specific meaning in logic books) any statement that is thrown your way? What would you have to say to negate "All IB candidates are compassionate"? How about "all metals expand with heat", "all even numbers are divisible by two", "all politicians are trustworthy", and "all goobles are fingfangs"? Don't be concerned with whether the statement or its negation is true or false (if one is true, the other will necessarily be false). Instead, focus your attention on the form of the statement "All P is Q", and the form of the statement you've used to contradict it.

Solely from the form "All P is Q", we can immediately infer—deduce from reasoning—the form of the statement that will negate it, which is: "Some P is not Q". Every single time you see a statement in the form "All P is Q", you can negate it by asserting that "Some P is not Q".

For your own protection, do not teach these rules of negation, below, to your younger sibling. We'll use P and Q to stand for any category you like, in the same way that the variable x in algebra can stand for any number.

It is always the case that:

1 An "all" statement—All P is Q—is negated by a statement of the form "Some P is not Q" and vice versa.
2 An "all" statement—All P is Q—is negated by a statement of the form "No P is Q" and vice versa. (Which negation is easier to apply in practice?)
3 A "some statement"—Some P is Q—is not negated by another "some" statement, "Some P is not Q" and vice versa.
4 A "no" statement—No P is Q—is negated by a statement of the form "Some P is Q" and vice versa.

There are also other inferences we can make, just from the form of statements starting with "all", "none", or "some". Here's one of them:

5 An "all" statement—All P is Q—implies the "some" statement "Some P is Q".

Working individually, test the five rules above by replacing P and Q with words that make the "all" or "no" statements true. Compare with examples offered by your classmates. Why is "the majority rules" not a good criterion for accepting these five rules?

Validity and truth

You now know how to negate every "all", "some", and "no/none" statement that comes your way, no matter what it is referring to. The source of the statement, the context in which it was stated, and even its truth or falsehood don't matter: you are able to negate any of these statements, solely based on the form they take.

Logical implication

The term "implication" appears in criterion C of the TOK essay assessment criteria.

An implication is a logical relation between two ideas, stated in the form "A implies B" or "If A, then B".

For any valid implication, if idea A is true, then idea B cannot be false.

This powerful role of form in deductive reasoning leads to the notion of validity. Validity depends solely on the form which a statement or a chain of reasoning takes, not on its content. Thus, validity is very different from truth. Sometimes the expression "that's logical" is used to express agreement or to convey, "that makes sense". "That's logical" used in this manner usually means "that's true", not "that's valid", so be aware of the ambiguity of language as you use these terms.

It is very important that we keep the terms "validity" and "truth" separate in our minds; they each have precise meanings that we'll be building upon.

Now let us re-test the first three rules listed above, but this time replacing P and Q with words that make the "all" statements false. Do you continue to agree with the statements?

Let's use P = men and Q = females, and examine our three statements.

1 "All men are females" is negated by "Some men are not females".

2 "All men are females" is negated by "No men are females".

Do these make sense? It would seem so. If a man were told, "all men are females," he could point at himself and say, "no, I'm not". And in this case, the false "all" statement is so absurd that even the second case—"no men are females"—could be used in practice to negate the "all" statement.

3 "All men are females" implies that "some men are females".

Despite the fact that both sides of the implication are false, the implication itself is a *valid* one, as was demonstrated by your examples in the previous section when you used a true "all" statement. It continues to be valid, no matter what we are talking about.

If, however, we were to state that "Some P is Q implies that all P is Q", this would be an *invalid* implication. The conclusion doesn't necessarily follow. For example, "Some IB students have an IQ of 152 implies that all IB students have an IQ of 152". The implication is invalid, for every category P and Q you may wish to consider.

Truth applies to the general and particular statements that we are reasoning about. To determine whether a statement is true or false, we need to examine its content and its meaning. We need to look at evidence, justifications, and reasons why we consider the statement to be true. We will discuss truth in Chapter 3.

Validity applies to the reasoning process. "All P is Q" implies "Some P is Q" is a valid implication. If it is true that "All P is Q" then it is also true (because it logically follows) that "Some P is Q".

The relationship between the validity of an argument and the truth of its premises—which we will call the *key assertion of deductive reasoning*—can be stated thus:

**If the argument is valid and all premises are true,
then the conclusion *must* be true.**

Notice that this is an implication in the form "A and B together implies C". If A (the argument is valid) is the case and B (all premises are true) is the case, then, necessarily, C (the argument's conclusion is true) is the case.

We can also state this key assertion in the opposite direction:

**If the conclusion of an argument is *not* true, then either the argument
is invalid or at least one of the premises is false.**

The second form of the key assertion can be useful when you are testing arguments for validity, or checking your own writing.

The blender metaphor for validity and truth

The relationship between validity and truth is a very powerful one. A valid deductive argument enables us to derive logically, or deduce, true conclusions from true premises.

Though the conclusions are already embedded in the premises, the valid linking of the premises in the argument allows new insights to surface. Think back to "The IB Genie", and the fact that the answers to the puzzle were contained in the poem before you even read it.

Let's explore this relationship a little further. Imagine that the reasoning process is a blender, that true statements are food that is good to eat, and that false statements are spoiled food.

A valid argument is like a blender that works well. If you place fresh milk and chocolate ice-cream (true statements) in this blender for a few minutes, you will **certainly** get a delicious chocolate milk-shake (true conclusion) at the end.

If you place sour milk (false statement) into this blender, no matter how many other fresh ingredients (true statements) you include, your milk-shake will probably not taste too good (false conclusion). However, you could also end up with good food (true conclusion) at the end, such as sour-milk griddle cakes (see www.cooks.com/rec/story/121/,

or search the web for "sour milk recipe"). There is no way to know what the result will be if one of the premises is false. There is no guarantee of success as there was above.

Finally, an invalid argument is like a blender that has a mind of its own. Anything can happen with any food you put in it. The results are so unreliable that you don't even bother to try to use the blender; you go and eat out instead.

The key assertion of deductive reasoning:

**If all premises are true and the argument
is valid, then the conclusion *must* be true.**

Validity applies to the reasoning process. If the thinking is done correctly, the argument is valid.

Truth applies to the content of the statements.

If the statements used as premises are true, and the reasoning has been done correctly, then the conclusion is also true.

If any of the statements used as a premise is false, the conclusion will be false—except in cases of lucky accidents.

When is an argument not a fight?

"Stop arguing, you two! Get along". The parental voice of the world equates an argument with a belligerent dispute. An argument in reasoning, however, is entirely peaceful. It is a clear and orderly progression from the assumptions (or premises) that we start with to the conclusions which we draw from them.

In the real world, arguments can be hidden within long paragraphs, and it may take some effort to identify their premises and conclusion. Here are some points to pay attention to, as you attempt to analyse an argument:

- There will usually be more than two premises.
- Some premises considered obvious won't be stated explicitly.
- Words or phrases such as "because", "for", "since", "if", "when", and "in view of the fact that" indicate that what is said next is a premise.
- Words or phrases such as "therefore", "so", "then", "hence", "thus", "consequently", and "it follows that" indicate that what is said next is a conclusion.

Exercise: Find an argument in an editorial published in today's newspaper. Identify its premises and conclusion. Identify any implicit premises as well. Exchange your argument with a classmate's, and check each other's analyses.

In order to introduce you to some of the key ideas and vocabulary you will need for TOK discussion (and essay writing), we'll offer you only two very simple deductive arguments called "syllogisms". If you're interested in learning how to analyse syllogisms yourself, or pursue more complex forms of arguments, we recommend an excellent text such as Irving Copi's *Introduction to Logic*.

A very simple deductive argument with two premises (often called assumptions) and one conclusion is represented below. The line separating the premises from the conclusion is a symbol for "therefore". (Note: The terms "argument" and "assumptions" appear in criterion C of the TOK essay assessment criteria.)

Argument 1
Premise 1 (major premise)
Premise 2 (minor premise)
Conclusion

All IB Diploma candidates are geniuses.
I am an IB Diploma candidate.
I am a genius.

The major premise is a general statement and the minor premise is a particular statement. The premises attempt to support the truth of the conclusion, which connects the particular case (me) to the general categories mentioned in the first premise (IB candidates and geniuses).

If you attempted to tell people point blank, "I'm a genius, you've got to believe me!" you would probably be laughed at. If, however, you were to offer people reasons—preferably good reasons—to believe you, you would have a far better chance of making your point. Herein lies the power of reasoning as a method of justification, which we will discuss in more detail in Chapter 3.

Typically in a deductive argument, some of the premises will be general statements, and others will be particular statements. We begin from a general statement such as how things are in the world, and construct an argument that enables us to arrive at a conclusion about a particular instance.

In the context of the arguments in the editorial articles you have been analysing, take a few minutes to discuss the following questions in small groups, then come together as a class to compare answers. Read the comments below the questions only after you've had a chance to tackle and discuss them first.

1 Is the major premise of the argument true? How can you find out?
2 Is the argument valid? How do you know?
3 Assuming that the minor premise is true, is the conclusion true? How do you know?

Comments on question 1—How to determine if the major premise is true

Examining the truth of general statements again illustrates the interplay between general and particular which we mentioned at the beginning of this chapter. One way to check the truth of the statement would be to examine many particular cases of IB Diploma candidates and determine if each is a genius (we will discuss this inductive process later). Much more will be said about ways to investigate truth as we proceed with our exploration of TOK.

Comments on question 2—How to test the validity of arguments

As we have seen, to determine validity we need to examine the form of arguments. A valid argument follows a certain structure, order or pattern, moving from step to step, that is, premise to premise, in a correct fashion. If an incorrect "move" is made, the argument is invalid, independently of whether or not the premises are true.

Comments on question 3—In this case, is the conclusion true?

This is a valid argument, so we know, from the key assertion of deductive reasoning, that the conclusion must be true if all the premises are true.

Here's another deductive argument, this time an invalid one.

Argument 2

Premise 1 (major premise)
Premise 2 (minor premise)
Conclusion

All IB diploma candidates are intelligent.
Stephen Hawking is intelligent.
Stephen Hawking is an IB Diploma candidate.

(Stephen Hawking needn't be the famous physicist and could be the name of your pet chameleon, but either one illustrates the mistake in reasoning here.) Notice how the form of this argument differs from the first. In that one, the connection between the major and minor premise was made from the category that immediately followed "all", leading to validity. In this one, the connection was attempted with the term "intelligent", which is further from "all", leading to invalidity.

A fallacy is a mistake in reasoning such as this one. In this chapter we're discussing formal fallacies, which derive from the form the argument takes. In Chapter 4 we'll be discussing informal fallacies, which are mistakes in reasoning due to things other than form.

Exercise: Test further categories for P and Q in the following structures, which replicate the examples we discussed. Specifically, try several combinations of true and false premises with both arguments, to get a feeling for the power of the key assertion of deductive reasoning.

Argument 1 (valid)
All P is Q
<u>R is P</u>
R is Q

Argument 2 (invalid)
All P is Q
<u>R is Q</u>
R is P

Counter-arguments and counter-claims
The key assertion of deductive reasoning:

**If all premises are true and the argument is valid,
then the conclusion must be true.**

This key assertion states a logical implication: if the part following the "if" is the case, then the part following the "then" *must* be the case. Thus, this assertion provides us with a way to ensure—a very powerful word—that we can infer true conclusions from true premises. For example, assuming you reasoned validly while solving the IB Genie puzzle, the (assumed true for the sake of the game) information embedded in the poem allowed you to reach several new conclusions (true within the context of the game).

The key assertion also gives us two tools to counter-argue the conclusion stated in an argument:

1   you can counter-argue that the reasoning is invalid, or
2   you can counter-argue that one of the premises is uncertain, questionable, or false.

If you succeed with either tool, the original conclusion doesn't necessarily follow.

Exercise: Find another argument in the editorial section of a newspaper. What counter-arguments could you use to weaken the stated conclusion?

"Counter-claims" as used in criterion C of the TOK essay assessment criteria are similar to counter arguments, but far more interesting. Instead of your attempting to weaken someone else's argument, you attempt to weaken your own. By asking "what can be said against my argument?" and addressing its weaknesses yourself, you strengthen your argument by demonstrating that you've carefully and thoughtfully considered your own premises and chain of reasoning.

Exercise: As you watch the news on TV, keep your ears open for the use of counter-claims. You might wish to watch a news programme that goes deeper than mere "sound bites". How do you respond emotionally to a speaker who addresses counter-claims, as opposed to one who does not?

As you write your own arguments and analyse those written by others, keep in mind that a strong argument is:

- *valid*—the form of the argument is such that the argument's conclusion logically follows from its premises—and also
- *sound*—the argument is valid and all its premises are true.

Inductive reasoning

Where do the true general statements we use as premises in our sound deductive arguments come from?

In mathematics many of our arguments (also called mathematical proofs, based on deductive reasoning) use premises such as "All right-angled triangles have a 90° angle". Mathematics is rife with such conventional definitions, similar to those in language. A general statement based on such a definition is easy for us to accept as true, at least for the sake of argument. However, when the statement addresses things that happen in the empirical world—things we can perceive, measure, or experiment with—it becomes a bit more complicated to arrive at a true general statement.

For each example below, consider (a) how you know the answer to the question, and (b) on a scale of 0–100%, how certain you are that your answer is true.

1   Will the sun rise tomorrow?
2   Will you eventually die?

Inductive reasoning methods are used in the natural and human sciences, and allow us to make generalizations based on observations of individual instances. Inductive reasoning is also used in areas of human endeavour such as marketing, business administration, farming, government, education, and telecommunications—pretty much in any circumstance where we need to gather data about a large number of objects, people, places, or events over time, in order to find out what happens in most cases. In the course of a normal day everyone uses inductive methods many times, even though most of us may not be consciously aware of using them.

We can be 100% certain that all future cases of a right triangle will have a right angle, because if something doesn't have a right angle then it won't be called a right triangle (yes, definitions are circular, by definition). In contrast, the inductive methods we will discuss here—classical induction, statistics, and analogical reasoning—will not provide us with generalizations that are applicable to all possible present and future instances, even if we often have excellent reasons to trust them despite that.

If you are disturbed by the idea of not having 100% certainty through inductive reasoning, consider the fact that you already trust a huge number of generalizations about things in the world, about which you can have a greater or lesser degree of certainty when you apply them to a specific case. Do you take any kind of medicine? Ride in a car, bike, or public transportation? Eat any kind of processed food, or follow a nutritional plan? Follow any kind of exercise routine? If you said "yes" to any of these questions—if you don't live under a rock, in a coma, by yourself, inside an isolated monastery—you are, in practice, already relying on a countless number of inductive generalizations. If they didn't work, or worked so infrequently that they couldn't be trusted, you would be very aware of them indeed.

One of our challenges with inductive reasoning is thus to decide how much we can trust the inductive generalizations about the world that we and others make. To do that, we need to take a look at how the different inductive methods operate.

Classical induction

Whereas deductive reasoning begins from a general statement, induction starts from observations. Here is a classic example of inductive reasoning:

I saw a swan and it was white
I saw a second swan and it was white
I saw a third swan and it was white

…

I saw an "Nth" swan and it was white
All swans are white (A general statement is the conclusion)

How many cases of white swans do you think you should notice before legitimately concluding that all swans are white? How many instances of sunrise do we need to see to believe that it occurs every morning, and that we can trust the sun to rise tomorrow? When we repeatedly observe instances of a particular phenomenon, it might not seem to be a tremendous leap of faith to cross the line and draw a generalization. But it is.

There is no magical number that can tell us when we have enough evidence to safely conclude with an inductive generalization of this kind. Imagine taking a voyage around the globe to observe swans. After tens of thousands of instances of white swans in Africa, Asia, and North America you arrive in the UK, take a walk in a central London park and there on the river, right before your now expert eyes, is one (just one!) black-necked swan. One false instance is enough to topple over the general conclusion you had painstakingly reached. As Bertrand Russell stated, "The man who has fed the chicken every day throughout its life at last wrings its neck instead".[32] The chicken cannot trust its experience of the inductive process, but perhaps it is humans it shouldn't trust.

Despite not offering 100% certainty, classical induction works quite well. Much of our knowledge about the natural sciences is based on generalizations backed by repeated observation of phenomena. Some examples are objects falling to the ground with an acceleration of 9.8 m/s^2, mitosis demonstrating specific phases occurring in a specific order, and chemical reactions consuming the same proportions of each compound each time. Finally, no case has ever been reported of a person who hasn't died by age 123; unless a great scientific breakthrough happens soon, it is extremely likely that we too shall pass.

Activity

Consider your group 4 subject. Review some of the discoveries you have studied and in particular the generalizations that have been the result of classical induction.

Statistics

Life insurance companies exist because we believe that we are mortal. Life insurance companies thrive thanks to statistics and professionals who specialize in actuarial science. Actuaries figure out how long people in our age group (and similar to ourselves in other ways considered to be relevant to our longevity) are expected to live on average. That is an important question for life insurance companies; answering it correctly means that on average we the insured will pay the company a larger premium than they will pay to our heirs in the event of our death, which is necessary if they are to make a profit.

When we discussed the terms "all", "none", and "some", we mentioned the possibility of using numbers to describe the infinite interval between "none" and "all". Statistics does exactly that. It makes statements about an entire population using data based on a random sample. Statisticians are very much aware that they seldom have access to an entire population, and have built their science upon that premise.

Enter a random percentage in an Internet search engine, and you will find a statistical result based on that number. Examine the statements below to get a feeling for the pervasiveness of statistics in our knowledge about the world.

● Women initiate 91% of divorce.[33]
● 91% of emails in India are spam.[34]
● 82% of cancer patients report "chemo brain" during, after treatment.[35]
● By 2009, 74% of all corporate phone lines will be VOIP.[36]
● 56.2% of software developers use Open Source.[37]

Each of the quantitative measures of "some" listed above comes with a story behind it (which is far more complex than the swan counter's notes, with entries such as "Monday: 21 white swans. Tuesday: 15 white swans..."). Each result is based on an experimental design (how was the random sample selected?) and on a methodology (how was the data analysed?) that need to be examined critically, to allow us to trust the results.[38]

Statistics enables correlations to be drawn between things that are observed in the world and possible factors that contribute to their occurrence. This is crucial information to medical practice and research—drug development, cancer research, health maintenance, evaluation of surgical procedures, for example. Other academic fields that use statistics are economics, psychology, sociology, engineering, and agricultural and environmental science. Statistics are used in the manufacturing, business, and marketing industries, as well as many others.

More than merely providing quantitative snapshots of a moment in time (for example, a future study might find that spam emails in India have decreased to 78%), statistics can go deeper. It can enable correlations to be drawn between things that are observed in the world (such as lung cancer) and possible factors that contribute to their occurrence (for example, exposure to cigarette smoke). Numbers and statistics can convey a lot of information in a condensed form and might seem to you to be the most neutral of all possible ways of representing reality, the epitome of information in its most indisputable and bare of forms. Does this assessment stand up to your scrutiny? Or are numbers and statistics just as susceptible as the other forms of symbolic representation—maps, photographs, natural language itself—to interpretation, bias, exaggeration, and manipulation?

Nizkor, Nizkor et achinu veachyotenu…*
by Chen Arad

Almost since I can remember myself, I can remember these few words, words that originate in a religious Jewish prayer, read every year in "Yom Hashoa", the Israeli Remembrance Day for the Holocaust. Every year, all over Israel, infants, youth, adults and elders all mention the murder of six million Jews in the Holocaust. Six million victims; this inconceivable number is emphasized time and again, specifically during this day, but all year long as well when talking about the subject, everywhere, by dedicated educators, by loving parents, by publicist media and by charismatic politicians. The consequence of this, which can be debated, is that when asked about the subject, any child will easily utter the number. Even if this will be followed by true sadness and a shed tear, a question must be asked: if this child, even if genuinely and truly sad, can really grasp the pain, sorrow, tragedy and remorse that this calamity, represented by a number, holds in it? Does his sadness truly come from a realization that six million living, unique stories with unique motives, needs and loves were systematically brought to death? To what extent are we all, experienced and educated as we may be, small children when we refer to such a complex, intriguing, yet deeply disturbing point in human history with a number?…

*The Hebrew word "Nizkor" means "we will remember".

As a critical thinker increasingly aware that ways of knowing can have an important impact on what we believe and assume to be knowledge, read the extract from a TOK essay (above) and ask yourself, as did the candidate who wrote it: "What's in a number?"

Both in the context of 20th-century history and of Jewish culture, six million is no mere number: it is shorthand for a tragedy of numbing proportions. In your mind compare for impact, precision, accuracy, detail, and truth this statistic to reading a testimony by a

Holocaust survivor, or observing a family tree marked with stars of David above the names of those who died in concentration camps. On your own or in a small group in your classroom, discuss the conclusions you reached about six million as a number. Think about the connotations of other statistics and numbers that might have been taught to you as a child, about your nation, religion, or region.

Mark Twain famously attributed to Benjamin Disraeli the remark that "there are three kinds of lies: lies, damned lies, and statistics".[39] When misused, distorted, and misinterpreted, this can indeed be the case with statistics. The strength of well-applied statistics, however, is that it does not attempt to generalize beyond what the data allows, and offers us a measure of that uncertainty.

Analogical reasoning

Classical induction requires that we observe very many instances, and statistics requires complex methodologies. In practice we cannot do either quickly enough when there is the need to make an immediate decision. Analogical reasoning is based on two steps: (1) there is a recognition of similarities between two or more things, and (2) there is an assumption that if two or more things are similar in one way, they will also be similar in other ways.

If I need to buy a pair of shoes for a party on Saturday, I'm not going to choose where to shop by conducting a poll amongst my friends to determine which store is best and then statistically analyse the results, nor will I want to visit every store in town. I'm more likely to return to the store where I bought shoes a few times previously, considering that I got good wear from shoes I bought there, that prices were reasonable, and that the salespeople were helpful. I will base my decision on a few past experiences, in the hope that conditions haven't changed. Alternatively I will ask my friend, who provided me with good recommendations in the past, to recommend a shoe store now, assuming he continues to know my taste and know his stores.

You are likely to study for an exam based on the kinds of questions your teacher (or the IBO) has asked previously, in the hope that the test you take will be similar to past ones. We buy an unknown music CD or download a song by a band we enjoy, in the hope that we will also enjoy their new music. Examples of analogical reasoning abound in our daily lives.

Analogical reasoning is commonplace in medicine, especially in diagnosis. The doctor's knowledge of medicine consists to a great extent of generalizations based on statistics—"this symptom manifests itself in 72% of patients"…"this medication is effective 97% of the time, but patients who take this other drug are susceptible to…" Even though these numbers are not applicable to any individual's body in particular, it's likely that your body is similar enough to most bodies used in the study to justify the analogy. Thus the doctor is able to make an educated guess of what ails you, and prescribe a treatment that is likely to work.

Sometimes we reason analogically not because we don't have enough time, but because we don't have enough information. For

Vocabulary box
inductive reasoning
deductive reasoning
analogical reasoning
creative reasoning
logical reasoning
statistics
general vs. particular
generalization
negate
counter-example
counter-claim
implication, implies
"it follows"
inference, infer
validity vs. truth
invalid
argument
premise
assumption
conclusion
conjecture

example, some of us imagine that life may exist on other planets in other solar systems, because it exists here. These kinds of analogy provide scientists with hypotheses they can pursue. The history of science is rich with stories of new discoveries based on analogical hypotheses.

Hypothetico-deductive reasoning

Here's a fun way to observe the interplay of induction and deduction. Play the game below, or another game,[40] in class or with a group of friends.

The Crazy Captain's game

You and the other members of your group live in a small community in a cosy bay on the Pacific Ocean. Usually nothing much happens over the summer, when most of you listen to the lap-lap of the gentle waves against the shoreline from the comfort of your deck chairs near the communal docks. But today is different. Because this summer has been so hot and dry, a forest fire is spreading from the mountains towards your community.

Choose now one member of your class (or the teacher) to act as Captain of the Evacuation Boat, waiting at the docks to take you all to safety. Imagine that the Captain has assured you that you have just enough time to run home and pick up a few belongings, those that you cannot bear to lose forever to the flames. Take note, though, your Captain is quite peculiar, since she will allow you to bring on board only items that conform to a rule—a rule that only she knows. You must guess it to be able to grab quickly your permitted personal treasure before you climb aboard.

Captain: you should now invent a rule. The rule could be based on the characteristics of the objects, on arbitrary features of the names of these (for example, items starting with S, having double letters, starting with the same letter as the name of the person proposing it). Or the rule could stipulate features of the way the proposal has to be made (with a "please") or even numerical patterns in answering (every five proposals gets a yes).

All of you should then take turns suggesting what you would like to bring, and listen to the Captain's replies. Based on the Captain's yes's and no's, your mission is to discover the rule. However, when you think you know the rule, do not shout it out. Just keep taking turns until everyone who is playing is on board ready to sail to safety.

Exercise

Give three examples of reasoning by analogy. How likely are you to trust your results, on a scale of 0 to 10?

Like natural scientists doing research on the fringes of their disciplines, when beginning this game you did not know the nature of the pattern you were seeking—the Crazy Captain could have invented any kind of rule. However, as you accumulated evidence— more and more instances of suggestions of particular items, which the Captain either accepted or rejected—you further refined your guess about the rule she had made.

The hypothetical-deductive method is a continual interplay between deductive and inductive reasoning, mediated by testing done in the real world.

The first step is inductive: based on only a few cases, you formed an initial hypothesis which was a generalization (for example, "The Captain wants on the boat only things that are good for the beach").

The second step is deductive: You chose a particular instance to test (for example, sunscreen). Think back to the valid and invalid arguments on pages 72–5. Your hypothesis served as the major premise, and the item you chose served as the minor premise. You built yourself an argument, whose conclusion you tested next.
The third step is a test of the particular instance which you chose in

the second step. You asked the Captain, "is the conclusion of the argument I constructed true or false?"

If the Captain rejected your object (false conclusion) you knew there had to be something wrong with your major premise. (Think back to the key assertion of deductive reasoning: Why is that the case?) So you had to go back to step one, and reformulate your prior generalization—or formulate an entirely new one—to use as your next hypothesis.

If, on the other hand, the Captain accepted your object (true conclusion), you went back to step two, choosing another particular instance to test. How many times did the Captain accept your object, before you were sure you'd discovered the rule? What made you feel sure you had the solution?

Perhaps what attracts people to the natural sciences is that they enjoy cracking puzzles. Your experience during this game was to some extent similar to what scientists experience as they test their hypotheses with individual cases, in laboratories around the world. Nature is a bit more reticent with its answers than the Captain was, as we shall see in Chapter 5, and there are other differences in practice which we will explore later.

Creative reasoning

As you played the game, you might have wondered if you weren't overlooking a pattern you weren't expecting to find. It may seem counter-intuitive that sometimes, in order to discover a logical pattern, one has to "think outside the box", so to speak, which is quite different from deductive reasoning. Think back to how you worked on the IB Genie puzzle, or to the most recent set of maths problems you solved without a calculator. Every step must be correct, logically following from the previous steps.

In creative reasoning, however, this plodding linearity is not strictly necessary; in fact, it can be a hindrance. According to one of its main exponents, creative reasoning is "like building a bridge. The parts do not have to be self-supporting at every stage but when the last part is fitted into place the bridge suddenly becomes self-supporting".[41]

In pairs or on your own, solve the mind twisters in the box below. (Don't peek—the answers are found on page 87.)

Wrap your mind around these!

1. A man is found dead hanging from a rope around his neck in the centre of a room with no furniture. A small puddle is on the floor below him. He had no apparent way of hanging himself but the police declared it a suicide. Explain.

2. A woman had two sons who were born at the same hour of the same day of the same year. But they were not twins. How could this be so?

3. There are six eggs in a basket. Six people each take one egg. How can it be that one egg is left in the basket?

> Question: Think of a child playing hide-and-go-seek. To what extent is he using the hypothetico-deductive method?

> ### Creative reasoning quiz
> Think, for a moment, about each of the following professionals. Assume they are extremely successful in their fields. Which of them might use creative reasoning?
>
> 1. a natural scientist
> 2. a mathematician
> 3. a historian
> 4. a human scientist
> 5. an artist
> 6. a lawyer
> 7. a medical doctor
>
> The correct answer is upside down below.

Answer to the Creative Reasoning Quiz: All of them.

Classification

As we enter a discussion of how we classify our perceptions, emotions, and ideas, you will surely recognize many concepts already raised regarding grouping and categorizing. Examining sense perception, we considered the way that we associate new sensations with past ones in both involuntary interpretation by the brain and more conscious interpretation. Examining language, we considered the way words create categories for our perceptions, emotions, and thoughts, and the variability of those categories for different cultures and different communication purposes. Examining reasoning, we recognized the interplay between the general and the particular, the category and the thing within it.

Profoundly significant for what and how we know, classification merits our further attention, as it has implications in all areas of knowledge.

The following group activity invites you to consider how we classify.

Scheming to classify

In advance, designate one person to collect 12 objects with as much diversity as possible. These should be placed on a surface so that everyone can see them. Get into groups of 3 or 4 people. Each group's mission is to classify those 12 objects into categories. These are the rules:

Rule 1: Create three or four categories that will accommodate all the objects. Describe each category with the label "Things that are [...]".

Rule 2: Each category must have two or more objects (no orphans or empty categories!).

Rule 3: Each object must belong to one, and only one category (this is the difficult part!).

Rule 4: Be as creative as you can. Groups are encouraged to handle the objects in order to get the creative juices flowing.

After 15–20 minutes of discussion, each group should describe their classification scheme using a table or chart, on a medium that can be viewed by the entire class. The class then critiques each group's scheme. Among the few schemes that will survive close scrutiny (Rule 3 will usually be the killer), the scheme that best satisfies Rule 4 is deemed to be the winner.

After you've done the exercise (and only after that!), continue reading below.

Imagine Carl Linnaeus in the 1730s, starting to develop his impressive *Species Plantarum* and *Systema Naturae* (kingdoms/phyla/classes/orders/families/genera/species), aimed to classify all the elements of the natural world. This was arguably the most complex problem of sense perception ever faced. He was determined to include in his classification system animals, plants, and minerals. But on what aspect of them should he focus? What should his criterion of selection be? Weight, colour, density, texture, shape, symmetry, or even smell—any of these could have qualified as important distinguishing features of the vast array of elements he meant to classify. He probably considered them all, and probably some others too. Over a period of 35 years, Linnaeus continually revised his system, including new plant and animal species. He had a significant insight about what features were important when, in the 10th edition, he decided to classify whales as mammals instead of as fish.[42]

It wasn't just the professor's keen and observant eyes and great personal interest that were at play in the construction of this system.

Linnaeus had to use reasoning skills every step of the way. How many species do we need in a particular genus? How many genera do we need in a particular family in order to accommodate all the objects we placed in an order? Reasoning had to be used continually to test the scheme against rule 3 of the classification exercise, "Each object must belong to one, *and only one* category". (Why is this a requirement for any useful classification scheme, by the way?)

Finally, Linnaeus was also faced with a linguistic challenge, having to find names for all the different categories he created. (His *Species Plantarum* (1753) listed approximately 8,000 plant species from around the world, while his *Systema Naturae* (12th edition, 1758) includes some 4,378 animal species.[43]) For other people to understand and be able to use our categories, we need to name them. In turn, other people need to agree to use those names to refer to the same characteristics as we did. We have already seen that language is a conventional system of symbols—"conventional" because people agree that the word "dog" denotes that four-legged kind of creature (and not a rock or a piece of cheese), and "symbol" because a word is not the thing it symbolizes, but *stands* for that thing.

Think back to the exercise you did in discussion of language, when one person gave a word and others noted their associations. If the word was "dog", for example, the first thought that came to your mind might have been a particular dog you know, perhaps your family dog. It is a specific dog, with an individual name, in the same way that you have a name but are also a member of *Homo sapiens*, according to Linnaeus. However, you also know the abstract concept of "dog", which everyone who speaks English shares with you. The word "dog" represents creatures that range from the chihuahua to the English mastiff, and it is useful to a veterinarian to know that he can diagnose and treat all dog breeds similarly despite the fact that they appear to be quite different. What makes a dog a dog, or stated differently, what do all dogs have in common?

Linnaeus based his classification scheme mostly on the way things look—their shape—which is why he classified both humans and simians as "primates" (and got into trouble with the local Lutheran archbishop, but that's another story). More recently, nucleotide sequencing has extended our perceptual tools, and is allowing scientists to refine Linnaeus' taxonomy in quite surprising ways. Thus, classification schemes are subject to change when more information becomes available, or when objects that don't fit into a pre-existing category are invented or discovered.

In the classification exercise you did, it is common for people to classify objects based on their uses, though also on the material from which they are made, their colour, or their usual place in a house or office. In the real world, specific industries would focus on the objects' weights or volumes, their market prices, or their electrical conductivities, schemes that might be of interest, respectively, to shipping and moving companies, insurance companies and stores, and engineers.

Reflection: Can you think of some examples of new classes being defined, and new classification systems superseding the old? (Hint: Paying attention to new words can often provide insight into these processes.)

People, too, can be classified in numerous different ways. Just take a minute to think about it. Your school's database might classify you by your grade, age, nationality, sex, latest standardized test scores, IB Diploma Programme courses, and projected graduation year. Your doctor's office might classify you by height, gender, blood type, race, and kinds of allergies. Marketers might be interested in your household's yearly income, how many people live there, how many microwave ovens, computers and televisions are in your home, whether your parents or guardians are single or married, the highest educational level they achieved, their political affiliation, the magazines they subscribe to, and their hobbies. Think about what characteristics might be of interest to: police departments; jeans or automobile manufacturers; the military; politicians; researchers of all kinds.

Classification

Let us pause to summarize some of the ideas about classification we have considered so far in this book:

- Classification is interpretive. It is our brains that make the associations and group our experiences.
- Classification may be deliberate or not. In your classification exercise you, like Linnaeus, constructed your categories deliberately, looking for the common features. Anyone moving house, however, might doubt the deliberate nature of the category "things that belong to me".
- Classification is passed on from generation to generation by naming in language, with different languages possessing differences in their categories.
- Classification may be very specific to context, giving the people in a particular group a specialized vocabulary for their needs, whether for making cheese or for investigating sub-atomic particles.
- Classification may depend on the classifier when it comes to relationships of relative terms. Are you "international"? Are you "foreign"? Vague words such as "tall" or "strong" are also relative.
- Classification schemes exist at higher or lower levels of generality, as Linnaeus recognized as he constructed boxes within boxes. That dog you were asked to think about is boxed in multiple

layers: your dog Waggles, a dog, and an animal.
- The criteria for classification, or the points of similarity, provide the system of boxing. Waggles could be grouped with brown things, your possessions, or things that need to be fed. Many classification systems may intersect for a single thing.
- Classification may be ambiguous. If you were asked to classify people by ethnic or cultural identity, what difficulties might you have, even on a very factual level? Would you have difficulty placing yourself?
- Classifications, like the words that hold them in place, have denotations and connotations. It is not always easy to distinguish between a factual category and one imbued with values. Sometimes, however, it is. Can you think of an incident of feeling insulted to hear yourself or anyone else called a ------?
- Classification may be elastic, as we saw when discussing inductive reasoning, or rigid. People may find it difficult to change their ideas in many areas of life—from having trouble modifying what belongs in the category of acceptable dress or music to being unable to absorb the unfamiliar classifications of a new scientific theory. One sub-category of a rigid classification is prejudice.

Open any of your textbooks, or think about what you memorized for a recent evaluation at school—and identify some the classification schemes involved in these cases. We are continually classifying things and ideas, in every discipline, in everything we do. Our perceptual and cognitive apparatus forces us to group the things in our physical and mental spaces, to help our brains keep track of every individual thing.[44]

We need to remain aware, though, that there's nothing necessarily permanent or universal about any particular classification scheme. Classification schemes are adopted because they are considered useful by a community of knowers. When the scheme ceases to be relevant to our needs or thoughts, we may change or abandon it—though many of the traditions and idioms of our cultures may still preserve its traces.

Other classification schemes are entrenched by power or overthrown by revolution. Still others may be negotiated through courts of law: legal rulings may change the category criteria for who is entitled to certain benefits. Think for a moment of the examples you identified yourself of new verbal categories. Why did new schemes supersede the old?

A striking example is the Person's Case. In 1876, a British ruling excluded Canadian women from being considered "persons" for full participation in public life. The ruling was invoked in 1916 to attempt to disqualify the first female judge in the British Empire, in the province of Alberta. She, with other professional women similarly challenged, took their case through all levels of court, to win it finally in the British courts in 1929. The unanimous decision was that "the exclusion of women from all public offices is a relic of days more barbarous than ours. And to those who would ask why the word 'persons' should include females, the obvious answer is, why should it not?"[45]

Stereotypes and prejudice

For many people throughout history there have been generalizations more difficult to challenge than this ruling on women, which at least had a legal forum. One black swan, we are told, is all it takes to overturn the generalization that "all swans are white" (page 77). Yet thousands of black people were not enough to overturn the European generalization that "all human beings are white". At the time of the African slave trade, "white" was no longer treated as part of the *description* of human beings but part of the *definition*, with the generalization closing firmly against any implications that black people should be treated in the same way as white people. (Conflicting beliefs about the slave trade, with their justifications, implications, and lingering world consequences, could make an interesting class presentation.)

Evidently, people do not always classify each other inductively, sensitive to the counter-evidence and the uncertainty of conclusions. Sometimes the classifications have already been taught, closed, and emotionally pre-judged. As we considered in discussing sense perception, people then tend to notice and confirm what they expect.

Stereotypes abound. They simplify a complex world for us and, in some contexts, create humour or effective satire. However, they also encourage us not to see the grouped people as they really are and not to recognize individual variability within the group. Thus, we may exaggerate some features of a group in a disproportionate way, see only certain features, or assume the existence of characteristics

"Categorization is not a matter to be taken lightly. There is nothing more basic than categorization to our thought, perception, action and speech. Every time we see something as a kind of thing, for example, a tree, we are categorizing. Whenever we reason about kinds of things—chairs, nations, illnesses, emotions, any kind of thing at all—we are employing categories…And any time we either produce or understand any utterance of a reasonable length, we are employing dozens if not hundreds of categories: categories of speech sounds, of words, of phrases and clauses, as well as conceptual categories. Without the ability to categorize, we could not function at all, either in the physical world or in our social and intellectual lives. An understanding of how we categorize is central to an understanding of what makes us human."[46]

George Lakoff, *Women, Fire and Dangerous Things*

even if we have never noticed them ourselves. Can you think of stereotypes in your society for different groups—for dentists, or car salesmen, or feminists, or peace activists, or politicians, or businessmen, or different religious or national groups? When is a stereotype harmless? Have you ever felt insulted by stereotypes held about a group to which you belong yourself?

When the stereotype is held with negative emotion, whether felt in silence or expressed in hostile language, it has escalated into full-blown prejudice. *All those people* in that category are believed to have certain features in common—and those are undesirable ones. Unfortunately, it is painfully understandable why many groups in the world hold deep prejudices against each other, especially in regions of continuing conflict. It is very difficult to break a self-perpetuating cycle of negative images and hostile behaviour between groups who see each other as the historical enemy. Examining how perception, language, emotion, and reasoning combine to give us our beliefs about the world, however, may be one step toward understanding prejudice and setting the stage for dismantling it.

Solutions to "mind twisters" on page 82

1 He stood on a block of ice to hang himself, which has since melted.

2 They were not twins because they were two out of a set of triplets (or quadruplets).

3 The sixth person took their egg away in the basket.

On racism

by Vivek Bammi

First, read this passage from A.C. Grayling, *The Meaning of Things*.[47]

Almost everywhere one looks among present societies, race and racism make angry welts and deep wounds on the body politic. It is an irony that although racism is a reality, and a harsh one, race itself is a fiction. The concept of race has no genetic or biological basis. All human beings are closely related to one another, and at the same time each human being is unique. Not only is the concept of race entirely artificial, it is new; yet in its short existence it has, like most lies and absurdities current among us, done a mountain of harm.

The first classification of humans into races was mooted by Linnaeus, who recognised it as a mere convenience with no basis in nature. He employed the same criteria as in his botanical classifications, namely, outward appearance, giving rise later to the simplistic typing of all humans into "Caucasoid", "Negroid" and "Mongoloid". But advances in genetics have demolished such taxonomies, by taking DNA as the criterion of classification…

In human terms DNA analysis dismantles the idea of race completely. "Race has no basic biological reality," says Professor Jonathan Marks of Yale University; "the human species simply doesn't come packaged that way." Rather, race is a social, cultural and political concept based on superficial appearances and historical conditions, largely those arising from encounters with other peoples as Europe developed a global reach, with the slavery and colonialism that followed…

All human beings have the same ancestors. Human history is a short one; it is less than a quarter of a million years long, with the first migrations from Africa beginning half that time ago. The physical diversity of human populations today is purely a function of geographical accidents of climate and the isolation of wandering bands. The distinctions which have since been drawn between peoples are therefore arbitrary and superficial, even those relating to skin colour—for as a moment's attention shows, there is simply no such thing as "white", "black" or "yellow" people; there are people with many shades and types of skin, making no difference to any other aspect of their humanity save what the malice of others can construct…

After reading this text, discuss racism in terms of the ways of knowing studied in this chapter. How do words and their connotations, categories and classifications, metaphors and emphases affect our perception of people? Is there sufficient evidence that the notion of race is based on false premises? What upholds racist beliefs and racist policies? How does or can developing empathy and emotional intelligence combat racism? If you were a racist, is there anything someone could do or say to open your mind? What would that be? Answer these questions (a) in the light of the excerpt above and (b) in the context of a *specific* conflict that you have studied or can now investigate, in which race was or continues to be an issue.

 If you are interested in doing a class presentation on this topic, consult Chapter 7 for guidance.

Project Implicit: our hidden assumptions

During TOK class or at home as a homework assignment, go to Project Implicit's web page at www.implicit.harvard.edu. This page is composed of a series of Implicit Association Tests (or IATs). Given that people don't always speak their minds—especially in psychological tests—the purpose of IATs is to scratch beneath the surface of what we say to draw out our hidden assumptions about people who are (or we think are) different from us. As the site claims, "IAT measures implicit attitudes and beliefs that people are either unwilling or unable to report".

Take the Race IAT and then take at least one more test—you can choose from IATs on sexual preference, religion, ethnicity and age, amongst some 90 possibilities. Take note of your results on both the Race IAT and one further test to use in your class discussion.

In his book *Blink*, Malcolm Gladwell argues that our attitudes toward race, gender, and ethnicity operate on two levels. On a deliberate, conscious level, we choose to believe and adopt certain values, for example, believing that all people are born equal or that a certain group is inferior to our own. But IATs also measure attitudes on a second level, what Gladwell defines as a level of rapid cognition, "the immediate, automatic associations that tumble out before we've even had time to think". According to Gladwell, "the disturbing thing about the test is that it shows that our unconscious attitudes may be utterly incompatible with our stated conscious values."[48]

Discussion of Project Implicit

- How did you react to your results? Were you surprised? Angry or hurt? Pleased? Discuss what you felt and why you think you felt what you did.

- Do you believe that your test results say something about you that you should pay attention to? Why or why not?

- Do you think that these tests are valid? When you first saw your results, did you question or accept the test's validity?

- Give examples of the cultural messages that may support attitudes linking a dominant group in your nation or culture with "good" or "superior" attributes and a subordinate group with "bad" or "inferior" ones. Are these attitudes generalizations that can be called stereotypes? How can generalizations be distinguished from stereotypes?

● If some of our consciously held beliefs, attitudes, and values are undermined by what Gladwell calls rapid cognition (others call this intuitive thinking or even gut feelings), what do you suggest we can do to combat jumping to (false) conclusions?

Follow-up reflection

Based on what you have learnt about ways of knowing, identify as many things as you can that you and your classmates can do to combat racism. If you aren't sure where to start, try to write tips about automatic thinking, language, and generalizations.

If you are working alone or if you would prefer to do so on this occasion, you could try writing an essay with the title "My Journey with Prejudice". Include examples of prejudice that you have encountered in your life, and conscious and unconscious attitudes of prejudice that you are aware of (in yourself and/or others). Conclude by considering the avenues by which a critical thinker like yourself may overcome or tackle the roots of prejudice in your attitudes and behaviour.

Who's in the centre?

In many ways, our knowledge resembles our maps of the world, as we considered in Chapter 1. Some of a map's features, such as the existence and location of lakes and mountains, can be checked against the world and corrected in the process. Other features, such as the choice of map projection, even when checked against the world, leave different interpretations and representations as options. Some features, like grids of latitude and longitude, cannot be checked against the world at all, as they are systems that we have invented which can be evaluated only for their internal consistency and usefulness. A comparison between a map and our knowledge can prepare us for some of the distinctions we will be making in this chapter and later ones. Can you already identify different areas of knowledge that seem to you to have the three features of maps just mentioned here, such as some of the subjects that you are taking in your IB?

However, knowledge is not a map—and a comparison, if taken too far, can become misleading. Since you have just been thinking about questions of classification, step back now to notice what we have done. We have taken features in common between one category—"maps"—and another category—"knowledge"—and highlighted their characteristics in common through a metaphor. Of the three roles of metaphor identified on page 46, we have used the first. We have deliberately chosen maps for their explanatory role, because they provide you, the reader, with a quickly accessible image for particular features of knowledge that we want you to notice.

As you become increasingly aware of your role at the centre of your own knowledge (another metaphor, with a diagram on page 19) as a critical and reflective thinker, we encourage you to notice such choices—to recognize the values that guide the books you read, the strategies of communication they use, and the purposes they serve.

Evaluate this TOK book using the questions below, which you will recognize in part from page 43:

1   Out of all possible topics or ideas regarding knowledge, what have the authors selected to give you?
2   Out of those topics and ideas treated, what have they emphasized, and how?
3   What kind of language have they used, and what emotions or values do you identify in the word choice? What images of photographs, drawings, or diagrams accompany the text, and how are they, too, selected and used?
4   What is the context in which the book is written—by whom, for what purpose, and within what framework of declared and implicit values (such as TOK and the IB)?

No book can ever be complete in its coverage of a large topic or be completely neutral in its treatment, even if it were to adopt completeness or neutrality as its goals. As you take ideas into your

---

Yeshey Lhaden, Bhutan

Respect for knowledge is a Buddhist principle, and in Bhutan we are deeply affected by Buddhism in all we do. In Dzongka, our language, one form of "knowledge" is gained through schooling. Education is valued. Just as an example, I would never knowingly step on or step over a book, because it holds learning. The other form of "knowledge" is gained through experience. The older person has seen more of life and has more wisdom.

Most highly respected is the wisdom gained by lamas. Some lamas go on solitary retreats for as long as three years, talking with no one and not washing or cutting their hair. They come back wearing just old rags and are detached from the superficial world. They gain control of emotions, thoughts, and actions so they can advise us on how we can live a virtuous life. They are on the pathway to enlightenment.

own mind, we urge you to be aware of where they come from and what they contain—and to process them with your own reflection.

What is knowledge?

As we approach the concept of knowledge, we are suddenly right back into the topic of classification. What goes into the category "knowledge" and what is excluded?

At the beginning of the course you drew a map of the world that you carry in your mind. Now, in a variation on the classification exercise on page 83, try to develop a new kind of "map". This map will describe a territory that consists of ideas, and will use language instead of an image. The exercises below will allow you, through the patterns that will emerge, to make generalizations about knowledge that will be useful later. Prepare to discuss them with classmates.

Classifying knowledge ideas

1 I know my friend.

2 I know how to solve problems between my friends.

3 I know that I am a student of theory of knowledge.

4 I know that if I drop my pen it will fall to the ground.

5 I know Mexico City really well.

6 I know that I am required to do a class presentation for TOK assessment.

7 I know how to play the piano.

8 I know how to solve problems in maths.

9 I know anger.

10 I know that many people become angry at times.

11 I know that Italy won the World Cup in 2006.

12 I know that the second world war ended in 1945.

13 I know that a right triangle has a 90° angle.

14 I know that atoms have protons and electrons.

15 I know that the sun will rise tomorrow.

16 I know that some day I will die.

17 I know that rotten eggs have a pungent smell.

18 I know what the word "knowledge" means.

19 I know when I know something.

20 I know when to stop arguing about something.

Classify the statements into categories in the way that makes most sense to you. Feel free to create more than one scheme. You may use a diagram, table, or definitions in language, whichever you please. The objective here is to recognize and explore different ways of grouping knowledge ideas.

Have a volunteer from the class start discussion by sharing his classification scheme in such a way that everyone can see it. What criteria did he use? As a class, discuss each scheme in turn, focusing on the common features of the statements that each scheme correctly stresses. Does the scheme make sense? How are other people's schemes similar to your own? How are they different?

With such an abstract word as "knowledge", it would be unlikely that each student in a class, every culture, and every language group around the world classified ideas in exactly the same way.

Your discussion has been in English. In French and Spanish, for example, there are two words for "know" that immediately place knowing a person or a place in a different category from knowing information.

Let us be clear on what we are doing when we classify statements that deal with knowledge. We are dealing with ideas, not pointing to things that have independent existence outside our minds (if anything has). There is no such thing as "knowledge" lying around in the world waiting for us to notice it, pick it up, and weigh and measure it. We create knowledge ourselves, through our four ways

Lindsay Lloyd, Nunavut, Canada

In Nunavut, knowledge has changed a lot from my grandparents' generation. They lived on the land, hunting, fishing, following animals. They didn't need a GPS to know their way around because they navigated by the stars. My grandmother was a teacher in traditional skills like preparing skins and beading.

We still learn about the land, and there's a school programme on learning traditional skills. But this kind of knowledge is not the most important now because going to school and finding out about the world around us is what we need. We depend on the Internet in a big way because the population is so small and so spread out that we can't have a large library anywhere. The solution is having the legislative library and the territorial newspaper online. We depend a lot on technology, including radio and satellite TV, for education.

When I was around 3 or 4 I remember our computer arriving. It was frozen so we had to let it thaw out before we could use it.

Yes, we're losing our culture. It's an oral culture so very fragile. With no trees we had no paper to write things on and no photos—no archive—and with the land frozen we have no large archeological remains. We're losing our culture, but we're making a new one.

Mohamed Youssef, Egypt

In the Arabic of the Koran, there are many words for knowledge. There are five stages of knowledge, with different words. The first means just an introduction, just starting to notice. Then the second one means finding out more, learning. The third and fourth mean reaching knowledge, but to different degrees, as if you arrive first with one foot and then arrive more fully with the second. The fifth means that you have fully arrived and absorbed the knowledge, as if you have stayed there and sat down. There is a big gap between these five and the next stage, wisdom, which involves not just having knowledge but knowing how to use it. With this high level of knowledge the word "light" is introduced. "Enlighten me" is how we express our desire to know.

of knowing—our sense perception, language, emotion, and reasoning. Then we use these same ways of knowing, in differing combinations and balances, to judge whether or not certain statements are appropriately called "knowledge".

Let us now try to sort our words and concepts in a way consistent with usage outside your classroom so that you will be able to communicate more effectively within TOK and beyond the IB. In the process, we will not be determining, in any way other than definition, what knowledge is, but we will prepare ourselves to talk and think with each other.

> Now, based on the insights you've gained up to this point, please take a piece of paper and write down your own definition of "knowledge".
>
> Again, discuss with your classmates. Are there points in your definitions that you all agree on?

Knowing: introduction to a classification scheme

In this course, we treat knowledge as falling into three categories—ones that influence each other and intersect but which do, nevertheless, have characteristic features.

1 Knowing through direct experience

If, in sorting the 20 items, you put "knowing my friend" and "knowing Mexico City really well" in the same category, you have grouped them in a way some languages do, giving this kind of knowing a separate word from knowing facts. Knowing a person, a place, or an action through your own direct experience, with all the personal familiarity that it brings, is our first category.

2   Knowing how

Knowing how to solve maths problems, knowing how to solve problems between friends, and knowing how to play soccer could readily be sorted into different areas of your life, but we are placing them together for their common quality, skill in doing something.

3   Knowing that…

Knowing that something is the case is our third category, grouping statements for their common quality of making a claim. The claim may take anything as its subject matter—for example, information from your personal life ("My bank account number is…"), assertions made the media ("On Tuesday the President met with the delegation from…"), or a law given by science, but must be an assertion presented as being true.

Other ways of classifying that you use yourself may become relevant in future discussions, but for now let us examine and apply this triple one.

What does the girl in the photographs know?
by Anita Holt

She knows Hampton Court Palace.

She has been there herself. She has walked through it, touched it, and shared the experience with a friend.

In what ways is her knowledge different from that of someone who has just seen pictures and read about it?

She knows how to play football.

She has the skill. She can kick the ball effectively, play as part of a team, and score a goal.

In what ways is a skill different from the other two forms of "knowing" pictured here?

She knows that she is taller than her grandmother.

She knows also that they are both women, that they are part of the same family, and that they both like chocolate.

In what ways is "knowing that" different from the direct experience of knowing her grandmother?

1   Which ways of knowing—sense perception, language, emotion, and reasoning—are most relevant to each of the categories above? Consider each of the three in turn for each of the four ways of knowing.

2   If you say, "I know about that" or "I've heard about that", in which category will you place the statement?

3   In which of the categories is it relevant to talk about "true" and "false"?

4   Do you consider "wisdom" to be a particular blend of these three categories, or another kind of knowledge entirely?

Knowing in your IB Diploma Programme subjects

Now take a sheet of paper and make a table for yourself. Down the left-hand side list your IB Diploma Programme subjects, spacing them out. Then make three columns, marking them at the top "Knowing/direct experience", "Knowing how/skill", and "Knowing that/knowledge claims". Fill in the sheet, considering to what extent and in what ways each of your subjects contributes to each kind of knowing. The six groups are: literature; second language; individuals and societies; experimental sciences; mathematics and computer sciences; the arts.

An example for group 1, language A is shown.

	Knowing/direct experience	Knowing how/skills	Knowing that/knowledge claims
Language A1 and A2, Literature	Gaining experience: being able to follow a novel with frequent time shifts without being confused, identifying with characters unlike yourself, responding to a powerful poetic image…	Gaining skills: knowing how to write an essay, knowing how to be both sensitive and analytical in a commentary, knowing how to read more critically…	Gaining information: knowing that tragedy has certain characteristics, that blank verse is unrhymed iambic pentameter, that alliteration is a device…

When you are finished, look over what you have written, and move into discussion with your class group. Consider the following questions:

1   Would it be fair to say that you gain all three categories of knowledge from all subjects?

2   Do different subjects offer you a different balance of these three? Do you think there is any general tendency toward particular balances and blends in the different groups of IB Diploma Programme subjects: literature; second language; individuals and societies; experimental sciences; mathematics and computer sciences; arts?

3   The International Baccalaureate aims to give you an "international education" and to encourage you to become more "internationally minded". In what ways are your own IB Diploma Programme subjects contributing to such education in these three categories of experience, skill, and information?

Knowing in your CAS activities

Extend your discussion now to your CAS activities. You will recall the reflections of students on their service projects earlier in this book (see page 63). Based on their comments, those of students pictured here and overleaf, and your own activities, what do you consider to be the balance in CAS of experience, knowing how, and knowing that?

Emily Myles, Canada on CAS

"Step back a bit," my Mom used to say to me when we looked at paintings together. I still hear those words and follow her advice whenever I look at a painting, and each step back I take, I see the work in new and different ways. One of the main ways I have of mentally stepping back and seeing the big picture in my everyday life is through my CAS activities.

Through all of the CAS activities in which I participate in the course of an average week, I am acquiring a range of skills thanks in large part to the experience and expertise of the activity leaders. Of course, how well I apply these skills depends entirely on myself. While the leaders meticulously explain and demonstrate how to do a "roll" in my kayaking activity or how to use movie editing software in my media activity, I can only know how to do these things myself with practice, tenacity, and maybe a little luck. Along with the rest of my section in choir, I have to learn the alto part of songs so that all the sections can sing in harmony; while volunteering at a local community house, I have to know how to help and interact with children and the elderly, people whose experience differs vastly from my own.

While I gain all this theoretical and practical knowledge from the activities in which I participate, the most important type of knowledge I gain from them is far less concrete. I can reach a state of knowledge that goes far beyond hitting the right notes, keys, or strokes. It happens when I share with a group of kids the simple joy of doing arts and crafts. It happens when I am singing and feeling a gospel song, not alone, but in harmony with a whole choir. It happens when, afloat in the mouth of the bay, I am overwhelmed by the raw, open beauty of the ocean, the trees, the wildlife, of the distant city and mountains.

Our classification scheme revisited

1 Knowing/direct experience

Directly experiencing something leads to a kind of knowing that ultimately remains personal and private. The girl who "knows" Hampton Court Palace by having been there herself will always have a different experience of it from those of us who saw it only in films. The student who sings in the choir, hikes in the mountains, or does a service project with children will have gained something he could never have gained from books.

In some ways, direct experience may be considered the "raw material" for the other forms of knowing—knowing how and knowing that—which draw on the experience for skills and information. It may also offer something a little difficult to talk about, but perhaps expressed as "depth of understanding" and often treated as an aspect of wisdom.

Characteristically, this kind of knowing—the direct experience of a storm or love or motherhood or building a bridge or doing chemistry labs or caring for elderly patients in a hospital—cannot be fully communicated. If a person is good at drawing, or excellent at taking pictures or filming, or highly fluent in a shared language, he might communicate much of the experience, but cannot give it to others as he experienced it himself or continues to experience it in his memory.

We often find connections between ourselves and others emerging from our private experience, however, if we accept ambiguity and uncertainty in communication. Sometimes another person, with a look or a gesture, can assure us "I understand", even if neither of us

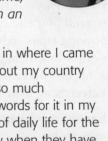

Kevin Muriuki Mwenda, Kenya *on a CAS project in an orphanage in Nairobi*

The project was a real eye-opener for me. It was the first time I was exposed to situations in my community that I had only seen on TV or merely heard about.

I discovered that in addition to the hands-on practicalities of the project, interaction with the children enriched me emotionally and physically too. The daily interaction with very young children was quite a new experience for me, and at first I did not think I could develop the tolerance required to handle such situations. The stench of soiled diapers, the crying and screaming of the babies almost tore me apart, but I took it positively…I reduced it to just a small twitch of the nose! With time I found out that when I gave sufficient attention to individual babies, less crying and screaming resulted, and I got emotionally attached to some of them.

My daily experience with the babies increased my confidence in handling emergency situations and being the only one available to do a certain task. I also developed discipline and integrity when doing certain jobs because I understood the impact that they had on the community.

could pin down exactly what that understanding might be. Sometimes, too, a song of loss or a dance of joy may touch emotions apparently shared, or a painting may capture a shared imaginative vision. Often it is in the arts that we find a powerful sense of recognition that others may have had private experiences akin to our own.

2 Knowing how/skill

In "knowing how" to do something, there is similarly a private experience that no one but the doer can possess. We watch the Olympics on TV with recognition that the top athletes can run or swim in a way that even their closest competitors may never approach.

Yet the skill has a name that we recognize presumably because of the aspects of it that are public. Only a few will win Olympic medals, but many of us know how to swim. The criteria for having the skill are included in its name. For example, the definition of "swimming" necessitates at least knowing how not to sink or drown in water, and knowing how propel oneself through it.

In skills, there is a strong element of demonstration in learning, teaching, and testing. Do you know how to make a cake? Make one. Do you know how to snorkel? A student, about to be dropped in deep water at considerable distance from the boat, asked, "What do I have to do to pass this test?" The instructor's answer was simple. "Come back."

Naja Hendriksen, Greenland
Naja describes fruitlessly trying to convey to others, across a huge gap in experience, her own direct personal knowledge. Between the two years of her Diploma Programme, she did a year of volunteer work in an orphanage school in Uganda.

The children were really interested in where I came from, but how could I tell them about my country without mentioning snow? I have so much experience of snow and so many words for it in my language, since it is so much part of daily life for the Inuit. But how could I explain snow when they have no experience of it at all? It's on the top of distant mountains in Uganda, but the children had never seen it.

I could have taken them to a local shop where there was a freezer and shown them the ice and frost, but that still wouldn't have given them the experience of snow. I tried to explain in English. Later, a little girl in the class looked up at a cloud and called to me, "Look, Madam. Snow!"

With less instantly observable skills such as thinking critically or getting along well with people, demonstration may be mixed with a higher proportion of theoretical understanding. Yet there is still the expectation of application.

Because skills can be observed, analysed, and demonstrated, they can be publicly shared and duplicated. Not only can skills be passed on through demonstration, they can also be taught through language. Athletes have coaches. You have your IB teachers.

3 Knowing that/knowledge claim

The knowledge claim ("I know that…") may arise from direct familiarity or skill, but differs from them in significant ways.

First, the knowledge claim is expressed in language. Gestures, photographs, music—all of these communicate between people. However, with language we move our thoughts and feelings (even if they lose something on the way) into a more "public zone" of defined terms (even when ambiguous) to share them with other people.

Second, the language of the knowledge claim is an assertion. It is not a question (Am I taller than my grandmother?) or an exclamation (How tall I am!), but a statement: "I am taller than my grandmother." The words "I know that" or "He/she knows that…" or "They know that" may be placed in front of the assertion. They do not have to be present, however, because the sentence form of the assertion implies them: "(I know that) I am taller than my grandmother."

Third, the knowledge claim is exactly that—a claim. It is presented as being true. Even if it is an error or a lie—a deliberate falsehood—it takes the form of a statement that something actually is the case.

Since the knowledge claim is made public through language, it can be examined. "Precisely what is being claimed?" it can be asked. "What," it can be asked further, "supports this claim? Should I believe it? Is it true?" The public nature of a claim allows it to be questioned, supported, refuted, or reformulated. It allows it to be published and archived, debated, and used by others in their own work.

All of these features of the knowledge claim merit closer examination.

Suggested class exercise

Cognitive psychology has determined that the kinds of knowledge discussed here, "knowing through experience," "knowing how" and "knowing that" are actually stored differently in the human brain.

Research the following terms: working memory, long-term memory, procedural memory, declarative memory, and episodic memory. Share with your classmates how these terms relate to the kinds of knowledge mentioned here. Focus on the kinds of evidence used by cognitive psychologists to draw conclusions about these different kinds of memory.

Voodoo Doc Dances up a Storm

15 MARCH 2006   by Ken U Bleevit, correspondent

BRAZIL. Doc Juru may be the greatest wonder of the world. The Amazonian medicine man appears to possess the power to change the weather patterns of the planet.

"It's easy," says the Doc through an interpreter. "I dance hard and fast, I make it rain. I spin, I make a hurricane."

Scientists are baffled by the powers of this quick stepping witch doctor of the Pira tribe, deep in the Brazilian jungle. They have been closely observing his dances ever since 2004 when the tribe was first discovered by adventurous anthropologists.

"I wouldn't have believed it," declares Dr Hans Wolfgang of the Climate Change Commission. "But our data show consistent correlation between the steps of his dances and the weather across

the world. I was a skeptic but now I feel I have to accept that there's something here that we just don't

understand with our current science."

Doc Juru, the medicine man of his tribe, is held in great respect by all the Pira. He is a descendent of an ancient line of weather makers who have preserved the jungle's climate for longer than anyone can remember.

"We have to keep his location confidential," says Dr Wolfgang. "Can you imagine how many groups would like to get their hands on this guy and his powers? He's worth billions."

Doc Juru himself is untroubled by all the attention. He is far too busy dancing daily, resisting outside influences such as jive, hip hop, and ballet. He is also very happy with the gifts he has been given by his paleface visitors, especially the shiny wristwatch and the chewy chocolate bars.

Billionaire Sunbather Bursts into Flames

COTE D'AZUR, FRANCE. The spontaneous combustion of oil tycoon Harold Hammer has French police shaking their heads. "There is no evidence of foul play," insists the Chief of Police. "One minute he was soaking up the sun and the next minute he was a ball of fire."

Eyewitnesses to the bizarre barbecue are still in shock. Pierre Blanc, ice cream vendor, saw the human bonfire. He wonders still whether eating an ice cream might have cooled the oily oil magnate enough to save his life. "I will have to live always with asking myself if I could have prevented this catastrophe. But these fat billionaires, they soak up so much. Maybe this was divine justice."

The knowledge claim: do you believe it?

We are presented with so many knowledge claims—in class, in the media, in shops, at work, in all the institutions and social circles of our lives. Does it matter if they are true? Is there any harm in believing nonsense?

Let's start with nonsense. In considering whether to accept or reject it, and whether it matters, you may quickly notice the beliefs you hold about truth and the skills you already possess to filter out nonsense.

Before reading the article "Voodoo Doc Dances up a Storm", you may want to know where it came from. It is written in imitation of articles in a particular kind of newspaper that sells at ordinary supermarket check-outs in Canada and the United States. This kind of tabloid abounds in reports of aliens on Earth, sightings of Elvis Presley alive, strange mutant births, and amazing discoveries of lost civilizations. Students have often been heard to make deploring comments about the stupidity of these papers and the people who buy them. At the same time, they can be seen to reach past a serious newspaper to read the stupid one in preference. And they can be heard laughing.

Now read the main article closely with these two questions in mind: Do I believe it? Why or why not? When you have had a chance to assess the article, the following questions may be useful in guiding discussion.

1   Look at the overall visual presentation of the article. Even before you read the words, are there features that would make you inclined either to accept or doubt the information? What background knowledge of media are you drawing on for this evaluation?

2   When you read the article, is there anything about the way it is written that might make you inclined to accept or reject it?

3   "Do you believe it?" the heading above asks you. But what is the "it"? Identify the knowledge claims made in turn by Doc Juru, Dr Wolfgang, correspondent Ken U Bleevit, and the *Daily World News.*

4   Do you consider those making the knowledge claims to be reliable sources? Why or why not? How can you check their reliability?

5   Are you able to check the information given in this article? Why or why not?

6   What stereotypes of indigenous people do you recognize in this article? Is Dr Wolfgang also a stereotype? Are there any others?

7   The article on Doc Juru is placed next to another about an unfortunate bonfire. Does association with this second story affect your inclination to believe—or reject?

8   What reactions do you find in yourself? Are you inclined to dismiss the article with impatience or irritation? To laugh? To be offended? To look for the possible bits of truth in the article? Do you find that your own prior beliefs about science, magic, and the unexplained, or about human groups, their cultural practices, and their interactions affect how you respond?

Does it matter if you believe it?

In the case of this particular article, does it make any difference whether you believe the knowledge claims or not? Could believing them affect your thinking or your actions?

Now leave the Voodoo Doc behind. Take your pen, paper, and about 20 quiet minutes to think and write more generally in response to this question:

Does it matter if what we believe is true?

Give reasons for your response.

Believing nonsense

What harm can it do to believe silly stories? Don't we seek out fiction that will entertain us and enjoy absurdity as humour or social comment?

If we do recognize nonsense as nonsense, then we can enjoy it or reject it without seeing it as threatening. We do, admittedly, have to be on guard against the residue it may leave behind: encountering a stereotype again and again, we may be less inclined next time to reject it as ridiculous. But if we become conscious of how we might be affected, we are less likely to be so.

Most knowledge claims, however, do not fit neatly and obviously into the category of "nonsense". If we want to seek out the truth we have to go a lot further than rejecting stories about Dr Wolfgang and the Voodoo Doc.

You are actually well on the way toward stories of greater subtlety. If you have given reasons for rejecting the Voodoo Doc, you have probably already identified in discussion three Truth Tests of which philosophers speak. You may already have gone further and seen both their strengths and their limitations. In dealing next with three different approaches to truth, we may well be summarizing points you and your classmates have already raised.

Knowledge claims: tests for truth

"True" and "false" are tidy categories, but as we learn about the world and ourselves, we quickly find them far too simple. Rejecting obvious nonsense can help us to identify our reasons for considering some claims false, but most knowledge claims do not earn quite such a clear "fail" grade in our truth tests. Testing them may involve a scale of probability or likelihood as we evaluate their merits in a more complex and sophisticated way. As you meet the coherence, correspondence, and pragmatic tests for truth, you are encountering assessment tools that should themselves be assessed for their strengths and problems. They are not ways of stamping most claims "false" or "true" in order to toss them swiftly and neatly into different piles, but they can help us to place different claims in their positions between these two extremes and illuminate reasons for our doing so.

1 Coherence test
(Think! Does this fit with what I already know?)

If you said, "That's ridiculous. No man can control the weather," then you were using the coherence test. Coherence demands the harmonious fitting together of all of the knowledge claims without contradictions. You test the truth of the new claim on the basis of

Does it matter if what we believe is true?

Some student voices

Not always, because…

- When it comes to some claims, I don't really care if they are true. It doesn't make much difference to me whether my friend's uncle drives a truck.
- Some claims can't be proven anyhow, and I prefer to believe. Believing in God gives my life meaning so I'd rather believe even if I'm wrong.

Generally yes, because…

- I just prefer truth. I don't want to mess up my mind with lies. I want to feel truthful inside.
- I think I'll make better choices based on truth. I want to take medicine that will actually cure me and apply to universities that are likely to accept me.
- I think that the way people treat me would be better if they didn't accept stereotypes. It's really insulting sometimes. And I wouldn't like to treat other people ignorantly, either.
- I want to pass my IB exams, so I hope the examiners have the same version of things that I do!
- It's kind of pointless to be studying stuff that's false. How can that be knowledge?

other claims that you believe already. You test the truth of reports and records by whether they agree with each other.

We use this test often, whenever we judge how likely a claim is to be true. When we hear a report about someone's behaviour, about political or military action, or about divine or supernatural intervention, we ask, "Is this claim plausible?" "Is it consistent with what I know, or what others claim?" "Does this make sense to me?" We can apply this test simply by thinking.

But think about it!

- What are some problems that you can identify with using a body of beliefs already held to judge the new claim?
- Why is it possible for two people using the coherence test to reach different conclusions?
- Sum up the strengths and weaknesses of this truth test.

2 Correspondence test
(Go and check!)

If you said, "Why should I believe this? There's no evidence given and no way of checking the facts," then you were using the correspondence test. This test demands that the knowledge claim actually match or correspond to what really happens in the world. You examine what is being claimed, with attention to the language, and then either go and look for yourself, or check what observations others have reported. Is there enough evidence to make the claim reliable? You cannot apply this test simply by sitting and thinking. You have to go and check.

Think about this test, too.

- What problems can you identify in establishing truth on the basis of sufficient evidence?
- Is it possible for two people using the correspondence test to reach different conclusions?
- Sum up the strengths and weaknesses of this truth test.

3 Pragmatic test
(Does it work?)

If you said, "This claim about weather control by some man in a jungle—it doesn't lead anywhere that gives a practical outcome" and turned your mind away, then you were using the pragmatic test. You evaluated the knowledge claim for whether it could be applied effectively in practice, and rejected it.

We use this test in accepting assumptions: we may not be able to prove that we exist to someone who doubts, but consider it useful to assume that we do. We accept methods that work in areas such as the sciences and the applied sciences and test by observable results: "The airplane flies." The pragmatic test gives a tentative, not an absolute truth, asking not for evidence but for what the practical consequences would be of accepting the knowledge claim.

Think about this truth test, too.

- What problems can you see with a society accepting what works for it, and calling it truth?
- Is it possible for two people using the pragmatic test to reach different conclusions?
- Sum up the strengths and weaknesses of this truth test.

Claims and the truth tests

If the truth tests were perfect, we could clear away so many uncertainties. Yet the uncertainties do not prevent us from continuing the search for truth—or even possibly finding the search more interesting because of—not in spite of—the complexities. Our awareness of the tests' imperfections can help us remain open to new information, new knowledge, new ideas, new theories, and prevent us from falling into the complacent attitude of believing we know it all. In spite of their imperfections, our truth tests work quite well.

Consider the areas of knowledge we cover in TOK, and the IB Diploma Programme subjects you are studying. Copy the table below and put a tick in the column if the subject uses a certain truth test, and an X if it does not. Keep your answers and review them after you complete Chapter 5.

We do use the coherence test, and accept what fits—what makes sense to us within the context of the body of knowledge claims we have already accepted. Our cultural and personal worldviews, although they may contain some contradictions and frictions within, generally integrate our interconnecting beliefs into a harmonious whole. In areas such as the natural sciences, chemists, biologists, and physicists also seek knowledge within a coherent conceptual framework or theory that integrates the data into the best explanation. In mathematics, too, we rely on the coherence test, and seek logical consistency and freedom from contradiction.

We do use the correspondence test, and accept what seems well supported by observation using all our senses. In sciences, we test our claims this way: we suspend judgment when the evidence is slight, reject conclusions if there is strong counter-evidence, and accept the version with the greatest evidence.

We do use the pragmatic test, and accept claims that seem fruitful for our understanding, ones that make a difference. Not only in our obviously practical areas such as applied sciences but in all areas of our lives, we want what works.

Subject of study	Coherence test	Correspondence test	Pragmatic test
Math (group 6)			
Natural sciences (group 4)			
Human sciences (group 3)			
History (group 3)			
Literature (group 1)			
The Arts (group 6)			
Ethics			

Dëgge
vërtetë
Sự thật
VERDAD
ความจริง
igazság
Añete
DINA
KEI
NA
DODONU.
Katotohanan
真实
Tâpwê
Chokwadi
Ilumoortoq

Liciniso

真実

Still, do we need any truth tests at all? After all, if someone says "I believe it", he is implying that he thinks it is true. He would certainly be unlikely to say "I believe it but I think it is false." So, in a personal and subjective way, he may equate truth with belief: "I believe it, so it is true—for me."

And why not accept true-for-me as our notion of truth? Two of the tests can readily support the personal true-for-me: the coherence test allows one to accept only the claims that reinforce beliefs already held, and the pragmatic test can be interpreted to allow one to accept whatever is personally useful. Even the correspondence test, which tries to go outside the individual mind, does not prevent subjective interpretation of evidence: the world is seen by many Jews, Christians, and Muslims as evidence of the existence of God, but not seen so by followers of non-theistic religions or atheists.

However, if "truth-for-me" is the same as "belief", then "truth" is an empty idea which adds nothing to our understanding. Let us, therefore, recognize "true-for-me" as a personal and subjective concept, but in our discussions accept a more meaningful concept: general truth, truth for all.

Let us enlarge our circles of coherence beyond the particular individual to communities of knowers—or ideally all people; let us consider pragmatically what works for all and cancel out the particular self-interest; let us establish criteria for our evidence for correspondence, and restrict its conclusions to the physical world. As we have seen already, we cannot expect perfection in our tests, but if we hold truth to be general, it can act as an inspiration and a goal. On the imperfect route, though, to our ideal goal, we will have to modify the clear and tidy categories of "false" and "true" to accept a more gently calibrated scale: the claim may not be certainly false, but it may be unlikely; it may not be certainly true, but it may be plausible or even probable.

Certainty

In accepting plausibility and probability as the achievable goals for most of our knowledge claims, we lay aside the expectation of finding absolute, unmistakable truth; we lay aside an expectation of certainty. We hesitate before we say "It is certain" regarding any knowledge claim.

It is entirely possible, however, for individuals or groups to be totally convinced, to believe a knowledge claim without a shadow of a doubt. When completely persuaded, we may not hesitate at all before we say, "I am certain." This form of certainty applies not to the claim but to the believer. It is not epistemological certainty but psychological certainty.

What is it that can persuade us so fully at times when the truth tests cannot give complete

THE OPENING AND CLOSING CEREMONY OF THE ANNUAL DOGMA DAY PARADE

Three truths and a lie

The trick

First, write four knowledge claims—about yourself. They can be of any kind, but should be quite varied. Some examples:

I am 130 cm tall, I never drink tea, I have two brothers, I am in pain right now, I have a good sense of humour, I won a dance competition when I was 12 years old, I have been twice to South America, I had an argument with my friend yesterday, I want to be an engineer, I believe that poverty is the most important issue facing the world today.

Here is the trick. Three of your claims must be true and one of your claims must be false. Yes, you are being asked to lie.

The interrogation

Divide yourselves now into groups of three or four. It's time for the interrogation. Can your classmates, by clever questioning, discover which of your claims is the lie? Can you, by your own clever questioning, discover the lies that your classmates have given you? (Note: "clever questioning" does not include directly asking, "Is your third claim true?")

Each person in your group, in turn, is in the "hot seat" answering the interview questions. Someone else in the group is appointed to watch the time. The interviewers have no more than 6 minutes maximum to ask their questions of each person and give their guesses on which statement is the lie.

The reflection

Now return to the full group. The big overarching question you must face together is the central one of the theory of knowledge course: How do we know?

Let it sink softly into the background of your mind as you discuss the following:

- What kinds of knowledge claims were the easiest to test with your questioning? Why? What statements were difficult? Were any of them impossible?
- What questioning strategies seemed to work best? Did they differ with different kinds of claims?
- What did you consider "evidence" for a truth—or a lie? What kinds of reasons seemed to be most convincing to you?
- Did your relationship with the person in the "hot seat" affect your questioning or your conclusions?
- In judging the truth of the claims, did you use only language, or did you find other clues in body language or tone?
- Is it acceptable for the person in the "hot seat" to answer the interview questions with lies? If anyone did lie, how did you figure out that he was not honestly answering the interview questions?

Look back now to the truth tests. Did you use them?

- Coherence: Did you judge the knowledge claims by whether they were plausible—that is, whether they made sense in the context of everything else you knew?
- Correspondence: Did you judge them by the quality of the evidence?

Look ahead now to "justification". What did you find a persuasive reason for believing the person on the hot seat? What was not persuasive?

assurance? Even when we are not psychologically certain, what are the reasons we might give for accepting one claim rather than another? How do we know? Keep this question in mind as you play the game above.

Justification: "good reasons" for belief

What is a "good reason" for believing a knowledge claim?

Read the nine situations described below and the questions that follow them, For each of the nine, discuss with your classmates possible responses to these two key questions:

- "What truth tests can I apply and with what conclusion?"
- "What reasons (justifications) can I give for believing or not believing?"

1   Your friend has just told you that a vending machine for soft drinks has been installed today in your school. Do you believe her? Why or why not? Do you ask her questions in order to evaluate her claim?

2   Your friend has just told you that the math test was extremely difficult. Do you believe her? Why or why not? What exactly do you believe? Are you more inclined to ask her questions than you were in situation 1?

3   Your friend has just told you that she really regretted not having studied harder for the math test and that she feels sure she will fail. Do you believe her? Why or why not? What exactly do you believe? Does knowing your friend affect your conclusion?

4   Your friend, a student in mathematics standard level, has just told you that the probability of tossing a fair coin 10 times and getting heads every time is less than 1 in 1000. However, if the result of the first 9 tosses is heads every time, the probability of heads on the 10th toss is still 1 in 2. Do you believe her? Why or why not?

5   Your friend, obviously very upset, has just told you that 15 little green men have landed in a flying saucer in front of the main school building. Do you believe him? Why or why not? Would you be more inclined to ask your friend questions than you were in situation 1?

6   Your chemistry teacher told you that one mole of any substance contains 6.02×10^{23} molecules. Do you believe him? Why or why not?

7   Your biology teacher has just told you that biology is the most fascinating subject in the world. Do you believe her? Why or why not?

8   Your parents have always told you that it was important never to be rude to your elders. Do you believe them? Why or why not?

9   Religious leaders have told you that there is a God. Do you believe them? Why or why not? (Note that in this question you are not being asked to comment on anyone else's belief, but solely to reflect on what your own reasons might be for accepting or rejecting the claim yourself.)

- What is the difference between making a false statement and lying?
- What is the difference between being sincere and being right?

What kinds of claims are they?

Within the nine statements above, you have encountered different kinds of knowledge claims, which prompt quite different reasons for believing (or not).

Rational claims: These claims are steps in rational thinking, such as $x^2 + x = x(x + 1)$. They are justified by reasoning, and tested for their consistency within a system by the coherence truth test. Rational claims also include definitions, which are also steps in thinking within a system as they use words in order to define other words.

Observational claims: These are statements about what we can observe with our sense perception. These kinds of claims are justified by observation, including observation extended by technology, and tested by further observation, using the correspondence truth test.

Are the following two assertions observational claims or value judgments? What difficulties, if any, do you find in classifying them?

1   The food that people eat in the United States is better than the food that people eat in impoverished Bangladesh.

2   The gold medallist in the men's marathon is an excellent runner.

Value claims or value judgments: These claims embed evaluations on a scale that is not calibrated in measurable units. Some examples of scales are tall–short, hot–cold, easy–difficult, good–bad, beautiful–ugly, just–unjust. "It is 30 degrees Celsius" is an observational claim; we agree on the scale and can look at the thermometer. "It's hot today" is a value judgment; someone from the Caribbean is likely to have a different "scale" for what is hot compared with someone from Iceland. If a summer day reaches 42 degrees Celsius, few, if any, would disagree that it is a hot day, but it is still a value judgment. Until the claim is put in observational terms, it is not fact but opinion.

Metaphysical claims: These are statements about the nature of reality outside physical reality, such as claims about the nature of time, the soul or God. These claims differ from observational claims in that they cannot be tested with sense perception. We cannot do the God lab: we cannot use litmus paper or a chemical reaction to demonstrate the existence and characteristics of a Supreme Being. We cannot weigh the soul or calculate the trajectory of reincarnation. The very absurdity of the idea underlines the nature of these claims: they are "meta"—that is, "beyond"—the physical. Like value judgments, they can have large numbers of people agreeing (or disagreeing) with them, but by their very nature cannot be proved true or false by our truth tests. The idea of truth we have adopted, you will recall, is not "true-for-me" but true for all.

Now, sort the nine claims on page 105 into categories by writing their numbers in the appropriate column under these headings:

Rational claims   Observational claims   Value judgments   Metaphysical claims

These categories are useful for making distinctions and clarifying differences, but do not include all claims we might make. Our claims are often, moreover, a mix or blend. Does any of the nine claims fit poorly into these categories? Which? Why?

Playing with knowledge claims

1 Claims and categories

Cut a piece of paper into four pieces. On each one write one claim, without identifying its category, until you have the four categories covered:

1   rational claim

2   observational claim

3   value judgment

4   metaphysical claim.

Pair up with a classmate and exchange papers. Identify the category of your partner's claims while they do the same to yours, then check the results with your partner. If you do not agree, wait until everyone has finished and submit your disagreements to group judgment. The conclusion is less important than the reasons for difficulties in categorizing.

2 Cards and categories

Divide into groups of roughly five people and share a pack of cards amongst the groups. In each group, place the cards face down and take turns pulling out a card. If you pull a spade, you must give a rational claim, if a club an observational claim, if a heart a value judgment, and if a diamond a metaphysical claim. If others think that you have given a claim that is not an example of the category pulled, they must help you to reformulate it until it is. Do two quick rounds.

Changing your mind: reflections on your own beliefs

by Sue Bastian

A Name one thing that you used to believe and now do not.

B Name one thing that you believe now and believe that you will believe forever.

For A, ask yourself:

- What made you believe it in the first place?
- How did you come to change your belief?
- What beliefs do you have now that may be similar, but so far have not changed?
- What might occur to make you change these beliefs and make them weaker?
- What might occur to make these beliefs stronger?
- Bonus question: Did you change your mind for a cause or for a reason?
- Double bonus question: What is the difference between a cause and a reason?

For B, ask yourself:

- What made you believe this in the first place?
- Is there anything you can imagine that would change your mind?
- Is this belief rational or emotional or both or neither?
- How many other people would think this belief is rational?
- How many other people would think this belief is emotional?
- What difference would it make in your life if this belief turned out not to be true?

Justifications for belief

Why do we believe some knowledge claims rather than others? Usually, we believe because we think we have a good reason for doing so—a justification for belief. Not all forms of justification are equally convincing to all people, though. We tend to converge in accepting claims of reasoning and observation, in which the justification can be demonstrated publicly, and to diverge in those areas where the justification is more private. All four ways of knowing are evident through these different justifications.

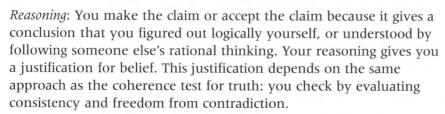

Reasoning: You make the claim or accept the claim because it gives a conclusion that you figured out logically yourself, or understood by following someone else's rational thinking. Your reasoning gives you a justification for belief. This justification depends on the same approach as the coherence test for truth: you check by evaluating consistency and freedom from contradiction.

Observation: You make the claim or accept the claim because it describes something you saw with your own eyes, heard with your own ears, or touched with your own body. Your sense perception of the world gives you a justification for belief. This justification depends on the same approach as the correspondence test for truth: you check by observing. The observations of others, reported or recorded, are also a justification, with the added complexity that you are accepting the report through language without having had first-hand observation.

Not all justifications will persuade all people

Some justifications can be demonstrated to others. For example, observation as a justification of a claim can be public. "Look. Everybody, look!" Now all the others have also seen it, with their own eyes. Reasoning is also public justification.

Some justifications remain private. For example, faith as a way of justifying a claim is "inside" and not demonstrated directly to other people. Although it may show "on the outside" in words or actions, others seeing the signs will not, as

a direct result, experience your faith. Emotion is also a private justification.

Some justifications are a combination of other justifications. "Evidence" is not, for example, listed as a justification. Is it a combination of other justifications, or does it have distinctive features that ought to earn it a category of its own? What do you think?

Emotion is placed in a category separate from the others. Could you make an argument for emotion being a part of some of

the other justifications?

Intuition is grouped with emotion as a way of knowing. Could intuition be argued to be better classified with perception?

Write your own list of justifications for belief, grouping and arranging the ones given here in the way that makes sense to you, and supplementing with others you consider equally important. Be prepared to give good reasons for your list.

A reliable source: You accept the claim because you heard it from someone you trust or from a printed or electronic source that you trust. All claims are expressed in language, which gives you access to other people's observations, reasoning, and emotions. Particular cases include believing an

● *expert source*: a person or organization which is considered appropriately knowledgable and trustworthy, and

- *general consensus*: a combination of sources in agreement with each other, and hence passing the coherence test for truth.

Memory: You make the claim or accept the claim because you remember previous claims and their justifications, or you remember the other kinds of knowing (direct experience, and knowing how/skill). Your memory allows you to carry and use the other justifications. With change or passing time, it may become the only justification that you can give for some claims. Your memory, like your emotions, is directly accessible only to you, through introspection as you "look inside" yourself.

Emotions: You make the claim or accept the claim because you feel that it is right, even if you cannot put your reasons into words easily and even if you cannot show others why you believe, as you could more readily do with observation as your justification. This justification may arise from "knowing" as direct personal experience or familiarity. Among the feelings may be:

- *intuition* (a hunch that you cannot fully explain)
- *faith* (an acceptance without the demand for further justification).

Revelation: You make the claim or accept the claim because God (or another divine or supernatural power) showed himself to you or communicated with you. This justification applies only to metaphysical beliefs and gives rise to further private justification in the form of sacred texts or holy books.

The knowledge claim: when does "I believe that…" become "I know that…"?

It is time to gather up all the distinctions that we have been making and knit them together. Almost all of this chapter has dealt with classification of our concepts in language and their relationship with each other.

Before we reach this conclusion, though, we have to intrude further upon a very intimate relationship, the one between belief and knowledge. Out of all the beliefs that I have, which ones can I rightly call "knowledge"? What makes a statement of belief ("I believe that…") become a knowledge claim?

- Is it the degree of confidence with which I believe?
- Is it the degree of intensity with which I believe?
- Is it the degree of significance that the claim holds in my life?

"Intuition takes us beyond the limits…"

David Pinel, IB graduate 1987, has an MSc in Rural Planning and Development and extensive experience as a guide trainer and community planning consultant.

Whether in adventure activities (e.g. deciding to stay on shore or make a kayak crossing in changing sea conditions) or in strategic planning discussions (such as deciding to put money into a reserve or expanding operations), listening to something deep down inside—a gut feeling—allows us to perform on a line of optimal tension that is safe, exciting, and responsive to many rapidly changing variables. Intuition takes us beyond the limits of information, skill, and experience.

We're taught and encouraged to "gather all of the information" prudently before "evaluating the information and options" then deciding. In the discipline of planning, this is described as a "rational comprehensive" approach. Unfortunately, during the time it takes to find supposedly comprehensive information, the conditions and variables tend to change and the information originally gathered becomes insufficient. At some point, responsible and responsive planning requires intuition to flag that "we have enough information (or skill, or experience)" to make and act on a decision in a timely manner—that more information (or skill, or experience) won't necessarily lead to a better result. And this is what most of us do consciously, and less consciously, all of the time in work, leisure, and routines.

Ironically, "intuition" is rarely taught or encouraged, and is often relegated as a insufficient justification for actions, and an unreliable form of knowledge. Yes, intuition doesn't always lead to the best or optimal outcome, but the same is true for information, skill, and experience. Together, however, they make a powerful quartet!

It could be argued that we say "I know" when we feel very sure. But there are problems. I was so sure I had returned the library book, but I was wrong. I was so sure that the computer would run the new software, but I was wrong. No matter how confidently I assert that Toronto is the capital of Canada…it isn't. I can draw a map with personal conviction that it reflects the world accurately, and I can be wrong.

It could also be argued that we say "I know" when we care intensely about the claim, accepting it passionately and feeling it to be very significant. Yet people have believed passionately in many claims: some groups believed so passionately in the claim that the world would end in the year 2000 that they prepared themselves to die. It didn't, and they didn't.

So, what *does* make "belief" into "knowledge"?

Now, let us put together the terms we have been discussing in this chapter to propose a working definition of knowledge for the TOK course. As you take in this definition, recall:

- forms of *knowing*: knowing of direct experience, knowing how, knowing that
- tests for *truth*: coherence, correspondence, pragmatism
- *justifications* for belief: reasoning, observation, reliable sources, memory, emotion, revelation
- *kinds of knowledge* claims: rational claims, observational claims, value judgments, metaphysical claims
- intensities of *belief*.

We are going to give a definition of knowledge that combines these terms, and ask you to examine its strengths and weaknesses.

Definition of knowledge

> Knowledge, first, is a sub-category of belief. It is a claim that you have accepted, regardless of your degree of confidence, emotional intensity, and sense of significance. I can say, "I believe that the book is on the table" or "I believe that the meaning of life is to reduce suffering"—and both statements, widely unlike, are together in the same category of statements which I have accepted psychologically.
>
> Knowledge is a belief that is true—not just "true for me" (or in other words, believed) but true for all. Already you are aware of some difficulties here: the truth tests are imperfect, and they do not work on all the claims that we can make. Perhaps it would be better to rephrase: knowledge is a belief that is held in areas where the truth tests work, and true as far as
>
> we can tell using them. It cannot, at least, have been proven false. In light of the over-simplicity of the true/false distinction, it may be that we should keep "truth" as an ideal guiding concept and, in determining the difference between belief and knowledge, give more attention to the concept that has gradation and degrees built right into it: justification.
>
> Knowledge is a belief that is justified—justified by methods that can be demonstrated to others such as reasoning and observation. Already you are aware of some difficulties here, and will meet more later in the course. The idea of holding a belief for good reasons, though, or the best reasons you can find, is central to a definition of knowledge.
>
> *Definition:* Knowledge is belief that is publicly justified and currently passes tests for truths.

Knowledge, in this definition, is public. It includes rational claims and observational claims, if they withstand truth testing and examination of justification. It does not include value judgments and metaphysical claims, for which the truth tests do not work and for which, arguably, justification cannot be demonstrated publicly. (We will return later to possible justification for ethical judgments and consider arguments against this last statement.) This definition does not reject value judgments or metaphysical claims as false or even less worthy than knowledge. It places no value judgments on them. It simply does not include them within the category of "knowledge".

Indeed, some of the beliefs that are most important to us in our lives are not, in this definition, "knowledge". Keeping them in the category of "belief"—or accepting them instead as the private knowledge of direct experience—does not in any way diminish their significance.

Put together the concepts: draw them

Here are the key terms we have talked about so far:

Belief   **Truth**
Justification   **Knowledge**

Draw: Using a picture or a diagram, put the four key terms in relation to one another in connections that make sense to you and that you can explain to others. Add any other terms that you need.

Discuss: Compare your drawings as a group by using a blackboard or other means. Discuss both any major convergences and any major divergences and your reasons for them.

It is not essential that you accept the definition given in this book. It is not essential nor even likely that we will all think of knowledge in the same way. It is essential, though, that we can use the terms and explore the concepts together.

Knowledge, in this definition, involves an exchange of knowledge claims. You are given knowledge claims and asked to believe them. You might reject them and say, "That is not true. That is not knowledge." Or you might accept them—believe them. If you test them for truth (as well as you can) and if you justify them through reasoning and observation (as well as you can), then they become part of your own knowledge. They contribute, then, to the claims that you might make yourself.

- Is this a perfect definition? No.
- Is it the only possible definition? No.
- Is it one which connects concepts usefully for us to be able to talk with each other? Is it one which will allow us to throw rocks at it and examine its imperfections and complexities in a way which will illuminate the nature of knowledge? Yes. It is.

Knowledge, nonsense, or something in between?

We started this chapter looking at knowledge in three forms— "knowing" through direct experience, "knowing how" of skill, and "knowing that" of the knowledge claim. We then zoomed in more closely on the knowledge claim, opening with nonsense in the story of the Voodoo Doc. From that point, involving your responses and closer examination, we looked at three tests for truth and several forms of justifications for belief. Finally we have concluded with a definition of knowledge, pointing out in the process some of its ambiguities and limitations.

Why do we not just tell you, firmly and clearly, what knowledge is and cut all this stirring up of ambiguity? Well, we could. We could make it so easy. Yet precision and clarity can come at a great cost:

they ignore the fuzziness and shadow around the words with the consequence that we may remove ourselves from the way we actually use them in the world. Acknowledging complexity, ambiguity, and variability right from the beginning probably forestalls greater difficulties of communication in the long run. Concepts that are meaningful are not necessarily precise.

With awareness of the imprecision of our tools—the words we use to deal with ideas—let us return now to how we apply them to knowledge claims. When you read an article, do you believe what it claims? Is it giving you truth, falsehood, or a mix or blend of something in between? What is the justification for the conclusion you reach?

The following example of the Bosnian pyramids is not fictional. The following article on the "Seductions of Pseudoarcheology" draws distinctions between "observable evidence, baseless speculations, and ideologically driven pseudoscience" and comments on some of the problems media face in presentation of archeology. Read both the claims below and the article and consider how best we can sort through all the claims to judge what is most reasonable to believe.

Thinking critically

The Bosnian Pyramid of the Sun[1]

- Semir (Sam) Osmanagic, Bosnian-American, claimed in 2005 that a large hill near Visoko, northwest of Sarajevo contains a pyramid built possibly as early as 12,000 years ago. As evidence he points to the shape of the hill, some blocks of stone he interprets as a paved entrance plateau and tunnels he interprets as ventilation shafts.
- He reports that he has been joined by experts in his assessment of the hill.
- Osmanagic studied the pyramids of the Americas for 15 years, and has published a book entitled *The World of the Maya*.

…or just a big hill?[2]

- Curtis Runnels, a specialist in the prehistory of Greece and the Balkans at Boston University, notes that 12,000 years ago, when Osmanagic claims the pyramids were built, the people in that part of the Balkans did not have the tools to build them. He also points out that Osmanagic's claims are not supported by artefacts, photographs, or any other kind of evidence presented in a way that would allow trained experts to examine them.
- Mark Rose, the executive editor of *Archaeology* (publication of the Archaeological Institute of America) writing in 27 April 2006 in *Archaeology*

Artist's impression. See www.bosnianpyramid.com.

points out that passages in Osmanagic's book on the Maya claims they were descended from the mythical lost continent of Atlantis. He calls the pyramid claim a "farce".[2]

- Anthony Harding, president of the European Association of Archaeologists, visited the site and concluded that the hill was not man-made but natural (*National Geographic News*, 13 June 2006).[3] He expressed concern that the "absurd theory" could attract funding that could be better used to preserve Bosnia's genuine cultural heritage.

If the story is absurd, why was it published in the media?

- What is the appeal of such a story for the media?
- What difficulties do reporters and publications face in deciding whether to run such a story?

Seductions of pseudoarcheology: far-out television

by Garrett G. Fagan[4]

What to think when Atlantis is just one click of the remote away…

While easy to dismiss, programs propagating pseudoarchaeological speculations—the mystical powers of pyramids, ancient astronauts, Atlantis' role in human development, etc.—air on an increasingly regular basis not only on the niche cable channels (Discovery, The Learning Channel [TLC], and The History Channel) but also occasionally on the networks (ABC, NBC, and especially Fox). "Hybrid" productions are also quite common, where good information is freely mixed with pseudoscience.

Mysteries of the Pyramids offered pseudoarchaeological propositions side by side with reasonable deductions about pyramids, and the transition between the two styles was seamless. A viewer lacking previous knowledge about the sites presented or how archaeology works would not necessarily see any distinction between rational deductions drawn from observable evidence, baseless speculations, and ideologically driven pseudoscience.

There is little doubt that presenting science (and archaeology) on television is a difficult business. The slow pace of change in scientific thinking, the habitual lack of consensus among academics about details, and the often complex nature of the arguments involved place special pressures on producers. For science to work on television, the program needs to tell a story. The best stories are about people, so good science shows usually highlight the human element by focusing on a researcher or team of researchers, interposing expositions of scientific reasoning as an element of the narrative.

In the case of archaeology, there are added difficulties. The unspectacular and painstaking nature of the discipline does not make for particularly scintillating television. For how long will viewers sit through scenes of dirt-sifting amid knee-high ruins? A further problem is that archaeology deals, in essence, with dead people, who somehow have to come alive for the viewers. One solution is to use computer graphics to re-create now-ruined splendors. Such sequences are increasingly de rigueur in the genre. Other newly popular options include having actors portray figures from the past or emphasizing pragmatic considerations an audience can relate to. Michael Barnes, producer of the PBS series *Secrets of Lost Empires*, assembled teams of archaeologists and engineers to re-create spectacular achievements of ancient technology—building a pyramid, raising an obelisk, and firing a medieval trebuchet. His series kept a human focus on the teams of experts while reanimating the past with a set of ancient but immediate practical problems that demanded solutions. We know the ancients did these things, but how? "Trying something out in practice beats all the armchair talk," says Barnes. There are other ways archaeology can be jazzed up for presentation on television. Compelling hooks emphasize the "mysteries", "secrets", and "treasures" of now-lost worlds.

Unfortunately, the format favored by television archaeology perfectly suits the exponents of fringe ideas. For starters, pseudoarchaeologists uniformly present themselves as tackling some terrific mystery or secret of the past, one they claim (often incorrectly) has long baffled specialists. In "solving" this great mystery, pseudoarchaeologists love to strike the pose of the unappreciated genius. There is often the promise of treasure at the end of the quest, the treasure of lost ancient knowledge that somehow will be of value for humankind. The wide-ranging nature of pseudoarchaeological speculations frequently requires visits not to one but to many exotic locations in a single show, as the "argument" jumps from Egypt to Peru to Easter Island, and so on. There is another powerful storytelling feature in this genre, one usually lacking in good archaeological television: a villain. For in many pseudoarchaeology shows, the villain is archaeology itself.

After considering that truth is defined in different ways and tested imperfectly, that justification for beliefs takes many different forms which are varyingly persuasive to different people, and that knowledge, in its most publicly demonstrated form, is not fixed and certain, do you give up the search? Do you say, "It's all uncertain, and all equally so," conclude that enquiry and the pursuit of knowledge are useless, and turn away? Please do not do so. Please consider that complexity can be far more interesting than simplicity, and that our ways of knowing, though imperfect, have allowed us to develop quite amazing areas of knowledge. Let us acknowledge—and accept—imperfection, but try to believe as truly as we can. Let us try for the best version possible.

Do I believe it?
The three S's: a guide to evaluating knowledge claims

Source	Statements	Self
• Does the source (person, publication, organization, etc.) have any recognizable motive for conscious or unconscious deception? • Does the source have a reputation for being honest and accurate? • Does the eyewitness seem to have senses which function normally for an act of observation and which are free from the influence of substances that might affect perception (e.g. drugs)? Does he or she seem to have a sound mind for interpretation? • Is the source an expert relevant to the topic under consideration (e.g. a medical researcher on medical issues)? • Does the source acknowledge counter-claims or limitations of its own knowledge? • Is the source in accord with, or consistent with, other sources with which its claims can be checked (coherence truth test)?	• What is the context of the knowledge claims—their social context, for example, or their publication or web context? Does the context give you any insight into whether the goal of the knowledge claim is to report or to persuade? • Are the background, values, and goals of the writer or speaker openly stated? Are values observable in the selection of details, emphasis placed on those details, or connotations of word choice in the knowledge claims? • Do the claims use any graphs, photographs, paintings, or other visual accompaniments? Are they relevant? Are they emotionally affecting? • Are the claims supported by evidence (correspondence truth test)? • Are the claims internally consistent, free from contradictions and logical errors (coherence truth test)?	• Do I recognize in myself (not easy!) an inclination in advance to believe or reject a particular source or statement? • Do I apply critical thinking to what I want to believe as well as to what I do not want to believe? • If I use my own past experience and understanding as a basis on which to judge the plausibility of new statements (coherence truth test), how reliable is that past experience? • Is it possible to separate my beliefs into private beliefs, based on whatever justification convinces me personally, and public beliefs based on justification which must convince others as well? • What is my attitude toward belief? Should "Do I believe it?" be instead "Should I believe it?" Is there an ethical dimension to what one *should* believe or reject?

4 Persuasion and propaganda

Trying to believe the best version possible: that seems a modest goal and a practical one. To achieve it, though, is a lifelong challenge. Thinking critically, as we have just seen, demands active evaluation of claims in order to accept those that persuade us for good reasons and to reject those that seek to persuade us without such justification. In this chapter, we will reinforce your current skills by directing attention to common failures of everyday thinking.

Please consider these questions now, and return to them at the end of this chapter:

How can you tell the difference between persuasion and propaganda?
Why might it be important to distinguish between them?
Why might the distinction sometimes be difficult to draw?

Sense perception

Sense perception as a way of knowing depends, as we have seen, on how we integrate sense information into our body of beliefs. Much of persuasion depends on influencing what we take in from all the sensory clutter that surrounds us.

Questions for discussion

Quickly review the summary at the end of the section on perception in Chapter 2 for some of the factors that affect what we sense and what we remember from our observations. Now imagine that you want to publicize an event within your school.

a How would you make the most effective visual display for a noticeboard, poster, or magazine or web advertisement? What do you take into account? What differences arise when you are creating not a static display but a moving image?
b How else would you advertise the event?

If you have already had experience in publicizing events, what did you find worked most effectively? What did not work as well as you had expected, and why?

Trying your own hand at publicity develops a keener awareness of how information and persuasion reach and affect us. In upcoming activities on maps, photographs, and statistics, recall the four principles of representation which you have already applied in Chapter 2 to connotative writing:

- selection of what is to be represented
- emphasis on certain aspects of it
- emotional colouring of language or image
- its treatment in context to support a perspective.

> ### *Planning your TOK presentation*
> If you have not yet done a TOK presentation or familiarized yourself with its expectations, we urge you at this point to read Chapter 7 on assessment for the TOK course.

Persuasion with maps

In the following two exercises, be as subtle or as flagrant as you wish as you use maps of the world to support your point of view. Consider such choices as projection, centring, evocative colouring, borders and names, and overlaid graphics. Divide into groups of 4 to 6 people. Your group should plan together both parts A and B of one of the persuasion exercises, then divide into two smaller groups to design the two maps in detail. When you are ready, present your results and identify your tactics of persuasion.

Persuasion exercise 1

A   You are the president of a European country. You want to test nuclear weapons in a region in the South Pacific despite the protests of much of your own population and many other countries. You want to persuade Europeans that the faraway nuclear testing does little damage and certainly will not hurt Europe. What kind of map do you use to persuade them? Design it.

B   You are a leader in a worldwide environmental organization. You are distressed that the president of a European country is testing nuclear weapons in the South Pacific and want to communicate the damaging impact of the blasts on both the immediate region and the rest of the planet. You want to support the protests that are already coming from many countries. What kind of map do you use to persuade them to protest more strongly? Design it.

Persuasion exercise 2

A   You are the leader of a small country threatened by the strength of a neighbouring one which has recently been showing far too much interest in your natural resources. You want to persuade the rest of the world to pay attention to your problem and to side with you in case of threatened invasion. What map do you use to awaken interest and sympathy? Design it.

B   You are the leader of a large country with a great need of natural resources. A neighbouring country, fairly small and militarily insignificant, has a concentration of exactly the resources you need. You are considering various ways to gain them—through trade or possibly through invasion. You want to prepare your own population and the rest of the world for a "merger" of your country with your neighbour. What map will you use? Design it.

Persuasion with photographs

1   Photos take one scene in one moment and cut it out of its context. Which moment will you select from the four shots shown here:[1]

   a   if you support the speaker as a candidate for election?

   b   if you oppose the speaker as a candidate for election?

   Write a caption or headline for each to support the effect.

2   If you have access to cameras and a computer program for cropping and modifying images, divide your group as you did in the persuasive exercise on maps. First choose two different interpretations of events or relationships between groups in your school and then, working as two opposing teams, seek out photographic evidence to support each

interpretation. (It is considered appropriate in many contexts to ask permission to take or use photos of people.) When both teams are ready, present the contrasting results to the rest of the class and identify specific tactics you used.

Finally, discuss as a class the following question:

● A photograph does not make explicit statements that can be judged true or false. Can a photographic record, then, ever lie?

3 Choose one photograph which you find particularly powerful in communication or pleasing to look at, taken from any source. Describe your own response to the image and consider how some of the following might affect that response: centring, angle, focus, colour, and shapes in composition.

Finally, discuss the following question:

● A photograph, as we have just said, does not make explicit statements that can be judged true or false. Can a photographic record, then, ever tell the truth?

> " *Whatever the limitations (through amateurism) or pretensions (through artistry) of the individual photographer, a photograph — any photograph — seems to have a more innocent, and therefore more accurate, relation to visible reality than do other mimetic objects. ... But despite the presumption of veracity that gives all photographs authority, interest, seductiveness, the work that photographers do is no generic exception to the usually shady commerce between art and truth. Even when photographers are most concerned with mirroring reality, they are still haunted by tacit imperatives of taste and conscience.* "
>
> Susan Sontag[2]

Language

In language, communication is constantly affected by the four principles of representation, regardless of its goal. Glance back to your exercise in Chapter 2 (page 44) and consider how easy it is to support different points of view in your account of an event. Then give your attention to the following further devices for persuasion.

1 Repeated affirmation

Effective communication sometimes repeats key points, and teaching often does so. (You will meet the four principles of representation again before this book is done.) The device of repeated affirmation goes further: it coins catchy slogans or emotionally powerful key words and repeats them until they are drummed into the minds of the audience. Problems arise when the repetition of memorable phrasing replaces analysis, evidence, or thoughtful argument. In our era of high speed communication and media sound bites, we are vulnerable to reiterated glib and simplified assertions.

Repeated affirmation: Hitler

from Adolf Hitler in *Mein Kampf*, 1925

"[Propaganda's] effect for the most part must be aimed at the emotions and only to a very limited degree at the so-called intellect. We must avoid excessive intellectual demands on our public. The receptivity of the great masses is very limited, their intelligence is small, but their power of forgetting is enormous. In consequence of these facts, all effective propaganda must be limited to a very few points and must harp on these slogans until the last member of the public understands what you want him to understand by your slogan."[3]

2 Jargon

The specialized vocabulary of any field may be called its jargon. It becomes a device of persuasion only when it is lifted out of its appropriate context and used not to communicate but to impress. Dazzling and incomprehensible, it may give the audience the illusion that the speaker or writer is an expert and stun into silence their capacity to ask penetrating questions.

3 Innuendo

This device of indirect suggestion is sometimes used to imply faults in an opponent or a target without the risk of direct assertion or accusation. (Have you ever met Iago in Shakespeare's *Othello*?) Reading "between the lines", the audience picks up the inference without necessarily noticing that no claim has been made. "Is it possible that he is a racist? I would be sorry to think so."

4 Persuasive metaphors

Look back to "Metaphors as pervasive figures of thought" in Chapter 2 (page 46). Analogies between unlike things can serve a useful explanatory function, but can also be used to encourage us to think and interpret in a certain way. For example, if a political leader presents his enemy or a situation he opposes as a disease and himself as prepared to remove the cancer, you might be persuaded to think of him as a healing doctor and give him your support.

Persuasion with metaphor

Now write your own metaphors, placing yourself in the position of someone who wishes to persuade others.

Round 1

Choose one undertaking or product to promote, and then choose one metaphor to present it positively and persuasively.

Suggestions for the product: a luxury product such as diamonds or furs, a cosmetic product such as hair dye or lipstick, a brainwashing cult that appears to love all its members while draining their financial resources, a car or refrigerator, or any ideology. Do not limit yourself to these examples if you have better ideas.

Suggestions for your image: ("Just as ___, so too ___.") Nature is a good source of images. You might use the waxing and waning moon, the changing seasons, life-giving rain, interdependent species of an ecosystem, a beautiful bird, a river thundering powerfully between its banks or flooding the plains, or the shine of the moon upon the ocean.

Round 2

Change your metaphor now to counter the persuasion you attempted in round 1. For example, if the ocean tides were rising inevitably to represent the growing force of your ideology, can you flip the image around so that the ebbing tides represent its fading and failing? If your metaphor does not lend itself to such reversal, develop a different metaphor to present the undertaking or product negatively but equally persuasively.

Emotion

In influencing the conclusions we accept, little could be more powerful than a direct appeal to our emotions. Advertisers promote their products by playing on some of our deep desires—for love, security, status, sexual pleasure, or eternal youth. Pity and fear, the grand emotions of tragedy, are tapped to solicit votes or peddle mouthwash.

1 Appeal to pity

How can compassion, that concern for others that motivates kindness and generosity, ever be used as a mere gimmick for persuasion? Unfortunately, sometimes our most admirable feelings can be exploited in persuasion, deflecting our attention from fact and argument. The embezzler, caught with his hand in the piggy bank, wells up with tears over the bad news just given him by his doctor; the political leader, caught in wrongdoing, presents himself as pitiably under stress. If the appeal to our pity seems to have some genuine basis, we may be inclined to soften our judgment of the person. But the key question to be resolved depends not on feelings but on facts: did he, or did he not, do what he is accused of doing?

More complex is the appeal to pity on the part of those who present themselves as victims. Compassion may be appropriate for their distress but not a sound basis to conclude, for example, that they genuinely have been wronged by the boss, the family, a divorcing spouse, or another ethnic group. In many conflicts, both sides compete to present themselves as victims rather than perpetrators in order to gain sympathy and support. When the hardship is well supported with evidence, the appeal to pity becomes a major thread in a complex argument. However, hardship in itself does not prove a claim of innocent vicimization.

2 Appeal to anxiety or fear

Fear, we are told, is one of the most basic and primitive of our feelings, going back to the fight-or-flight response for survival. Indeed, we are legitimately afraid of many people and forces in our world, and perhaps even insufficiently afraid in the face of such looming catastrophes as environmental destruction. Fear is often a motivator toward prevention.

It is also, however, an emotion easily exploited for less constructive persuasion. The appeal to fear may come as an implied threat: "Are you really planning to expose the Minister of the Public Purse? Doesn't she own the bank which holds the mortgage on your house?" Or, more pervasively, it may take the form of generating and nurturing anxieties—anxieties about our personal appearance that persuade us to buy innumerable products, for example. Many businesses thrive on selling us peace of mind by first nurturing and directing our anxieties. Similarly, some political leaders thrive on becoming saviours of the people, but may first create the fear that gives them that role. Historically, leaders of many countries have secured their positions in part by focusing the attention of their people on a common enemy and exaggerating the threat. Indeed, the fear and reactions based on it may end up creating the reality.

3 Appeal to belonging

Surely almost as basic as pity and fear is the deep human desire to belong to a group and to be accepted. But what group? By buying certain brands or fashions, advertisers encourage us to believe, we will gain that elusive acceptability. By buying a particular car, we can achieve a desired and admired identity, perhaps membership of an elite group. In some forms, the appeal to belonging is only marginally different from an appeal to fear—the fear of rejection.

This device also uses the confident voice of the insider calling to other insiders, emphasizing a bond that creates a sense of trust on the part of the people to be influenced: "We Serbians/Americans/workers/Christians/Moslems/women can no longer tolerate this affront to our rights/dignity/religion/way of life. We must take the following action: ____." Conversely, it can appeal equally forcefully to class, caste, religion, nationality or other forms of belonging to arouse suspicion of the outsider and to incite and justify hostile action. Patriotism and religious faith create communities of belonging, but can be exploited to create antagonism toward those outside.

4 Borrowed associations

This tactic depends on creating an association in our minds between the undertaking or product and something desirable. Naming and quoting respected figures introduces fine sentiment into a campaign and creates the impression of trustworthiness; using music in the background of an advertisement suggests quality, particular status or emotions such as joy; using celebrities to endorse products or campaigns, even ones whose talents are irrelevant to what is promoted, both attracts attention and borrows something of their allure. Indeed, in contemporary television advertising, it is sometimes a guessing game to figure out what product is actually being promoted when the emphasis falls upon a tender family moment, a beautiful woman, or the glorious freedom of the wilderness.

Borrowed associations are also used to discredit an undertaking, a group, or an ideology, often working in combination with other devices such as innuendo or the appeal to fear. The figures quoted or named are ones regarded with fear of loathing; the music is discordant; the shadows in the photograph deepen.

5 Misleading use of sources

Citing a particular person, publication, or organization as a source can be one of our major ways of justifying knowledge claims. Unable to research every field ourselves, unable to witness the major events of the world personally, unfamiliar with the perspectives of people with quite different life experiences, we have to depend to a large extent on the reported knowledge of others. We seek out reliable experts in many areas of our lives, and do not consult those we do not trust. As a means of persuasion, then, an appeal to the source may be entirely sound.

When does such a citing become dubious or even devious? The answer to this question depends on your evaluation of the relative reliability and expertise of the particular source and the way that the source has been used in the context of an argument. You might want to flip back to the conclusion of Chapter 3 for some of the criteria for judgment summarized there.

The appeal becomes truly dubious when the sole justification given for a claim is the source. "He said it, so it must be true." "He said it, so it must be false." We are encouraged to accept or reject a belief based solely on the reputation of the source without being given further evidence or the possibility of checking the claim. Moreover, that reputation may be irrelevant to the issue under discussion.

Historically, a major thrust of ideological persuasion has been to create not simply reputation of a source but also an emotional

---

Emotional appeals

Which do you personally find most persuasive of these emotional appeals, and why? Which ones do you see most often in advertising and politics?

Find examples of at least two of these appeals in newspapers, magazines, the Internet, or any other source available to you. Share and evaluate them with classmates. Are they subtle or blatant? explicit or implicit? Do the tactics you identified work alone or in combination with other appeals?

Citing the sources

Why does the IBO, like universities and publications, insist that sources for essays be footnoted? Why is it considered so important that a reader be able to see where ideas and words come from?

Who selected the resources for your IB courses? Ask your teachers why they chose a particular textbook or recommended a particular journal or website for support.

"If I have seen further it is by standing on the shoulders of giants," said Sir Isaac Newton in 1675.[4] What attitude toward prior sources of knowledge is implied in his statement?

A librarian's guide to evaluating Internet sources

Sherry Crowther, Librarian of Lester B Pearson College of the Pacific, spoke to TOK students on using critical thinking in research. Below is some of her advice.

The web has brought "publishing" to the masses and is a wonderful place to begin research. Be aware, however, that authors and publishers want to be paid for their work, so not all published materials are available free online. For academic research, it is important to include published materials, so use the library to access journal databases, books, and reference sources such as encyclopedias.

Since a large portion of online materials are self-published and the work has not been vetted through an editorial process, it is important that users learn how to evaluate the quality of online sources. Listed below are a few general tips on how to assess the reliability of a site.

1 Who is responsible for the site?

Check to see if the author can be identified. Is there an email address or other contact information? Are credentials/qualifications listed? If not, type the author's name in a search engine such as Google to get more information about him/her.

Check where the site is hosted. Research information hosted on a university server may be better than information on a commercial site that is trying to sell something. The URL (web address) may give you some clues. Even though they are not completely standardized, domain suffixes may help you differentiate between the different kinds of sites.

.com = company, a commercial site

.org = non-profit organization

.edu = educational website

Truncate the URL to check the organization hosting the site. For example, for the following web address: www.lib.byu.edu/~rdh/wwi/links.html, simply try going to www.lib.byu.edu.

2 How accurate is the information?

Check to see if the online document contains a bibliography of sources. Can you verify the information used? The types of materials cited may be an indicator of quality. For example, citing a published, academic journal would be more credible than citing information from a personal website.

3 How current is the site?

Check whether there are dates on the site. When was the site created or when was the site last updated? Is the site recent enough for your field of study? When was the document published on the web?

4 Gain further information on the website

Check information on who has registered the site, what other sites link to it, and who visits it. Having lots of other websites linking to the page may be an indicator of quality. Check the kinds of sites using this link. Useful search terms are "whois" and "wayback".

---

allegiance or hostility. Huge photographs, reverent quotation, and songs of praise, for example, contribute to the lustrous image of a charismatic leader with infinite wisdom and infallible authority. Discreditable stories and abusive cartoons and jokes, conversely, contribute to the vile image of an enemy whose every word is to be doubted. Softer versions of authorities and villains abound in everyday life, with presentation of irrelevant or fictitious details of the source's personal life often used to deflect the audience's attention from what he is actually saying.

This appeal to the source similarly raises questions of its dependability when the person or organization cannot be identified. While cases do exist of reliable sources remaining anonymous for personal reasons, in many cases the device depends upon vague terms or feigned secrecy. "Scientists say...." "An observer close to the President alleges...."

Reasoning

In gaining and testing knowledge, reasoning is a powerful way of knowing. Yet common errors in thinking—often called logical fallacies—abound.

1 Problematic premises

As you will recall from Chapter 2, the premises of an argument are its opening statements, the assertions to which deductive reasoning will be applied. In the example "All Asians are...." "Yi is Asian." "Therefore Yi is....", the premises are the first two statements, a general statement and a specific case. If the logical processing is correctly done (valid argument) and the premises are true, the conclusion is necessarily true.

What are the implications for both the process and the content, though, when the premises are not given? Without premises as the starting point, there can be no argument. Yet identifying them in ordinary discussion can be challenging. In Chapter 2 you identified the argument in the editorial of the day's paper, but may have found it difficult to pin down the premises as they are often unstated and blended with many other background assumptions.

Unstated premises are entirely characteristic of any exchange of views. When you jump into the discussion of any issue, are you able to articulate *all* the assumptions that you are bringing to bear on the question? Are you even aware of all the assumptions that you make? Many of our basic practical assumptions, such as our own existence or the reliability of sense perceptions, may be invisible to us. Other assumptions may be so much part of our culture or our personal web of beliefs that we recognize them only when they are challenged. Behind the premises that you are able to state, therefore, lie many other unarticulated assumptions. Moreover, even those premises that you can articulate with a high level of awareness are often the conclusions of previous arguments with their own premises.

A key skill of critical thinking, therefore, is being aware of unstated assumptions when listening and reading in order to understand the bases of differing perspectives. Understanding an editorial or any other kind of commentary, a debate on any issue, or even a discussion between friends may demand a keen attention to what is *not* said. You may often be able to infer the underground assumptions through your awareness of both biases of language (Chapter 2) and the differences between types of assertions, for example statements of fact and value judgments (Chapter 3). Resolving conflicts—the most common conflicts over information, relationships, values, or procedures—may depend in large part on uncovering the differing assumptions that furnish premises for opposing arguments. Differing premises, after all, change all the logical conclusions that follow thereafter.

Only when the premises are identified can the essential question be asked: "Is this premise *true*?"

The *dubious premise*—possibly true, possibly false, and certainly contestable—plays an important role in persuasion. If someone

Recognizing invisible assumptions of culture

1 A German IB student and an Argentinian IB student are sharing a room in an international residence. Both make a real effort to be friends at first, but for some reason things go wrong.

Argentinian: I've really tried to get to know her, but she's very cold. She hardly even greets me. I've tried to include her in conversations with my friends, but they don't feel very welcome in our room either. When it comes to the 10:30pm privacy time, she tells them to leave even if we're in the middle of a conversation. I think she cares more about rules and schedules than about relationships with people.

German: I want to share a room, but she wants it all. She's noisy and intrusive. I don't like her kissing me hello all the time but not really caring about my feelings or respecting my space. She has her friends in the room all the time and they play their music loudly. Even when it comes to 10:30pm, when we're supposed to have privacy in our room, I have to speak to her friends before they'll leave. She doesn't even care about the code everyone's agreed to.

What cultural behaviour does each of these students notice in the other? Try to identify the assumptions that each makes, including the values according to which each judges the other.

You might find it useful to consider some of the following concepts, which are aspects of culture: sense of time, sense of space, sense of fairness and justice, sense of individual or group identity. You might also consider greeting patterns and relative explicitness of communication.

2 An American student and a Japanese student are going on a school trip by bus. The American student values open honesty, expects frankness in communication and disagrees with others comfortably in public. The Japanese student values harmony, expects understanding of indirect suggestion and would not expose someone else publicly as making a questionable statement. Can you imagine their discussion over whether the bus window should be open or closed? The American student wants it open while the Japanese student wants it closed. Will it end up open or closed?

claims firmly that immigrants are a drain on the economy then it is only a short step from that premise to an assertion that the country should accept no more foreigners. Once the premise is accepted and combined with other such firm statements ("We have to take care of our own people first.") then the conclusion follows. A counter-argument depends in part on contesting the initial claims.

The *implied premise* is also sometimes used to influence attitudes or conclusions. "Have you stopped cheating in IB exams? Give me a direct answer—yes or no!" Try it. No matter which answer you give, you confirm the buried premise that you have cheated in IB exams in the past. This device can plant suggestions about a person or a situation that are difficult to dispute without drawing greater attention to the implicit assumption. Consider another example:

"Are things better now between you and your husband?" The insinuation of gossip is not unlike the implied charges of many a political exchange: "Can we trust this government to improve its record on handling of land issues?"

2 Flawed generalizations

What evidence and how much evidence is sufficient for a sound conclusion? You will recall this question from the treatment of inductive reasoning in Chapter 2, and will hardly be surprised that it is a central question in Chapter 5 on areas of knowledge. Let us touch here on only three weaknesses in using evidence, simply because they are common.

a   *Argument from ignorance.* This first flaw in the use of evidence makes no sense at all when you examine it. Why would anyone believe a claim on the basis of no evidence at all? Yet life and death examples of the argument from ignorance have been part of the pageant of history. Claims have been believed and acted upon because there was apparently no evidence to the contrary. Accused of being witches, many women during the Inquisition in Europe were put to death by drowning or burning at the stake, because they could not prove they were not witches. But how could they possibly do so? Similarly how could a husband, accused of fantasizing about women other than his wife, prove otherwise? And how could a country charged with possessing and concealing illegal weapons prove that it had none, if the absence of evidence for weapons is interpreted as evidence for the effectiveness of their concealment?

b   *Hasty generalization.* A second flaw, the hasty generalization, is a conclusion reached on the basis of insufficient evidence. Often quick to infer patterns from scant data, people can jump to conclusions after only one or two examples—conclusions about the availability of taxis in a particular part of town, the likelihood of a particular person showing up drunk at a party, the relative honesty of an entire group of people. With further experience, many people will confirm or revise their first judgments. Unfortunately for the truth, and sometimes for relationships, the first judgment sometimes blocks recognition of the later exceptions.

As a device for persuasion, the hasty generalization may be fueled by striking stories of particular experiences. One or two atrocity stories may encourage negative beliefs about entire groups of people. One or two miracle stories may sell a health product or a religious cult. By the power of narrative, what is called "anecdotal evidence" may persuade people to believe more effectively than many a carefully administered general survey.

c   *Manipulation of statistics.* A third flaw in use of evidence depends on the interpretation of statistics, on which we often depend to overcome the limitations of anecdotal evidence. Like other forms of representation, they can be used for well-founded or ill-founded justification. Play with persuasion in the activity below in preparation for a fuller discussion of statistics in Chapter 5.

Persuasion with statistics

The government of your country, trying to encourage equal employment opportunities to the Red group and the Blue group, has promised a financial bonus to any company that demonstrates that it treats the two groups equally.

A You are the Red owner of a company hiring from both the Reds and the Blues. You want to demonstrate that you give equal employee benefit to each group in order to gain the government bonus. Your claim: "I treat Reds and Blues equally, and if I have any leaning at all it is toward giving greater benefit to the Blues." Present and justify your argument as persuasively as possible.

B You are a Blue worker who wants to demonstrate that the company does not treat employees equally, and does not deserve the bonus. Your claim: "Reds and Blues are not treated equally in this company. Reds have much greater job opportunity." Present and justify your argument as persuasively as possible.

You may want to take into account any of the following:

- your definition of "job opportunity" and "equal treatment"
- the average salary calculated as the mean (the sum of all the salaries, divided by the number of wage earners), the median (the mid-point salary), or the mode (the most commonly occurring salary)
- the mean average salary for Reds and for Blues separately
- inclusion or exclusion of the owner's income in averages
- the number of workers of each group, and their distribution across the hierarchy
- the ratio of salaries to each other between individuals and groups.

Company incomes	
100,000	owner, Red

Red and Blue employees: salary and distribution	
50,000	Red, Red, Blue
40,000	Red, Red, Blue
30,000	Red, Red, Blue, Blue
20,000	Red, Red, Blue, Blue, Blue
10,000	Red, Red, Blue, Blue, Blue, Blue, Blue, Blue, Blue, Blue

3 Slips on the grey scale

Not only do we often fall into error in generalizing from evidence, but we may also be inclined to over-emphasize certain positions on the spectrum of interpretation of evidence. Again, these weaknesses of everyday thinking can foster poorly justified conclusions or allow deliberate manipulation.

The metaphor of a grey scale between opposing interpretations helps to illustrate three main fallacies of thinking.

a *Black-and-white thinking* is a form of oversimplification that presents opposing views as the only possible alternatives. The range of possible views between the extremes is not recognized, and no mention is made of alternatives outside that particular scale. "You are either with us or against us" is a typical example. If groups are opposed to a particular conclusion, does it necessarily follow that they are in support of the opposite? The issue may not even be of concern to them. Polarized thinking is often coupled persuasively with an appeal to belonging. If those supporting a speaker's stand are called "true patriots", then what are the others? In propaganda, black-and-white thinking is often used to present *our* heroes and *their* villains.

As you will already have observed, the fallacies identified here are often applied jointly. Which ones can you name in this pair of Nazi posters?[5] On the left, the artist uses Christian religious imagery of the dove and radiant light to show Hitler as a divinely endorsed leader and associates him with a love of Germany. On the right, the artist makes "the eternal Jew" look ugly and distorted, with his hand outstretched for money. Hitler aimed for effective persuasion. A glance at history shows his success.

b *The argument of the beard* denies such extremes, obscuring real differences between opposing positions by considering only shades of grey. How many hairs make a beard? Not three? Not four? Not seventy? By insisting that there is no point at which one hair tips the balance, this argument denies the very real difference between a shaven face and one with a shaggy beard. Thinking in small increments in this way can be surprisingly seductive; it is the procrastinator's plague and the dieter's delight. "I'm so late with handing in this essay, what harm can one more day do?" "Just one chocolate won't make any difference." It is far too easy to blur the difference between a job done and a job not done, or a full box of chocolates (or bank account) and (oops!) an empty one. Turned to persuasion, this fallacy can be used to sell cars or vacation packages, for instance, as the purchaser is encouraged to add just one more little feature (not expensive) and then another (not expensive) and then another.... It can also be used as a defence against charges of wrongdoing, from lying to committing war crimes, for surely, on a sliding scale of grey, perpetrators' offences are seldom worse than those of others they could point to!

c *Truth is in the middle* is the last in this trio. Although compromise or a moderate middle way are admirable in many contexts, they can be applied erroneously when the truth is on one side. Between the claims that $5 \times 7 = 35$ and $5 \times 7 = 41$, would it make sense to conclude that the correct answer is the mid-point of 38? Does it make sense to call a woman "a little bit pregnant" or the targets of a bomb "a little bit dead"? Sometimes the truth does lie at either black or white on the spectrum. Mid-point averaging of opposing claims deflects attention from the weight of evidence. How can an honest person or a trustworthy organization preserve its reputation in the face of false allegations, if onlookers conclude that between the allegation and the denial there must be moderate wrongdoing?

4 Flawed cause

"Why?" How we answer this question will be a major topic of the next Chapter on areas of knowledge. So, for the moment, let us touch just briefly on two common errors in thinking and their role in persuasion. Both try to establish a cause–effect relationship between variables when none exists, or when the possible causal connection has not yet been tested and established.

a   *Post hoc.* The first confuses a sequence of events in time with a causal sequence. This fallacy is usually known by its Latin name of *post hoc ergo propter hoc,* meaning "after this, therefore because of this", and shortened to *post hoc.* This faulty connection of variables is the basis of many superstitions. A person walks under a ladder and then later has an experience that he interprets as bad luck. So what does he do? He blames walking under the ladder for the bad luck. He does not reflect that he also ate breakfast, opened his mail, and talked to his friends, and considers none of them to be the possible cause. In persuasion, *post hoc* is used variously—to attribute the recovery of health, for example, to the bracelet that the patient started to wear (which can, of course, be purchased for a bargain price) or to blame the crisis in the economy on an irrelevant decision taken earlier by an opposing political party.

b   *Confusion between correlation and cause.* In the second error of thinking variables are placed in relationship with one another and a faulty conclusion is drawn. The world around us abounds with situations in the process of change: the unemployment rate rises or falls and so do divorce rates, frequency of natural catastrophes, number of new infections from HIV/AIDS, numbers of deaths due to hunger, or sales of chocolate bars. Are variables that change at similar or inverse rates necessarily linked in any causal way? "In 2005, the percentage of students in North America taking the International Baccalaureate rose by 15%. So, too, did the incidence of youth crime in the streets surrounding this IB school." Even if both these statistics were accurate, would you conclude that, to reduce youth crime, it would be advisable to discontinue teaching the IB?

Persuasion through correlation

When you played earlier with metaphors for persuasion, you found points of comparison between unlike things and then extended the image for argument. Can you now make a similar move with correlations, using a possibly arbitrary relationship of variables in two areas to argue for a causal connection?

Conclusion

Because we depend on perception, language, emotion, and reasoning to gain our knowledge, we become better critical thinkers when we are mindful of how misuse of these ways of knowing can lead us into error. Now that you have examined some common devices for persuasion, return to consider more fully the opening question:

● What is the difference between justified persuasion and the persuasion of propaganda?

As your final activity, read the following passages in which the author comments on beliefs and persuasion in wartime. Do you recognize in his description of persuasion some of the weaknesses or tactics treated in this chapter? His conclusions are inescapable: what we are persuaded to believe has implications for our relationships and actions in the world—for good and, sadly, for ill.

Persuading toward war

In War is a Force that Gives Us Meaning *(2002),[6] Chris Hedges reflects on his long experience as a war correspondent to document and deplore "the myth of war" which glorifies a cause and "the drug of war" which provides a heady and addictive sense of purpose. The antidotes, he suggests, are humility and compassion. In 2002, Chris Hedges was given the Amnesty International Global Award for Human Rights Journalism and was part of the* New York Times *team that was given the Pulitzer Prize for Explanatory Reporting.*

"War makes the world understandable, a black and white tableau of them and us. It suspends thought, especially self-critical thought. All bow before the supreme effort. We are one. Most of us willingly accept war as long as we can fold it into a belief system that paints the ensuing suffering as necessary for a higher good, for human beings seek not only happiness but also meaning. And tragically war is sometimes the most powerful way in human society to achieve meaning." (p. 10)

"States at war silence their own authentic and human culture… By destroying authentic culture – that which allows us to question and examine ourselves and our society – the state erodes the moral fabric. It is replaced with a warped version of reality. The enemy is dehumanized; the universe starkly divided between the forces of light and the forces of darkness. The cause is celebrated, often in overt religious forms, as a manifestation of divine or historical will. All is

dedicated to promoting and glorifying the myth, the nation, the cause." (p. 63)

"Historical memory is hijacked by those who carry out war. They seek, when the memory challenges the myth, to obliterate or hide the evidence that exposes the myth as lie. The destruction is pervasive, aided by an establishment, including the media, which apes the slogans and euphemisms parroted by the powerful. Because nearly everyone in wartime is complicit, it is difficult for societies to confront their own culpability and the lie that led to it." (p. 141)

"The cultivation of victimhood is essential fodder for any conflict. It is studiously crafted by the state." (p. 64) "War finds its meaning in death. The cause is built on the backs of victims, portrayed always as innocent. Indeed, most conflicts are ignited with martyrs, whether real or created. The death of an innocent, one who is perceived as emblematic of the nation or the group under attack, becomes the initial rallying point for war…." (p. 114) "The cause, sanctified by the dead, cannot be questioned without dishonoring those who gave up their lives." (p. 145)

"Until there is a common vocabulary and a shared historical memory there is no peace in any society, only an absence of war…. But reconciliation, self-awareness, and finally the humility that makes peace possible come only when culture no longer serves a cause or a myth but the most precious and elusive of all human narratives – truth." (p. 81/82)

Traditional logical fallacies

Many of the errors in thinking or tactics of persuasion treated in this chapter have a long history, to the extent that some are still known by their Latin names. In order to make them more effective tools for thought for TOK students, we have made a number of modifications here to traditions of teaching fallacies: the errors and persuasive devices have been classified according to the ways of knowing of the

TOK course, fused or grouped in relationship to each other on the basis of common features, considered in relationship to legitimate justifications that they resemble, updated with names meaningful in a contemporary context, and supplemented with others common in our own era.

However, recognizing some of the common names when you encounter them elsewhere might help you to connect what you have learned in TOK with that other context—and perhaps give you the pleasure of seeing today within the framework of many yesterdays. The following list, which contains fallacies both modified and preserved here, is unfortunately by no means complete: errors in thinking fill many a book.

false analogy: revised as persuasive metaphor. Language 4.

argumentum ad miseracordiam: appeal to pity. Emotion 1.

argumentum ad baculum: appeal to fear. Emotion 2.

argumentum ad populum: appeal to the people and **wrapping oneself in the flag**: patriotic appeal. Both overlap with appeal to belonging. Emotion 3.

argumentum ad verecundiam: argument based on authority and *argumentum ad hominem*: argument based on the man rather than the argument: treated within misleading use of sources, Emotion 5.

missing premise, false premise, argument in a circle: fused as problematic premises. Reasoning 1.

hasty generalization: Reasoning 2b.

argumentum ad ignorantium: argument from ignorance. Reasoning 2a.

black-and-white argument, oversimplification, and false dilemma: fused as black-and-white thinking. Reasoning, slips on the grey scale 3a.

argument of the beard: reasoning, slips on the grey scale 3b.

truth is in the middle: reasoning, slips on the grey scale 3c.

non causa pro causa: mistaking something not the cause for the cause, here treated in the specific form of correlations mistaken for cause. Reasoning, flawed cause 4b.

post hoc ergo propter hoc: a sequence in time mistaken for cause. Reasoning, flawed cause 4a.

Further reading
- The Media Education Foundation online
- Poynter Online, a website of the Poynter Institute
- Reporters without Borders, online
- O'Reilly on Advertising, a CD set available at the Canadian Broadcasting Company shop online

Introduction

How many castles are there in this drawing? Count them and be prepared to explain your response.

Is any of the towers completely separate from the others? Is any completely out of contact with the ground on which the entire structure rests?

Evaluate this visual analogy to interconnected areas of knowledge. Do you consider it effective? Or is it limited, or even misleading?

The ivory towers of learning

"The ivory tower" is a metaphor sometimes applied to universities, suggesting that they are lofty and beautiful but quite remote from everyday life. The notion that gaining knowledge can be a pursuit that lures one away from life is disturbing. Surely a better educated understanding of how the world works is an ideal preparation for informed and effective involvement in it.

Already we are preparing in TOK not to retreat from life but to become engaged in it. We have brought to the discussion our ways of knowing and recognized some common failings in well-based persuasion. Now, within the framework of ideas of justification and truth, we will consider how people gaining knowledge use the ways of knowing to create knowledge in different areas. By the end of this chapter we hope to have given you an overview of how the areas of knowledge fit together, an overview that is likely to be immensely useful to you in your lifelong learning. We will follow with a chapter applying all of your critical thinking skills and all of your understanding of areas of knowledge to a world issue, to develop a general approach that you will be able to take with you beyond your IB graduation. Asking "How do I know?" is a question that immediately takes you to the ivory towers of learning, but simultaneously places you firmly on the ground.

However, do you accept the assumption that knowledge has value only if it has evident practical benefit? Do you reject learning for its own sake? With a mind alive and questioning, you are likely to find great pleasure in joining and adding to a knowledge conversation that has gone on for centuries. From the very tip of the most elegantly carved spires, you may survey the world with greater insight and understanding—and realize that you have never really left it. Even the most lofty tower has a solid base on the earth, and climbing it gives you a splendid view.

Questions for reflection

1   What knowledge, to you, seems the most useful? Why?
2   Is there any knowledge that is useless? How do you know that?
3   Is usefulness the highest value to place on knowledge? For what else do you value knowledge?

Areas of knowledge

Before starting a chapter that categorizes areas of knowledge for discussion, consider your own understanding of how different subjects fit together. As you did in the classification exercise near the end of Chapter 2, take the subjects listed below and shuffle them into categories, either in lists or in a diagram, according to a consistent principle that makes sense to you. If you wish to add more subjects, feel free to do so.

sports   information technology   philosophy   mathematics
biology   chemistry   dance   literature   physics   anthropology
theatre   medicine   psychology   economics   history
political science   music   painting   geography   film

Now, share your classification with others and justify it. As a group, are your principles for classification and your categorizations similar? Keep a note of these preliminary reactions in order to return to them after you study in this chapter the classification given by the TOK guide. You may wish at that point either to revise or to strengthen some of your initial ideas.

The IBO's TOK guide offers the following categorization not because it is the only one possible, but because, for one thing, the writers of the guide considered it to be an extremely useful one for bringing out common and contrasting features of areas of knowledge. Usefulness is not its only justification, however. In this chapter, reasons for this classification will be given and questioned.

● mathematics
● natural sciences
● human sciences
● history
● the arts
● ethics

What does this list leave out? Where would you place any omitted knowledge you identified in relationship to these categories?

Arguments, persuasion, and justification

Notice that we have asked you to do the same thing that we are doing in this book—to think about categories and distinctions between them that make sense to you and then to argue in favour of them, giving your reasons. Much of the exchange of knowledge works in this way, with people persuading each other to believe knowledge claims or to think of them in a certain way. We communicate to others how we conceptualize our ideas, and when they respond we have a chance to evaluate our own justifications. We also learn what others believe, and through this exchange of perspectives we end up (we hope) with our ideas clarified and better grounded. Reflection and exchange are ways of expanding and deepening our knowledge.

As we engage in these exchanges, we need to consider how we accept or reject knowledge claims. What justifications are acceptable for overthrowing a knowledge claim held true for a long time by a large number of people? What makes a person in any field an authority, whose opinion we take more seriously than other people's? Does the responsibility for justifying research claims rest with the person who puts them forward or with the whole knowledge community?

As we ask these ordinary questions that are central to knowing, we find that the answers depend on which area of knowledge we're examining. Researchers in each area use different kinds of justifications for their knowledge claims, gained through methods appropriate to their fields. As we move now through the six areas of knowledge of the TOK course, you will have the chance to ask numerous questions yourself and consider how others answer them.

Creation of areas of knowledge

Knowledge does not simply *happen*. Real people create it, individually or in groups, affected by the social context in which they live and the natural world which surrounds us all; that context may provide a background influence or may become itself the subject of study. The works they create—from a proof in mathematics, to a research paper in physics, to a novel or symphony in the arts, just for example—are received and evaluated by members of their own knowledge community. That community may be peers, specifically the peers in quite similar fields who are able to understand and evaluate the work. That community also includes the general public, who are involved in judgment of it to differing extents and in differing ways in different areas of knowledge. With their effect on the public, then, works of knowledge in any field contribute to the evolving social context within which further knowledge is created.

This brief account of the creation of knowledge leaves a lot out in order to highlight certain connections, ones to which we will return in the pages ahead. To start with an overview, consider this diagram and the questions that follow it. As you read this chapter, return to this page as you finish examining each area of knowledge. You may be intrigued by the interconnections you find between parts of this diagram and the similarities and differences between the areas of knowledge.

Knowledge Creation Diagram

within context of the natural world

| knowledge creator(s) | work(s) of knowledge *(math proof, research paper, novel)* | knowledge community *(peers, critics general public)* |

within social context

How are the answers to the questions below similar or different, as you consider the six areas of knowledge of TOK?

1 Knowledge creators
Who are the knowledge creators? What knowledge, skill, and talent do they need? What motivates them, supports them, restricts them? What social conditions (e.g. moral values, funding) influence them in their process of creating knowledge? Do they share the same goals as each other and the same goals as their critics?

2 Works of knowledge
What are the characteristics of a work in this area? What kinds of knowledge claims are made? How are they justified? Is there a method that distinguishes the area? What tests does a work have to pass in order to be accepted as a work appropriate to the area? What are the internal formal features which the work must have?

3 Knowledge community
Is there a community of peers? Who are the critics who evaluate the work for its strengths, weaknesses, and degree of contribution? Are they peers, experts, or even experts in criticism? What is the attitude of the critics toward variability and change? To what extent does the general public take part in the criticism? How much power does the knowledge community wield, in determining which works of knowledge are produced and which are not?

4 Context of society
In what ways do societies influence knowledge creation within them? How do the historical time, the economic conditions, and the cultural worldview, for example, affect what knowledge is created and how it is judged? To what extent does the created knowledge affect its social context? To what extent does it contribute to a cultural and historical record?

5 Context of the natural world
To what extent does the natural world influence what gets studied and how? Is the natural world the subject of study itself? Are attitudes toward it the subject of study? In what ways does the creation of knowledge have an effect upon the natural world?

6 The diagram as a whole
Remember that lists and diagrams are tools for thinking and drawing distinctions, but should be viewed critically for what they emphasize and what they leave out. Here, notice the artificiality of some of the divisions, created to clarify or emphasize certain points in a general argument. Surely the creators and critics often exchange roles, and both groups are part of their society. It is a perpetual challenge in simplifying not to *over*simplify in a way that might even distort. Please view diagrams in this book, like all others, as tools for the mind, to be approached critically. The influence of diagrammatic pictures and metaphors on our thinking is worth some reflection as a knowledge issue.

As we move in this chapter through broad general surveys of entire areas of knowledge, we will in our overview touch on or trace numerous such *knowledge issues*, those intriguing questions that attract the mind to question how knowledge is created and judged, open different perspectives and, we hope, invite exploration. This book, in a few pages, can only gesture toward the territory and hand you (metaphorically) a map. It is up to you, if you will, to do (metaphorically) the exploring.

● ●

Mathematics

Have the lights brightened? Have the shadows melted away? Far away, as perfect circles spin in crystal spheres, celestial music sounds in perfect harmony. On a screen the shifting shapes of symmetries and sequences, intricate filigrees, white out softly and vanish into pure abstraction. We have entered the realm of mathematics where the rational mind is at work, at play.

These images may not be what come first to your mind as you do your math assignments. Is there any other picture or image that conveys your experience in this area of knowledge?

When most abstracted from the world, mathematics stands apart from other areas of knowledge, concerned only with its own internal workings. It retreats, it seems, to the most remote of the ivory towers, in order to think in peace, undistracted by the world.

But for all its removal into abstraction, mathematics, at other times, also gets around companionably in the world. It has developed intimate relationships with other areas of knowledge, helping them to think, express ideas, draw new connections, model the real world, and create new knowledge. It becomes almost part of the family in the natural sciences and the human sciences and is welcomed in professions as various as engineering, veterinary medicine, marketing, and architecture.

You have probably welcomed it yourself into your own family home. From managing a budget to managing your time; from filing income taxes to deciding how much to trust an experimental medical treatment; from calculating the amount of carpet you'll need to purchase for your living room to estimating the ingredients for a shopping list, you may already have found reason to appreciate mathematics. Even if you go into a field that relies minimally on mathematics, being an educated adult in modern society will ensure that mathematics will permeate many aspects of your personal life.

Mathematics gives a splendid entry point into our TOK areas of knowledge.

Is mathematics "the language of the universe"?
Generally speaking, mathematics is the study of patterns and relationships between numbers and shapes. Symbolic and abstract, it takes us into our minds and back out to the world.

No matter what one believes about the origin of mathematics—some philosophers of math continue to engage in the age-old argument about whether we invent mathematics or discover it as we do scientific laws—it is undeniable that mathematical equations can describe the physical universe extremely well. We can truly feel a sense of wonder that the area of knowledge which takes us closest to abstract thought simultaneously provides us, very often, with the symbolic system with which we can talk most precisely about the world.

Two very special irrational numbers illustrate this amazing connection between the abstract and the concrete. Pi (π = 3.14159...) and Euler's constant (e = 2.71828...) show up in many equations in the natural and human sciences, and within mathematics itself.

Pi appears when we consider the circular shape, and is defined as the ratio of a circle's circumference to its diameter. It naturally appears whenever knowledge about circles and spheres is invoked, even within physics formulae.

The formula e = 1/0! + 1/1! + 1/2! + 1/3! + 1/4! + ... (infinite series) provides one way to calculate Euler's constant, and uses factorials (e.g., 5! = 5 × 4 × 3 × 2 × 1; 0! = 1 by definition). As students of calculus learn, the function e^x has very peculiar properties. It is even more peculiar that a number calculated with an infinite series would naturally appear in equations describing phenomena as diverse as radioactive decay, the spread of epidemics, compound interest, and population growth. Finally, within mathematics itself many consider Euler's equation, $e^{i\pi} + 1 = 0$, to be one of the greatest equations of all time. Not only does it uncannily connect the five most important numbers of mathematics (e, π, 1, 0 and the imaginary number i), but "what could be more mystical than an imaginary number interacting with real numbers to produce nothing?"[1]

We do not know why natural phenomena are so well described by mathematics, which is sometimes called "the language of the Universe". Novels like *Contact* by Carl Sagan (in the book this is made more explicit than in the namesake movie) presume that any intelligent extraterrestrials we encounter will be able to understand our mathematics. This belief was also shared by the very real scientists who included in the cargo of the Voyager 1 and 2 spacecraft (launched in 1977 and now moving beyond the solar system) phonograph disks which require that our mathematics be deciphered.[2]

Pure and applied mathematics

The main difference between pure and applied mathematics, as some universities classify their departments, is in the application of the knowledge they develop. (The qualifier "pure" to describe one kind doesn't imply that the other kind is impure or inferior; according to one practitioner,[3] a more fitting name might be "theoretical mathematics".) Researchers in pure mathematics—which includes abstract fields such as algebra, analysis, geometry, number theory, and topology—are not concerned with the direct practical applications of their labour. Applied mathematicians, on the other hand, focus on developing mathematical tools to enable and enhance research in other areas of knowledge. Applied math fields include numerical analysis, scientific computing, mathematical physics, information theory, control theory, actuarial science, and many others.

As is usual with classification schemes, some of the distinctions between "pure" and "applied" are fuzzy. The very establishment of applied mathematics resulted from the successful application of pure mathematics to real-world problems. As Nikolai Lobachevsky once said, "There is no branch of mathematics, however abstract, which may not someday be applied to the phenomena of the real world."[4] In the 1970s his assertion was verified yet again with the application of the fundamental theorem of arithmetic—considered useless for more than 2,000 years!—to cryptography, in order to enable secure electronic communications.[5]

A second degree of fuzziness occurs when we consider the distinction between applied mathematics and the areas of knowledge they support. For example, many advances in physics—perhaps even most advances—did not result from fitting a mathematical expression to experimental data points. To derive the equation $E = mc^2$, for example, Albert Einstein applied Lorenz transformations to what he believed was true about light and logically deduced, one step following the other, his theory of special relativity. Thus, it is sometimes difficult to distinguish clearly between applied mathematics and theoretical physics. With the pervasiveness of computational techniques applied to modelling and simulation in various fields, today the boundaries have become even more blurred.

Whether we're speaking of pure or applied mathematics, both deal solely with ideas, at a level of extreme abstraction. The number 2 symbolizes not just two objects of any sort but the idea of two-ness, and the place of two-ness in a number line of other abstractions going to infinity and back to negative infinity—an idea even more abstract. In set theory there can be an infinite number of infinities, and mathematicians can manipulate them through the symbols and the rules they've established to govern their use.

A mathematical world?

The world abounds with patterns that can be described in mathematical terms. How would you describe the examples pictured here?

- *top*: face, the phases of the moon, the pattern of a flock of birds in flight
- *left column*: starfish, buttercup, snowflake, sea anemone, sunflower
- *middle column*: butterfly, pansy, crab, drainage pattern (or...?), leaf, feet
- *right column*: snail, cochlea of the inner ear, water going down a drain, hurricane viewed from above, galaxy, iris of the eye.

To what extent is the naming system in biology affected by characteristics of living things describable in mathematical terms?

In these examples, what kinds of patterns appear within all three categories of animals, plants, and non-living things?

What other mathematically describable patterns in nature can you add to these examples? What, for example, is the Fibonacci series?

The sketch on p. 136 starts and ends with parts of the human body, mathematically describable in number and symmetry. Do we interpret the world as mathematical because we ourselves can be described so, and hence are inclined to see the world in our own terms? Or are patterns describable in mathematical terms part of the world independent of our own minds—a mathematical world of which we are only a part? Even without expecting to answer it, you may find the question quite intriguing, as have others before you.

Mathematics as a language

You have learned many mathematical symbols in your lifetime—all the numbers you can imagine, and many others. Take a few moments to write down ten mathematical symbols (other than real numbers, which would be too easy). Note how each symbol has a very precise meaning.

Are you allowed to combine these symbols in any way you wish? No. In the same way that the string "there go pretty me went I" uses English symbols but is not grammatical, a string such as "x + 2)(= >" is not grammatical. It is meaningless.

Because it is symbolic and can be manipulated into meaningful statements, mathematics has many characteristics of language. Although it does not have the range of functions of language and, arguably, depends on being consciously taught through language, mathematics has features which make it far superior to language as a symbolic system for abstract, rational argument:

1 It is precise and explicit. 3 is always 3, whereas "a few" can mean two, three…or even many, as in "I just need a few minutes!"
2 It is compact. Considerable thought can fit into a few lines. To see the difference for yourself, explain the Pythagorean theorem, $c^2 = a^2 + b^2$, using English.

Now, write down a few of the rules with which you manipulate mathematical symbols and statements. Examples include the commutative property, cross-multiplication, not dividing by zero, reducing a fraction, factorizing a polynomial, and many others. Note that these rules are general. The introduction of rules leads us to two more features of mathematics as a symbolic system:

3 It is completely abstract. It manipulates its statements solely with its own rules.
4 In a way similar to a valid deductive argument, mathematical statements can be manipulated in a step-by-step fashion according to clearly defined rules, leading to new conclusions that were not readily apparent.

Note that when these abstractions are applied to the world, the meaning of mathematical statements gains a concrete dimension. I can abstractly know that the equation $c^2 = a^2 + b^2$ is applicable to every right triangle, but when I'm buying fencing for my garden, determining the shortest drive between two points, or calculating the resultant force in a physics problem, a, b and c have different and very specific meanings.

For mathematicians, this precise, compact, abstract, and transformable symbolic system provides the vocabulary and grammar which enable us to talk about abstract relationships such as symmetry, proportion, sequence, frequency, and iteration. Thus, mathematics simultaneously provides a way of analysing not just patterns found in the world by the sciences but also those created from the world by the arts.

Can you speak mathematical "language"? Three activities

1   If you are interested in visualizing mathematical ideas, investigate the artworks of M.C. Escher, which tease and puzzle sense perception while they play with mathematical concepts. You may wish to pair up with someone else in the class or form a small group to look closely at his art and its relationship with mathematics, and share what you have found with the rest of the class. Images and mathematical commentary can be found on the Internet.

2   If you are a musician familiar with compositional analysis, share with the rest of your class some mathematical principles in music. You may wish to pair up with someone else in the class or form a small group to present your ideas. Live performance or recorded music add pleasure to exploration of this topic.

3   Try to write a poem in mathematical language, just for the fun of it. Students before you have done so with results that are quite entertaining. Concepts of nothingness, difference, union of sets, and infinity, for example, seem to lend themselves to poetry— but they are merely the start. When you have exhausted your capacity to unite mathematics with your poetic imagination, consider whether what you have written could be considered mathematics or, rather differently, language using mathematical imagery. Think back also to the comparisons you drew between different symbolic systems in Chapter 2 (see page 33).

With such a wide range of applications in the world, what is it that mathematics cannot do as a "language"? Why is the IB never likely to offer mathematics A as a group 1 subject?

Building upon foundations: creating an axiomatic, deductive system

Mathematics is frequently spoken of as having foundations, rather like a building with a strong stone or concrete base. If the foundations are solid and unshakeable, the construction that is built on top rests secure. For mathematics, assumptions known as axioms provide the foundation, and through the process of deductive reasoning, step by step, often over a span of many centuries, mathematicians carefully erect a building.

Different mathematical fields such as geometry, algebra, set theory and number theory are axiomatic, deductive systems. Each of these fields is based on a different set of axioms, but relies on the same method to develop new knowledge. By using the axioms at the foundation as premises and applying valid deductive reasoning to them, mathematicians obtain—through a process called mathematical proof—new statements called theorems. These, in turn, are used as additional premises to build further theorems, which are in turn used as additional premises…ultimately giving rise to entire structures consisting of interconnected mathematical statements.

But what is missing from this picture? Think back to reasoning as a way of knowing and the blender analogy discussed in Chapter 2. Recall that in order to generate true conclusions, a deductive argument requires not only valid reasoning, but also true premises. How do we know if the axioms used by mathematicians as the foundations of their structures are true? That question turns out not to be simple. Actually, it is a critical knowledge issue in mathematics.

Historically, geometry was the first axiomatic, deductive system to be developed. It was Euclid, 2,300 years ago, who identified the first known set of axioms, only ten of them (the fewer, the better!). He considered these axioms (which he called "postulates" and "common notions") to be true, derived from experience and requiring no proof.[6] With one proof at a time—some less formal than others, because Euclid "assumed details and relations read from the figure[s] that were not explicitly stated"—Euclid's system of plane geometry was built. Students worldwide continue to study it in schools today.

For over 2,100 years, Euclidian geometry was considered to be perfect knowledge. It was regarded not just as valid but as true—true not only in its logical consistency (coherence test for truth) but also true in the world (correspondence test for truth). Even more significantly, Euclidean geometry was considered to be eternally true.

No challenge came to the perfection of Euclid's mathematical system until the 19th century, and even then the challenge was not to its validity but to its truth. What if Euclid's axioms, the very foundations of his system, were not true—or were not the only possible truth?

The first four of Euclid's axioms seemed self-evident because they could be verified by drawing figures on the sand. The first required joining two points with one, and only one, line segment; the second required imagining that this line segment continues forever on the flat ground; the third required constructing a circle centred on a point; and the fourth required only that people compare right angles they could easily draw, and conclude that the angles are congruent. But the fifth axiom—known as the "parallel postulate"—was more problematic, even for Euclid, who only invoked it upon proving his 29th theorem.[7] How could anyone ensure that you can draw only one line through a point P that is parallel to a given line? Verifying the truth of that axiom would require someone to accompany the line forever, to ensure that it never intersects the first line. Mathematicians tried to prove the fifth postulate as if it were a theorem, and failed.

Independently of these quirky little technical problems, countless generations benefited from knowing one of the theorems proved by Euclid, that the sum of the angles of a triangle is 180°. They found in geometry's established truths easy ways to solve their everyday problems, such as determining how much wall to build around a perimeter or calculating the area of their fields. Meanwhile, mathematicians continued to struggle with the fifth postulate, mainly by trying to prove that Euclid's system was foolproof.

It was Carl Friedrich Gauss in the early 1800s who first noticed that a geometry could be built without including Euclid's fifth postulate. Gauss paved the way for the non-Euclidean geometries of Nikolai Lobachevsky and later that of Bernhard Riemann. Lobachevsky replaced Euclid's fifth postulate with the idea that through a point P next to a given line, at least two lines exist that are parallel to it. Riemann, on the other hand, assumed that no parallel lines exist through P, which logically implied that he had to adopt modified versions of Euclid's first and second postulates as well. (To understand why, imagine Riemann's geometry happening on the surface of a sphere instead of on an infinite plane surface like Euclid's. On a sphere's surface, more than one line can be drawn between two points, and lines cannot be extended indefinitely.[8]) These non-Euclidean geometries—consistent and valid, though based on different axioms—shook the very foundations of mathematics.

Mathematics: definitions and playing by the rules

A farmer called an engineer, a physicist, and a mathematician and asked them to fence the largest possible area with the least amount of fence.

The engineer made the fence into a circle, and proclaimed that he had the most efficient design.

The physicist built a long, straight line of fence and proclaimed "If we were to extend this length around the Earth, we would have the largest possible area."

The mathematician just laughed at them. He built a tiny fence around himself and said, "I declare myself to be on the outside."

It had been assumed that Euclidean geometry was true according to the correspondence truth test, accurately describing space. How could other consistent geometries be built using different axioms, geometries that didn't have any bearing on reality? Were mathematical systems not necessarily true? The answer to these questions changed the whole notion of mathematical truth. Mathematical truth came to be understood as truth within a system: mathematical statements could be true within the Euclidean system, or true within the Riemann system. The only truth test relevant was the coherence test, or in other words the consistency of every statement with every other statement within its own axiomatic system.

Though Lobachevsky's geometry hasn't been shown to apply to the cosmos, in 1916 Riemann's geometry did find a practical application. The curved space of Einstein's theory of general relativity is well described by Riemann's geometry.

We now consider axioms to be not "self-evident truths" but to be the assumptions, premises, definitions, or "givens" at the base of a mathematical system. We still use the metaphor of foundations, but recognize more than one possible construction. Euclid's geometry is more useful in building a house, Riemann's is more useful in flying an airplane, and Lobachevsky's, in accordance with his own quoted words a few pages ago, might one day find a practical application…or not.

With the failure of Euclidean geometry to describe physical space as had been expected, a vast amount of room opened up for the creativity of mathematicians. Today, they do indeed have the freedom to declare whatever they please, independently of whether their assumptions have any bearing on the real world or not.

Once a mathematician adopts any specific set of definitions and rules, however, he must play by them—very, very strictly.

Reflections on mathematics

For class discussion

In what ways does the general public—like you and your family—benefit, directly and indirectly, from the products of mathematical research?

Make a list of the ways in which you're classified based on the numbers associated with you (e.g. your number among other telephone owners). What parts of your life do numbers enter? If you seem to have more numbers attached to you than others do, what has created this difference?

With the pervasiveness of computers, might we as a culture have become too attached to representations of the world in quantitative terms? Consider the following statement about world hunger: "…how we understand hunger determines what we think are its solutions. If we think of hunger only as numbers—number of people with too few calories—the solution also appears to us in numbers—numbers of tons of food aid, or numbers of dollars in economic assistance."[9] Do you agree this might be the case? What would support this argument? What would counter it?

For research and class discussion

Identify three formulae or algorithms which you find interesting in your current mathematics textbook. Research who developed them, and when and where they were developed. Why did you choose these specific three? Do they have anything in common? Share your insights with classmates.

Investigate some of the specializations in which applied mathematicians collaborate with researchers in other fields. Does any of these fields appeal to you? Does it surprise you that being a mathematician doesn't necessarily imply working within a university?

Mathematical proof: challenging and beautiful

Euclid and Riemann both created knowledge by means of the characteristic method of justification in mathematics: the proof. To create a proof, as we have seen, the mathematician takes as his premises the foundational axioms and all subsequent theorems and proofs based on them. Then, with a problem or conjecture in mind, he reasons toward a new conclusion, taking immense care to avoid error in any step. In manipulating ideas in a process of pure thinking, he creates new knowledge. That new theorem, in turn, provides a base for further reasoning.

Mathematicians, taking pleasure in such abstract creation, are the more delighted if the proof goes beyond merely being valid. It should be, as they say, elegant. The elegant or beautiful proof is incisive and ingenious. It is economical in using as few steps as possible and holds a little jolt of surprise as ideas fall neatly into place. A swirl of a cape, a flash of a rapier and—voilà—proved! Or so the mathematician would like.

When we liken mathematics to a game with its own internal rules, we do not mean that it is trivial. Games can be very serious.

However, mathematicians are not always very serious. What is the invalid step in this proof?[10]

What's wrong with this proof?

Given: $A = B$

Multiply both sides by A: $A^2 = AB$

Subtract B^2 from both sides: $A^2 - B^2 = AB - B^2$

Factorize both sides: $(A + B)(A - B) = B(A - B)$

Divide both sides by $(A - B)$: $A + B = B$

Since $A = B$, $B + B = B$

Add the Bs: $2B = B$

Divide by B: $2 = 1$

A new proof, no matter how beautiful it is, does not enter the realm of mathematics until it becomes public knowledge: the truth of the claim must be justified to the relevant knowledge community which, through the process of peer review, must come to believe the claim's truth.

A good example of peer review at work is the rejection, for almost four centuries, of all attempted proofs for what came to be known as Fermat's Last Theorem (FLT).

In 1637, Pierre de Fermat, as the story goes, was reading for pleasure a book of ancient mathematics, a French translation of Diophantus' *Arithmetica*. Mathematicians still do not know what was going through his mind when he wrote in the margin of the book the message, "I have a truly marvellous demonstration of this proposition which this margin is too narrow to contain."[11] Without ever sharing his proof, he died. Published posthumously by his son in 1655, the note remained. Fermat had a solid reputation as a mathematician, so it could not be dismissed lightly. But what was his "marvellous demonstration"? Fermat had left to his successors the most famous unsolved problem in the history of mathematics.

We know from working with right triangles that many trios of integers can satisfy the equation $c^2 = a^2 + b^2$. What Fermat postulated was that no trios of integers exist that can satisfy equations such as $c^3 = a^3 + b^3$, or $c^4 = a^4 + b^4$, and so forth, for powers greater than squares. Many mathematicians tried and failed to find a proof. Even more just turned away to work on problems more likely to be fruitful. Why waste time on FLT?

When a proof was announced, it caused a sensation. It was in 1993 that British mathematician Andrew Wiles first announced he had proved FLT. Wiles presented his 150-page paper at a conference as a "traditional mathematical proof", which omits routine logical steps and assumes that knowledgable readers can fill in the gaps. Such proofs rely on intuitive arguments which can be easily translated by trained mathematicians into rigorous deductive chains. Proofs are usually presented this way because too much formality would obscure its main points, much like watching a movie frame by frame would distract the viewer from enjoying, or perhaps even understanding, its storyline.

Peer review went to work—and this version of Wiles' proof was found to have a flaw. In Wiles' own words, "It was an error in a crucial part of the argument, but it was something so subtle that I'd missed it completely until that point. The error is so abstract that it can't really be described in simple terms. Even explaining it to a mathematician would require the mathematician to spend two or three months studying that part of the manuscript in great detail."[12] Wiles went back to work, creating still more mathematics in order to remedy the error.

In 1994 Wiles presented his amended proof. Again peer review went to work—and this time the mathematical community accepted the proof. Wiles became a celebrity overnight, surrounded by public excitement over the solution of such a famous and longstanding problem. Intriguingly, though, his proof of Fermat's Last Theorem cannot have been Fermat's own, as the 20th-century mathematics on which it is based was unknown, back in 1637, to Fermat.

The story of this proof illustrates many characteristics of mathematics as an area of knowledge. For one thing, it shows something of its humanity—the fascination, the challenge, the creativity, the aspiration, the disappointments, the sense of triumph. At the same time, though, it reflects characteristics of more ordinary mathematical endeavour—the level of care and detail demanded, the peer review and its difficulties when the work is new and complex, and the respect given to achievement that the lay public does not understand and for which there may be no apparent practical use.

In 2006, Wiles' proof of FLT has not yet been developed into a rigorous or formal proof, showing every single deductive step. Computer scientists have now been challenged to "formalize and verify" it, and one of them estimates that he expects this problem to be solved in about 50 years.[13]

(Indeed, contemporary mathematical proofs are rarely brief. In 2003, Russian mathematician Grigory Perelman announced that he had solved a classical problem within the field of topology, the Poincaré conjecture. In 2006, Perelman's traditional proof was confirmed after peer review.[14] It was roughly a thousand pages long.)

Clearly, the relationship between the mathematician Diophantus of ancient Greece, Pierre de Fermat of 17th-century France, and

Dr Andrew Spray,
IB Diploma Programme mathematics teacher
and examiner

Why do you love mathematics?

The challenge in replying is that it is hard to give
one single reason. Among the features that are very
endearing are:

- The elegance of the logic behind many classic mathematical
  proofs.

- The unexpected connections between apparently distinct areas of
  mathematics. e.g. e appearing in probability problems, π
  appearing in summing the inverse powers of numbers, the classic
  $e^{i\pi} + 1 = 0$.

- The beautiful patterns, usually unexpected, that arise between
  numbers. e.g. 3 cubed + 4 cubed + 5 cubed = 6 cubed (or
  $3^3 + 4^3 + 5^3 = 6^3$).

- The fact that areas of mathematics developed solely for the sake
  of pure mathematics turn out to have very useful applications in
  the real world, for example complex (or imaginary) numbers,
  group theory.

- The joy of being able to solve a complex problem and prove you
  are correct.

I love mathematics for all these reasons, and more, but perhaps it is
the patterns, the searching for them and the joy of discovering them,
that captivate me most.

contemporary Andrew Wiles of Britain (who developed his work in
the United States) highlights certain features of mathematical
knowledge. Its challenges and its products can last over centuries.
Yet once it is satisfactorily proved, the proof is permanent in all
places and all time, and the proven knowledge claim earns its place
as yet another brick in the edifice of mathematical knowledge, built
across boundaries of time and culture.

Placing the spotlight on the successful proofs, however, may obscure
the contributions of the failures. Have their failures really been
failures for mathematics? After all, the development of mathematics
relies on failed attempts at proof as well as successes. Much new
knowledge is generated in attempts to solve problems; many
interconnections between mathematical fields are established. As
Wiles said about his own effort, "The definition of a good
mathematical problem is the mathematics it generates rather than
the problem itself."[15]

Mathematics and its critics

With the creation of considerable mathematical knowledge through
the past century, mathematics is evidently flourishing. However, as
an area of knowledge with its characteristic means of justification,
mathematics has also faced criticism of its very foundations.

The growth of mathematical knowledge: exercise

by Manjula Salomon

In the following exercise, you will take on a research topic, find out about it, and share your findings. Be prepared to identify your findings according to historical time and place of origin.

Divide your group so that someone is investigating each of the following topics. Allow at least 20 minutes in the library or on the Internet for the investigation. For finding the most crucial details, your best source may be an encyclopedia.

- abacus
- Ramanujan
- calculus
- Omar Khayyam
- geometry
- algebra
- algorithm
- infinity
- decimal system
- probability
- Pythagoras' theorem
- chaos theory
- zero
- Euclid
- trigonometry

Create a timeline on the board or a large poster. Each person or group should report the information obtained and place the relevant information on the shared timeline.

Questions for discussion

1 What interdevelopments do you see between the various topics?

2 To what extent does your research suggest that mathematics is an international area of knowledge? How would you compare it in this regard with other areas of knowledge?

3 Does your research challenge any of your previous assumptions?

4 The development of mathematical knowledge is often illustrated by a tree diagram (that is, roots labelled as arithmetic, the trunk labelled as calculus, etc.). Mathematical scholars often select the banyan tree as the best tree for such an illustration. Why might this be so?

Note: Conventional division of the mathematical history timeline separates it into periods: earlier times to ancient Babylonia and Egypt, the Greek contribution, the Far-Eastern and Semitic contribution, and the European contribution from the Renaissance onward.

Consider now the diagram at the beginning of this chapter for its application to mathematics.

We have considered the creators of new knowledge, the characteristics of mathematical work, the role of peer review in the process of public justification, and mathematics' relationships with the natural and social world depending on whether we are speaking of pure or applied mathematics.

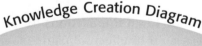

Knowledge Creation Diagram

within context of the natural world

knowledge creator(s)　　work(s) of knowledge *(math proof, research paper, novel)*　　knowledge community *(peers, critics general public)*

within social context

Let us look more closely now at the role of the critic, who applies critical thinking to a balanced examination of the justifications of the knowledge claims, seeking to appreciate both their strengths and their limitations. The critics of mathematics, those who evaluate each new mathematical work, are themselves mathematicians—peers of the knowledge creator(s). At a higher level of abstraction, though, are those mathematicians who evaluate the entire area of knowledge, examining its knowledge claims for their nature and their bases. Sometimes philosophers, sometimes highly reflective mathematicians, sometimes meta-mathematicians, these critics concern themselves with such issues as the reliability of the foundations of mathematics and the nature of proof.

In the early 20th century they reached a shocking conclusion: that mathematical knowledge has flaws and limitations, implying that mathematicians do not have an absolutely unshakable basis for their knowledge claims. Mathematicians had thought they had possessed that solid basis before the development of non-Euclidean geometries, and were hoping to restore the status of mathematics as a field providing absolute, eternal truths.

So, after mathematicians realized that mathematical truths must be evaluated using the coherence truth test (which implies that the axioms they use as foundations need to be logically consistent), they turned their attention to studying axioms more attentively. Could mathematics reach a state of completeness—a state in which it would be whole, having all its necessary elements or parts? This translated into another two questions. First, can all propositions be proved or disproved from axioms within the system? Second, can the consistency of the axioms be proved (can we be sure they don't contradict each other)? Bertrand Russell, working with Alfred North Whitehead, had been trying to deduce the entire field of mathematics from the principles of logic alone. They started with arithmetic, by attempting to construct the real number system using mathematical sets as a tool.[16]

In 1901, they were disturbed to discover a contradiction regarding those sets which are, or are not, members of themselves. If the set is a set of chocolate bars, for example, the set is *not* a member of itself. However, if the set is a set of all those things that are not chocolate bars, then the set is a member of itself. Russell discovered that he could easily create a contradiction, no matter what objects he was including in the set, by creating a set of all sets that are not members of themselves. Hence a member of the set would have to be (a) a member of itself, because it is part of the set and (b) not a member of itself, because that is what the set is—a set of things *not* members of themselves.

Russell's paradox had implications for all mathematics: if mathematics is an intellectual game played by its own internal rules, and expected to be complete and free of contradiction, then what claim to knowledge can it have if there is an inconsistency within it? Russell and others, including Gottlob Frege and David Hilbert in the 1920s, attempted without success to eliminate paradox from mathematics.

Verbal analogies to self-reference and contradiction may give some sense of what these mathematicians experienced. Self-reference, after all, is not unusual in itself. Singers sing songs about singing songs, poets write poems about writing poetry, and painters have been known to paint paintings of painters painting. Every time you use "I" you are using self-reference. Even reflection on knowing in TOK is often self-referential. Still more so is the research of cognitive psychologists, who use their brains to think about the thinking of the brain. (If you wore a self-referential T-shirt, what would be the

Jest for fun

Mathematics is made of 35 percent formulae, 35 percent proofs, and 35 percent imagination.

There are three kinds of people in the world; those who can count and those who can't.

design on it? If you took a self-referential photograph, what would it show?)

When self-reference creates contradiction, the results can be quite witty. The writer Oscar Wilde once quipped, "I can resist everything—except temptation" and on the basis of similar cleverness became a favourite party guest for a while. Depending on your sense of humour, you may find paradox quite entertaining as it jams your mind with contradiction: "Disobey this command." (Just try doing that!) Ancient paradoxes live on to perplex us largely because we enjoy them: Epimenides, from ancient Crete, uttered the claim, "All Cretans are liars" or, in another version, "I am lying." Well, if he is telling the truth, does that mean he is lying? If he is lying, does that mean that he is telling the truth? This kind of paradox, many find, is immensely entertaining. But mathematicians did not burst into laughter when Gödel made a similar move in mathematics.

In 1931, Kurt Gödel published what is now known as "Gödel's Incompleteness Theorem", which basically states that the dream of having mathematics reach a state of completeness is impossible to achieve. There cannot be a guarantee, within any axiomatic system, that the axioms adopted will not give rise to contradictions. There will always be, in any formal system, statements that are not decidable within it. Thus, no axiomatic system can ever prove its own consistency.

Gödel had no intention of knocking the supports out from under mathematics—and also its hope of being the only area of knowledge able to achieve absolute certainty because of its reliance solely on reasoning. Gödel intended exactly the opposite, actually—to ground the axiomatic approach to mathematics the more firmly on logic. With considerable ingenuity, though, he followed where his reasoning led him, creating through a numbering system a means of self-reference within mathematics that led to internal paradox and, ultimately, to the Incompleteness Theorem.

Despite having been shocked into the realization that mathematical knowledge has limits, mathematicians survived, and kept on working. The dream of absolute certainty is not attainable in mathematics, nor is it attainable in the natural sciences, as we shall see in the next section. But that doesn't prevent us from learning as much as we can, including learning to judge how much we can trust the knowledge we glean. The revelation of the flaws in mathematics has not stopped mathematics. On the contrary, it has given it a new understanding of itself, new problems to solve, and new directions for the mind.

G.J. Chaitin, a contemporary mathematician who stated that any given number cannot be proved to be random,[18] recently looked back on the Incompleteness Theorem as almost inevitable—as a step in mathematical progress now absorbed into further thinking. Like Alan Turing's later work and Wiles's more recent proof, for him the Incompleteness Theorem becomes clear in hindsight: "So you see, the way that mathematics progresses is you trivialize everything! The way it progresses is that you take a result that originally

> "*A mathematician is a person who can find analogies between theorems; a better mathematician is one who can see analogies between proofs and the best mathematicians can notice analogies between theories. One can imagine that the ultimate mathematician is one who can see analogies between analogies.*"
>
> Stefan Banach[17]

required an immense effort, and you reduce it to a trivial corollary of a more general theory!" He speculated that in a century or two, Wiles's proof, hundreds of pages long, will be reduced to a single page and understood readily in the context of mathematics developed after its time. "But of course that's the way it works. That's how we progress."[19] So maybe, after all that is said and done, we'll finally figure out what proof to his last theorem Fermat had in mind when he wrote that note in the margin.

The ivory tower revisited

Mathematical progress—perfect or imperfect—surely takes us to its ivory tower, remote from the world in a realm of pure thought. It is a particularly intricate tower, carved and incised with immense care for detail, and elegant in its shape. Within it, pure mathematicians build their proofs with little concern for practicality, while many practitioners of other areas of knowledge wait, hoping that they will produce the mathematical knowledge and language that will be useful within their own fields. The remote tower, after all, has never lost its connection with all the others.

Let us give the final word on mathematics to someone passionate about it, IB graduate (1999) Gergana Bounova of Bulgaria, who concluded an essay in TOK with a personal declaration about this area of knowledge:

> *Ultimately, I am certain about one thing—mathematics is extremely beautiful. Only a few can truly appreciate it. Beauty is not in the eye of the beholder. Beauty is in the mind of the beholder. Mathematics is a sophisticated toy you can play around with until reaching total intellectual satiation. It is unbelievably perfect and this is why I feel it is not the universal language. The world is an interesting but imperfect place and needs something to balance it. So let's dream in mathematics and wake up in the real world.*

Final question for TOK reflection

Has the study of this section changed your understanding of, or your feelings about, mathematics and mathematicians? If so, in what ways?

Fun math tricks and games
The Magic Gopher:
www.learnenglish.org.uk/games/
magic-gopher-central.swf.

● ●

The natural sciences, human sciences, and history

As we move from mathematics to the sciences and history, the clear light becomes increasingly dappled with recognizable shapes of the world—trees, animals, and passing human beings. We have left the realm of pure thought and are entering the world and the areas that study it.

In your diagram or lists at the beginning of this chapter, what connections did you make between physics, chemistry, biology, psychology, economics, anthropology, and history? In TOK, the first three are natural sciences, the second three are human sciences, and history stands on its own. However, for the moment, we will consider all of them together.

What would justify claiming that these areas of knowledge are different from mathematics? Consider the following two statements and compare mathematics broadly with the natural sciences, human sciences, and history.

- Pure mathematics is concerned only with the connection of abstract ideas. What, in comparison, is the subject matter of these three areas?
- The only justification for knowledge claims in mathematics is reasoning and the only truth test is coherence. What justifications and truth tests, in comparison, are used in these three areas? (If you need to review justifications and truth tests, see Chapter 3.)

Keep a record of the broad comparisons that you draw at this point. As you are asked once again to classify, you are probably increasingly conscious that the very process of grouping and drawing distinctions contributes to seeing characteristics of the components more clearly. The classifying never ends as you gain knowledge and recognize the processes that lead you to it.

Answering the question "why?"

Science, a famous scientist once said, is merely a refinement of everyday thinking. He was not talking specifically about categorizing, nor specifically about wondering why, but he could have been. Surely few reach the age of maturity of Diploma Programme students without having thought quite a lot about what has caused our own lives and the world around us.

Take time now to ask yourself the question, "Why am I here in this particular place at this particular time?" Consider all the possible answers you might give and select those that you think give the best explanation. Write reflectively for 20 to 30 minutes, gathering ideas.

Now share your answers with classmates, building up as many responses as possible collectively. Appoint one person to take notes for your group, preferably on a board or flip chart where all can see the notes.

You may have stories to tell of how you happened to end up in this place or how things might easily have been otherwise. You might recall "turning point" moments in your own life, involving personal decisions or the actions of others. ("If it weren't for X, I wouldn't be here.") You might consider, too, what background situations had to exist for the particular events to have happened as they did. Do you feel that your being here, now, is pure accident or chance, or do you consider there to be some purpose or plan for your life in the form of destiny or the will of God/Allah?

"Why?": How do we explain?

Please read these questions only after you have completed your discussion on why you are *here*, *now*. Use them to reflect on your own answers and the answers that emerged from discussion with your class group.

1 Did your explanation involve or even emphasize *your own decisions*? Did you feel it relevant to give the factors that in turn affected the choices you made, and to explain why they were important to you? Do your expectations of the future affect your decisions in the present?

2 Did your explanation involve *actions by other people*? If so, did you think of the effect those people had on you mainly in terms of their actions or also in terms of their intentions?

3 Did your explanation involve *negative causes*, things that did not happen to prevent the present? Many people have stories of times when they (or their parents before their conception and birth) might have died from illness, accident, or violence, for example, but did not.

4 *How far "back"* in time did explanations within your group go? Did they move back in time to the lives of your parents and grandparents? How did your mother meet your father? Is their story part of your own? Did you go further back into the lives of your ancestors? Did you assume that cause was a linear sequence, metaphorically going back and back to a beginning, perhaps the Big Bang theory and/or a First Cause as God/Allah?

5 *How far "out"* did explanations within your group go? How much within the present background came into discussion of cause? Did you feel it relevant, for example, to include the existence of the International Baccalaureate or your school, or the political, economic, and cultural background of your region that affects the educational context?

6 What did you consider "cause" to be? Was it the *biggest influence* (even if it is in the background), the event or influence that stands out as *most unusual*, or the one that happened *last* to provoke your being in the particular place at the particular time?

7 Did your explanation include *metaphysical influence* in any form? Does your personal understanding of cause and effect involve, for example, destiny, karma, or God?

In the natural sciences, human sciences, and history, which seek to give explanations for different aspects of the world, questions of cause are extremely important. Which of the questions above would *none* of these areas consider, and which ones would only *some* consider?

Metaphysical or spiritual explanation

In Chapter 3 we identified a number of justifications for belief— reasons for belief that are persuasive to the believer. Some justifications could be demonstrated publicly to all (reasoning, evidence), while others could not (revelation, faith) and remained private. That sub-category of beliefs which is given justification in a public way is called "knowledge", while the rest remain as "belief" or as "private knowledge". As we will see in dealing further with areas of knowledge, this division between "knowledge" and "belief" is neither precise nor stable. However, it provides a useful distinction between knowledge claims that deal exclusively with reasoning and the material world and those which deal with the immaterial or spiritual.

In public knowledge we tend to converge, while in private knowledge we often diverge. An atheist, a Buddhist, a Christian, and a Muslim can work together on the same research team, converging in their knowledge: they may have the same level of doubt or questioning regarding the knowledge claims of their field and the same skills of investigation. Each *knows* the same thing. However, each may integrate that knowledge into the coherent whole of all his beliefs and *understand* the knowledge differently. For the atheist, the scientific explanation has no spiritual resonance—none, at least, in the form of a god. For the non-theist Buddhist, the explanation may be part of an understanding of a universe where cause and effect are of central significance, where all actions create good or bad karma that will come back to affect the doer and others. For the theist Christian and Muslim, the explanation may fit into a conception of the world where God/Allah is the cause of all—the Creator, the causal force behind the events of the world (God's will or plan), and a force that may intervene in life in response to prayer. The four researchers do not differ in their knowledge. They differ in the meaning they attribute to it and the place they give it in their larger worldview. An examination of where we converge in our knowledge may be incomplete without a complementary recognition of where we diverge in our understanding.

Indeed, it could easily be argued that for many people their private beliefs are more personally significant than those public ones called "knowledge". The answer to "What is the purpose of my life?" or "What happens to people when they die?" may be valued more highly than the answer to "What is a true description of the world I live in?" even though the answer to the latter, involving everything from growing crops to taking medicine to making political decisions, affects well-being or survival.

Yet the beliefs of a spiritual worldview, it seems, are often difficult to speak about and are often held with emotion that makes discussion sensitive. Do you possess the sensitivity and respect for the views of others that would make such discussion rewarding? If so, you may find that a TOK class presentation provides an effective framework in the form of the expectations of the assessment criteria and the terminology of the course (belief, justification).

 If you have a diversity of spiritual worldviews within your group, you may wish to consider what justifications persuade people to believe their own metaphysical explanations (why?) and what the implications are for a real-life situation. In a class group with a dominant worldview, the challenge will be to gain further perspectives, and to gain them from the "inside". It is not the Christian's view of the beliefs of Islam that your class seeks, for example, but the Muslim's view, and vice versa. Questions of spiritual belief are not the central ones of this chapter or this course, but they potentially thread through discussions and affect interpretation.

● ●

The natural sciences

We enter the natural sciences first in terms of what they are not: they are not mathematics, in that they *do* study the material world, and they are not a spiritual worldview in that they study *only* the material world.

What, though, *are* the natural sciences? In your broad comparisons of natural sciences, human sciences, and history with mathematics, already you will have picked out several characteristics of this area of knowledge. Let us stand back a moment, though, just as we did with mathematics, and try to capture what we think of most when we turn to the sciences. What comes to our minds as they sweep over this broad field of physics, chemistry, biology, environmental science and their combinations?

Try the class activity. Do not turn the book to read the instructions until your whole group is prepared with paper and pen and you are given a collective go signal. The activity will take only a couple of minutes, though discussion of it will take rather longer.

Activity

Do not turn this book to read the instructions until everyone is ready and you are instructed to do so.

Identify in advance who will be the time-keeper, allowing 20 seconds for each of the activities.

---

1   Draw a hand.

2   Draw a house.

3   Draw one thing that you think represents mathematics.

4   Draw one thing that you think represents the sciences.

5   List as many words as you can that you think describe a scientist.

6   Bonus challenge: draw a scientist.

When everyone is finished, turn ahead to page 156 for questions for discussion.

The sciences and the search for pattern

It looked as though we were leaving mathematics behind as we entered the sciences, and indeed we are—up to a point. However, mathematics is an area of knowledge that always seems to come along to everyone else's party. If you glance back to the beginning of the section on mathematics, you will recall that it actually gets invited—largely because of what it brings along to make the party better. It brings its elaborate web of interconnected statements that turn out to be very useful in finding and talking about patterns that occur in nature.

And that's what the sciences are after: those recurring patterns, the regularities of nature about which they can generalize. The natural sciences provide statements about all bodies falling to the ground…all plants…all chromosomes…all liquids…all ecosystems…They attempt to make generalizations about entire collections of things. The search for pattern has taken inquiring minds toward the neutrino of the subatomic world and to the stars of the universe, toward the study of inanimate crystals and to the study of living cells. Scientists search for the regularities and recurrent relationships that exist within the physical world, both to *describe* and to *explain*.

Of course, describing things in general terms is not the province of scientists alone. As you think back to earlier discussions you are already aware of how we use all our ways of knowing in classification every day (page 83): we associate and group our sense perceptions and our emotions with other similar ones; we use reasoning to make and apply generalizations; we use language to name the categories. You are also aware of some of the common errors in generalizing and classifying, and their potential use for manipulation (see Chapter 4). Sciences start with everyday critical thinking and develop it with care. As Albert Einstein once declared, making a huge generalization in the process, "The whole of science is nothing more than a refinement of everyday thinking."[20]

The periodic table is a diagrammatic representation of a general pattern that chemistry has found in the world; in visual terms, it describes the world. What would you say is the relationship between *description* and *explanation* in the natural sciences? Does the periodic table help you, as a science student, *explain* what is going on in experimental work or in the work treated in your textbook?

Learning science

Any student of science with a handy textbook has reason to feel grateful to language as a way of knowing. There it is—a solid and accessible book, a record of what many knowers have gained from their investigation of the world and passed on, publicly. It is not necessary for the next generation to start back at the beginning.

The science textbook, though, does not often give the moving picture of science in the process of creation: it is not the film but a frame taken from it. Rarely does it give its pages to the past, to old science, as it teaches the current ideas and methods of investigation. You may be quite glad not to have a 10-volume set of books for your IB science course, books encompassing ideas proposed and believed along the way, but now left many, many frames behind. It is far more useful, as you learn science, to have the current frame. This current frame, of course, is already moving into the past as you learn. Unfortunately, though, the book's very solidity can sometimes lead students to believe that science is a body of knowledge that is true beyond doubt, and final.

In IB Diploma Programme experimental science, however, there is a counter-balancing emphasis: as a student you are learning not only the information but the process of science, not only "I know that…" but also "I know how…" With this emphasis comes a more balanced picture of science, not as a static body of knowledge but as knowledge in process, with continuing inquiry into the regularities of the world. Even though you are not a professional researcher creating new knowledge, in IB sciences you are learning something of how scientific investigation is done.

Activity: your own IB Diploma Programme science course

Divide up your class into smaller groups according to which IB science you are studying—physics students together, chemistry students together, and so forth. Subdivide if necessary to have groups of four or five. Have your science textbooks and notes handy to consult. In order to respond to the following questions, draw on your own IB Diploma Programme science course and your group 4 project, if you have already done it. First prepare group answers to the questions below, and then return to the full class group in order to report and compare.

The central question for your group to answer is this: *How do the natural sciences gain knowledge of the world?*

Try to deal, at a minimum, with the following questions:

- The natural world is immense, the current background knowledge is vast, and the concept of cause and effect is immensely complex. Where does a contemporary scientist or research group even begin?
- What are the relative roles of previous knowledge and current conjecture, or hypothesis?
- What makes a hypothesis a good hypothesis?
- Does your textbook tell you of any particularly ingenious experiments in science? Has your teacher described any in class?
- What does the researcher or the research group do with the results?
- How are other scientists, besides an individual researcher or a research group, involved in the creation of scientific knowledge? What does it mean to say, "Science is public knowledge"?

As you build up a collective class description of how science works to gain its conclusions, what are the features you find in common between your science courses? What are the differences between

Obsolete science: the condensed version

Conduct a mini research exercise, for a look at what does *not* appear in your current textbook. Work individually or in pairs, preparing a short report for the rest of your class.

Your report should give a brief explanation of the outdated science and attempt to answer the following three questions:

1 Why did people believe these theories?

2 Why do people no longer believe these theories?

3 Which of these obsolete theories is now irrelevant to science, and which has led to refined versions currently accepted?

- spontaneous generation
- maternal impression
- miasma theory of disease
- recapitulation theory
- caloric theory
- phlogiston theory
- anomalous water
- luminiferous aether
- steady state theory of the universe
- Rutherford model of the atom
- N-rays
- cold fusion
- flat Earth theory
- the Open Polar Sea
- alchemy
- astrology
- phrenology
- numerology

them? Scientific inquiry has common features but can take a variety of forms, with some clever problem solving along the way.

Creating science

In your IB Diploma Programme science course, you are learning about science—its methods of inquiry and its currently accepted information and theories. Imagine now the limits of science—that grey region of knowledge that hovers between what we think we know and what we're sure we don't know. In that fringe, the formulae and facts are not known, and are being sought with the same passion and determination as the proof to Fermat's Last Theorem.

Imagine that you're an *experimental scientist*. Your research team (very few scientists work alone these days) designs an experiment which you hope will be able to measure something you are seeking. Nobody has ever done this experiment before. If the experiment works, you will be amongst the very first humans to observe, in the laboratory, what you're hoping to observe. For example, will it be with this experiment that you'll be able to find experimental evidence that strings actually exist, helping to validate the beautiful mathematics of string theory?

Or maybe you're a *theoretical scientist*, working mostly with mathematics, writing equations with pencil on paper or, more commonly these days, performing complex mathematical calculations which you have arduously programmed into the computer. You have a pile of research papers on your desk, reprinted from venerable publications that only publish peer-reviewed articles. You also have some data on your desk which your experimental collaborator across the world sent you, rough data his team collected via extensive interviews and tests performed with pairs of identical twins. Your research team will analyse and try to explain data that nobody has managed to explain before. For example, what are the factors that cause one identical twin to develop Alzheimer's disease, but not the other?[21] Might your team be able to contribute to answering this question?

Or maybe you're a *field scientist*, going out and observing natural phenomena. Perhaps, like researcher Roman Dial, you're using a new method you've developed to propel yourself directly from tree to tree in the canopy of the Borneo jungle, and applying a new laser technology to help you map the jungle in a way never done before, using a technological extension of sense perception (see page 25). For the first time ever someone is able to map the canopy structures, and you're "investigating how they relate to the animals that live there".[22]

Just as in the distinction made in mathematics, all the scientists in the examples above are "basic" or "pure" scientists, in that they're not attempting to develop specific technologies. In very rough terms, basic science attempts to answer the question "why"—why does this happen like this or that?—whereas applied science attempts to answer the question "how"—for example, how can we do this or that more effectively or in a way that is less expensive?

The sequence of development can go either from pure to applied, or from applied to pure. The laboratory discovery of X-rays by Marie and Pierre Curie led to development of X-ray machines that enable the health of your lungs to be checked; Einstein's theory of special relativity led to knowledge about how to produce electricity using nuclear energy. In the other direction, the invention of the steam engine led to extensive knowledge of thermodynamics.[23]

Scientific method?

No fixed "scientific method" of a common sequence of steps unites all of these kinds of natural scientists, working in very different ways on very different problems in very different aspects of the natural world. Scientific papers are written in a certain order—the same order in which you are asked to write lab reports—but that is not really the way that discoveries are made or explanations are created. Hypotheses may be generated in many different ways, some of them involving creativity too elusive to grasp.

Research exercise

Divide up your group to investigate the following examples of quite different "methods" of creating scientific knowledge.[24]

- serendipity and methodical work: Roentgen's discovery of X-rays
- detailed background and dreamlike vision: Kekulé's discovery of the structure of benzene
- idealized models and mathematical calculations: discovery of band structure in solids
- exploration and observation: Von Humboldt and the biogeography of ecosystems
- hypothetical-deductive method: Edward Jenner and the discovery of smallpox vaccine.

Whatever the specific method of the natural scientist, however, the broad approach outlined within your Diploma Programme science courses still prevails—combining background knowledge, creative conjecture, testing, and finally publishing. However generated, the hypothesis must be tested. If it is repeatedly found flawed, it is laid aside—though, even if it "fails", it may have led to new information coming to light in the process of testing. It may, otherwise, be modified for further testing. If testing seems to confirm the hypothesis, it is not accepted until it has been tested further—ideally rigorously and repeatedly, with the possibility of other scientists also testing it, directly or indirectly, if it is relevant to their own work.

Into which of the three categories above—experimental scientist, theoretical scientist, or field scientist—would you put the scientist you are about to meet? Read the following interview with a nuclear physicist—who is an IB graduate. Consider as you read what he is saying about aspects of science in the process of creation: imagination, testing, models, metaphors, the role of technology, and common features across sciences. The interview is followed with some further questions.

Stereotypes?

Discussion on your class activity (see page 152)

Drawings 1 and 2: Compare within your class your drawings of the hand and the house. Are they very similar to each other? If so, why do you think this is so?

Students from all around the world, with hands that move into many positions and home dwellings of many different kinds, tend to draw hands and houses in almost exactly the same way. (This general tendency may, of course, not be the case in your own particular group.)

Drawings 3 and 4: Compare your drawings. Do some images or symbols recur? What characteristic features of mathematics and the sciences do your drawings reflect?

Wordlist 5 and drawing 6: Share your words and compare your drawings. What impressions of the scientist emerge from the group? Is there any indication of one of the common stereotypes—a middle-aged white male in a lab coat, with glasses, wild hair, and the slightly crazed look of a mad inventor?[25]

Are there any other recurrent features in your verbal and visual impressions?

How would you find out whether these general images of the scientist are sound generalizations or stereotypes?

Science, technology, and the subatomic world

Interview with Dr Patrick Decowski, IB graduate 1991

Patrick Decowski has an MSc in Nuclear Physics from Utrecht University, the Netherlands, and a PhD in Nuclear Physics from the Massachusetts Institute of Technology. He is currently a researcher at the University of California at Berkeley.

Would you please explain what you are researching?

My research focuses on a subatomic particle called the neutrino, one of the particles emitted in radioactive decay. The neutrino does not have electric charge and very little mass. We do not know the exact mass yet, but it is for sure 100,000 times less massive than the electron, the lightest particle of "ordinary matter". The neutrino is copiously emitted by the Sun, but very difficult to stop: more than a hundred billion neutrinos pass unhindered through your thumbnail every second! The neutrino is still one of the least understood subatomic particles and many current and future experiments aim at unravelling its mysteries.

I work on a project called KamLAND. The experiment is located in an old zinc mine in western Japan. The experiment consists of a large, 18-metre diameter container filled with 1,000 tonnes of liquid scintillator (essentially baby-oil with a fluorescence) that is viewed by 1,800 light-sensitive detectors. About 40 times per second particles interact with the liquid scintillator and give off light flashes that are recorded by the light sensitive detectors and stored for later analysis. It turns out that the vast majority of the light flashes we see come from background events. Using elaborate computer algorithms, we can identify particle light flashes coming from neutrino interactions with the liquid scintillator. Our project has been very successful; based on our measurements we have gained a much better understanding of the properties of the neutrino.

When we discuss the natural sciences in TOK class, we talk about it as a study of the natural world—the physical or material world. If what you are studying is a particle far, far, far too small to see, are you still studying the physical world? Should we change the way we talk about science?

The neutrino (or any other subatomic particle for that matter) is indeed far too small to see directly. We always study these particles through their interactions with other particles, "amplifying" their presence and inferring their existence. Also, once you get to subatomic length scales, you are firmly in the quantum world and you can no longer talk about particles being objects of a defined shape or form.

At the same time, although we do not see these particles, they are part of the physical world. We can make accurate predictions of what we expect to see and then perform the experiment to test the hypothesis. Indeed, one of the great triumphs of particle physics was when the quark model was developed (quarks are the building blocks of protons and neutrons that make up the atomic nucleus). The quark model not only describes how protons and neutrons behave, but it also predicted the existence of a certain short-lived particle. When physicists looked for this particle, they found it. The material world is not limited to entities that we can see or touch. As a matter of fact, the vast majority of our material world turns out to consist of vacuum, with only every now and then a tiny particle that determines the properties of the material. Additionally, in recent years we have discovered that we interact and see only 4% of the total mass of the universe! 26% of the mass is so-called "dark matter" and the other 70% is "dark energy". We currently do not understand this stuff and it is subject to intense study.

Models, from what you say, really help you to conceptualize particles and their relationships. Do you have other ways of conceptualizing them, perhaps using metaphors?

It really depends on what questions you want to ask. Different theories work as different metaphors in science. To give an example, when studying properties of a gas, the gas particles (which can be single atoms) can be thought of as being little billiard balls. It is not that they are really little billiard balls, but that metaphor allows us to make certain predictions for the gas that are validated by experiment. But one must not confuse that metaphor with reality. When looking at the gas particles at a smaller scale than the overall gas (such as what I am doing in neutrino physics), the billiard ball metaphor breaks down and we really have to think in quantum-mechanical terms. It turns out that viewing particles as waves is a much better metaphor at those length scales. Even the mathematics that sits underneath all of our theories can be seen as "quantitative metaphors". Just because there is currently a correspondence between these equations and the physical world, does not mean they are one and the same.

What is the role of computer modelling in your research? Can you do "experiments" within a computer?

Computer modelling is extremely important in most branches of science nowadays. In subatomic physics it is particularly important. Most experiments cannot be interpreted without a significant amount of modelling, to understand both the behaviour of the detector and the physics being studied.

Doing experiments in computers has also become very popular, because specific hypotheses can be tested relatively quickly for their consequences. A hypothesis with a set of starting conditions can be stepped through in time inside the computer and then tested for violation of specific physical laws (such as energy conservation) and discarded if it does violate some important law or does not match observation. The great advantage is that computer simulations allow us to study theories that are otherwise hard to test. The modelling helps in fleshing out the theory, but the computer predictions have to be compared with real, physical world experiments.

Computer modelling has become a very important branch in physics. These types of modelling are not done only in nuclear physics and meteorology, but also in astrophysics, biophysics, climate studies, and so on. Computer modelling really has revolutionized the way we do research and the current generation of scientists spend considerable time in front of computer screens.

Einstein has been quoted as saying that imagination is more important than knowledge. In your kind of scientific research, what is the role of imagination?

I think that what Einstein meant was that you have to have an open mind and think out-of-the-box. It is extremely important to have imagination in physics. When seeing some unexpected effect, you have to use your imagination to try and understand what you are seeing. Is it a detector effect? Is it due to the environment? Could it be new physics? This is usually where we spend most time, in interpreting the data. You try to vary some accessible parameter

in the experiment and ask, "Is the effect changing?" The imagination is necessary for coming up with hypotheses, but this is always followed by testing.

Why do you find your research so interesting?

I have always had a fascination with how things work. Over time I realized that what is even more amazing is that nature itself works so well and that I wanted to understand it better. Certain "themes" come back in areas that superficially do not have anything to do with each other. Why is it that ocean waves and light rays can behave in similar ways? Why do the same equations describe a mechanical and an electrical oscillator? There are similar "themes" and symmetries at the very smallest particle level. This led me to become interested in subatomic particles and the neutrino is one of the least understood and most fascinating particles.

The fundamental nuclear physics that I do is in some sense similar to what astronomers do when they look at stars. They look upwards at the large scale, whereas I look downwards at the very small scale. My research does not have any direct application—just like knowing how stars shine does not have any obvious application. We are studying it purely for the knowledge and trying to understand what is behind it. This is in many respects similar to the reasons why people enjoy art. Science is captivating.

Questions for discussion

1 Patrick speaks of "our project" and "our measurements". In a field such as his, would you expect scientists to be working alone or in research groups? Why?

2 What is the role of technology in his group's experiments? Does your own science course depend extensively on technology?

3 What does he say are the roles of imagination, models and metaphors, and testing? Do his comments also apply to the science you are studying for the IB?

4 He describes both the correspondence test for truth and the coherence test for truth (see pages 100–101) in action, though without giving them these names. What is the role of each in his experiment? In your most recent experiment for your science course, what truth test were you using?

5 From his description, what resemblances do you find between scientific research and detective work?

The natural sciences: the whole picture

The knowledge creators

"Why is it that ocean waves and light rays can behave in similar ways? Why do the same equations describe a mechanical and an electrical oscillator? There are similar 'themes' and symmetries at the very smallest particle level."

Patrick Decowski echoes in this interview on research in physics a fascination with patterns so often also expressed by mathematicians. You may recall the words of Andrew Spray (scc page 144), speaking of why he so loves mathematics: "it is the patterns, the searching for them and the joy of discovering them, that captivate me most." In the natural sciences, the search for pattern takes a form different from that in mathematics, and gives a different kind of justification for the knowledge claims it brings back from its search. Yet, for many minds, it exerts a similar magnetic pull.

The kinds of pull that draw scientists into this area of knowledge, however, are as various as the individuals. As one Nobel Prize winning scientist said, surveying his colleagues, "Among scientists are collectors, classifiers, and compulsive tidiers-up; many are detectives by temperament and many are explorers; some are artists and others artisans. There are poet-scientists and philosopher-scientists and even a few mystics. What sort of mind or temperament can all these people be supposed to have in common?"[26]

The picture of "the scientist" becomes even more fuzzy in contemporary science because our knowledge creators work in teams—teams of physicists, chemists, biologists, environmental scientists, and increasingly, interdisciplinary teams of them—experimenting in laboratories, observing in the field, or working in offices connected to very powerful computers.

Knowledge Creation Diagram

within context of the natural world

| knowledge creator(s) | work(s) of knowledge *(math proof, research paper, novel)* | knowledge community *(peers, critics general public)* |

within social context

The scientific work

The knowledge creation diagram, by now familiar to you, moves us on from the scientists to their work, of which we are already gaining an idea through the examples we have seen.

Science, as we have observed repeatedly, is a public area of knowledge, with work contributed to a kind of living public archive through the channels accepted within science—the published paper, the conference paper, and to an increasing extent an online computer archive of what work is in progress.

The new assertions published by natural scientists are usually not very dramatic—rarely the revolutionary discoveries that make the news or dramatic fiction. For example, one of the authors of this book, Lena Rotenberg, spent three years of her life as a research physicist studying a polymer that had been modified by a chemist. She measured its properties as a function of its temperature, and then had to explain why the graph she obtained did not comply with the expectations of a model presumed to work for similar samples. She had to come up with an alternative explanation in order to publish the paper—something like "this material appears to be X, but it's behaving like Y, which might be due to factors (a), (b) and (c)". When she finally had the "aha!" moment which enabled her to explain the data, it was a very exciting feeling: nobody had ever gone to the fringe with that particular material before. In the context of the edifice of science hers was a very, very minor result— she hammered a small nail in a small room in a forgotten hallway on the side of a very huge house (the house is a metaphor for the theoretical construct) of solid state physics. But that's how the majority of the basic natural sciences are developed—with small, particular results cumulatively added to each other in an international, collaborative effort. Most scientific theories are supported by hundreds of thousands, if not millions, of such small observational nails, hammered into place by scientists over many centuries.

More dramatic works achieve the kind of generalizations that the natural sciences seek, the identification of regularities. Every so often a scientist manages to identify a pattern in the specific, minor results published by large numbers of scientists—manages to see a causal connection—and can show that "if P, then Q". An example is Boyle's law, mathematically expressed as "PV = constant at a fixed temperature", which asserts that "If a rarefied gas is kept at constant temperature, then there is an inverse relationship between its pressure and its volume." A few of the research papers produced by scientists do propose such generalizations, called scientific laws.

Major scientific work: scientific theories

Even more seldom than laws, natural scientists produce scientific theories, the overarching constructs that encompass and explain many laws. It is sad that the popular fictional detective Sherlock Holmes used the word "theory" so lightly to refer to any conjecture that came to his mind. When people use the phrase "it is *just* a theory" in regard to a scientific theory, they are discounting a tremendous amount of evidence, as we mentioned above. It is also confusing that the result of a mathematically-based work with no experimental evidence (such as string theory now, and quark theory until quarks were finally detected a few years ago) uses the same name.

The best scientific theories have several characteristics.[27] They:
- encompass scientific laws, which are deducible through them
- make existential or factual claims, such as "electrons exist and have a charge of minus one", or "ideal gases consist of a very large number of atoms with negligible size, in random motion, which collide elastically with one another"
- refer to unobservable entities or properties that stand behind the measurements we make: for example atoms, natural selection, the curvature of space, strings
- are interrelated in such a way that they explain not only a particular law or phenomenon, but whole ranges of each—such that apparently diverse laws or phenomena can be explained within a common framework

" Music is the favourite art of the scientist. And so it should be. It allows us to see new worlds with our eyes closed. "

John Polanyi, Nobel Prize in Chemistry, 1986.[28]

● provide an enormous predictive power (including phenomena which were previously unknown).

Scientific explanation: your own natural science course

Class activity

Form groups within your class, as you did earlier, according to the particular IB Diploma Programme science course you are studying—chemistry students together, and so forth. If most in your group study the same science, break up into subgroups of four or five. It would be very useful to have your science textbook and class notes to consult.

First, answer the following questions within your group. Then, as a class, exchange what you have found and compare your understanding of how science seeks to explain.

1 From your own science course, find examples of each of the following:

   a *a scientific hypothesis*: a conjecture, based on evidence, interpretation, and imagination of a causal relationship.

   b *a scientific theory*: an explanation based on evidence of causal relationships found in the world, which accounts for phenomena already observed and provides a framework, shared by the scientific community, for further investigation. Can you identify theories used within the science you are currently studying? Do they possess the characteristics of the best theories, outlined above?

   c *a scientific model*: an image or three-dimensional object that represents things or processes that we believe to exist in the world and that selects some relevant features to clarify relationships.

   d *a scientific law*: an expression of a causal relationship established on the basis of evidence and tested sufficiently extensively that it is considered reliable and spoken of as true.

2 Do these four elements of scientific knowledge describe the world or explain it? What is the relationship between them?

Description and explanation may be seen as different kinds of patterns that scientists search for in nature. The description is the map: "this is what it looks like". The explanation, though, involves something we do not perceive through our senses but construct with our minds: cause. We do not *see* cause. We *infer* it from repeated correlation of events, tested until we are confident of the nature of their connection. In practice in science, the two kinds of pattern are completely interconnected.

Of all the patterns that science has discovered in recent decades, perhaps the ones that have been absorbed most strikingly into the awareness of the general public are fractals—not only because they represent a breakthrough in science but because they please our eyes.

Fractal patterns: mathematics, science, technology...and beauty

*Interview with Dr John Dewey Jones, P.Eng.,
School of Engineering Science, Simon Fraser
University, Vancouver*

As an engineer, did you first become attracted to fractals through the mathematics or through the technology?
I was inspired to start creating fractals by Dewdney's "Computer Recreations" article in the August 1985 *Scientific American*. Creating fractals was computationally intensive by the standards of that time, but as an automotive engineer working for General Motors, I had access to one of the fastest supercomputers in North America (roughly as powerful as a modern digital watch). It was very exciting to watch the complex organic patterns of the Mandelbrot set emerge on the screen, the image building up line by line; and to add to the excitement was the risk that someone from GM management would come by and notice that I wasn't designing cars.

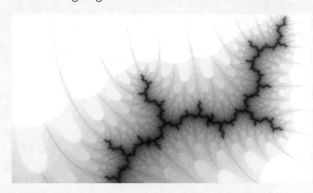

Frosted branch

They are, as you say, "complex organic patterns". Are they really simply the results of equations fed into a computer?
Despite their dissimilar appearance, both "frosted branch" and "diatom" show the results of repeatedly applying the transformation

$$z_n = z_{n-1}^2 + z_0$$

to a range of complex numbers z_0. In each case, starting with a small complex number z_0, we square the number, add the original number to the result, and repeat until the absolute magnitude of the result exceeds 2. The differences between the two pictures all stem from a small difference in the complex numbers we started with.

These pictures, like all computer pictures, are made up of a large number of pixels—the phosphor dots making up the computer screen. Every dot in the picture corresponds to a single complex number—its position on the horizontal axis corresponds to the real part of the number, while its position on the vertical axis corresponds to the imaginary part. We assign each pixel a shade of grey depending on how long its magnitude takes to grow greater than 2.

What kinds of patterns do you see yourself within your mathematically generated images?
The image "diatom" looks symmetric, but if we look more closely, we see that while the lower half is indeed a mirror image of the upper half, the left and right halves of the image are not perfect opposites—the lines separating the left and right halves both trail off to the right, for example. We also notice that these lines are studded with small blobs. Each blob, if we magnified it, would turn out to be a complete figure as complex as "diatom" itself—and each of these diatoms would in turn contain blobs, which, if magnified...

Despite the almost graph-like symmetry of this figure, it does rather suggest a section through a cauliflower floret. This is a recurrent characteristic of fractal images, and we see it again in "frosted branch". Just as frost, formed by the simple physical process of freezing, can produce intricate, plant-like forms, we see here that the even simpler mathematical process of iteration can mimic both frost and organic plant life.

This, perhaps, is why fractal images fascinate and intrigue us—by showing the immense complexity and beauty that can result from a few simple rules, they hint that the world's complexity and beauty may also be the product of laws that we can discover and comprehend.

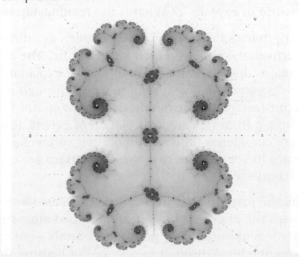

Diatom

Fractal images and chaos theory: some characteristics of science

The receding, self-duplicating shapes of the fractal image give a pattern that emerges from chaos theory—a theory with a particularly catchy name. Paradoxically, the theory of chaos is in many ways a theory of order: it reveals a new kind of pattern within the turbulence of nature, with limits on the degree to which it can be predicted. In its development, chaos theory offers a good example of some of the characteristics of science at work.

For one thing, natural scientists do not make their observations randomly, but purposefully seek pattern where the predominant theory suggests that it would be most fruitful to do so. In doing so, they have the advantage of being able to research and communicate within a common conceptual framework of theories, models, laws, and vocabulary. However, they also have the disadvantage of being directed away from patterns not illuminated within that theoretical framework. "The phenomenon of chaos could have been discovered long, long ago," commented one scientist involved in its recognition. "It wasn't, in part because this huge body of work on the dynamics of regular motion didn't lead in that direction."[29]

For another thing, there may often be a great difference between the way that *science* accepts change and the way that *scientists* do. After all, "science" is an abstraction, representing a vast base of provisionally-accepted knowledge and procedures. When we say that "science changes its mind" we are using an image, personifying a system of knowledge that, actually, has no mind to change. Scientists, however, do have minds to change—and like other people often have difficulty doing so, especially after having worked for a long time with one familiar way of perceiving things. In the early days of chaos theory, its proponents faced considerable resistance, verging at moments even on hostility.[30] Understanding and acceptance of the new theory was slowed, too, by its having no home in any particular discipline but instead crossing many disciplines, being applicable to, for example, weather patterns, fluid dynamics, populations in biology, and electrical activity of the heart.

Chaos theory, moreover, illustrates the intimate relationship between developing science and developing technology. It was the amazing computational power of the computer that enabled scientists to see the considerable long-term consequences of tiny changes in initial values of the variables. This sensitive dependence on the starting data has been dubbed "the butterfly effect", another very catchy name which captures the sense of tiny differences that can add up to affect the course of events in the future. Unless we have perfectly precise knowledge of every influence in the present, no matter how minute, our predictions become increasingly off the mark as we cast them farther into the future. And such omniscience is quite beyond us. Nevertheless, the computer technology that exposed the limits of prediction simultaneously revealed patterns within the unpredictable. "The system is deterministic," observed one of the early chaos scientists, "but you can't say what it's going to do next."[31]

The butterfly effect

The butterfly effect is the particularly charming name given to the idea that tiny, unmeasurable events can accumulate to cause major ones. Even the breathing of a butterfly in the Caribbean contributes to conditions that can result in a hurricane in another part of the world.

In addition, chaos theory demonstrates graphically the idea of pattern that recurs through many areas of knowledge—through mathematics in the patterns created rationally by the mind, in the sciences in the patterns found in the world of sense perception (often using mathematics and technology), and through the arts in the patterns created from all the raw material of experience. In all of these areas, their practitioners are apt to have moments of pure admiration: "It's beautiful!"

Finally, chaos theory, like many other theories in science, also has its effect on the public, in the way that it influences how we understand the world and speak about it. It is tempting to apply the idea of the butterfly effect, as novels and films have, to an idea that probably came up in your class discussion of why you are *here*, *now*: if it weren't for that one small event in your life, it might have been otherwise.

Natural scientists, their work, and the world: truth?

A scientific work may be beautiful, and may be persuasive. But is it true? In the knowledge creation diagram, the natural world is the context within which we all live, but for natural scientists it is also their subject of study. They identify patterns not for their beauty— though they may appreciate it—but for their truth.

Consider the diagram now with this question in mind: How do natural scientists test for truth? With your own personal experience of IB science, the class activities of this chapter, and the supporting text and interviews, you should by now be seeing this diagram as a schematization of a living process. As scientists test for truth, are they checking exclusively the connection between the work itself and the natural world, or between the work and the knowledge already shared with the knowledge community? To what extent is the knowledge shared between the creators and their peers both a help and a hindrance, in a way characteristic of the interplay of mind and eye in sense perception?

Knowledge Creation Diagram

within context of the natural world

knowledge creator(s)

work(s) of knowledge
(math proof, research paper, novel)

knowledge community
(peers, critics general public)

within social context

As you consider the way the natural sciences work and the kind of knowledge they give, what other relationships do you begin to draw between the components of this diagram?

How do scientists evaluate their work, or test it for truth? Read the following quotation from Peter Medawar, who won the Nobel Prize for Medicine in 1960, and who has written extensively to provide the general public with an understanding of the natural sciences:

Scientific theories (I have said) begin as imaginative constructions. They begin, if you like, as stories, and the purpose of the critical or rectifying episode in scientific reasoning is precisely to find out whether these stories are stories about real life. Literal or empiric truthfulness is not therefore the starting-point of scientific enquiry, but rather the direction in which scientific reasoning moves. If this is a fair statement, it follows that scientific and poetic or imaginative accounts of the world are not distinguishable in their origins. They start in parallel, but diverge from one another at some later stage. We all tell stories, but the stories differ in the purposes we expect them to fulfil and the kinds of evaluations to which they are exposed.[32]

What "kinds of evaluations" do the stories of science face, and how do they involve the components of the knowledge creation diagram?

Correspondence test for truth

The correspondence test for truth, you will recall (see page 101), demands that the statements we make correspond to what we observe in the world. To test, scientists examine the world and find evidence either directly through sense perceptions or via technological extensions of the senses.

They must offer evidence in the form of replicable results. It is essential that every time something is measured, the same result be obtained. For example, distilled water should boil at 100 °C at sea level no matter where in the world we are, and no matter when we make the measurement. Every time a scientist observes a phenomenon the results should be either the same or justifiably different (for example, we can predict the boiling point of water at different altitudes[33]). Mitosis occurs with the same steps in cells all over the world. If one scientist performs an experiment in Germany, a colleague in Tanzania should be able to replicate the results.

How much evidence is enough evidence for declaring a statement of the natural sciences true? As you will recognize from descriptions of how the sciences work, their statements are never assuredly true forever, in the manner of mathematics. Indeed, by the very nature of scientific generalization and inductive reasoning (see page 76), it is possible to refute statements—*falsify* them—but not to prove them true. Scientists work with probabilities and accept as true (for now) the conclusions best supported by the evidence available at the time. They call this *provisional* truth.

Coherence test for truth

The coherence truth test for truth (see page 100) demands that the statements we make be consistent with each other. To test, scientists look not at the world but at the knowledge claims themselves and, as mathematics does, examine them for consistency, freedom from contradiction.

Not only should the observations and measurements be consistent with each other, but, on a deeper level, the explanations that they give about phenomena should also be consistent with each other.

Yet how much consistency with each other do the sciences demand for explanations to be accepted? Sometimes the sciences replace older theories within which contradictions have appeared with new ones which integrate all the evidence harmoniously. However, at other times they accept more than one version, each internally consistent but not consistent with the other, as each has its area of applicability.

Consider the following two sets of theories, evolving through time.

Biology	Physics
1 spontaneous generation	1 Newtonian mechanics
2 Lamarckian evolution	2 Einstein's theory of special relativity
3 Darwin's theory of evolution	3 quantum mechanics

In the first set, spontaneous generation was shown not to happen—new theories replaced the old. In the second set, we continue to use Newtonian mechanics most of the time, to explain what happens in human size ranges and at speeds at which we usually move.

Which of the two models of the natural sciences shown is applicable?

The hope expressed by some natural scientists is that, with progress over time, the sciences will eventually reach a grand unified theory, as all scientific theories become merged into an overarching explanation that brings them all into harmony.

The natural sciences

 or

New replaces old through falsifying,   New coexists with old.

Pragmatic test for truth

The pragmatic test for truth (see page 101) demands that the statements work in practical terms.

The pragmatic truth test is also central to the natural sciences. We accept certain assumptions without empirical proof, like axioms, because they happen to work. For example, we *assume* that nature is regular and understandable.

We *assume* that Ockham's razor, also known as the law of parsimony, holds true: when we have two equivalent theories, we choose the one that is conceptually simplest, with the "most economical conceptual formulation". Phlogiston, for example, was not necessary to describe heat, and therefore the concept was discarded.

We *assume* that the laws of physics we develop are applicable all over the physical universe.

We *assume*, to an extent, that theories that are mathematically beautiful and symmetric are more likely to be true, and search very hard for experimental evidence to confirm them. We did that with Einstein's theory of general relativity and with Gell-Mann and Nishijima's theory of quarks, and we are now trying to find empirical evidence for string theory.

For many years we *assumed* that the scientific observer could stand outside the experiment and not affect it, but Heisenberg's uncertainty principle demolished that illusion. When we study the realm of the atomic and subatomic, we affect our data by the very act of trying to measure it.

The axioms of science, despite their occasional failure, serve us well. Look around you and realize how many results of science surround you, and how much you trust them without even thinking. You hop on an

airplane, get in a car, drink water purified by the city, and take medicines your doctor prescribes, trusting that all the science behind them will work.

Is the explanation that works necessarily true in an absolute sense? No. But at least for now…it works.

The natural sciences and their critics

As has been evident in these pages, criticism is an essential part of the process of the sciences, as works of the natural sciences are replicated and reviewed by peers. As in mathematics, it may be only the specialists within the particular field who understand and examine effectively the new work, but in principle the knowledge is open publicly to all.

As in mathematics, the sciences also have critics—scientists or philosophers—who examine the way the entire area works and the problems that it encounters in making knowledge claims. Like mathematicians, natural scientists have had their moments of distress on realizing the imperfections in the claims their area might make to truth. *Yet it is only if you expect to be perfect that you consider imperfection a failure*. The contribution of many critics of science has been to give science more realistic expectations than it had of itself at the beginning of the 20th century.

Criticisms have been various. Some have stressed the fallibility of sense perception, even when extended by technology, and the fallibility, too, of indirect technological observation. Others have stressed the limits of inductive reasoning, with the goal of making accurate generalizations about *all* phenomena limited by having access in study only to *some*; counter-evidence will overturn or "falsify" an inductive generalization. Still others have cited human fallibility in experimental methods, and the fact that scientists replicating flawed work may also, influenced by their expectations, replicate the flaws. More broadly, critics have pointed out the bias that comes with theory and observation; as in everyday life observation, scientists look where they expect to find and, when they see, interpret with the bias of previous knowledge. Finally, critics have emphasized the implications of some significant findings in science: the uncertainty principle, which tells us that the very act of observation may in some circumstances affect the thing that we are observing, and that we cannot expect to remove our own presence from an experiment; and the butterfly effect of chaos theory which emphasizes that the inevitable limitations of our knowledge of all things in the present affect the accuracy of our predictions into the future. All of these criticisms have been illuminating. And science, with a better understanding of itself, gets back to work.

Less thoughtful criticisms of science have come from other sources, such as pseudo-science. Lacking sufficient evidence to have their claims accepted as science, pseudo-scientists have often accused the "scientific establishment" of being close-minded or even prejudiced against them. Admittedly, the inertia of accepted theory and the difficulty scientists may have in reconceptualizing their explanations often do create resistance to new ideas. However, legitimate claims find their way through the resistance—by means of tested and replicable statements, based on evidence. These pseudo-science cannot provide.

How can we recognize pseudo-science? One commentator, a professor of physics, proposes seven "warning signs" of pseudo-science—while recognizing that "even a claim with several of the signs could be legitimate".[34] His warning signs can be summarized as follows:

1   The discoverer bypasses peer review to go directly to the media.
2   The discoverer claims that the scientific establishment, possibly as part of a larger conspiracy, is trying to suppress his work.
3   The evidence is extremely hard to detect.
4   The evidence takes the form of individual observations or stories, not able to be generalized.
5   The discoverer claims that the knowledge is ancient and hence more credible.
6   The discoverer has worked alone.
7   The discoverer needs to propose modification to the laws of nature in order that his findings be credible.

In trying to distinguish pseudo-scientific claims from the claims of the sciences, we affirm once again a basic principle of this book: that critical thinking requires a mind open to alternatives yet concerned to sift through them for the version that is the best justified. As critical thinkers, we expect to identify multiple perspectives, recognize their contribution to an understanding of the whole, and not reject them summarily. A contemporary emphasis on knowledge as culturally constructed and variable helps us see the significance of difference perspectives. However, the fact that there are many perspectives on something does not imply that all of them have equal claim to be accepted. Think back to the maps of the world that you drew at the beginning of this book. All of them were equally good as records of what you carry in your mind. But they were not all equally good as records of the world.

The natural sciences in their social context

We end these pages on the natural sciences with some reflections and questions for you, as a member of the public affected by the process and products of this area of knowledge.

- In what ways does the general public—like you and your family—benefit, directly and indirectly, from the products of scientific research?
- Do you consider there to be effects that are not beneficial? If so, where does the responsibility, if any, lie for reducing ill effects?

- In what ways are you personally affected by "scientific thinking"? In what ways do you think your society absorbs or resists the knowledge given by science?

In the natural sciences, the creators of knowledge and the critics of that knowledge are peers, sharing findings publicly within their own knowledge community—a community not geographically defined but crossing borders as readily as the exchange of knowledge.

This community has a set of values. What would you, as a student of science, identify as the values that are prized by the sciences in their way of working as a public area of knowledge? What code of conduct would you expect natural scientists to follow in their treatment of their work and each other? Why is fraud in the sciences considered to be such a serious breach of professional conduct?

The knowledge community of the sciences, united conceptually but fragmented geographically, consists of people who work and live in towns and cities, within countries and regions which affect their work and are affected by their work. Whether the sciences are supported and funded and by what organizations, whether they are controlled and by what organizations—these issues have an immense impact on science and scientists. Their work and their knowledge do not exist in isolation from their human context.

Read now the following interview on the knowledge community of the sciences, set within a social community. Dr Maarten Jongsma is a distinguished researcher—and a former IB student.

Respond to the questions that follow this interview. They may give you some thoughts—and possibly a presentation topic—to take away with you.

Science in its social context

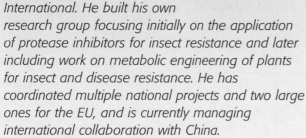

Interview with Dr Maarten Jongsma, IB graduate 1980

Maarten Jongsma has an MSc and PhD (1995) from Wageningen University in the Netherlands. He is currently working at Plant Research International. He built his own research group focusing initially on the application of protease inhibitors for insect resistance and later including work on metabolic engineering of plants for insect and disease resistance. He has coordinated multiple national projects and two large ones for the EU, and is currently managing international collaboration with China.

One of the stereotypes of science is that breakthroughs are made by the lone genius, the solo scientist following his own brilliant idea. How accurate is this picture of how results are achieved in science?

In my field of work (plant genomics and genetic engineering) the papers that have major impact and end up in *Science* and *Nature* are often the result of hard work and collaborations across different disciplines. A good example is the sequencing of the first plant genome (*Arabidopsis*). Another one is a recent paper in *Science* in which we describe how plants become attractive to predators of insects based on specific emitted volatiles. These results are considered important hallmarks, but to some extent they are expected, and part of the original hypothesis on which the grant money was obtained. To obtain the result your main task is to be a good manager to execute it and to arrange all the right collaborations if you have only part of the expertise.

Yet at the same time I can also give examples of the stereotype. Those results are never planned or expected and the result of inspiration based on unexpected results and requiring lateral thinking. Usually, however, the inspiration is immediately shared and tested with colleagues and incorporated into the usual line of research, requiring again the work of many to achieve the final top-rated paper.

Does it make sense to talk about the social context of scientific research being a "scientific community" beyond the immediate research group?

Certainly scientific research extends well beyond the immediate research group. Research would not happen without the consent of many due to the large amounts of money which it consumes. Many scientists in higher positions are constantly working on obtaining grant money and the proposals are nearly always peer reviewed. Furthermore, one of the most important and honourable platforms for the

169

research produced is the scientific conference. Excellent papers are invited for oral presentations leading to the further dissemination of the results. Also there is a lot of moving around of scientists. Often your best graduates will go to your competitor.

In research over which there is public controversy, such as your own work in genetic modifications, do you see the scientist as having any special responsibility to the broader society beyond the scientific community?

Certainly I believe that one has a social responsibility. However, I feel that scientists are often considered highly suspect due to the active propaganda issued by NGOs. My interest in participating in the debate is often to demonstrate the good that the technology can bring. An exclusive focus on the potentially bad sides with the aim of eliminating the technology altogether is a dead-end road, which, in my opinion, will harm society. I cannot avoid taking a stand in that debate.

What are some of the good sides?

Developing countries like India and China, representing nearly half the world population, have embraced plant biotechnology as one of the major ways to improve the yield and quality of their food crops such as rice, corn, pulses, potato, and vegetables. There is an urgent need for this in the light of their growing populations depending on the productivity of less and less suitable land. The greatest good the technology could bring is a world free of hunger, but it is no cure against the political and natural disasters which are often the true cause of the problem.

What do you see as the responsibility of the lay public within that debate?

In my view the most important responsibility of the lay public is to maintain their common sense at all times. I would define common sense as the outcome of balancing the good and the bad and choosing what is advantageous to society as a whole. Some NGOs still promote a complete ban on genetic engineering and put the scientist in the role of Dr Frankenstein. I think it is the role of the lay public to refuse such simple-minded representations, to demand a balanced debate, to deny the insult to their intelligence!

Questions for discussion

1   In the interview above, Maarten Jongsma is asked to give both factual description and opinion. Re-read the interview and consider the balance of fact and opinion at different points.

2   What are the values of the scientific community that are stated or implied in his description of how science works? On the basis of this interview and your other sources of understanding, what would you say are ideals that guide natural scientists in their work?

3   Maarten Jongsma says that one of the responsibilities of the lay public is "to demand a balanced debate" on controversial issues within science. To what extent do you consider knowledge of an issue from different points of view to be essential to a sound judgment? To what extent does a judgment involve, in the end, not only facts but values?

Suggested presentation topic

Taking genetic engineering or another controversial area of scientific research as your contemporary issue, consider the responsibilities of the researcher, scientific peers, the lay public, and political decision-makers in the face of new discoveries or technologies that pose ethical questions.

If you are interested in pursuing this topic, you are advised to present it only after the discussions of ethical criteria for judgment later in this chapter. You may wish to do a presentation specifically on the knowledge issues raised by genetic modification in the context of the larger topic of world hunger in Chapter 6.

The human sciences

It takes a while for a younger sibling to be taken seriously by the older members of the family. Ancient and seemingly eternal, mathematics has always thought well of itself. Joined merely centuries ago by natural science, it granted the newcomer its respect—but only very gradually. When human science came along much later, the older siblings were not at first very welcoming, even when the toddler tried as much as possible to be like them. Natural science, much closer in age and resemblance, was particularly condescending, pointing out all the clever things it could do itself but that human science just could not do. Then as human science grew up, it learned to talk back. Such family bickering!

"You can't control your variables," said natural science.

"Well, you can't ask your data any questions," said human science.

"And you can't replicate and generalize the way I can," said natural science.

"But who says I have to?" said human science. "Do you expect all human beings always to act the same?"

Fortunately, another ancient sibling was watching in the background. It was history, who gave the knowledge family a little bit of perspective.

The "family resemblance" claimed in this small story is close, in many regards, between the natural sciences and the human sciences. Human scientists share the broad goals of natural scientists—to describe and explain. However, there is one difference that has a profound effect on knowledge: human scientists study, as the name implies, human beings.

At moments, human scientists might well envy natural scientists, who do not have to take into account the sense of humour of their microbes, or ask what their plankton is thinking and why, or try to infer the cultural meaning of the behaviour of gases.

Might human scientists need to use the ways of knowing in a manner different from natural scientists, and even draw on some additional personal qualities not essential for physicists, chemists, or biologists? After all, they have data that stare straight back at them with awareness, react to being observed, and demonstrate the same capacity as their own to think and guess, and to reveal or conceal.

What do the human sciences study?

But what do human scientists actually study? In the natural sciences, researchers do not wander vacantly about, declaring, "I shall investigate the natural world!" They work within a field of science and with a specific research focus. So, too, do human scientists.

For your group 3 subject, are you taking a human science course? Are you taking psychology, social and cultural anthropology, economics? (Note that the IB classification scheme of subjects into groups is not identical to the TOK classification scheme of knowledge into areas.) Adapt the following activities to fit your particular class.

Class activity part 1: for groups with students studying human sciences

Divide into small groups according to your human science subject. If most in your group study the same human science, break up into subgroups of four or five. It would be very useful to have your course textbook and class notes handy to consult in order to prepare group responses on the following questions.

- What does your human science study? Can you sum up its subject matter in a sentence or two?
- What are its methods of gaining knowledge? Pick out examples you have studied of researchers at work and the approaches they have used to gain the knowledge they report.
- What methods does your human science seem to share with the natural sciences? What differences appear to exist in the methods they share? What additional methods are open to the human sciences?

Return to your full group to exchange descriptions of your human science subjects and to compare them for a broader understanding of similarities and differences within this area of knowledge.

Students in this photo were doing a presentation on knowledge issues of ethnocentrism—assumptions and cultural bias in interpretation.
Two anthropologists, in the background, interpreted the scene as a woman subservient to a man. However, in the culture role-played, only women are permitted to rest directly on the sacred mother earth.

Class activity part 2: for all groups

Regardless of whether or not you are taking a human science subject, you still have some idea of what the area studies and have some group knowledge to exchange.

First, working on your own, write the following, widely spaced, on a page: *psychology. anthropology. sociology. economics. political science.* Now use your pen to join them up in ways that show any interconnections. After you have had a chance to think about them, exchange ideas within your class.

- What does each one study? Do some of them overlap in what they study? Are any of them subcategories of others?
- What associations come to your mind for each of the human sciences? Are there stereotypes that you can identify?
- Do you consider there to be any significant omissions to the subjects in this list? If you are studying human geography or business, for example, where would you place your subject? Is it a human science?
- In what ways can *all* the sciences, both natural and human, tell us something about human beings? What can they tell us, for example, about our ways of knowing: sense perception, emotion, language, and reasoning? Is it biology or psychology that can tell us more about our emotions?

In this activity, the emphasis has been on what the subjects study, rather than how they study it—although it's likely that different methods of investigation came up in discussion. Consider briefly the following claim. To what extent do you accept it?

"Effective investigation depends on the relationship between the methods and the subject of the research. So interdependent are they for the successful creation of knowledge that they cannot be separated: tell me your methods, and I will tell you your subject matter; tell me your subject matter, and I will tell you your methods."

At the end of this chapter, after looking more closely at the subject matter and methods of the human sciences, return to this statement to assess it once again.

Identification of pattern: generalizations

Patterns in nature: that's what natural scientists, as we saw, are trying to discover. Natural scientists have identified some patterns so regular that they have generated laws describing how nature acts everywhere and at all times.

Patterns in human society and individual human actions: that's what human scientists are trying to discover, to the extent that their human subject matter will allow. The patterns that human scientists find are less regular than those found by their colleagues in the physical world, and give rise to no laws about how all human beings act everywhere and at all times. All beakers of hydrochloric acid can be expected to act in the same way under the same circumstances. Not so all human beings or human societies. Not only are exactly the same circumstances difficult to replicate, or in some fields impossible, but people cannot be depended upon to act in the same way even within closely similar circumstances.

It is not surprising that the human sciences have sometimes been described as existing in a state of tension between generalizing and particularizing perspectives. Across subjects that examine many aspects of human beings, human scientists hold different views on the level of generalization they can aspire to make. Some human scientists do seek highly regular patterns, for example studying perceptual characteristics common to all human brains or universal features that might structure all human societies, even though it is difficult to pin them down. Others expect to make generalizations not about all human beings as consumers, for example, but about most in a large group, or about the range of human abilities and responses. Still others hold that individuals or societies can be understood only in terms of their particular local conditions. Still others, and whole fields, such as cultural anthropology, argue that a comparative method provides the greatest understanding of human beings: particular societies are best understood within the context of the human range of possibilities.

Generalizations, for both description and explanation, demand the evidence of particular observations, and these the human sciences can provide—and provide increasingly as their records stretch back further in time. Like the natural sciences, the human sciences look back historically on theories that are now obsolete. Yet the very nature of the evidence in the human sciences increases the possibility of different theories co-existing, each with its area of applicability, each shedding light on different connections within a causal web. Different broad theories, or different perspectives, give rise to a fuller understanding of societies, or market places, or the workings of human minds.

Studying human beings: ways of knowing

In their studies, human scientists take a range of approaches, using all the ways of knowing. Some look primarily (or exclusively) at human beings "from the outside"—using sense perception in the form of careful observation and, in some fields, testing. It is in the "outside" approaches that human scientists resemble natural

Equal opportunity

"When I say GO, swim the river!"

What might be the purpose of this test? When might such a test be used?

What is wrong with this test?

What is right with this test?

A blink—or a wink?

Is this a blink or a wink? How do you know?

What is the difference between the cause of a blink and the cause of (or reason for) a wink?

Which area of knowledge is most relevant for explaining the cause of the blink? of the wink?

For which—the blink or the wink—is it relevant to talk about the action's "meaning"?

contributed by Anita Holt

scientists—though always with the added complexities of the subject matter. Moreover, they then face the challenge of inferring from the outside the *meaning* of the activities observed. Others try to study human beings "from the inside"—adding language as a way of knowing in methods such as interviews and questionnaires. In some fields, emotional empathy is also relevant. In both planning their investigations and in drawing conclusions from their evidence—and certainly in making the higher level generalizations—human scientists also use reasoning. None of the ways of knowing is excluded from the area as a whole.

If *you* wanted to know more about human beings, how would *you* do it? The following class activity gives you a chance to try different roles—of biologists and anthropologists. Note that advance planning is essential.

Observing the human world
contributed by Susana Leventhal

Observing an apple, a plant, or a rock are fairly simple endeavours. How easy is it to observe people, or even a specific human characteristic? In this activity, your group will observe people in different locations. Half of you will act as biologists (natural scientists), choosing a specific behaviour to observe, and half will act as anthropologists (human scientists), seeking to observe and report on a more ample range of behaviours.

Pay attention, while you are engaging in this exercise, to how sense perception, language, emotion, and reasoning influence your experiences, and your findings.

Prior to the exercise
1   (Individually) Investigate the research methods used by biologists and anthropologists. Compare the biologist's perspective with that of an anthropologist. What do they focus on? What kinds of observations do they seek to make? What kinds of conclusions are they aiming for?

2   Work in groups of four or five, and choose a place to which you will all go for about one hour. It has to be a busy place in which you are able to sit, observe, and take notes, and where you don't know any of the people. (Possibilities: a shopping mall, a restaurant, the school cafeteria during primary school lunch, a primary school classroom, the lobby of a public agency.)

3   In a notebook, vertically fold into half at least 10 pages, so that you can see two columns. Make sure that you don't run out of ink or pencils during the 25 minutes in which you will be taking many notes.

Your mission
1   Two people in your group will be biologists. Biologists: You will agree on a behaviour to observe that is also common to

mammals other than humans, but will not tell the other members of your group what you've chosen. (Possible behaviours: scratching self, touching own hair or face, coughing, crossing legs, etc.) You will sit close to each other but will work separately. Your mission is to keep track, for 25 minutes, of the number of times in which you observe the behaviour. Register as many instances as you can—it's not often that you get to observe this species!—in a factual way that can be confirmed by the other biologist in your team. Keep track of each instance using only the right side of the pages in your notebook.

2   Two (preferably three) of you will be anthropologists. Anthopologists: Your mission is to observe the people at this place as if you had no idea of what they're doing. (Imagine they are part of a culture that is very different from yours.) When registering their actions on the right side of the pages in your notebook, use language that demonstrates this factual stance. (For example, don't assume that a child holding an adult woman's hand is her son, and don't assume that someone "wants" something. Focus on describing only observable behaviours.) Sit close to each other but work separately. Make notes of what you observe for 25 minutes, registering as much as you can—it's not often that you get to observe this species!—in a factual way that will allow the other anthropologist(s) in your team to confirm your observations.

Team discussion after the observation

The whole team sits together and discusses their observations, in three phases.

1   The biologists speak, the anthropologists critique. The biologists start the discussion by comparing their observations of their chosen behaviour. On the left side of the pages where they took notes, the biologists note whether there is agreement or disagreement. During this discussion, the anthropologists act as judges, accepting or rejecting observations on the basis of their objectivity. Criteria for rejection of biologists' observations: the instance was not observed by both biologists, or was not described in precise, denotative terms. Points to pay attention to during this discussion:

   a   What troubles are the biologists having in their communication?
   b   What might they have done better?

2   The anthropologists speak, the biologists critique. The instructions are the same as above, except for the adoption of the following criterion for rejection of anthropologists' observations: inferences were made, or conclusions were drawn that weren't based on observed behaviours. Points to pay attention to during this discussion:

   a   What troubles are the anthropologists having in their communication?

 b What might they have done better?

3 The whole team prepares a report of their discussion, answering the following questions:

- How many observations by the biologists were accepted/rejected by the anthropologists? How many of the anthropologists' observations were accepted/rejected by the biologists?
- What difficulties did biologists and anthropologists face regarding (a) sense perception during the observation, (b) taking notes during the observation, and (c) communicating observations to their partners? What could they have done better?
- What were some of the feelings experienced by participants during this exercise and its discussion? How did these feelings affect both the observations and the discussion?

Discussion after the observation

(Respond individually to the following questions, then discuss in class.)

Establish similarities and differences between the methods of observation used by biologists and anthropologists. Give specific examples.

1 Why were the criteria for rejection of observations different for the biologists and for the anthropologists?

2 Where was there greater agreement—among the biologists or the anthropologists? Why do you think this is the case?

3 How was this activity affected by the different ways of knowing—sense perception, reasoning, emotion, and language?

4 What are some problems faced by biologists when observing people in an uncontrolled environment? What are some problems faced by anthropologists observing people in an uncontrolled environment (as they always do)?

5 How would this exercise be affected by observing not human beings, but a different species in their natural environment? Or in a lab?

6 What generalizations can you make about the work of biologists and anthropologists?

7 To what extent can you generalize these conclusions to other areas of the natural and human sciences?

People studying people: from the "outside" or from the "inside"?

In doing the class activity taking the roles of biologists and anthropologists, you will have recognized some of the complexities of knowledge gained through observation—limits of what can be observed and communicated, variability in interpretation, and the ambiguity of language.

If you had continued to observe people in your chosen place, you might also have found that your observations had to be modified even as you studied. People as individuals and as groups change their behaviour over time. Would anthropologists observing your grandparents at your age have reached the same conclusions about your culture as they would observing you? Perhaps. But perhaps not. Ethnographies in anthropology, for example, may have to be treated as historical records—not falsified by new observations that contrasted with the earlier ones, but rather becoming part of a larger record of cultures in the process of change, often deliberately studied at intervals of time.

Outside methods

How much easier it would be if human scientists could perform experiments on economies or cultures to find out what would happen if they changed this variable here, or that variable there! But they cannot do so. For one thing, human beings are enmeshed in such an elaborate web of interconnected variables that it would be impossible to change one variable while keeping the others the same. For another—well, human beings *object* to the idea of some kinds of tests being done on them. ("Let's remove their altars, and see what they'll do." "Let's declare a massive stock market crash, and see if it fulfills my hypothesis about the effect on the market.") Human beings in this case will use the word "unethical". Indeed, a sense of ethical responsibility is expected as a guide to research on human beings—respect for their rights, for example, or concern for the effect of the investigation upon them.

In some fields of the human sciences, however, such as certain areas of psychology, laboratory experiments are possible. (You may wish to read up on Milgram's experiment.) Laboratory experiments in psychology must be designed quite differently from experiments in the natural sciences. Think for a moment of a few experiments you've done in your group 4 subject. Imagine that you wish, for example, to find out what happens to people who are under psychological pressure (as opposed to a gas under physical pressure). What might an experiment to measure this pressure need to take into account? If you were to make a list, what would be on it?

Your list may have included concerns with validity: does the experiment measure what it claims to measure? Researchers need to agree on how to define "psychological pressure", to decide what kind of pressure to apply to human beings (observing ethical constraints), and to ensure that their operational definitions can be accurately communicated to other scientists who wish to replicate or compare results. They would also need to agree what they mean by

Activity

What do the following terms mean and what do they illustrate about human sciences? Go through the list together. If there are terms no one knows, have individuals or pairs look them up and explain them to the class:

- validity, operational definition, construct validity, triangulation
- reliability
- Milgram experiment, ethics codes
- dependent/independent variable, control/experimental group
- Hawthorne effect
- subject-expectancy/ observer-expectancy effect
- double-blind/triple-blind trials
- placebo, nocebo
- observation, verbal protocol, self-report
- participant observation, cross-cultural comparison
- cultural relativism
- random/representative sampling
- survey, census, questionnaire, interview
- qualitative/quantitative research
- experimental research, correlational study, case study, longitudinal study.

"what happens to people" under psychological pressure: which of several manifestations of responses to psychological pressure will they measure, and how will they measure it or them?

There are also many considerations about experimental design. Experimenters on human subjects can't reuse a sample over and over again as they can reuse gas molecules in a test tube, because human subjects have memories: the first experiment would affect successive ones. Thus, identical sets of human samples would have to be made available, raising the question of how many people should be in each sample, and how to ensure that they're similar enough in the characteristics that matter. (Thankfully, statisticians know a lot about how to obtain good random samples.) One sample—the control group—would need to be subjected to no psychological pressure whatsoever, to provide a reliable basis for comparison. All these considerations affect the reliability of the experiment: would results be consistent if the experiment were performed again? Two years from now? Fifty years from now?

In sum, people are not identical electrons, so human scientists have had to become aware of their methods in order to outsmart their subject matter. They recognize that people do not act the same way when they know someone is watching them (Do *you*?). They also recognize that people respond to being tested and may try to guess what the test is all about in order to comply with the researcher or resist him—consciously or unconsciously. To compound the complexity, people may fulfill not just the researcher's expectations, but their own expectations—created by the process of testing or by the announcement of results. In cases of medications being tested, for instance, patients have declared that the medication made them feel much better, even though the researcher may have given them nothing but a sugar pill as a placebo. People may also change their behaviour because a prediction is made; for example, economic predictions of shortage have in fact precipitated shortages because people, *in anticipation*, filled their shelves at home with the desired goods. As human scientists try to pin down human psychological reactions or make accurate observations about human cultures, they have to cope with the humanity of the data.

And then, too, human scientists have to cope with their own humanity. What are their own expectations that encourage them to make confirming observations—a temptation also for scientists studying the natural world, but heightened in studying people? What are their own psychological tendencies that might affect their interaction with the human beings they are studying? What are the cultural assumptions and biases that affect how they design a questionnaire, or what they notice in another culture and how they interpret it? The interaction between human observers and the observed adds up to a situation of quite extraordinary complexity.

The methods adopted by human scientists have to take all of these factors into account. In cultural anthropology, for example, they have developed participant observation and recognized its areas of fallibility. In psychology, they have developed blind trials, so that research subjects do not know, as they give their brand assessment,

Laws in the human sciences

Questions
- Why are there no "laws of science" in the human sciences?
- How would you test any of the following proposed "laws"?
- In what ways does the existence of humorous mock laws highlight a difference between the subject matter of the natural sciences and the human sciences?

Murphy's Law: If anything can go wrong, it will.

Ducharm's Axiom: If you view your problem closely enough, you will recognize yourself as part of the problem.

Cardinal Conundrum: An optimist believes we live in the best of all possible worlds. A pessimist fears this is true.

Swipple's Rule of Order: He who shouts the loudest has the floor.

Edelstein's Advice: Don't worry about what other people are thinking about you. They're too busy worrying about what you are thinking about them.

Jochen Van Den Bossche's Ratio: The amount of love someone feels for you is inversely proportional to how much you love them.[35]

which brand of soap they are using to wash their clothes. They have also developed double-blind trials, using control groups so that neither subjects nor researcher knows who is in the experimental group which is, for example, receiving the real drug. They have had to try to remove barriers of self-consciousness in some cases, outsmart their data in other cases, and in some cases even outsmart themselves. Clearly, the knowledge that the human sciences gives us is not solely the information gained through the methods but also an understanding of the methods themselves: both illuminate features of human beings.

Inside methods

Unlike the natural sciences, the human sciences are not confined simply to observing and testing. These "outside" methods are joined by "inside" methods of interviews, questionnaires, or polls. Not only can language be used for thinking and communicating to others in the knowledge community, but, in a way quite unlike mathematics or the natural sciences, it can become a research tool in interacting with the subject matter. What a bonus! But what a *complicated* bonus—as you will be aware from all you considered in Chapter 2 regarding ambiguities in definition, connotations of words and phrasing, language barriers, and the influence of a social situation on what people will say and how they say it.

"Inside" understanding involving emotional empathy may also be relevant in human science research—but as it is variable from interaction to interaction, it would be nearly impossible to construct it into a *method*. Nevertheless, tactful interviewers are more likely to gain truthful answers than clumsy ones, and sensitive participant observers in a culture, especially ones best able to share the cultural perspective of the group studied, are more likely to be given access to information and more likely to be able to interpret its meaning accurately.

The questionnaire

What skills must the human scientist possess to find out information through questioning? Perhaps nothing highlights the importance of skills more than does their *absence*. Consider the questionnaire below and its follow-up interpretation. Then consider how a professional human scientist would do it—better.

Questionnaire

Identify at least ten flaws that make this questionnaire and its following interpretation unlikely to gather accurate information.

Imagine that you graduated 10 years ago with your International Baccalaureate diploma. A researcher, trying to find out about the impact of international education, has decided to survey IB students of your graduation year, contacting those for whom their schools have up-to-date contact information. You receive in the mail the following questionnaire and, although you pick up your pen to fill it in, you quickly find difficulties in answering. What problems do you face?

Survey: your international education

1 What percentage of your IB education was international?

2 Under the heading "The influence of CAS on your life" you are asked two questions:

   a How many hours a week have you contributed to doing service within the past year?

   b How much money have you donated to international charities within the past year?

3 Rate, on the IB scale of 1 to 7, how much more international your outlook is, having taken the IB, than it would have been if you had not done so.

Several months later, you are sent a general report on the results of the survey. What difficulties do you face in accepting the researcher's conclusions?

Interpretation of results

1 Male graduates are more generous than female graduates. They have donated 15% more to charities in the past year than the women have.

2 IB graduates contribute on average 15 hours a week to doing service.

3 IB graduates are 17.69% more international in their outlook than are graduates of any other form of international education.

In assessing the questionnaire, did you find problems with any of the following?

- the method for gaining a sample of graduates
- the assumptions seemingly made
- the choice of the particular questions to ask
- the language, such as definitions
- the scales for evaluation
- the use of a control group (your alternative self)
- the likeliness of accuracy of memory in reporting
- the likeliness of accurate answers as people report about themselves
- the precision of the statistics
- the consideration (or not) of alternative explanations.

What advice do you think an experienced human scientist could give to the researcher who designed this study, on each point above? How are the issues raised here are also relevant to the method of interview?

Representing the conclusions

Now give your attention to how data is reported, often using pictures and graphs for more vivid visual communication. The following two graphs display results for an university entrance examination run in Chile until a few years ago. On the vertical axis of each are the examination points scored, and on the horizontal axis are the years of examinations (1996–2001). Both graphs represent the same school's results over the same period of time.[36]

Which graph, A or B, would be used by the school's director to demonstrate to the board of the school how well the students have been doing? Why?

Which graph, A or B, would be used by an angry parent demanding an explanation for the school's terrible examination results in 2001? Why?

A
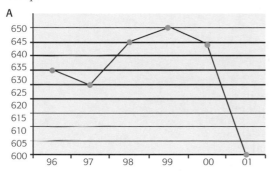

B
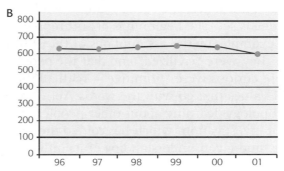

Activity

Choose an area of your own life which can be quantified and expressed as data (how many hours you spend studying, how much money or time you spend pointlessly, how often you are particularly helpful, how often you are in conflict with someone else, or so forth). Present the data twice—once in the way most flattering to yourself, and once in a way much less flattering. Do not change the data. Change only the way in which it is represented. The graphs above may give you ideas, but you may also have ideas of your own.

Share results with the rest of your class. Then discuss together the expression "the data never speaks for itself". What does it mean? How is it relevant to this class activity?

What are the implications of how we measure for the kinds of conclusions we draw?

Kipkorir Weldon of Kenya presents this topic to his TOK class, working with other students also taking IB Diploma Programme economics.

Presentation topic: How does our method of measuring poverty affect the knowledge we gain?

Quality and quantity: How do we try to quantify "poverty"? What do Gross Domestic Product (GDP) and the Human Development Index (HDI) measure and how do they measure it? What are the implications of accepting each of the methods of measurement, for world attitudes and potentially world decision-making?

Explaining the research

The observations of an anthropologist, the test results of a psychologist, the statistics of an economist—none of these, as we can see, ever "speaks for itself". Information has little explanatory value in itself. It takes a human being to interpret it—to understand its implications, to link it in correlations and conjectures about causal connections, to place it in the context of the larger explanations of theory. Understanding in these larger terms is an achievement. As one economist contends:

> An attempt to build an explanatory model that reflects every aspect of behaviour leads to a similar problem to that of a geographer who wants to draw a completely accurate map of a city, and finds that she can do so only by using a scale of one metre to one metre. A good explanation, like a useful map, tries to capture the essential features without becoming overburdened with detail.[37]

In capturing the "essential features", though, theories are both influenced by, and influence, the social context within which the area of knowledge is set. The beginnings of anthropology were influenced, for example, by the assumptions of the 19th-century Europeans that they were "civilized" and that the peoples about whom they were curious were "primitive"—with all the connotations of values that go with the words. Yet, subsequently, it has been anthropology, learning about other peoples and about its own methods of investigation, which has coined the word "ethnocentrism" and given understanding of its influence on what and how we know.

In economics, similarly, theories are not separable from the assumptions and values of a larger social context. The influence of our own age is possibly harder for us to see, though some assumptions about "essential features" of explanations are currently forced to our attention. The environmental crisis recognized at the end of the 20th century has not (yet) compelled people, governments, and corporations to transform how they act, but has generated considerable awareness of problems, and introduced new concepts of sustainability. A way of living long practised by many cultures in the past is becoming an ideal for the future. Notions of progress as industrialization, nature as resources, and growth as needing no restraint stand to be revised, and their revision puts pressure on economic theories to change accordingly. To consider some of the assumptions of economics, read the following interview with a development economist—an IB graduate.

Economics: assumptions, predictions, and "externalities"

Susan McDade, IB graduate 1983

Susan McDade is the United Nations Resident Coordinator in Cuba and oversees the development of assistance activities provided by the UN to support socio-economic development there. She has served with the United Nations Development Programme for 16 years, with long-term postings in Guatemala and China. Most recently she was in New York as an Adviser in the Bureau for Development Policy leading the Sustainable Energy Programme.

Susan is a development economist with a Bachelor of Arts from the University of Guelph in Canada and a Masters degree from the Institute of Social Studies in the Netherlands. She has lectured at Columbia and Princeton Universities.

In economics, dealing with human beings, is it possible to generalize and predict in the manner of the natural sciences?

Economics is not a pure science as its ability to predict price or market outcomes is limited. Moreover, many economic theories and analyses which have been developed to suit western European or North American social and market conditions are not easily transferable to developing countries.

What limits the ability of economics to predict?

Most economic theory used in western, or market-based economies, falls into the category of neo-classical economics. These theories have a number of assumptions in common. Although many of the assumptions can be pointed out to be weak or not always true, the line of argument goes that as long as the predictive quality of the theory holds true, or gives good results, it doesn't matter if the assumptions are not 100% true. This is a major weakness and limits economic analysis. We should not be surprised that sometimes the predictive ability of economic analysis is very limited—and this often is linked to the weaknesses in the baseline assumptions.

What are these baseline assumptions?

The underlying assumptions include things like: markets will clear when supply and demand are mediated by prices; markets are rational; information flows freely; and people are individual utility maximizers. These assumptions can be major limitations in many places. Information certainly does not flow freely, especially if you are illiterate or off-line—akin to the same thing as information technology permeates countries around the world. Moreover, consumers do not make their purchasing decisions solely based on what is best for them. Many consumers will make decisions that are guided by their community, the religious group that they belong to, or what they think might be best for their children, village, or ethnic group in the future. They may in fact maximize some other utility function than their own.

Things that are not easy to measure or which are thought to be outside economic systems are considered "externalities". Until recently, this included environmental inputs like fresh air or extreme storms, but now economists see that these types of things do impact the ability of economies and price systems to function.

A sad but useful example of the limits of economic analysis is how we measure the cost of traditional energy delivery in poor countries. Fuelwood if cut, gathered, and transported by a company with a truck has a price determined by the market in which it is sold. It reflects the cost of labour, the cost of the truck, and the fuel for the truck among other things. The same fuelwood collected by women and young girls, transported on their heads and backs, and consumed at home is seen to be "free". Economists can compute the "opportunity cost" of that non-traded fuelwood but in this mathematics it is easier to value the transport costs represented by a mule than by an 8 year-old girl.

Similarly, the loss of ecosystems from land degradation caused by over-harvesting that fuelwood is not normally calculated, nor is the cost of illiteracy in the lives of the girls that cannot go to school while they are out collecting wood. So in short, the wood that is "free" may in fact have very high economic, social, and ecological costs that price systems and the market do not reflect at all.

Economic analysis is useful in providing a range of information to policy makers to assist in decision making, but it is limited in its predictive value and will not capture transactions that cannot be easily observed, measured, or quantified.

Questions for discussion

1   Susan McDade identifies four "baseline assumptions" of neo-classical economic theory. Compare the use of assumptions in economic theory with the use of assumptions as axioms in mathematics.

2   Susan refers to "utility function" and says that people are not always "individual utility maximizers". What does this mean? What assumption does neo-classical economic theory make about human nature?

3   A theory is accepted, says Susan, if it gives good results. What test for truth is used in this case? What could or should make a theory fail this test?

4   What are "externalities"? Is it characteristic of theories in other disciplines that they illuminate only certain features and neglect others?

5   Is economics neutral or value-free? In what ways do the particular "externalities" that Susan identifies here have implications for values?

The human sciences: who's in the centre?

The human sciences not only gain knowledge about human beings but also provide, in reflection, knowledge about how human beings gain knowledge. Where do we place ourselves, psychologically and culturally, as we learn? In the centre, obviously. Where else could we be?

Thus, the human sciences have made a major contribution to our understanding of what is "obvious" to us, and the process by which it becomes so. As anthropologist Clifford Geertz has asserted:

> We [anthropologists] have been the first to insist on a number of things: that the world does not divide into the pious and the superstitious; that there are sculptures in jungles and paintings in deserts; that political order is possible without centralized power and principled justice without codified rules; that the norms of reason were not fixed in Greece, the evolution of morality not consummated in England. Most important, we were the first to insist that we see the lives of others through lenses of our own grinding and that they look back on ours through ones of their own.[38]

In our knowledge, we do look through "lenses of our own grinding". It is not a fault that we do so; we cannot do otherwise as human beings. Cast your mind back to the TOK diagram (see page 19), with the knowers—as individuals and as groups—at the centre. As we *know*, we do so using ways of knowing influenced by our own characteristics and perspectives, some of which you noted in the profile you wrote of yourself as the course began.

How can we recognize these personal and cultural influences on our knowledge? It may be that the only way is to gain more knowledge, and try to reflect upon it as we learn. It is not anthropology alone which has contributed to our capacity for recognizing our own perspectives—though we may appreciate the enthusiasm of the anthropologist quoted above. Many areas of knowledge contribute to our understanding of our own "centrism"—both in what they tell us and what we can interpret from it.

Consider, for example, the contribution of astronomy. Once, not so very long ago, we placed our planet in the centre of the universe. But we learned that the Earth is not in the centre of our solar system; we live instead on a planet that orbits the Sun. Then we learned that our solar system is not in the centre of its galaxy; it is in one of the spiral arms of the galaxy of the Milky Way. Then, most recently, we went one step further: our galaxy, in turn, is not in the centre of its part of the universe but "in the periphery of a cluster of galaxies".[39] Furthermore, as many galaxies recede from each other in an expanding universe, there is, apparently, *no fixed centre at all.*

Consider, too, the rather different contribution of geography, with awareness of alternative maps of the world. Think back to Chapter 1, to your own map and the differing cartographic representations of the world. Our different world maps, embedded with assumptions and conventions established by politics and power, do not falsify previous versions as did our successive astronomical pictures of the universe. Reflection on them leads us to a different conclusion: that we need not discard our own maps of the world but use them to position ourselves, with full awareness of alternative projections of the world.

A huge part of education is to open up understanding of other ways of thinking in this way: *knowledge* can lead to greater understanding of knowledge. To this process TOK contributes its part in two major ways. It encourages you to be *internationally minded* in your awareness of alternative perspectives. And it encourages you to be aware of knowledge *holistically*, so that no matter which area of knowledge you choose to pursue in the future, you will more readily position yourself within the whole, seeing from inside your knowledge circle but appreciating how your circle might be viewed from outside. Recognizing "centrism", of course, is a metaphor, one that helps in thinking about abstractions.

Metaphors in areas of knowledge

contributed by Julian Kitching

Metaphors are more than linguistic devices. They can influence the way we think about all sorts of things and, by extension, guide our actions. (Look back to Chapter 2 to refresh your memory on the distinction between the source of a metaphor and its target. The three functions of metaphor identified there are now applied specifically to areas of knowledge.)

1 Explaining and understanding

Metaphors use everyday words or technical terms from another discipline in order to make links that make explaining and understanding easier.

Example: communications in the human body

One way of conceptualizing some of the organ systems in the body is to compare them with aspects of a telephone network. The nervous system corresponds to land lines with fixed "cables", cells in the immune system correspond to mobile telephones that move around picking up signals and responding to them, and the endocrine system corresponds to transmitter stations that broadcast signals. Points of similarity and difference can be easily identified here. By integrating the three specific metaphors into a larger systematic one, a certain kind of understanding is forged that views all these systems as part of a larger dynamic whole. This can help us to see these three systems in a new way—overcoming, for example, the traditional western biological view that the body can affect the mind much more powerfully than the mind can affect the body. This traditional view is, of course, built upon the widespread idea that mind and body are somehow separate entities.

2 Challenging orthodoxy

Metaphors provide new and different ways of thinking through their "surprise value".

Example: the "selfish gene"

Since the British evolutionary biologist Richard Dawkins coined the term "selfish gene" in his book of the same name in 1976, the term has become a stimulus to thinking about the nature of living organisms in a certain way. Dawkins wanted to switch the emphasis in biology from the primacy of organisms to that of genes, and to do that he employed the new term in order not only to help people to understand what he was saying, but also to

challenge accepted ways of thinking. The behaviour of genes could best be explained by imagining them showing intentional behaviour, such as being selfish. When the metaphor is extended logically, it is clear that "selfish" genes would put their "interests" ahead of the bodies in which they found themselves, and that therefore bodies could be regarded as merely the vehicles for transmission of genes from one generation to the next. This was a powerful and influential new way of looking at biology. Nevertheless, there have been those who mistook Dawkins's metaphor for literal reality, and mocked his allegedly poor grasp of the subject! Once again, it is important to understand metaphor.

3 Conditioning thought and action

Metaphors are powerful as they can be used for deliberate manipulation of thought and action, or simply because they reflect basic aspects of our environment. They help to create structures of thought that are variously described as paradigms, conceptual schemes, or frameworks. Let's consider biological evolution as an example.

Example: "natural selection"

When Charles Darwin wrote of "natural selection", he intended the term to build on the more familiar concept of "artificial selection", in which plant and animal breeders influenced the make-up of their stocks by choosing individuals with desirable characteristics for breeding. This metaphor was very successful in emphasizing certain points of similarity, such as the gradual nature of change and the basic importance of individual variation, but has also contributed to 150 years of misunderstandings. "Selection" seems to imply a "selector", seems to invoke intelligence, and encourages the thought that the fundamental process involves positive selection of "fit" individuals rather than the elimination of "unfit" ones. It could be argued that Darwin's metaphor has been only partially successful in promoting public understanding of evolution.

If different languages use metaphors with different meanings, how might this affect the pursuit of knowledge?

Metaphors in IB Diploma Programme subjects

The table below contains terms that are important in particular IB Diploma Programme subjects. From which subject(s) does each term come? What is the *source* of the metaphor? What is its *target*?

It may be necessary to know some of the history of the subject disciplines in order to make informed judgments about what was borrowed from where, but, according to what you know, can you tell from which other subject(s) words or terms have been borrowed?

innate drive	computer virus
mRNA translation	concentration gradient
electric current	punctuated equilibrium
monetary inflation	computer hardware
Big Bang	work done

regime purge	natural selection
system firewall	cognitive dissonance
Netiquette	buffer solution
price elasticity	selfish gene
radioactive decay	group pressure
Great Leap Forward	eukaryotic cell
electrical resistance	Trojan horse
liberation front	nitrogen fixation
computer software	lock and key model
greenhouse effect	network topology

Can you suggest other examples from your studies in various subjects?

If some disciplines are richer in metaphor than others, is this the result of the subject matter with which it is concerned or more the result of the methods that it uses?

Does geography play a special role here in providing raw material for the construction of metaphor? If so, why might this be the case?

History

We met history some pages ago, when it was offering its siblings something it so often gives: a larger perspective on the issues of a moment.

In many ways, history resembles those younger siblings within the knowledge family. Like natural science and human science, it asks a lot of questions, tries to understand the causes of things, and likes to explain. Like them, it gives serious attention to evidence and interpretation—and tends to be rather self-critical in drawing its conclusions. Considerably older, though, history has watched the others grow up, as it has watched so much in the human activities of the world as they slide into the past.

In grouping and classifying areas of knowledge at the beginning of this chapter (see page 131), where did you place history? If you grouped it with the human sciences, you would be consistent with the IBO and many universities. Why do we treat history separately in TOK? What characteristics does historical knowledge possess which merit special examination?

Consider with the rest of your class the following comparisons as you enter a discussion of history, and return to them for further consideration as the chapter ends.

- In what ways do *all* areas of knowledge, not just history, depend on records of the past?
- What differences in knowledge are created by the fact that historians take the past as their subject for study?
- The human sciences and history both aim to describe and explain human activities. What are the differences between the kinds of descriptions and explanations that they give?
- A biologist is investigating birds flying north. A historian is investigating people who were fleeing north two centuries ago. Compare their methods of investigation and the kinds of conclusions they reach.

As we give our attention to the study of history, we are pulling together many of the threads of discussion of the whole TOK course so far: reliability of sense perception; variability of reports; the four principles of representation applied language, maps, photographs, and statistics as they form our records; reliability of sources; issues of identifying cause; methods of persuasion and propaganda; and complexities of studying human beings. You may want to create a flow chart of all the key TOK knowledge issues that enter into the study of history from the moment that events take place to the moment that some of them appear in history books—and then beyond, to you as the critical reader.

In this chapter we will start by considering the primary records of history, go on to historical interpretations, and end by trying to place the interpretations in a larger context of beliefs.

Activity

A team of researchers has suddenly taken a profound interest in your school. They want to compile a historical record, and seek from you, as eyewitness and participant, first-hand information about the past year.

Before you respond to their questions, identify as a class a public event in your school that occurred within recent weeks. It could be a school meeting, a performance or dance, an event involving the public, or anything of the sort where most of you were there.

Then write individual answers to the following questions. After everyone has finished, compare your replies and use the questions below as a prompt to further discussion.

Eyewitness to history

1 What were the most striking characteristics of the public event that your TOK class identified?

2 What would you consider the five most important events for your school during this past year?

3 What do you consider to be the three most important things which the group of students from your graduating year has gained from its time so far at the school?

4 One of the researchers asks you how you think he can best gain information on the events, culture, and ambience of 1999/2000 within the school. What would you recommend?

5 Who do you think is best qualified to write a history of your school: a graduate, a teacher, a member of the school board, a parent, or a local journalist? Why? Would someone else be better? Why?

Eyewitness to history: follow-up discussion

1 In identifying the most striking characteristics of the event, what do you think affected what you perceived and later recalled? How would a historian, for whom you are a primary source, try to overcome the limitations of eyewitness memory?

2 In picking out the five most important events for the school, on what values did you base your selection and emphasis? Do all of you in the class share the same set of values? Did you define "school" as the institution, its current population, or otherwise—and what are the implications of your definition for the selection you make? Is your principal or school head likely to show a different perspective in the definition and selection of events?

3 As the questions become more abstract and more overtly value judgments, do the responses within your class diverge increasingly? Why or why not?

4 What materials did you recommend? Do you expect historical researchers to look only at artefacts (such as trophies, artworks, clothing) and factual documents (such as enrolment lists and budgets) or, further, the more emotional and variable records such as school yearbooks and your own eyewitness reports in the three questions above? Would you expect a historical account of your school to include or exclude emotions and value judgments?

5 What are the main differences between, on the one hand, your own eyewitness records and the artifacts and documents of #4, and, on the other, an historical record? If events of the past few years are not yet considered "history", why not? What is a "primary source" and what is a "secondary source"?

COLUMBUS, WE'RE IN TROUBLE -- THE WORLD IS NOT FLAT!

THAVES 10-13
© 1997 by NEA, Inc.

Interactive Frank and Ernest @
www.unitedmedia.com
E-Mail: FandE Boot @AOL.COM

Perspectives in history

Direct your attention now to further consideration of the last question in your class activity—historians and the histories they write. Historians are facing a central challenge in the knowledge they give us: they cannot experiment or make repeated observations of the events about which they write. They cannot rerun massive famines or armed conflicts in order to view them from a different perspective, to replicate them in another part of the world, or to fill in gaps in their notes on a third try.

Only the records remain. But records left by whom? Not all groups within a society own the artefacts or write the records; not all lives are equally represented in the primary materials. Moreover, the primary materials are likely to be far more variable than your class records of events in your school, as they have probably been left by people with less in common than the members of an IB class in a school. To compound the challenges for the historian, much will have been lost from these records, destroyed over time. The historian is rather like someone trying to assemble a complex puzzle out of only scattered or patchy pieces.

Not all historians, though, are trying to create similar patterns out of the pieces of the puzzle. They research the past with certain interests or questions in mind, pick out only the pieces that are relevant to their investigation, and assemble them in different ways. Admittedly, many historians do converge in the pictures they build up, and do generalize to a certain extent in the manner of natural scientists: in using words such as "empire" or "revolution", they do find common features that justify the application of certain vocabulary. Indeed, finding similar features between human experience of the past and human experiences of the present is one of the ways in which history contributes to our understanding of some of the patterns of our lives. However, the ways in which different historians connect even a shared understanding of events may vary considerably. The same period of the past may yield numerous histories, each with its own centre of interest and emphasis.

Historians return repeatedly to epochs of the past, using the works of other historians as secondary sources, combined with the primary materials, in order to answer new questions that become of interest within their own time. After all, if they are asking the question "How did we get here from there?" the changing features of what we consider to be here generate new questions about the route from there.

Historians tracing that route are creating it out of causal connections, with all the interpretations involved. The route is not a single super-highway along which all historians move but rather a number of different paths intersecting, as different historians trace different connections within epochs of the past or between the past and the present. Already in TOK we have considered many of the knowledge issues surrounding cause, particularly in our discussions before we turned to the natural sciences, and have examined the methods used by the natural and human sciences as they answer the question "why?" In history, where variables cannot be controlled and tested, and where the subject matter is the past, the causal links that historians make between there and here demand considerable interpretation. A work of history becomes an argument for a particular interpretation, justified by evidence with different characteristics from that of the sciences.

The particular arguments we accept influence how we understand our own societies in the present. The following questions, consequently, are significant ones for you to consider with your class.

● How do we know whether a particular history is telling us the truth? What truth tests are relevant, and how would you apply them?

● If there are historical interpretations of the past that are not only different in centre of interest but actually conflict, how can a critical reader determine which to believe? How can we deal with differing versions in a way that gives us the best understanding of the past?

If your class contains students of Diploma Programme history, they could act as resources for the class in sharing examples and issues from their own history course.

History presentation, introductory skit

Latin American colonization: two perspectives

Indigenous: Michelle Soto Maldonado, Ecuador
Spanish: Angela Garrido Retamal, Chile

Spanish: Oh! I remember those times, our glorious days in history when we, the Spaniards, colonized America.

Indigenous: Oh! I remember those times, our tragic days in history when the Spaniards colonized us.

Spanish: Yes! Everything started when we discovered America.

Indigenous: Yes! Everything started when they thought they had discovered a new land, but we had been there long before their arrival.

Spanish: The new continent was full of savages, real savages! They wore almost no clothing. All sinners! Practised polygamy and…they didn't know God!

Indigenous: They arrived with a lot of things that we had never seen before, huge weapons that made horrible noises, dishonouring the land of our gods.

Spanish: We had to do something about it. We had to convert the savages into Christians. But…would they listen to us? Oh no! We had to use force in the name of God.

Indigenous: We had to do something about it. This was our land! In the name of a god that we didn't even know they killed many of us! And of course we fought for our land and our people.

Spanish and Indigenous: Yes! We fought.

Spanish: We colonized them!

Indigenous: They colonized us!

Spanish and Indigenous: And there was death.

Spanish and Indigenous: But…we were right.

Spanish and Indigenous (to each other): What? We were right!

Knowing the past: interview with historian Charles Freeman

Charles Freeman is a recognized freelance academic author of Egypt, Greece and Rome, Civilizations of the Ancient Mediterranean *(Oxford University Press, second edition, 2004),* The Closing of the Western Mind *(2002), and several other books about the ancient world. He is an examiner in both IB Diploma Programme history and TOK.*

In your study of ancient Egypt, Greece, and Rome, you are dealing with eras for which, surely, most of the records have been lost. What is the nature of evidence when studying times so long ago?
Traditionally scholars studied the surviving texts in Greek, Latin and, following the decipherment of hieroglyphics in the 1820s, Egyptian. There is an excellent range of writings but naturally they represent the voices of

the literate elite. There are very few women's voices and none of slaves. In the past twenty years, there has been far greater interest in, and effective use of, material remains, statues, pottery, buildings and the traces of human activity in the landscape. Balancing and assessing these sources is not easy but a much fuller picture of the ancient Mediterranean is emerging and the subject is academically a very lively one.

When information is missing, how do you close the gaps?

One of the most important attributes for the historian of any era is common sense. You must understand what humans are and are not capable of and how the natural world conditions human activity. So the story you create must, in the first instance, reflect what is humanly possible. Next you cannot make any assertions which contradict reliable evidence. There is a mass of interlocking evidence, for instance, that the major pyramids at Gizeh in Egypt were built about 2400 BC.

There are some pseudo-historians who claim they were built in 12,000 BC by a superhuman race who aligned them with star patterns. These historians appeal to the credulous. In the last resort the historian must tell a plausible tale, one which realistically reflects the evidence. Obviously there is room for creative imagination here and history comes alive when there is debate between different possible interpretations of an event.

History is sometimes described as a being mid-way between science and literature. In what ways do you see yourself as following the methods of a scientist as you reconstruct the past?

Science, in the traditional sense of the word, is increasingly used in the study of the ancient world. For instance, there was an important volcanic eruption of the island of Thera in the Greek Mediterranean which was probably followed by a tsunami which must have done a lot of damage to coastal cities and may even have temporarily destroyed the Minoan civilization in Crete. For decades there was controversy over the date but now an exact one, of 1628 BC, has been proposed on the basis of the analysis of wood samples and other debris. Once a date has been securely fixed, a lot of archeological sites which suffered destruction at the same time can also be dated. This is laboratory work. In a broader sense, a scientific approach is useful in proposing hypotheses from the existing evidence and testing new discoveries against the hypothesis, although, unfortunately, one cannot carry out experiments by rerunning the past. In short, one has to be aware of what science can achieve in analysing material remains and also be ready to apply deductive logic to evidence.

To what extent do you agree that history resembles literature?

History is about the activity of human beings, as individuals and within societies. They have stories to tell of themselves and we can suggest our own stories of their lives. The great historians are those who can convey the motivations of those who created the past and allow us to empathize with them. This is, in essence, a literary skill and it is essential if history is to be communicated in an effective way.

You say that history deals with causes and motivations. Is explanation the major goal for historians?

For me personally, the excitement of history lies in trying to offer explanations for developments. The greatest satisfaction comes from reviewing the evidence and realizing that it can be rearranged to produce a fresh interpretation of an event. For instance, in my study of the fourth century AD, *The Closing of the Western Mind*, I found a lot of texts which denigrated reason in favour of a commitment to faith. When I put these together, I was able to offer a new approach to the decline of intellectual life in the late Roman empire. I found it absorbing, especially when I found other historians supporting my thesis.

In your study of the role of reason and faith, have you found it difficult to put aside your own beliefs as you researched and wrote?
We all have our beliefs and no historian achieves complete neutrality. (Could one write a history of the Holocaust which is free of all emotion?) Myself, I am committed to the idea that a society which enjoys freedom of speech is not only a much healthier society in itself but achieves a much higher standard of intellectual activity. That is why a lot of my work recently has concentrated on times when freedom of speech has been eroded by governments or religious dogmatism.

This does not mean I am against religion per se—it obviously fulfils important human needs—but in my latest book, *AD 381: The Turning Point that Time Forgot*, I am arguing that spiritual life was also diminished by the imposition of religious orthodoxy in the fourth century by the emperor Theodosius. Everyone, religious and non-religious alike, suffered by not being able to enter into free discussion.

Studying our era is presumably quite unlike studying ancient Greece and Rome, in that there are perhaps too many records. How do you suppose historians in the future will be able to make sense of our era?
Every era has its own problems of interpretation and it is often only in hindsight that we can begin to spot the important trends. The present day is similar to that of antiquity is that the vast majority of voices go unrecorded, however many paper and electronic records the elite produce. However, one does feel that there are more fragmented societies today, societies split apart by globalization, deteriorating environments and the lure of the west. It will surely be hard for historians to reflect the totality of any modern society.

What advice would you offer a student of history?
First, don't stick to one single period. Ideas, knowledge and skills learned from the study of one era can often be transferred to help provide a fresh approach to another. The best historians, such as Simon Schama, have written on a wide variety of subjects, in Schama's case, 17th-century Holland, the French Revolution, slavery, and a history of Britain.

Second, realize that evidence does not come only from texts. I have learnt a lot from looking at the art and architecture of the periods I have been studying. It tells you a great deal about how a society presents itself and what it considers important to spend resources on. One of the most important moments in the history of Christianity came, for instance, when the emperor Constantine transferred the pagan custom of spending a lot of money on temples into Christianity so that the religion of the poor became the religion of the big builders. Every major European city was transformed as a result! Always be ready to see everything from coins to the writings of philosophers as potential evidence. A broader approach makes the subject more interesting and will help deepen your understanding of a period.

Questions for discussion

1 Charles Freeman says that "there is room for creative imagination" in history. What two or three things does he suggest, on the other hand, that restrict the creative imagination?

2 Charles Freeman presents emotion as acceptable in the writings of history, both in emotions associated with historical events and in the empathy with the lives of people in the past. What is your own expectation of the role of emotion in the *content* of the historical records, the *process* of selecting and filtering the evidence, and the *writing* of the resultant history? In what way is emotion relevant in the response and understanding of the reader?

3 What are the relative advantages to the historian of studying the recent past or studying the more remote past?

4 Charles Freeman says that today, still, "the vast majority of voices go unrecorded, however many paper and electronic records the elite produce." Everyone in your class is likely to have the ability to leave a historical record on the Internet, so is it accurate for a historian to consider you as part of the elite?

5 "Realize that evidence does not come only from texts," Charles Freeman reminds us. What other sources does he suggest? What further sources of information would you add to his list? Are there others unimaginable to historians of the past but made possible by contemporary science?

History in the context of other areas of knowledge

As we considered the distinction earlier in this chapter between the natural sciences and the human sciences (page 173), we commented on differing approaches to generalizing. We ventured at that time to suggest that natural scientists use their records to make generalizations applicable everywhere, but that human scientists are, by the very nature of their human subject matter, held in tension between generalizing and particularizing perspectives. Consider the spectrum below, in which history moves further away from generalizing and closer to particularizing.

GENERAL ⬅━━━━━━━━━━━━━━━━━➡ PARTICULAR

mathematics   natural sciences   human sciences   history   the arts

- Why is mathematics placed as the most general of all areas of knowledge?
- We described the human sciences earlier as held in tension between generalizing and particularizing perspectives. Would it be reasonable to describe history in the same way?
- What differences exist between the human sciences and history that might justify their relative positions on this spectrum?
- Glance briefly ahead to the arts. Does it make sense to you that they be placed at the particularizing extreme? To what extent are the stories of literature like the stories of history, individual narratives from which we may infer more general ones? In what ways are they different?

- To what extent do the arts provide particular works about which history might generalize? What kind of social records do such arts as literature, architecture, sculpture, and painting provide for historians to interpret?

This spectrum is yet another of the many images and metaphors that we have given you in this chapter, to suggest ideas for you to consider critically. What other criteria might you use to order these areas of knowledge, forming different spectra?

From common systems to multiple perspectives

Mathematics	Natural and human sciences		History
Axiomatic deductive systems are simultaneously valid.	New theory replaces old through falsifying, *or*	new theories coexist with old. Perspectives differ more in human sciences.	Multiple perspectives coexist. Interpretations may cohere or clash in interaction.

This picture reinforces the spectrum of general to particular, seen in a slightly different way. Again, a diagrammatic simplification emphasizes particular features but ignores others. Be critical.

The forces of history?
Consider now a different kind of diagram, from a physics textbook.[40]

- What are the differences between the forces studied in physics and the forces studied in history?
- To what extent is the metaphor of "the forces of history" useful to historians? To what extent does the metaphor suggest a particular perspective on history as moved by impersonal forces beyond human control? To what extent, on the other hand, is it used more loosely as an image that sums up many causes?

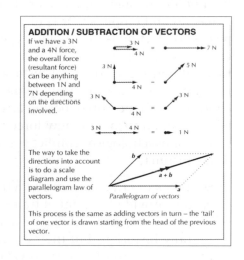

ADDITION / SUBTRACTION OF VECTORS

If we have a 3N and a 4N force, the overall force (resultant force) can be anything between 1N and 7N depending on the directions involved.

The way to take the directions into account is to do a scale diagram and use the parallelogram law of vectors.

Parallelogram of vectors

This process is the same as adding vectors in turn – the 'tail' of one vector is drawn starting from the head of the previous vector.

History and arguments for patterns
Facts in themselves do not lead to understanding in *any* of the areas of knowledge that aim to explain, as we have seen in the sciences. In history, historians are dealing with facts that are different from those of the natural and human sciences—facts that are established not by direct observation but by records. And facts have no life of their own. The historian must interpret them in order to reach any understanding, and then use that understanding to *argue* for a perspective or point of view. No historical account can possibly be a neutral record of the past "as it happened".

That is not to say that historians are free to invent the past. Some events in history are very well documented, and some are not. But whatever the quality and quantity of the records, historians must develop interpretations based on the records and consistent with them.

Nevertheless, historians cannot describe *everything* any more than you can—even regarding a single day of your life. They must select information relevant to the stories they want to tell, in response to the questions they want to ask, in the context of an audience of their particular place and time. During the late 20th century, for example, many historians researched the lives of people marginalized in previous histories, contributing new perspectives on the past through, for example, black histories or women's histories.

As they research and write, historians have still further choices to make, consciously or unconsciously. How will they classify their subject matter? For example, will they treat human beings as **individuals**, as do liberals, with an emphasis on individual motivation and particular views of human nature; or as **social groups**, as do Marxists, with an emphasis on group dynamics, specifically the class struggle? Will they classify societies into abstracted **types**, such as democracies, and treat them in terms of the abstracted ideal? Will they treat forms of social relations, such as barter and trade or gender relations, as historically rooted in a time and place—or universal? Indeed, like other human beings, historians may simply *make assumptions* about the right approach without noticing or questioning them, particularly if surrounded by a society with which they share the assumptions.

As they develop and argue for their interpretations, historians may also be influenced by their beliefs about the larger patterns of history within which they place their own accounts. How big is history, and what is its shape? Is history a cycle, with events repeating with some kind of identifiable sequence or rhythm, like the rise and fall of dynasties and empires? Or is history linear? If so, does it give a picture of decline from a golden age in the past, or progress to a golden age in the future? Or is it, instead, the story of Great Men who influence the course of history (while the women, invisible in this history, presumably stay home and cook)? Or, rather, is history continually shaped by opposing forces which fuse together, only to be opposed in turn by a new force that arises? Or is it, instead, a record of psychological conflict between the life instinct and the death instinct?

These kinds of large patterns, whether *assumed* to exist or *argued* to exist, can provide conceptual frameworks for the particular stories set within them, and influence the interpretations they are given. It is not only historians but their entire societies that may embrace particular patterns of history to validate their own visions of themselves and give a positive interpretation to purposes that could be construed otherwise.

Take, for example, the picture of history as linear, with human life improving as it goes. Much of European history from the 19th into the 20th century is enmeshed with the idea of progress. What could have been described as imperialist conquest and exploitation of lands and peoples was told as a story of progress: Europeans carried enlightenment and the true religion to dark places of the world, and nobly took on the white man's burden of civilizing primitive peoples. Even scientific theories, such as the theory of evolution, were drawn into the large story of progress when evolution was treated, disregarding its science, as a source of metaphor. The idea of progress, also associated with industrialization of the "developed" world, continues to have impact on the world today: what constitutes progress, and what changes are beneficial to a society, are issues for debate within contemporary approaches to development.

Imagining history as progress, though, is only one possible way to find pattern and meaning in the records of the past. Take another example. Is history the story of Great Men who change its course? If so, it can be used to justify and glorify the strong leader, or to support a cult of personality around figures in power. As we considered in Chapter 4, the Leader can be a creation of effective propaganda.

Great Man interpretation

The Great Man picture of history places an emphasis on powerful leaders as the strongest forces of history. How does a leader gain and hold power? A study of power in history includes a study of propaganda and justifications for belief.

The poster reads: The sunlight of Mao Zedong's thought illuminates the road of the Great Proletarian Cultural Revolution.

History as progress

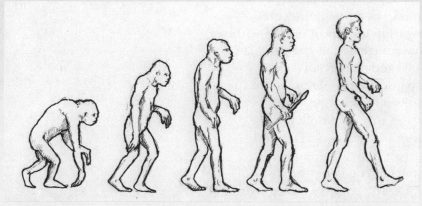

The familiar image of the "march of progress" takes certain ideas from Darwin's theory of evolution and frames them with meanings foreign to biological change—suggestions of purposeful "progress", ideas of evolving civilization, and racist notions of white superiority. The image carries associations of many strands of thought, all coherent, for example, with a European self-image in an age of imperialism. The implicit biases were no more evident to those who held them than were the biases of their Mercator map.

The idea of "survival of the fittest" that often accompanies this image has likewise been used without concern for its scientific meaning. "Social Darwinism" justified the gap between rich and poor by interpreting the rich as more fit to survive and thereby making power self-justifying.

Historians of an age are influenced by the ideas of their age. It falls to later historians to look back on secondary sources, reinterpreting them in hindsight in their own work.

The interpretations that we accept of history may affect us deeply in the way that we live in the present, as in many ways they provide a collective memory for a social group. The version of history told within families and communities is part of the cultural identity of the group. The stories told may be of shared blood that makes events of the past belong to a group in the present as their heritage. They may also be of group entitlement, destiny or mystic connection with a particular piece of land: "We have been victims in the past and are therefore owed _____." "Many of us have died for this cause/this land and we owe it to them to _____." The stories of a living past may also emphasize the characteristics in which the group takes particular pride, perhaps their honesty, or their capacity to endure hardship, or their sense of responsibility: "We are the kind of people who have always ____ and therefore we must ____."

Similarly, the version of history taught within a school system is always a choice of what is considered most important for the new generation to know, in order not to be ignorant of their own society and the rest of the world. Students from parts of the world in conflict have often been surprised, though, to find how different are the versions they learned in school. Indeed, versions of history taught in schools have often reflected not only the inevitable biases of each part of the world but also deliberate attempts to create distorted visions of the country or its enemy. History, in the history of the world, has often been used for the purposes of propaganda.

Would we ever wish to leave our history behind and somehow start afresh? It is only when considering grim events that we might ever wish to do so. In recent years, some world attempts to overcome some of the negative impacts of history serve to emphasize how significant to us is the record of our past. For example, several governments have made public apologies to groups of people within their own societies for the ways they were treated in the past. The apologies have been treated as symbolic and significant—even though neither the people apologizing nor the people to whom the apology is given were necessarily involved in the injustice or even alive at the time. Another, even more striking, example is the attempts of some countries such as South Africa to declare and record the brutal events of the recent past in a "truth and reconciliation" tribunal, in hopes that acknowledging the truth of events of the past would help people and the country to deal with their devastating effect.

Clearly, the versions of history that we accept influence how we understand our present. In our day, we have been offered one version of history as the clash of civilizations. We can hope that this version does not encourage us to accept clashes as inevitable rather than as the result of decisions and choices, or blind us to what we can do ourselves to influence our futures.

In considering further the way that historical interpretation is done, take now the role of the historian yourself, sifting through the records of the past to understand them and to present an argument based on that understanding. The follow-up questions at the end of the following activity ask you to consider the role of argument in historical interpretation, and the implications of those arguments for understanding of the present.

Did the Chinese discover America before Columbus?

contributed by Vivek Bammi

In a book published in 2002, called *1421: The Year China Discovered America* (William Morrow, New York), a retired submarine commander in Britain's Royal Navy, Gavin Menzies, claims that the Chinese discovered America about 70 years before Columbus. Under Emperor Zhu Di, China in the early 15th century was a great seafaring nation. Huge Chinese ships, commanded by Admiral Zheng He, and bearing silk, porcelain, and other treasures made expeditions to Indonesia, India, and as far as East Africa. Menzies says he has found proof that the Chinese ships sailed further—around the Cape of Good Hope in Southern Africa and all the way to the Americas, with some ships even crossing the Pacific back to China. He insists not only that the Chinese beat Columbus, but that European explorers who reached the Americas did so with maps copied from the Chinese. The book has created controversy, and many scholars have questioned the claims of Menzies.

In this activity, we will look at evidence for and against Menzies' thesis, and then you can reach your own conclusion on the question: did the Chinese discover America before Columbus?

Evidence for the claim

1   In 1421, China was more powerful than any other nation. The Ming Emperor Zhu Di had a vision of discovering and charting the entire world and bringing it into Confucian and Buddhist harmony through trade and diplomacy. Serving him was one of the greatest admirals the world has ever known, Zheng He, a Muslim eunuch and one of the king's closest advisors.

2   The whole world was accurately mapped by 1423—*before* European voyages of discovery started. A map said to date from 1418 was recently displayed in Beijing by a Chinese lawyer. The map shows both North and South America in unusual detail. The lawyer claims that the map proves the Chinese explorer Zheng He had been to America many years before Columbus, and also shows the Chinese understanding of the entire world. Moreover, there was only one nation at that time with the wealth, the scientific knowledge, the ships, and the seafaring experience to have carried out voyages around the world, and that was China.

3   Zheng He's fleet for the expedition to the western lands from 1421 to 1423 consisted of more than 300 ships manned by over 28,000 people. Each of the 62 flag ships of the fleet was roughly 450 feet long and 190 feet wide. By comparison, Columbus' flagship, the Santa Maria, was 75 feet by 25 feet.

4   In the official history of the Ming Dynasty it is recorded that Zheng He led excursions to Java, Sumatra, Vietnam, Siam, Cambodia, Philippines, Ceylon, India, Yemen, Arabia, and Somalia. As a clear demonstration of his travel to Africa, he brought giraffes and lions back to China as souvenirs. The official history also mentioned "Franca" (the term to describe today's France and Portugal) and Holland. The Hollanders were described as tall people with red hair and beards, long noses, and deep eye sockets. If he did meet with Europeans in their native countries, the only way would be to navigate around the Cape of Good Hope (the Suez Canal was only built in 1869).

5   Local people in the Pacific and the Americas have left descriptions of Chinese or Asiatic peoples who settled amongst them before Europeans arrived. In Northern Australia there are references to "honey-coloured people" settling, the Maoris of New Zealand refer to "light-coloured settlers", and in Greenland it's recorded that "people from Cathay have visited here". Carvings in the New England and Mississippi areas of North America show foreign ships and horses, an

animal that became extinct in the Americas in about 10,000 BCE. Studies using DNA suggest connections between the Chinese and American Indian groups in South America.

6 Plants indigenous (original) to one continent were found on another by European explorers.

   • From China to Australia: lotuses and papyrus; to North America: rice, poppy seeds, roses; to Amazon and Mexico: rice.

   • From South America to China and Southeast Asia: maize (corn); to Pacific islands: yams, sweet potatoes; to Philippines: potatoes and maize.

7 The Newport tower in Newport, Rhode Island (USA) was, according to Menzies, actually built by the Chinese as it resembled a lighthouse built in China in the 13th century.

Evidence against the claim

1 There was strong opposition to the ocean voyages in China, especially from the Mandarins (ruling officials), who felt that the voyages resulted in wasteful expenditure and affected the country's finances. They believed that the emperor should focus on dealing with the poverty of the millions of Chinese farmers and to build up China's internal strength. They also feared merchants and foreigners as threats to their privileged place in Chinese society. Emperor Zhu Di's son and successor, Zhu Gaozhi, agreed with them, and in 1424 he ordered a halt to all ocean voyages, the destruction of the large Chinese fleet, and the burning of the records of Zheng He's expeditions. As a result, we have no direct evidence to support Menzies' claim that the Chinese discovered America in 1421.

2 Unlike the European explorers, armies and governments from the 15th to 19th centuries, who sought economic and political control of new territories, the Chinese had no interest in direct colonization of the areas that their fleets visited. Rather, the Chinese voyages aimed at gaining scientific knowledge and displaying the wealth and power of their civilization and the emperor, the "Son of Heaven". Most of the products brought back to China from other countries were dismissed as "trifles" compared with the sophistication of a country that called itself the "Middle Kingdom", or the centre of the world. Would this attitude support sustained exploration of the world?

3 Historian T. Furnish from Georgia (USA) points out that Menzies "does not read Chinese and thus *cites no primary sources*—a problem even if one accepts that the records were all destroyed". Professor Furnish accepts that "the most likely candidate for future world domination in 1400 certainly would have been China, with its huge oceangoing ships backed up by a sophisticated, prosperous, and powerful state; however, *that did not come to pass*".

4 The "original" map of 1418 claimed by the Chinese lawyer is probably an 18th-century copy. Some academics point to inconsistencies in the map, including the use of language that does not fit the style of Ming China, suggesting that it may be a fake.

5 In her history of the Ming voyages, *When China Ruled the Seas*, Louise Levathes wrote in 1994 that "most scholars are generally agreed that there appears to have been at least some Asian influence in the New World before the arrival of Columbus". However, she does not mention anything about the Ming fleets going around the Cape of Good Hope or circling the globe. "The farthest down the African coast any of the Chinese fleets are certain to have sailed…is near Madagascar."

6 Menzies never provides the DNA evidence which he claims shows links between the American Indians and the Chinese. DNA tests in the Atlantic and North American areas have not yet been carried out.

7 Other scholars claim that the Newport Tower in fact resembles an ancient Viking (Scandinavian) construction, supporting their thesis that the Vikings discovered America before Columbus. After a careful

study of the artefacts found near or under the tower, including pottery, iron nails, clay tobacco pipes, and buttons, it was found that all these items could be traced to Scotland, England, or the English colonies in America and they were made between the 17th and 19th centuries. The carbon dating of the mortar used to build the tower gives its year of construction as 1665. It would seem that this evidence does not support the case for either Chinese or Viking discovery of America before Columbus!

Discussion questions and reflective writing on 1421: The Year China Discovered America

1   Which of the evidence that was provided to *support the author's claim* that the Chinese discovered America before Columbus did you find the most convincing? Explain why you agree with that evidence in two or three sentences.

2   Which of the evidence that was provided *against the author's claim* did you find the most convincing? Explain why you agree with that evidence in two or three sentences.

3   After looking at the evidence for both sides, *which one do you agree with more*? Explain your answer in three or four sentences, referring to specific evidence to support your reasoning.

4   What does this debate about the discovery of America tell us about the study of history? (Remember, the word "history" comes from the Greek "istoria", meaning questioning or inquiry.) Is the question of the "discovery" of America an important one? Explain in three or four sentences.

5   If Menzies' claim is fully verified, how would that change our understanding of world history in the last 600 years? Explain in three or four sentences.

6   Zheng He's voyages are being used by the Chinese government today for political and diplomatic purposes, to back its claim that China's rising power will not threaten its neighbours. Why is history used by people in the present to support their viewpoints? Do you think this is a legitimate use of history?

7   The Ming emperors had a vision of a world brought together in spiritual unity through trade and diplomacy. Do you think this is an appropriate vision for our global community today? Are there alternative models of globalization you would suggest?

Areas of knowledge

Pause as we leave history as an area of knowledge to look back over all of mathematics, the natural sciences, human sciences, and history. Cast your mind ahead toward the arts and ethics, which we will treat next. With all areas of knowledge in mind, consider the knowledge issues that arise first from reflections on a rainbow and then from the tiny story of the ichthyologist.

The rainbow

contributed by Charles Freeman

Read the quotations on the following pages and then consider in class discussion the questions tht follow them. Rainbows can invoke, beautifully, nearly the whole of knowledge.

The rainbow

On the 27th day a rainbow whose brightness was very great stretched in the east … On the same day in Hiritu in the province of Sippar the troops of Babylonia and Assyria fought with each other and the troops of Babylonia withdrew and were heavily defeated.' Report by the royal astronomers of Babylon, 651 BC.[43]

Observationally the rainbow is a circular arc of several colours seen in rain or spray opposite the sun and centred around the shadow of your head … Optically, the rainbow is just a distorted image of the sun. Rainbows perform this rearranging of sunlight versus reflection and refraction.[44]

In the early church a rainbow was "but a manifestation of divine light reflecting the glory of Christ and seen particularly in holy visions, a further indication of the unworldly nature of these rainbows".[48]

rainbow, *n* (before twelfth century) 3) [fr. the impossibility of reaching the rainbow, at whose foot a pot of gold is supposed to be buried]: an illusory goal or hope.

rainbow, *adj* (1652). 1: Having many colors. 2: of, relating to, or being people of different races or cultural backgrounds.[49]

Nature, in all the varied aspects of her beauty, exhibits no feature more lovely nor any that awaken a more soothing reflection than the Rainbow.

John Constable[52]

Conventionally there are six colours of a rainbow; from the outside to the inside, red, orange, yellow, green, blue and violet. However, colorimetric analysis can identify 3,300 different colours in a rainbow and it is possible to argue that in fact the number of colours is infinite.[53]

I do set my bow in the cloud, and it shall be for a token of a covenant between me and the earth.

Yahweh[54]

But why should not the glorious rainbow be included among the gods? It is beautiful enough, and its marvellous loveliness has given rise to the legend that Iris [the goddess associated with the rainbow] is the daughter of Thaumas, the Greek god of wonder.

Cicero[46]

There was an awful rainbow once in heaven:
We knew her woof, her texture: she is given
In the dull catalogue of things.
Philosophy will clip an Angel's wings,
Conquer all mysteries by rule and line,
Empty the hunted air, and gnomed mine –
Unweave a rainbow.

John Keats[50]

An association of the rainbow with a serpent is found in many folklores, including those of the Australian Aborigines, the Igbo of Nigeria and the Toba Indians of the Argentine Chaco. The Estonian rainbow serpent sucks up water from rivers, seas and lakes and sprinkles it back to earth as rain. [51]

"The rainbow is the combination of yin and yang", the complementary female and male opposites contained in all life. From the Chinese I Ching, 12th century BC. Hungarian folklore tells how anyone who passes through a rainbow will change sex.[55]

Somewhere Over the Rainbow[45]

Somewhere over the rainbow
Way up high,
There's a land that I heard of
Once in a lullaby.

My heart leaps up when I behold
A Rainbow in the sky:
So was it when my life began;
So is it now I am a man;
So be it when I shall grow old,
Or let me die!

William Wordsworth[47]

The rainbow: questions for discussion

- What issues of knowledge arise from the rainbow in the sky?
- How many colours does a rainbow have? What knowledge issues regarding sense perception does this question raise?
- Distinguish what one can say with certainty about rainbows in general and one rainbow in particular. Is it possible to have certainty about a class of objects but to be able to say nothing of certainty about a member of that class?
- It is possible to describe a rainbow in factual terms. But can you see one without an emotional response? Are reason and emotion inextricably linked in response to perception?
- Do you support Keats' view that philosophy (by which he means scientific/mathematical understanding) conquers "all mysteries"? Has the development of science destroyed our awe of nature?
- What might the artist John Constable mean when he says that a rainbow is soothing?
- The Babylonian astronomers related a bright rainbow to the defeat of a Babylonian army. What knowledge issues of associating cause and effect does this example raise?
- Which is more real—the rainbow or what it represents? Can you think of other things for which their symbolic meaning may be more gripping to our minds than the things themselves?
- Is the natural beauty of a rainbow of a different kind from beauty in art?
- Do you have any personal associations with rainbows that you would be prepared to share with the rest of your class? Do you think these personal associations change your *knowledge* of a rainbow?
- If you can find the music for "Somewhere Over the Rainbow", play it in class. In the song, what feelings are associated with the rainbow? Do the song and the quotations here affect your feelings about rainbows? Do they affect your *knowledge* of a rainbow?
- Some of these statements about rainbows reflect the observer's religious and cultural beliefs. Why might we view rainbows differently from the way they were observed one, two or more thousand years ago? Do we *know* what a rainbow is in a fuller sense than we once did?

The ichthyologist[41]

Let us suppose that an ichthyologist is exploring the life of the ocean. He casts a net into the water and brings us a fishy assortment. Looking at his catch he proceeds to generalize and arrives at these two propositions:

- No sea creature is less than 2 inches long.
- All sea creatures have gills.

These are both true of his catch, and he assumes tentatively that they will remain true however often he repeats it.

An onlooker may object that the first generalization is wrong. "There are plenty of sea creatures under 2 inches long, only your net is not adapted to catch them."

The ichthyologist dismisses the objection contemptuously.

In applying this analogy, the catch stands for the body of knowledge which constitutes physical science, and the net for the sensory and intellectual equipment which we use in obtaining it. The casting of the net corresponds to observation, for knowledge which has not been or could not be obtained by observation is not allowed in physical science.

"Anything uncatchable by my net is *ipso facto* outside the scope of ichthyological knowledge, and is not part of the kingdom of fishes which has been defined as the theme of my knowledge. In short, what my net cannot catch is not fish."

Sir Arthur Eddington[41]

Some questions for reflection

1. What ways of knowing does the ichthyologist use in this story? In what ways?
2. What comment is Sir Arthur Eddington making on the natural sciences through this analogy? In what ways do you consider his analogy to be appropriate? In what ways is it limited?
3. To what extent does the analogy also apply to the human sciences and history?
4. Would you apply the analogy, either as it stands or in a modified version you propose, to any of mathematics, the arts, or ethics?

The arts

Can you hear the sound of music and laughter? There—in the centre of the village, the women sway and shift their feet in unison while a ring of villagers clap rhythmically and cheer them on. Someone bursts into song and others take up the chorus. The scene fades.

Over there—a different scene. People chat as they approach a house of worship, decorated to lift the mind beyond the material world. Is the decoration carved figures or is it abstract tile patterns? It's hard to make out as the scene fades.

A third scene. On a platform, a man raises his voice in anger to a younger man, who hurls back his defiance, whirls about, and strides away…to step behind a hanging curtain. People gathered watch raptly, caught up in the story the two actors are playing.

How can all three of these scenes represent the arts? How can forms as various as music, dance, sculpture, tile work, and theatre all cluster together into a single category? How can they be joined by opera, photography, novels, poetry, painting, film, and architecture? Is there room for flower arranging, calligraphy, pottery, weaving, and silverworking?

The sheer variability of the arts challenges their classification together. Indeed, not all languages, even those with a flourishing tradition of music, dance, and the visual arts, have the generic word "arts" to contain them all. Even in those languages where the word has long indicated a conceptual category, the territory has borders much less guarded than those of mathematics or the sciences as new forms question the membership criteria and demand to be let in. Yet, despite the looseness of the category of the "arts" and the immense variability within it, they are held together by family resemblances.

As we enter this family of the arts, critical thinking demands that we neither be swept along unthinkingly into its pleasures, nor summarily reject it as knowledge according to the criteria of another area. It demands that we be aware of what the arts try to do, how they do it, and how they affect what we know.

More than any other field, though, the arts may foster a resistance to critical analysis—perhaps because the creator and the critic in this area are not necessarily using criteria of judgment universally accepted within their knowledge community, or perhaps because the experience of creating and enjoying the arts can be so personal and emotional. Even those who expect close scrutiny to be given to works of science have been heard to protest, "I just know whether I like it, and that's enough. Why do we have to tear it apart?" As we move to thinking about the arts, we will try to use critical thinking just as we would in any other area of knowledge, not destructively but respectfully. Being appropriately critical is a way of being appreciative of the knowledge of any area.

Nathan Bowman, Kentucky, USA

The banjo is the most obnoxious instrument in the world. It's loud and twangy and addictive. You just can't quit playing.

I grew up playing traditional blue grass with my whole family, including all my cousins, with all of us playing several instruments. The banjo is my eleventh instrument. For me, music is like another language. I can't legitimately claim to be bilingual, or to be fluent in music, but that's how I think of it.

I don't play because I want to express things. I don't play my angst out into my songs! But I can get lost sometimes and realize that four or five hours have passed on the clock and I have holes in my fingers. I have to consciously limit myself to an hour and a half a day.

Arts from the perspective of the creator

We enter the arts through your own personal experience. In the IB, you are asked to develop your creativity within CAS and also given the opportunity in group 6 subjects to develop your practice of an art. Outside the IB, you might play in a band, dance, write creatively, or engage in any of the other arts.

Would you be willing to share with others in your class a sample of what you do, and talk about it with them? Ideally, several volunteers from your class will bring their paintings or poetry, for example, or an instrument to play. If you do not feel comfortable sharing samples, feel free in any case to join in discussion about what actually doing an art means to you.

The following questions can be useful in guiding discussion.

- What motivates you to do it?
- What do you get out of it?
- What knowledge do you need to do this art form?
- For you, is your art a way of communicating with others?
- Do you think someone from a different culture or another epoch would understand any communication from your art?
- What do you come to know through doing your art—perhaps information but perhaps also something about yourself or others?

> " *Despite many ardent attempts to be anything but a musician, I finally gave in to this deepest of desires. As a teacher (and as a student, which I still am) I am forever struck by what it means to 'find your own voice'. More than anything else, even more than my passion for the music itself, it is this metaphor which motivates me in my work.* "
>
> Douglas Millar, IB graduate 1987. Operatic bass-baritone, music teacher[56]

Mona Aditya, Nepal

My dance talks about the ironies of life so it's a bit sad, but the rhythm makes me jump and keeps me happy. I have to balance between the rhythm and the meaning.

The gestures and steps have meaning. Some of the steps are obvious, but others are more like a non-verbal language. Since the language is not known to people in Canada where I'm now studying, I try to make my movements very clear. In the dance I put on a bindi to be beautiful as I do make-up in the mirror, but the dance says that life is as fragile as the image on the mirror.

I can't say that the dance represents Nepal because we are so diverse, with 70 dialects and 36 ethnicities.

But it reflects a part of Nepal. Dances are an important part of our culture. We learn them originally in school and put on performances on occasions such as Parents' Day.

The arts and ways of knowing

As we play music, dance, or paint, we are not confined to that part of ourselves that favours the logical and explicit. We may tap into all forms of knowledge (see page 95) and draw on all of our ways of knowing without exclusion. The arts embrace our sense perceptions and our feelings, our thoughts and our critical perspectives. They reflect worldviews and feelings —and also create them.

In creating feelings and beliefs, the arts certainly do not avoid making knowledge claims—and they can make them powerfully. In literature, writers often treat social or political issues, for example, with a goal of revealing problems or arguing for solutions. The means is fiction but the goal is a claim: "This is how it is" and "This is what is wrong with it." They can also convey such a convincing sense of human psychology in fictional characters—in action, in speech, in reflection—that we, too, may be inclined to declare: "This is how people are." The arts make not only *observational* claims such as these, but metaphysical ones as well. Religious paintings, for example, represent key moments of the life of a god or a vision of an afterlife: churches throughout Europe show again and again the crucifixion and resurrection of Jesus Christ to testify both "This is what happened" and "This is its significance." And, certainly, the arts also make *value judgments*: apartheid is unjust; the proletariat are glorious in their work; the coronation is triumphant. All of these kinds of knowledge claims within the arts can be articulated, such as those made through character debate or the author's voice in a novel, or, as in art forms that use no language, they can be implied and often ambiguous.

Both explicit statements and ambiguous suggestions, though, can affect our attitudes and values with persuasive power. The arts are capable of stirring deeply both our senses and our feelings. A photograph of a lone child in a war zone, a song of aching love, a painting of serene nature—all of these can touch our feelings, stimulate associations of thought, and even after we do not consciously remember them may continue to influence how we think and feel about what they have shown us. It is not surprising that the arts have often been enlisted in the service of propaganda in an attempt to bypass rational and critical thinking. Neither is it surprising, in traditions of thought which treat emotion as suspicious at best, that the arts have often been marginalized as knowledge.

For an understanding of the arts as an area of knowledge, however, it is necessary to put aside such suspicions in order to recognize the complementary nature of reasoning and emotion. To understand the experience of the arts demands some detachment from our experiences of works of art in order to study or analyse them—to *describe* common features from which generalizations can be drawn and to *explain* the interactions between artists, their works, their knowledge community, and the context of society and the natural world within which the interactions are embedded. Regardless of the immense variability within the arts, reasoning can help us recognize broad patterns and the place of the arts in our knowledge.

> " *The music and literature courses, the fine arts events, the choir and the numerous shows all had a very strong impact on me. They made me realize how much music was the true centre of my life and could become my personal contribution to the world. My dreams of making a better world could this way be fulfilled by composing the best music I can.* "
> Martin Laliberté, IB graduate 1982. Composer, music professor[57]

> " *My exposure to the concepts of the international understanding, service to the community and social justice have definitely affected my musical and personal life in a positive way. I have consciously and lovingly opened myself up to music and cultures of the world, playing Salsa, African, Klezmer, Reggae, Blues, Jazz, Funk and many other styles of music with equal love and respect. I always have time to do benefits for worthy causes, and often bring my saxophone to anti-war rallies and peace marches.* "
> Richard Underhill, IB graduate 1980. Composer, saxophonist[58]

But so, too, might sense appeal and emotion. Being moved by music or responding with imaginative identification to characters in literature can create a sometimes startling awareness of common humanity—of sharing our experience as human beings. In a way which is utterly personal and which lends itself to no kind of totally rational test, through the arts we may feel our own lives in the lives of others—and recognize human experience that just might be "true for all".

Follow-up question

Reference is made above to trying to study or analyse the arts. What would be the relevance of the following in such study: biology, psychology, cultural anthropology, and history? Give examples. Are there other subject areas that you think also contribute to understanding the arts?

Knowing the arts from the perspective of the audience

If you participate in the arts, you probably find yourself drawing on your own feelings, thoughts, personal taste, training, cultural background, and so forth as you create or perform. If you *evaluate* what you have done, you will be trying to take a different perspective—trying to see your work as someone else (or several different people) would see it and trying to put your own performance in context of expectations of form, technique, or expression. The outside critical perspective, difficult though it may be to achieve, can be illuminating and possibly influential for your continuing work.

As the *audience* of the arts, you may be interested solely in having your own personal response, without ever trying to take an outside perspective on it—as is frequently the case if you like or dislike a song, for example, and feel no pressure to analyse your own responses or justify them to anyone. Why should you? It can be one of the great pleasures of the arts that you are able simply to enjoy them or to be affected, whether positively or negatively, and not have to explain.

If, however, you wish to gain a greater understanding of your experience, you will try to see yourself and the artwork from an outside perspective, one that may reveal features of the artwork itself, of yourself, and of the context in which your experience is set. Becoming critically aware in the arts, just as in other areas of knowledge, involves some consideration of how the area works.

In the next activity, you will be asked to look at artworks selected in large part for their variety. As you examine and learn about them, you will also be asked to stay aware of your own reactions and whether they change as you learn more. When the four steps in the activity are complete, you and your class will be better prepared for class discussions that follow. May the process be a pleasure!

Activity on arts from around the world

Divide into teams, one for each of the six artworks pictured here. Try to choose the one least familiar to you. Your goal initially will be to find out about it, share the information you have gained with the

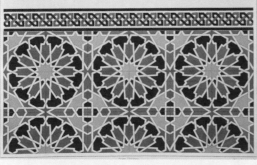

209

rest of your class, and stay aware of how growing knowledge may affect your response.

Step 1: Before you begin to talk with your team, write down your own immediate reaction to the work you will examine. What is your understanding of what it represents? What do you like or dislike about it?

Step 2: Get together with your team and discuss your reactions. Do other people's thoughts change the way you respond to the artwork yourself?

Step 3: As a team, find out as much about the artwork as you possibly can in the time you have. Prepare yourselves to give a short report to the rest of the class, making sure that you deal as fully as possible with the following questions. You may find that not all the questions readily apply to your particular work.

> You will be able to find information on the Internet. However, for one or two images you may not find the exact one given here and should direct your investigation toward the generic form and what it represents.
>
> Simone Martini, *The Annunciation*. Christian, Italy
>
> *Vishnu and Lakshmi, with conch and lotus*. Hindu, India
>
> Bill Reid, *The Jade Canoe "The Spirit of Haida Gwaii"*. Haida, Canada
>
> Picasso, *Guernica*. Spain
>
> Tiles, arabesque pattern, Mosque of Cheykhoun. Islamic art, Egypt
>
> Terracotta Warriors of the Emperor Qin. China

a Who was/were the artist(s)? Can you find any information on what motivated them, and within what circumstances they were working? If there is no apparent artist whose name you can find out, why not?

b Who was or is the audience? What role might the artwork perform in their lives? Can you find out anything about audience reaction to it at the time it was done? Can you find out what reactions are to it today?

c What is the meaning of your artwork within its cultural background? In trying to answer this broad question, consider the relationship between the image and relevant cultural stories, cultural practices, or historical events. Try to find out about any symbolism.

d Look at the work itself. How are the shapes balanced structurally, for example, or space handled? Do you find it pleasing? Is there any special significance associated with its form?

e Do you consider this work to be a work of art? Why or why not?

Step 4: Return to your full class group. As each team gives a report on its particular artwork, compare your answers to the questions above and your responses to the works.

Activity follow-up discussion 1

What is the role of the arts in our lives?

Appoint a scribe to take notes on the various ideas that teams raise and to ensure that everyone gets a copy. You will need these notes later. As you try to identify what the arts do in our lives, keep in mind all the artworks you have just examined and make sure that their apparent roles are reflected in your notes. Feel free, however, to think beyond these six examples.

Creation and criticism

In examining works of art, learning about them, and commenting on what they do, you have taken a major step toward developing critical perspectives. You have already, as well, recognized the variability in their goals and the cultural contexts that make their works meaningful. Our knowledge creation diagram frames once again a set of dynamics between its component parts and invites comparisons between the arts and other areas of knowledge.

Overview questions for comparison

To what extent do all the knowledge creators and members of the knowledge community share the same criteria for evaluating the work of art? What other areas of knowledge do the arts most resemble—and most contrast with—in this regard?

To what extent is the social context—the political and economic organization, the history, the cultural practices, for example—something to be overcome and effaced in the creation of knowledge in the arts? What other areas of knowledge do the arts most resemble—and most contrast with—in this regard?

In what ways do creators in the arts build on each other's work? In the relationship of new works to previous works, to what extent do the arts resemble other areas of knowledge? What other areas do they most resemble—and most contrast with—in this regard?

What knowledge precedes judgment?

In the knowledge creation diagram, the knowledge community of the arts includes peers, critics, and the general public. In the arts, as in other areas, creators may often become critics, and peers may often evaluate each other's work. More than in other areas, however, the role of the creator and the role of the critic may be taken by different people. And more than in other areas, too, are you, as a member of the general public, involved in the role of critic. This involvement highlights an issue of knowledge relevant to all areas. To what extent is it important to have knowledge of the works of an area before you can expect to judge them? What and whose judgments should be taken seriously?

In other areas, the need for specialized knowledge before evaluating works is evident: the works may be incomprehensible to those who are not creators or peers within that particular field. The general

Knowledge Creation Diagram

within context of the natural world

knowledge creator(s)

work(s) of knowledge
(math proof, research paper, novel)

knowledge community
(peers, critics general public)

within social context

public is involved in evaluation of the natural sciences, for example, not in judging whether a specialized research paper contributes effectively to its field but in judging, within the social context, the broad direction of the natural sciences and the ways in which the knowledge should be used. Moreover, although opinions on the direction of the natural sciences may abound, those which are informed by an understanding of the area are taken, it seems, more seriously. As members of the general public, we listen to those speakers, panellists, columnists, writers, and so forth who seem to us to understand the implications of the research. Or so a critical thinker might hope.

Is specialized knowledge similarly essential in judgments placed on works of art? Is it important to critical thinkers to have informed voices of critics interpreting for us the significance of works and their implications for, say, the direction of the area of knowledge and its impact on us?

As you have probably seen in examining the six quite various works, background knowledge does increase understanding and (depending on how that knowledge affected you) probably also interest and pleasure. As we can recall from discussions of the human sciences, there is a difference between an outside perspective and an inside one; the meaning of an action or an artwork for its own creator or context is different from its meaning for someone unfamiliar with either.

Activity follow-up discussion 2

What knowledge should precede judgment?

Consider the following two arguments:

- *Surely,* a response that is based on some understanding of the meaning of a work within its context—the context of the culture and the context of expectations of that particular form of art—is a fuller response, and an informed judgment more worthy of being taken seriously.
- *Surely,* on the other hand, one of the characteristics of the arts is that they are able to make us respond and understand even if the particular art form is unfamiliar or if we know very little indeed about its context.

Read the two countering arguments raised above and consider your own expectations of knowledge and judgment. With the six works you investigated in mind, respond to the following questions and exchange your views with your classmates.

To what extent is it important to have knowledge of works of art—their cultural context and the expectations of the particular art form—before you can expect to judge them? What and whose judgments should be taken seriously? Does your answer change depending on whether you are thinking of painting, music, or literature?

If works of art can be understood without critical explanation, why is that? Does understanding without explanation characterize some kinds of knowledge?

As you formulate your own thoughts on these questions, try to apply them beyond the arts to the other areas of knowledge that we have also discussed.

Taking critical perspectives

With questions of how we respond to the arts and evaluate them still lingering in your mind, consider your own thoughts, which you discussed earlier, on the roles of the arts.

Activity follow-up discussion 3

First, find the notes taken by your scribe in follow-up discussion 1 on the purposes of the arts and their roles in our lives. Try to associate each of the ideas suggested with some part of the knowledge creation diagram.

If you said that art gives a representation of important cultural stories, for example, that statement is relevant to a work's social context. If you said that art expresses the emotions or the beliefs of the artist, to what part of the diagram is that statement most relevant? Did you suggest that the arts please our senses or intrigue our minds, or entertain us, or provide social and historical records, or bind us together in social identities, or teach us our culture, or give us a picture we should face of the problems of our societies, or give us works of beauty, or…? As in other areas of knowledge we have treated previously, you may find that the diagram is useful for clarifying ideas, but at the same time freezes, as if separate, components constantly in dynamic interaction.

In associating your own reflections on the role of the arts within this framework you are placing your ideas within major perspectives on the arts. These perspectives do not exclude each other and, although each provides criteria for evaluation that are unlike those of the other perspectives, one cannot demonstrate another to be false. Although artists and critics themselves often argue for one perspective over another, as we look at the world's art over centuries, we realize that each is rather like a spotlight illuminating a somewhat different part of the whole.

As you read about each of the following critical perspectives, consider the extent to which it resembles your own. Feel free to disagree—and argue for your own point of view.

1 Do you evaluate the artwork with emphasis on the artist?
(Critical attention focuses on the biography of the artist, the artist's intentions and the creative process, and the expressive quality of the work.)

Some critics emphasize the artist's role—the mysterious creativity that energizes the arts, the inspiration and intentions of the artist at work, and the frustrations, pleasures, and growth of the process. This perspective highlights the expressive role of arts for the creator.

From this perspective, some critics further argue that the essential criterion for a work to be considered "art" is that the creator must have intended it to be so. The implications of this particular argument are that we cannot be sure that a work is "art" unless we are sure of the artist's intentions. A further implication is that creative products made with a practical or social purpose, or those of cultures with no general concept of art, are eliminated because their creators did not have the intention of creating art.

From this perspective, which of the six works of art from your earlier activity would be disqualified as art? Which would be most strongly affirmed to be art?

2 Do you evaluate the artwork with emphasis on the artwork itself?

(Critical attention focuses on the formal features of the work, its composition and technique.)

Some critics stress above all the work of art itself—the text of the poem on the page, the arrangement and quality of sounds in music, the movements in space of a dance. Many critics argue that aesthetic form is the essential criterion for a work to be art. It must be beautiful.

Whether it treats ugly or troubling subject matter, as do many works of literature, film, and painting, is irrelevant to its aesthetic appeal. A work is aesthetically beautiful if it is beautifully composed and has mastery of technique. *Guernica*, for example, with its grotesque and distorted figures, possesses a composition that holds the tormented individual images in balance. Notice the strong sense of form and pattern that underlies the work, and the balance of light and dark.

The aesthetic approach to the arts is often held to be contrary to any that involve the emotions, as a formal response is described as contemplative, even rational. It is a recognition of pure pattern. If you did the exercise on mathematics and music (see page 138), you will recall the use of mathematics as an ideal language of pattern with which to do compositional analysis. Interestingly, in works that people find aesthetically pleasing, certain mathematical ratios recur, for example the proportions called the golden ratio or the golden section.

You are not unfamiliar with this criterion at work. In your IB literature course, the commentary portion stresses (along with features that fit other perspectives here) the formal aspects of text— the "shape" of the work, and the way technical devices, handled skilfully, create their meaning and their effect.

From this perspective, is any of the six works from your activity disqualified as art? Is any, in your view, strongly affirmed as art?

3   Do you evaluate the artwork with emphasis on the
      knowledge community (peers, critics, general public)?
      *(Critical attention focuses on the effect the work of art has on
       the audience.)*

Many critics argue that the intention of an artist is irrelevant to evaluating an artwork, and that what is of primary or even exclusive importance is the impact the work has upon its audience—the peers affected in their own work, the public moved to rapture or extreme annoyance. Some critics argue that art exists only within this response.

This perspective highlights, for example, the way a piece of music may make people sing along with pleasure, or the way its experimental features may challenge an audience to join the adventure into new territory. It brings attention to the impact of social criticism or satire, the popularity of certain forms, and the continued popularity of many works which pass the "test of time" and continue to "speak" to people long after their creator has gone. It is also the perspective that most emphasizes ethical issues over what should or should not be treated in art, and how.

From this perspective, is any of the six works from your activity disqualified as art? Is any, in your view, strongly affirmed as art?

4/5 Do you evaluate the artwork with emphasis on the context
     of the natural world or society?
     *(Critical attention focuses on the effectiveness of the work in
      representing its context, and its role as a social and historical
      document or artefact.)*

Many critics give attention above all to the way the arts can give a vivid portrayal of the world. Literature, for example, may reflect keenly observed details of psychological and social interactions or depict our societies with all their flaws and glories. Painting may catch light as it plays across water or a woman's face, or pick out revealing moments of our societies in action. It is from this perspective, in combination with that of the reaction of the reader or audience, that we most recognize the capacity of the arts to take us imaginatively into the lives of other individuals and other societies.

Moreover, the artwork can, in capturing a record of people, places, and times, provide a kind of evidence of their tastes, values, and experiences.

You are not unfamiliar with this criterion at work. In your language A1 course, the works you read take you into the lives of people and societies, some of them crossing cultures in the process.

From this perspective, is any of the six works from your class activity disqualified as art? Is any, in your view, strongly affirmed as art?

What does "theory" mean in literature?

Becky Halvorson, IB graduate 1986

Becky Halvorson has a BA and MA in English Literature. She has taught English at university level at Capilano College in Vancouver, Canada and has taught IB English and Theory of Knowledge in IB schools in India, USA, and Canada.

Theories in science often compete in their attempts to explain the natural world, with old theories replaced by new ones that seem to explain better. How does theory function in a field like literature?

I'll answer with respect to the field of English literature and language studies, though many of its theoretical perspectives have been imported from other languages. The study of English literature in the 21st century supports many theoretical perspectives at the same time. These different approaches can interact with one another in collaboration or opposition in order to illuminate the effects of one approach on the other. Frequently an intact theoretical approach is applied to a literary text, such as a feminist reading of *Hamlet*. Sometimes in literary studies, though, the development of the theory itself is the main focus, with literature providing examples to illustrate abstract theoretical points about how language works, such as in deconstruction. Theories thus evolve and increase our insight into various relationships between language and literature.

Do any theories in literature remain unchanged over time?

The classic of literary studies is ironically called New Criticism, dating from the 1920s, which is so timeless and pervasive that it can be mistaken as the only theoretical approach to literature. It avoids any political, social, cultural, and historical context, and instead consists of close reading of literary devices ostensibly to reveal the work's objective meaning and our common humanity. The close reading techniques of New Criticism remain popular and valuable in literary studies.

What are some of the other theoretical approaches?

Other fields of literary criticism are also concerned with literature's context, and therefore ask fundamental questions similar to those of other subject areas. For example, when we read a poem, novel, short story, or play, we read not only the words on the page, but also infer the assumptions and values in it. Deconstruction exposes the implications of oppositions, and of what is included and excluded from a text, by examining how language itself constructs values. Biographical and psychoanalytic critical approaches are especially interested in the assumptions and values of the text's author, and we consider the same questions of ourselves as readers when we employ reader response criticism. We pay attention to the wider context of the writer and his or her work in New Historicism and cultural studies, with focus on social class in a Marxist approach, gender in feminism, and sexual orientation in queer theory. Postcolonial theory combines many of these perspectives, with a particular interest in race and culture in relation to colonization. These approaches encourage us to understand the climate that preserved that piece of literature for us to read today. As a result, we may realize the importance of literary studies not only as a source of aesthetic approaches to knowing, but also as a study of how literature reveals—and in fact contributes to—knowledge as a form of power in a society.

Question for discussion

In this interview, Becky Halvorson uses "theory" in the way it is used within the field of critical studies. In this TOK book, though, the word "theory" is replaced with the word "perspective" or "argument" in considering the arts. In what ways do you consider the perspectives of the arts, regardless of what name we give them, to be similar to theories in the sciences? In what ways are they different?

Expanding TOK reflection on the arts

In TOK essays on the arts, students commonly make only two comments—that they express the emotions of the artist and that they must be beautiful (with beauty being in the eye of the beholder). They tend to use as their examples only paintings of 20th century Europe. May this generalization quickly be falsified!

Parades, Parades

There's the wide desert, but no one marches
except in the pads of old caravans,
there is the ocean, but the keels incise
the precise, old parallels,
there's the blue sea above the mountains
but they scratch the same lines
in the jet trails—
so the politicians plod
without imagination, circling
the same sombre garden
with its fountain dry in the forecourt,
the gri-gri palms desiccating
dung pods like goats,
the same lines rule the White Papers,
the same steps ascend Whitehall,
and only the name of the fool changes
under the plumed white cork-hat
for the Independence Parades,
revolving around, in calypso,
to the brazen joy of the tubas.

Why are the eyes of the beautiful
and unmarked children
in the uniforms of the country
bewildered and shy,
why do they widen in terror
of the pride drummed into their minds?
Were they truer, the old songs,
when the law lived far away,
when the veiled queen, her girth
as comfortable as cushions,
upheld the orb with its stern admonitions?
We wait for the changing of statues,
for the change of parades.

Here he comes now, here he comes!
Papa! Papa! With his crowd,
the sleek, waddling seals of his Cabinet,
trundling up to the dais,
as the wind puts its tail between
the cleft of the mountain, and a wave
coughs once, abruptly.
Who will name this silence
respect? Those forced, hoarse hosannas
awe? That tin-ringing tune
from the pumping, circling horns
the New World? Find a name
for that look on the faces
of the electorate. Tell me
how it all happened, and why
I said nothing.

Derek Walcott

Show now a broader understanding of perspectives on the arts as you consider this poem written by Derek Walcott, from St. Lucia in the Caribbean, who won the Nobel Prize for Literature in 1992.

1   How does Walcott express his emotions? Now go further. Does the poem seem written to express the author's personal feelings *for his own sake*, while we as readers eavesdrop, or does it seem

that the personal voice is used as a *strategy* to reach and provoke others?

2   Is the poem beautiful? No. Let us, going further, rephrase the question to stress *aesthetic beauty* of form. Is the poem effectively shaped in its overall structure and technically adept in its use of language and poetic devices?

Now add the following questions.

3   In what ways does the poem comment on the society in which it is written, and stand as a social document itself? What is Walcott saying about the transfer of power in a former colony which has gained its independence? If you were interested above all in post-colonial issues, what might you say about it?

4   Do you *believe* the poet, and accept him as an authority on problems in the Caribbean? Are you inclined, when an author presents a point of view personally and vividly, to accept the point of view presented? If so, you might wish to reflect on the persuasive power of literature.

5   Look back now in addition to the other two poems to which you have been introduced in this book, "Sunlight on the Garden" by Louis MacNeice (see page 40) and "Grief" by Denise Levertov (see page 61). Although all three deal with very particular experiences and are quite obviously subjective, do they give or imply any general understanding relevant to broader experience?

Choreographer, dancer, and critic: roles in the arts

Fearghus O'Conchuir, IB graduate 1988

Having completed degrees in English and in European Literature at Magdalen College, Oxford, Fearghus O'Conchuir trained as a dancer and choreographer at London Contemporary Dance School. He has since performed internationally with companies including Adventures in Motion Pictures and Arc Dance Company. In 2001, he set up his own company, Corp Feasa and has made work for it that has been shown in Ireland and abroad. In 2005, he became Ireland Fellow on the Clore Leadership Programme.

As a choreographer, what are your main goals as you compose or design a dance? Is a dance in any way a statement or expression of knowledge?

Dance is a body of knowledge, an exploration of the knowledge within and between our bodies. When we learn a new language, when we learn to play an instrument, when we learn to love, our bodies grow and change: neural pathways are extended, specific co-ordinations of muscle-strength and flexibility are established and the physical sensations of a particular emotion are stored. The processes are not secondary to knowledge acquisition; they are the process of learning. However, many people are oblivious to this physical aspect of knowledge. In a western culture in which a strand of religious thinking regards the body as animal and reprehensibly distanced from the divine, and in which a Cartesian separation of mind and body privileges mind as the site of selfhood and consciousness, the ignorance of body knowledge is as unsurprising as it is unhelpful.

In choreographing I am trying to understand, express and extend the knowledge in my body and in the bodies of the dancers with whom I collaborate. When I share my work with an audience, I want to model for them the possibility of growth and understanding which they may not have experienced. Such growth is a moral imperative for me. If Socrates says that the unexamined life is not worth living, I suggest that the examination should start in our mindful bodies, in our embodied minds. Dance, among a range of mind and body practices such as yoga or tai chi, provides me with a framework for that study.

As both a dancer and a choreographer, you practise, in a sense, two different art forms. What, for you, is the relationship between the two?

There are similarities in the relationship between the composer and the musician and that between the choreographer and dancer. The composer decides what notes go where but when s/he writes a symphony s/he is not in a position to deliver all the notes. The distinction is usually drawn between the composer/choreographer as a creative artist and the musician/dancer as an interpretive artist. In much current choreographic practice, however, the dancer is expected to have a great deal of creative input, contributing movement ideas that a choreographer uses and shapes. Unlike the composer who may compose complex scores in the privacy of his or her room before ever encountering the musicians who will deliver the work, choreography takes place most often in a studio, evolving over time in relationship with the dancers who will perform the work. In these situations the dancers are more than interpreters of the work, they can be creative partners too. This creative contribution can be overlooked, however, because of the circumstantial power-differential which often exists between those titled "choreographer" and those called "dancers".

When I choreograph, I take responsibility for the work and by doing so hope to facilitate the free and creative exploration of the dancers. In my case, the environment I create and the atmosphere I foster is my greatest contribution to the choreographic process. The rest is open to chance, to discovery, to the inspiration of others. Instead of fleshing out something I already know, this is the way I learn something new.

I have danced for other choreographers and choreographed often for other performers, but at the moment I derive greatest satisfaction from performing my own work. This is not the case for many choreographers, some of whom would argue that it is impossible to consider how a work is taking shape, how it looks when one is inside it. But for me there are a number of reasons for wanting to be inside the performance, even if I use video technology in the choreographic process to allow me to see and shape the work from the outside: if I expect an audience to learn something from my work, in particular if I want them to better comprehend a way of being, I think it is my responsibility to face that challenge myself, to lead by example. I also want to be a direct part of the encounter with an audience, not simply authoring the work and abandoning it but learning from experience how an audience reacts to what I have made. The challenge to grow is two-way. It's a demand I make of myself as much as it is an invitation to the audience.

What do you see as the relationship between the dance creator and the dance critic? Do they have to possess different kinds of knowledge?

I think I've always wanted to be an artist or whatever I understood an artist to be, but it took me a while to find that dance could provide me with a form for artistic investigation and expression. I studied literature at university, was good at words and thought writing might be my art form. However, whenever I tried to write, I felt hampered by my critical knowledge. I was aware of my shortcomings, aware of how derivative my "voice" was. Later, when I began choreographing, I had no such direct critical knowledge and felt free to acknowledge the validity of the movement that came from me. Of course, the movement was derivative, unconsciously influenced by a lifetime of exposure to a variety of physicalities (Ukrainian dance, MGM musicals, sports, kayaking). Of course, I wasn't entirely without critical knowledge either, since the years of studying literature taught me many ideas about aesthetics, about form and structure, which I could apply indirectly to my new art form. The prerequisite for my creative process, however, is that critical knowledge doesn't precede and consequently dampen the creative spark that I need to ignite my work. Once that spark has been allowed to express itself, once it is outside of me and I can observe it, then all my critical and analytical faculties can kick in. The artist needs to be creator and first critic of his/her work; but without the moment of creativity, the critic's work cannot begin.

In general, what do you consider the relationship to be between the creator and the critic? What is the role of critical theory in an understanding of the arts?

The burgeoning of critical theories (psychoanalytical, feminist, new-historicist, post-colonial, queer, deconstructive, Marxist etc.) has provided new ways of reading and seeing and in doing so has altered how we experience the world. These ways of seeing seek to replace existing filters on our perception that have become so familiar as to be invisible. However, these radical theories very quickly become new orthodoxy. The danger with orthodoxies is that in allowing us to see some stories, they are blind to others. The artist's job is to keep exploring and expressing the widest range and deepest extent of stories possible. Attentive, informed and adventurous theory can help those stories be perceived; theory that has atrophied into dogma can hide them. But the stories exist in the art, waiting to be acknowledged.

Questions for discussion

1 In what ways is the "body knowledge" of which Fearghus O'Conchuir speaks related to the three forms of knowing identified in this book: knowing by experience, knowing how, and knowing that? Is it a blend of these, or is it something else entirely and largely neglected in this book?

2 Fearghus likens the choreographer to the composer. Are there other art forms in which this distinction between composer and performer is also relevant? What, do you think, is the difference in the kind of knowledge that each role demands?

3 On the basis of this interview, what ways of knowing would you say are involved in dance? What would you add from your own experience?

4 Fearghus speaks of wanting the audience to learn through his dance, but also growing himself in his relationship with the audience. What do you think you yourself learn from watching dance performance, theatre, live music, or any other form of performance arts?

What is *good* art?

The arts, clearly, can be appreciated from many perspectives. How, though, do we evaluate the quality of a work? The arts frequently make their own value judgments on human attitudes and actions. What value judgments do we now place on works of art? What makes a work of art *good*?

Various answers lie in various critical perspectives, in effective fulfillment of the expectations of each position. What, do you think, would make a work of art excellent for each?

- from a perspective that stresses the creator and the creative process?
- from a perspective that stresses aesthetic form?
- from a perspective that stresses the effect on the audience?
- from perspectives that stress the contexts of the natural world and society?

Moreover, of all of these perspectives, which is the most important? Perhaps, in response, we might think about the role of criticism in different areas of knowledge. In some areas, the role of criticism is to scrutinize a work closely to ensure that it meets the criteria of evaluation established and held in common by the creators of knowledge and their entire knowledge community. Criticism used in this way is essential to the creation of their knowledge.

In the arts the role of criticism is also to look closely at a work—but there is not a single set of criteria for judgment, nor need there be. A work of atonal music does not logically contradict a classical symphony, nor does a Cossack dance falsify ballet; two novels giving opposing depictions of the same society do not violate the coherence test for truth. And we do not add up the landscape paintings of the world and average them to find a general view. The arts give innumerable particular views and can simultaneously accept works quite unlike each other.

That does not mean that criticism is free of debate over criteria of judgment: musicians, writers, and others often disagree heatedly, and often clash with their traditions. The contemporary standards of judgment may reject works of art as pseudo-art, but it is the standards themselves that may be forced to yield. In the arts, knowledge is first the creation of the artist, and only afterwards—and in a different way—the understanding of the critic.

And neither creation nor criticism is fixed or static.

Examining shifting styles in the arts, crossing time, creates an appreciation of the arts slightly different from the one we gain by crossing cultures. We can look back on a history of obsolete scientific theories, significant in the present as stepping stones on the way to our current knowledge, but of no present worth in themselves according to the criteria of evaluation of the sciences. In contrast, a work of art may remain today just as valuable as ever: it may be just as aesthetically beautiful, as powerfully emotionally affecting, or as illuminating of people and society. It may be, admittedly, that we attribute to it a meaning different from the one it had in its original context—a different meaning, or even additional meaning as we look back within a tradition. But more than in areas of knowledge which aim for progress toward a common goal, we take the works of previous eras along with us into our present. We can look out over the immense wealth of the arts across cultures and across time, and feel a connection with a multitude of others sharing a common human experience.

Question for reflection

To what extent in areas of knowledge other than the arts do new works force the standards of judgment to change?

Ethics

Meeting ethics as an area of knowledge can give a strange sense of recognition. Haven't we met before? Isn't there a strong family resemblance with the areas with which we have already been spending time? The human sciences and history talk a lot about motives, decisions, actions, and consequences of actions. They also show us much about human moral values. What is it that makes ethics different from other members of this knowledge family?

First impressions, though, grow more complex at a closer look. Yes, there is a difference, and it does make ethics distinct. It is still studying human action—but studies not how human beings *do act* (human sciences) nor how they *have acted* in the past (history) but rather how they *should act*.

How *should* human beings treat each other?

Kofi Annan, Secretary General of the United Nations, looked back in 1998 at a century for which *Guernica* stands as an icon:

The world has changed since Picasso painted that first political masterpiece, but it has not necessarily grown easier. We are near the end of a tumultuous century that has witnessed both the best and worst of human endeavour. Peace spreads in one region as genocidal fury rages in another. Unprecedented wealth coexists with terrible deprivation, as a quarter of the world's people remain mired in poverty.[59]

Read his words closely. What are the values that he is either stating or implying for how people should treat each other?

Look again at Picasso's *Guernica*. The emotional outcry against violence and the pain of war need not be confined just to the bombed civilians of the village of Guernica. Could any values be inferred from his painting regarding how human beings *should* or *should not* treat each other? To what extent is it possible to infer a general statement from a particular image?

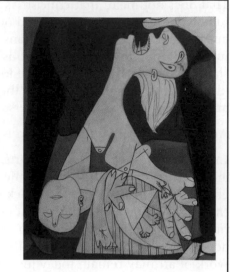

Ah. How very much like many works in the arts! Among paintings and plays, novels and dances are huge numbers which apply value judgments of "right" and "wrong" to human actions. They praise, condemn, or counsel; they declare or imply that people *should act* or *should not act* in particular ways.

Yet looking still more closely, we can again see differences within the family resemblance. Many works of art, such as an abstract painting or a lyrical flute solo, make no moral judgment at all. Moreover, the moral judgments that do run through the arts are particular to the works themselves.

Ethics, on the other hand, takes moral judgment as its only topic and seeks to be general—to comment not just on individual stories but to comment on them all—to give general perspectives that can apply to particular cases.

But what is it that ethics comments upon? Where are the works of ethics equivalent to new works of the sciences, or history, or the arts? In areas we have previously met, the critics comment upon the work of their own areas: critics of mathematics examine proofs and the nature of proofs; critics in the sciences scrutinize and test research findings, and critics in the arts evaluate creative works.

But what does the critic in ethics examine? It seems that ethics has no equivalent area that is specifically its own. It treats instead a specific aspect of all of the subject matter and methods of all the other areas of knowledge. It also examines our everyday decisions and actions from the most private and personal to the most public and political. It surveys all that human beings do and persistently asks these kinds of questions: "What does it mean to be good?" "What should I do (or not do)?" "How do we justify our moral decisions?" And then it explores possible ways of thinking about the questions and possible ways to answer. Ethics is essentially an area of criticism, or formalized critical thinking, applied to all that people do, and possibly even think.

In taking its approaches to criticism to the whole of life, it could be argued that ethics takes on the most difficult subject matter of any of the areas of knowledge we have met. It takes on the messy stuff of life—our emotions, our personal and cultural senses of identity, our religions, our ideologies—and tries to give us guides to sound moral decisions, to consider, further, how those guides might be given, and to reflect on the nature of moral choice. It may be one of the delicious ironies of knowledge that the questions that are most important to us as human beings to ask are the ones which least yield clear and certain answers. Yet the questions of ethics may be among the most fascinating in themselves and we could argue that the answers that do emerge are among the most significant to us in our lives.

Is or ought?

Statements of fact address the way things are. Judgments address the way things ought to be. Below are some statements about the use of force. Classify them as "is" or "ought" statements, carefully considering what kinds of evidence would be necessary to prove or disprove a statement of fact. (Note: The attribution list is at the bottom and may affect how you interpret the statements.)

1 "From pacifist to terrorist, each person condemns violence—and then adds one cherished case in which it may be justified."

2 "There is a violence that liberates, and a violence that enslaves; there is a violence that is moral and a violence that is immoral."

3 "The one means that wins the easiest victory over reason: terror and force."

4 "When a fact can be demonstrated, force is unnecessary; when it cannot be demonstrated, force is infamous."

5 "Against naked force the only possible defense is naked force. The aggressor makes the rules for such a war; the defenders have no alternative but matching destruction with more destruction, slaughter with greater slaughter."

6 "If you want to make peace, you don't talk to your friends. You talk to your enemies."

7 "The moment the slave resolves that he will no longer be a slave, his fetters fall. He frees himself and shows the way to others. Freedom and slavery are mental states."

8 "It is clear that the way to heal society of its violence…and lack of love is to replace the pyramid of domination with the circle of equality and respect."

Attributions:
1. Gloria Steinem; 2. Benito Mussolini; 3. Adolf Hitler, *Mein Kampf* (1924); 4. Robert G. Ingersoll, *Prose-Poems and Selections* (1884); 5. Franklin D. Roosevelt, message to Young Democrats Convention, Louisville, KY (Aug. 21, 1941); 6. Moshe Dayan; 7. Mahatma Gandhi, *Non-Violence in Peace and War* (1948); 8. Manitonquat.

Ethics, then, deals with moral choices—choices that we make that reflect our values. The choices themselves are called "moral choices". In everyday language, choices that meet with approval are called "moral" and those which are condemned are called "immoral". Here, we use the term "moral choice" to mean any choice in accordance with our moral values, whether we applaud or condemn the particular decision.

Almost any choice, however, has the potential to be a moral choice within a particular context: what we wear may be merely a matter of style, but can also, with the degree of exposure of parts of the body, come accompanied by social values; what we eat may be a matter of taste, but can also, as with some forms of vegetarianism, be grounded in values placed upon animal life; how we greet someone else may be a matter of custom, but can also reflect the value of respect for others.

Which argument do you find the most persuasive, and why?

Death penalty
a is moral because it's how my society has decided is the best way to deter and to punish murder

b is immoral because errors can happen and there's no going back

c is moral because my family welcomed the revenge and closure after the murder of my brother.

Female genital mutilation
a is moral because it is a cultural practice, and different cultural practices should be respected

b is immoral because I wouldn't want my daughter to undergo it

c is immoral because it inflicts pain on girls and removes potential for pleasure.

Terrorism
a is acceptable because terrorists think of themselves as freedom fighters

b is immoral because innocent human beings are killed

c is immoral because I am still in grief over my brother, killed in a terrorist attack.

Rape
a is immoral because one person is using another person against their will

b is questionable because consent is never clear

c is immoral because my little sister was raped and I know what it does to someone.

Cloning
a is moral because it can improve human life

b is immoral because it goes against God's will

c is questionable because we don't know much about its long-term consequences.

Eating meat
a is moral because people naturally eat meat for food

b is immoral because animals feel pain and have the right to a natural life

c is questionable because we need to find viable alternatives.

Although it is difficult to disentangle our *moral* choices from those which are *amoral*—which are subject to no moral judgment—a few characteristics have been proposed to distinguish them. Consider these yourself, and decide whether you think they draw the line successfully between the amoral and the moral.

Possible Criterion 1: For the choice to be subject to any kind of moral judgment, whether condemned or praised, it has to be a conscious and deliberate choice.

Possible Argument 1: If you accept this premise, you may argue that accidents are amoral. Knocking someone into the path of an oncoming car and knocking him out of danger are morally equivalent if accidental. Both are morally neutral, or amoral. You may also argue that actions taken under threat or force are amoral because again there is no choice. Caring for wounded patients and killing them are morally equivalent if you are acting under military command, in effect with a gun to your head.

Possible Criterion 2: For an action to be subject to any kind of moral judgment, it has to affect someone else other than the person acting.

Possible Argument 2: If you accept this premise, you may argue that self-mutilation, taking drugs, or joining an exploitative cult are amoral because the person acting affects only himself.

As you read these suggested criteria, you may be noticing a recurring keyword: argue. Argument is the method of ethics, with flaws in the assumptions or the steps taken from them generating further arguments in support or opposition.

Take each of the arguments above and offer counter-arguments— arguments for an opposing view.

Possible Criterion 1:
a   First accept the premise and oppose the conclusions that are drawn from it.
b   Then argue against accepting the criterion.

Possible Criterion 2:
a   First accept the premise and oppose the conclusions that are drawn from it.
b   Then argue against accepting the criterion.

In the examination of arguments and counter-arguments, the goal is to reach the conclusion which has the best reasons given in support. The method is argument and persuasion—persuasion based on reasonable assertions and coherent following of their implications.

Do not, however, confuse the persuasion of good arguments with some of the devices for persuasion considered in Chapter 4. In ethics, theorists attempt to be clear with their assumptions, apply them in analysis, follow their implications, and consider counter-arguments as they weigh the merits of differing analyses and conclusions. Remember that ethics is an area dealing not with material objects but with thought and judgment, so it uses the methods that are appropriate to its subject.

Ethics is the only area of the TOK course that remains a branch of philosophy, a subject with a long history of thought and argument— a subject which may be considered the mother discipline of many contemporary areas of knowledge. Most of the areas treated in TOK have gone their own way from philosophy, developing other methods, such as research, of gaining and justifying knowledge. However, the criticism within those areas of knowledge, as we have seen, continues to pose questions about the methods of justification and the nature of the knowledge, often in the manner of philosophy. The highest level reflective questions of their areas are often called their "philosophy", such as "the philosophy of science". TOK, similarly, has evolved from a branch of philosophy known as epistemology, which examines the bases of knowledge.

As we examine ethics in TOK, we will not be *doing* ethics any more than we were *doing* sciences or the arts when we discussed them as areas of knowledge; we will not be making or arguing for the knowledge claims of the field but seeing how they are made and

Environmental problems

" We all carry a responsibility.... "

Chico Viddi, IB graduate 1994
Chico is in the Graduate School of the Environment, doing a PhD on Environmental Science/Marine Ecology, at Macquarie University in Australia. He is cofounder of the Chilean NGO Centro Ballena Azul, where he is responsible for coordinating research on small cetaceans (dolphins and porpoises).

My great love for nature results from my mother's influence. She used to teach me when I was little to care about and respect all living creatures. But when I was 15 I realised that my love and passion for nature could be directed into actions, that I could dedicate my life to contributing to conservation.

Our world is facing all types of serious problems, and to me all of them are caused directly or indirectly by our society and our way of living. I believe that we all carry a responsibility, first to be aware of the problems affecting our world, and second to integrate in our everyday life, whatever we do, those small or great details to make a difference (from choosing the best option when behaving as consumers to deciding to spend most of your life actually doing something more specific to contribute to changing this world).

considering their implications for other knowledge and potential action.

The moral judgments you may reach yourself are only the raw material here for your further reflection. We ask you to bring your views into discussion but notice above all how you are arguing in their support. As the final area of knowledge in the TOK course, this one demands probably the most of you in terms of reflection on your own ideas, willingness to exchange views with others, and readiness, even if your own views are firm, to listen for what justifications persuade others. What touches us most deeply can be contestable.

If ethics seems at moments to be messy and confusing, it is not a weakness in ethics but a characteristic of what it takes as its subject. It is dealing not only with human beings but human value judgments and trying, despite the immense complexity, to give an understanding of moral choice.

What is the source of our morality?

We often use the words "moral" and "ethical" interchangably in everyday language. In TOK, we will consider morality to be our sense of right and wrong and ethics to be the area of knowledge that examines that sense of morality and the moral codes we develop from it. Since all of us are involved throughout our lives in moral decision making, ethics is an area of knowledge whose subject matter concerns us personally. And it is to your own thoughts that we next turn.

Answers to questions, as you are well aware, often raise more questions. Responses to sources of morality can take you to ideas that reward further investigation.

Reflection

Questions: How did you gain your own sense of right and wrong? How do you justify it?

Take time for quiet writing, responding to these questions.

Discussion: Exchange your ideas with classmates, looking for points of similarity and difference. Conclude by making a summary list of the sources suggested in your discussion.

Investigation: possible sources of morality

Divide up your class to do some investigation on the following topics, with small groups preparing brief reports for the class on what they learned. In this investigation, you will not be touching on all possible views, but representative ones or examples. Give a time limit to your research, though, because this is only one part of the TOK course and these questions could consume your lifetime.

1 The source of morality is human nature

a Human beings are naturally good and tend toward cooperation with others.

b Human beings are naturally selfish and find that cooperation with others maximizes their own benefit.

Although it has not been possible to demonstrate what human nature is without the influence of life experiences, many thinkers have suggested versions of what humans "naturally" are. Interestingly, the same result—a desire for a cooperative society—can be reached by reasoning from opposite assumptions, as above.

Investigate the following:

- biology: Dawkins' "selfish gene"
- psychology: Kohlberg and stages of moral development; Maslow's hierarchy of needs
- political science: Rousseau and natural man; social contract theory
- religion: Christian concept of original sin and redemption.

2 The source of morality is religion

Both theist religions and non-theist religions teach codes of morality based on the will of a Supreme Being (Jehovah, God, Allah) or other forces beyond the material world.

Investigate the following as examples of this perspective:

- What are the core moral teachings of the Abrahamic religions of Judaism, Christianity, and Islam? On what are they based?
- What are the core moral teachings of Hinduism and Buddhism? On what are they based?
- In what ways do the concepts of morality in these religions have implications for a life after death?

3 The source of morality is observation and/or reasoning

Thinkers seeking a human way of deriving moral principles have used the ways of knowing treated in TOK. Some have used reasoning as a way to recognize moral obligations and others have used observation and prediction as a way of anticipating the effects of our actions on others.

Investigate the following examples:

- Immanuel Kant's categorical imperative
- John Stuart Mill's principle of utility.

4 The source of morality is emotional empathy

Other thinkers have sought moral guidance not in the reasoning that leads to concepts of justice but the emotional concern and development of relationships that leads to nurturing and care for others.

Investigate the following:

- Carol Gilligan's ethics of care.

5 The source of morality is social and political: the traditions and laws of a particular society or international agreements that override them

Suggesting traditions and laws of a society as the source of morality raises questions of how those traditions and laws developed, whose interests they serve, and whether the way things are is the way they ought to be. Anthropology and history give us some perspectives on cultural traditions and change.

The debate between accepting traditions of societies or accepting a worldwide code arises in part from conflicting principles: on the one hand, it can be argued that it is essential to be tolerant of the differing cultural practices of the world's societies; on the other hand, it can be argued that human beings inherently possess worth and rights, and that worldwide practice should respect these.

Investigate some major attempts to establish worldwide codes:

● international human rights law, including the United Nations Declaration of Human Rights

● international humanitarian law, including the Geneva Conventions.

Justifying moral beliefs

In your class investigation, you have now been exposed to many key ethical arguments made by others. It is time now for you to argue ethically yourself—that is, to argue for moral claims with awareness of your assumptions and justifications.

In responding to the three questions below, give an answer and give your reasons.

Dilemma trio: set 1

1 Your friend has a beautiful and valuable ring. You want it. Is it right for you to take it? Why or why not?

2 You have accidentally broken your mother's favourite plate. She sees the broken pieces and, quite upset, asks you if you know what happened. You want to blame your brother. What is the right thing for you to do? Why?

3 You told your teacher that you would prepare a presentation for tomorrow's class. However, tonight you would rather watch television. What is the right action for you to take? Why?

In giving your justifications for your decisions in each of these three cases, you are probably acknowledging the difference between what you would like to do and what you feel you should do. It is possible, though, that your sense of what is right may override an inclination to act otherwise.

In many, many of the decisions we make each day, we are scarcely aware of the sense of morality that guides us and attribute our actions to our "conscience", our values internalized to the point of needing little conscious thought. Part of growing up and reaching maturity is gaining awareness of other people's feelings and control of our own impulses, so that most people would not even consider stealing from a friend, and, though we might consider evading responsibility for acknowledging a broken plate or fulfilling promised work, we would probably decide that it is right to tell the truth or to carry through on a promise.

As soon as we say "We would probably do this", though, we face the need for evidence to support our generalizations and we move toward the human sciences. In investigating how people *do* act rather than arguing for how people *should* act, the sciences add perspectives to ethical debate, though they cannot replace it. If you researched the so-called selfish gene (natural sciences) or Kohlberg's work on stages of moral development (human sciences) during your class investigation, you will have encountered attempts to examine and explain moral actions through observation. Yet the idea of morality and its definitions are not in themselves the material of the sciences.

A distinction between the natural sciences and ethics crystallizes in their various ways of treating laws. Natural sciences generalize on what things do under certain circumstances. All objects, when dropped anywhere on the planet, will fall to Earth. The law of gravity describes what happens. Ethics likewise generalizes and, depending on the argument, may apply its conclusions to all human beings. Yet it does not aim to describe but to prescribe: it does not tell us what people do but what people should do.

Thus, ethics may become the basis of another kind of law, the legislated laws of society which also prescribe what people should or should not do: they should pay their taxes; they should not rob stores. However, ethics is not the only possible basis for social legislation. One political system of legislation may generate laws for the public good (Obey the speed limit.) but another may generate laws to support the interests of the lawmakers (Blacks must live in the homelands designated for them by the ruling whites.). Speaking observationally again, we can see that people do not always obey social laws and that their obedience involves their will and choice: they may evade paying taxes; they may rob stores. Speaking ethically again, we might argue that people should not obey certain laws of society if there are ethical reasons for acting otherwise (e.g. defying the South African laws of apartheid).

Human rights

" If there is something that makes us all truly equal it is the universality and indivisibility of our human rights. "

Claudia Ricca, IB graduate 1985

Claudia has been a human rights advocate for nearly 20 years, first volunteering then working for Amnesty International. She has also been Programme Manager for Latin America and South East Asia for the Coalition to Stop the Use of Child Soldiers.

My interest in human rights advocacy began as an IB student in 1984. I remember being profoundly moved at news of the exhumations of some of the "disappeared" in Argentina, my own country. I decided then to get involved in making sure atrocities such as these never happened again, to anyone, anywhere.

The more I've worked in human rights, however, the more I've realized that this job is never done. Despite our best efforts, there will always be atrocities committed even in the name of peace, religion, national security, or self-defence. We live in an increasingly complex world, where the language of rights is being used and abused all the time: if you are infringing my rights then I have the right to defend myself, many say. And although that's a sentiment most people will sympathize with, many serious human rights violations are being committed in the process.

This has served to remind us all that our work is never over and that the preservation of human rights must be everyone's business. We are all involved, we can all be victims. But we cannot sit back and wait for someone else to fix it. If there is something that makes us all truly equal, it is the universality and indivisibility of our human rights, no matter who we are or what we believe in. And it's those qualities that make our work even more relevant in our troubled world today.

Consider now three questions rather parallel to the ones above, but placed in a larger political framework:

Dilemma trio: set 2

1   You are the leader of a country. A neighbouring country has territory with valuable oil fields which they are not developing and seem not to need. You want them. Is it right for you to invade and take them? Why or why not?

2   You are the chief engineer of a company that has accidentally spilled chemicals into a river. The government environmental agency detects the spill and asks you if you are to blame. You want to blame a rival company. What is the right thing for you to do?

3   You are the leader of a country which has signed a world agreement not to develop nuclear weapons. You are inclined, however, to do otherwise because possessing the weapons is in the interests of your country. What is the right thing for you to do and why?

Discuss these examples. Did you find that the ethical issues are quite similar to the original three? From your own experience and your knowledge of world politics, do you think that human beings adopt different moral behaviour on the small scale and the large scale?

What are the constraints on human actions to compel moral behaviour? On an international scale as on a smaller scale, the same issues apply—of ethical bases of law and appropriate forms of coercion. Your investigation on the topic of international law is relevant here.

Already, in giving your reasons for right action in the questions above, you have been arguing ethically. Let us now look closely at one more example, and then step back to survey our ways of arguing.

The ethical dilemma

Although ethics is often characterized as an area of conflicting conclusions and controversy, we venture to suggest that people tend to be much in agreement in most moral decision-making. It is when we face dilemmas, however, that we most often bring our values to consciousness and, in ethical argument, try to resolve what the moral action would be and why. If you face an ethical dilemma, you are facing a moral choice without being sure of what the right thing is to do. You have to think about it, clarify your own values, and then make your choice.

Now consider the following story in which a teacher faces a moral dilemma. Read all pieces of information carefully, decide what you think the right action is for the teacher to take, and be prepared to give your reasons. If you do not consider it to be a dilemma—that is, if you are quite sure what the right action is—consider why someone else might find it a dilemma. The conclusion you reach is less important than your reasons for reaching it.

Ethical dilemma: IB exam hall

A teacher, while invigilating an IB examination, sees someone indisputably cheating. (Note that the issue here is not one of perception and possible error. It is a given in this question that the student really is cheating.) In a frozen moment, various pieces of information pass through her head. Which ones are relevant, and what is the morally right action for her to take?

a   The student needs to pass the exam in order to get his IB diploma.

b   The student is predicted to pass the exam.

c   The student is very popular, so his friends will be upset over the incident if his cheating is exposed.

d   The teacher really likes the student.

e   No one else sees the student cheating, and at this moment he is not aware that the teacher has seen him.

f   No one else writing the exam is cheating.

g   The teacher has undertaken invigilation, or the prevention of exam irregularities of any kind, as part of her professional responsibility.

h   The student is under pressure to succeed from his family and his community, who expect him to bring them pride.

i   The teacher has heard it said that the student has cheated in the past in minor ways, but cannot recall the details.

j   The IB system of examinations is a means of comparing student performance worldwide with identical examination conditions.

Taking critical perspectives in ethics

The situation of the IB examination hall provides an example deliberately simpler than many situations we find in life. It may, however, bring out the major ways of arguing in ethics, not unlike the perspectives on works in the arts (see page 213) with successive emphasis on the artist, the work, the effect on the audience, and the social context.

1   Did you evaluate the action with emphasis on the moral actor, and intentions?

If so, did you consider only the intentions of the teacher, who is the one with the choice to make in the story, or also the intentions of the cheating student who has already made his choice?

Some difficulties arise when evaluating the morality of an action based on its intentions. As we considered emotion as a way of knowing, we recognized that it is difficult to know the feelings of others and that it is possible to lack self-knowledge about our own feelings. Similarly, how can we be sure that a person's intentions are what they claim them to be, or that we are identifying even our own intentions accurately? When intentions lie in complex human psychology, intertwined with beliefs and emotions, they can be quite difficult to pin down.

Still, if someone kicks you during a football game, your evaluation of his action is likely to be quite different depending on whether you

Knowledge Creation Diagram

within context of the natural world

knowledge creator(s)

work(s) of knowledge
(math proof, research paper, novel)

knowledge community
(peers, critics general public)

within social context

believe it to be accidental or deliberate. Even in a court of law where the codes are formalized, the apparent intentions of a law-breaker are often taken into account in the sentence. In at least some legal systems, premeditated murder, for example, brings a harsher judgment than a killing considered a crime of passion.

Indeed, one of the distinctions commonly made between a moral action and an amoral action is that the moral actor must have chosen the action. An injury to someone else that is purely accidental does not, in this line of arguing, bring condemnation. A further issue to be considered, though, is whether the person could have reasonably expected the damaging outcome or have taken precautions to avoid it. A drunk driver cannot excuse himself by saying, "I didn't mean to kill the pedestrian."

2 Did you evaluate the action with emphasis on features of the act itself, and principles of what is right and wrong?

If so, what principles did you take into account as you decided what the teacher should do in the examination hall? Did you consider the principle of telling the truth, for example, or fulfilling a promise? Did you take into account the obligations of the teacher as an invigilator to report cheating, or the obligation of the student not to cheat in the examination, both duties based on accepting promises that go with the roles?

Principles and duties can be derived in quite different ways. From your class investigation you will recall both religion and reasoning as sources of moral principles. Religious teaching gives some rules to follow, such as the Ten Commandments of the Abrahamic Old Testament telling followers not to lie, steal, or desire what other people have. Reasoning, quite a different source of justification, may also lead to rules and duties. You will probably recall Immanuel Kant's categorical imperative—his test of whether an action is ethical by using a generalizing thought experiment of wishing that everyone would act that way. Should I lie? Would I wish everyone to lie? The wish is rationally self-defeating, in destroying the notion of lying and telling the truth. So I must not lie. Whether the principle is gained from religious teaching (justified by faith, sacred text, or reported revelation from a Supreme Being) or derived from reasoning, it can act rather like an axiom in mathematics in providing a firm assumption from which further reasoning is done, deductively, as the general principle is applied to a particular example.

Such principles are absolute. Principles given by religion are considered by believers to be the will of God, and so to be followed without the debate that attends human conclusions. The variability of interpretation of the will of God by different religious groups, based often on which prophet is considered the most reliable source or what reading is given to sacred text, does not make the resulting commandment less absolute. Each religious group holds its own interpretation to be the will of God. Similarly, Kant considered duties, once recognized, to be absolute, no matter what the situation, so that it is always, everywhere, morally correct to tell the truth, not to injure others, or to protect life. "Deontology", as it is called, has been criticized for being inflexible. It is not difficult to imagine a situation in which telling the truth does not seem the most moral choice.

Dilemmas arise, for example, when principles that must be obeyed come into conflict with each other, giving a problem with no solution. Suppose that you promised a friend that you would keep her secret, but then what she tells you fills you with fear that she is in danger. Both keeping a promise and preserving life are your duties, but you cannot fulfill either one without failing to fulfill the other. Deontologists after Kant, such as W.D. Ross, have ranked duties so that some override others: you would be right to save your friend not because breaking a promise is morally acceptable but because saving your friend takes moral priority.

This approach to ethics through asserting some absolute principles lies behind the concept of human rights, which identify basic entitlements of all human beings, such as freedom of speech, freedom of religion, or freedom from being tortured. If your class did the investigation of the Declaration of Human Rights or the International Court of Justice, you will recall international attempts to establish codes that apply worldwide. They are established by ethical argument and then upheld by law.

3 Did you evaluate the action with emphasis on the effect on others—the consequences of the action?

If so, what consequences did you take into account?

- the immediate consequences on the teacher, the cheating student, and the others in the exam hall?
- the longer-term consequences on the student's reputation, education, and character, the teacher's reputation and character, and the relationship between teacher and student?
- the broader possible consequences on the school's reliability as an examination centre, the examination results of other students, and the school's ability to offer the IB in the future?

If others also argued on the basis of consequences, did you all agree? It is entirely possible to use the same way of arguing and reach different conclusions—for example that the consequences are worse if the teacher reports the cheating because the student's IB results will be compromised, or that the consequences are better if the teacher reports it because the student will learn not to cheat. A frequent response is, "Would you want to go to a doctor who had cheated his way through medical school?"

From your class investigation earlier, you will probably recognize that John Stuart Mill argued in this way with his principle of utility—that the most moral choice is the one which yields the greatest happiness (or benefit or utility) to the greatest number.

The difficulties of evaluating ethically according to consequences, though, become evident in this small story of the examination hall:

- How accurately can we predict the consequences of an action? Remember the butterfly effect of chaos theory and the problems, even in dealing with measurable data, of predicting accurately. How can we tell in advance what the consequences will really be

233

for either the student or the teacher? Will the student become haunted by guilt and never cheat again or, quite the opposite, go on to a career of cheating?

● What importance do we give each of the possible consequences, and how do we weigh them up against each other? We cannot quantify harm and benefit in grams and place them physically on a scale to compare them (5.37 grams of harm, 4.978 grams of benefit…). Is preserving the student's IB more important than preserving the teacher's honesty?

"Utilitarianism", as it is called, has been criticized for some of its implications. As it argues for the greatest happiness for the greatest number of people, it could possibly permit great harm to a minority if the majority is benefited. Is it morally acceptable to kill off a very small tribe of people if a very large tribe would benefit? The objection is a serious one. Nevertheless, even from a utilitarian perspective it could be argued that great harm to a minority counts more heavily on one side of the balance than the benefit for the majority does on the other.

Utilitarianism has also been criticized for being so dependent on the particular situation that it produces unpredictable decisions. Yet others point out that it need not be so. "Act utilitarianism" looks only at the specific case, for example whether the particular teacher in our examination story should report the particular student for cheating. "Rule utilitarianism", however, looks at all equivalent cases, for example whether all teachers should report all students for cheating. Whereas the act utilitarian will expect that the teacher could decide either way depending on her understanding of the consequences she is weighing, the rule utilitarian will insist that the teacher report the student, as the consequence of all teachers ignoring all cheating would be to undermine the examination system. Notice that the generalizing of the rule utilitarian resembles the generalizing of Kant's deontological categorical imperative, but is concerned not with reasoning and consistency but always with consequences.

What this ethical perspective of evaluating according to consequences cannot do, in the end, is to make ethics into a science. It does use observation, prediction, and attempts at quantifying and weighing of results, but it is dealing not with the material world but with immaterial value judgments.

What it can do, however, is to take into account the complexities of situations in which ethical decisions so often have to be made and to encourage a consideration of consequences beyond the immediate ones. It also gives moral guidance to practical decision-making. When resources of time, money, or equipment, for example, are scarce, utilitarianism would direct them to where they can provide the greatest happiness for the most people.

4 Did you evaluate the action with emphasis on the moral code of the surrounding society?

If so, what part of the society did you consider most important? Was it the network of the IB, with its system of examinations running worldwide and whose moral code for both candidates and invigilators is published and posted before examinations are run? (It says, "Don't cheat.")

Was it the society of the school, with its laws—or rules—and traditions? Or your own social group within the school? Or was it the context of the town or region in which you live?

A society or culture is rarely homogeneous, and it is entirely possible that in different parts of the social networks that surround you you will find conflicting responses to this dilemma. Some IB students of the past, considering not the teacher's choice but the student's, have argued that in their home context it would be considered immoral not to cheat, on the basis that friends should help each other and that it would be selfish of one student to succeed and allow friends to fail. Clearly, no absolute guide to moral action can emerge from emphasizing the traditions of the cultural context.

The tension between relativism and absolutism

In considering theories in human sciences, interpretations in history, and perspectives in the arts, we noted that different arguments made within areas of knowledge illuminated different features of the subject matter they considered. So, too, do all the different ethical perspectives we have considered so far. Yet it is probably the tension between the extreme arguments of absolutism and relativism that most serves to highlight the fundamental characteristics of ethics as an area of knowledge based on argument.

Ethical relativism argues that there is no such thing as right and wrong outside the values of the particular individual or, broadening the judging body, the values of the society. It points observationally to moral variability from person to person and society to society, as in point 4 above, and places emphasis on divergences. It also counter-argues any justifications for ethical judgments that transcend individual or group values. The weakness of relativism in logical terms is that it is self-defeating: if all ethical claims are just relative to the particular person or group, then so is relativism itself. Many would also find weakness in practical and emotional terms in that its implications are repugnant: it nullifies all general moral judgments and allows no possible grounds for generally condemning any actions, including slavery, infanticide, genocide, or torture. What relativism may contribute to ethical debate, with removal of any outside absolutes, is an emphasis on developing personal values and possibly tolerating those of other people.

Ethical absolutism, at the other end of the spectrum, argues that there is such a thing as right and wrong applicable universally. It uses arguments from principles, as in point 2 above, which identify moral standards that do not vary with the situation, the society, or the individual. Its weakness is that no moral judgments have been established to be held without exceptions across societies, so that it cannot be justified observationally. Its further weakness in practical and emotional terms lies at the other extreme from relativism's: it opposes the chaos of relativism, but argues for inflexibility. What absolutism contributes to ethical debate is its challenge to all systems to try to rise above immediate circumstances and establish a guide that would be applicable worldwide. It also challenges traditional codes of behaviour to be open to change.

The two positions, extremes in the ethical spectrum, remind us that ethics is not an area of knowledge where a right answer can be established that easily commands universal assent. It is not mathematics, where the reasoning of a proof can compel judgments to converge. It is not science, where the reasoning, applied to observation, can also make conclusions converge. In dealing with human beings, their emotions, and their worldviews, ethics applies its reasoning to subject matter that defies attempts to pin down a perfect right answer. Each of its ways of entering the debate, though, can add to the total of our understanding.

Back to the ethical dilemma

The choice of an IB examination hall was a deliberate one, in that it introduced limited complexities. Moreover, most of the ways of arguing ultimately lead to the same outcome— that the teacher should report the cheating student in the manner laid down by the examination system. The very choice of the artificial examination situation which people enter voluntarily makes the case much easier than many situations in the world.

Let us move now outside the exam room and vary the story. The issue resembles the one in the examination hall in that someone violates a rule.

Let us suppose that a mother is stealing a bag of flour from a shop. You see her do so. Should you report her? Add now the following information: her country has great extremes of wealth and poverty, and she and her family have been dispossessed from their land by a rich landowner wanting it for large-scale agriculture. Her children are hungry and she has no money for food. The punishment is five months in prison. Evaluate her action from each of the four ethical approaches outlined above and exchange views with the rest of your class.

As you did this ethical evaluation, which ethical approach did you favour? Did you find this situation more complex than the one in the examination hall? If so, why?

It has been argued that without justice within a society or the world as a whole, it is difficult to apply meaningfully notions of individual justice. Ethical ways of arguing may illuminate such problems rather than giving clear solutions. This failure to deliver tidy answers is not

Privilege and responsibility

" *I have opportunities and benefits that are mine without question…* "

Kate Neville,
IB graduate 2000
Kate is a Master of Environmental Science candidate at the Yale University School of Forestry and Environmental Studies, hoping to graduate in May 2007. She is an Alexandra Goelet Scholar and attending Yale with a Fulbright-OAS Ecology Initiative Award.

I have a strong sense that we have, absolutely, a moral responsibility to help others, and this is particularly true for those who are privileged. Being someone from the developed world (for lack of a better term), Canadian in particular, white from a middle-class family, I have opportunities and benefits that are mine without question, and often come at the expense of others.

My attempts to engage in the world around me in meaningful ways have taken various forms over the last few years. My current life is wrapped up in water: for my master's degree research, I have been looking at urban water management, specifically in the Philippines. The aim of my research is to advocate context-appropriate management strategies for water provision, with the broader goal of improving water access. Water is a vital resource, and incorporates natural science and ecosystem awareness with social organization and equity. It therefore seems to be an area through which I could make a measurable difference to people's livelihoods and well-being. By contributing, even in a small measure, to these projects and policies, it seems possible to integrate social and ecological responsibility into meaningful research and action.

a weakness in ethics but often its strength, in drawing attention to the complex and troubled world in which the judgments apply.

However, while illuminating the surrounding complexities, ethics often does deliver answers. The answer may be to create social justice, as ethics begins to fuse with politics. Justice, hardly surprisingly, is quite an ambiguous concept, and the justice of distribution of benefit is defined in a range of political ways: give to each equally, give to each according to his merit, give to each according to his need…Each perspective of political ethics can present good arguments for a version of social justice which may seem unjust from the perspective of others.

However, if societies remain unjust, the cause cannot be attributed entirely to different concepts of social justice. Ethics can give good advice. It is up to people in political and economic spheres of influence to follow it.

Convergences and controversies

Ethical dilemmas also highlight the frictions between beliefs within a society or within the world at a given historical moment. What issue at what time and place is controversial? Slavery was once controversial and is now resolved by world governments as unjust. Some of the arguments against slavery are now finding new forms to oppose child labour and exploitation of human beings in the sex trade. Is abortion a controversial issue? Whether it is a topic of public debate at all reflects the political system of decision making within a country and the existence, or not, of diverging values within a society.

While the controversies stand out as making the news, convergence of views is sometimes obscured. Terrorism is a striking contemporary case, and raises many ethical issues beyond simple moral condemnation. The question for ethical consideration is not whether terrorism is good. No ethical system and no religion argues that killing people, often involved in terrorism, is good in itself. There is enormous world convergence on this point.

Many individuals and societies, however, argue that killing is acceptable in some circumstances as a means to an end—as a way of achieving consequences good enough to outweigh the harm. Arguments for capital punishment or war take this line of reasoning. However, they stop short before arguing that the deliberately targeted killing of innocent civilians is justified. Terrorism does not. As is often said, one person's "terrorist" is another person's "freedom fighter", and for some "fighters" no cost is too high for "freedom".

But what then? Surely this kind of recognition of an alternative perspective does not close the ethical exploration. Surely it opens it. Is it possible that we ourselves carry some kind of ethical responsibility to try, for the good of all, to understand what persuades people of a perspective that approves the methods of terrorism? Should we give thought to arguments for killing and other violence being morally legitimate in some cases but not in others? Should we concern ourselves with definitions of "war", which is commonly thought to sanction violence, and who can declare it on whom? Can either terrorism or a "war on terror" be considered a "just war"—and on what grounds might a world consider it so, or not so? Should we concern ourselves, further, once a group of people have become terrorists, over how they became so—what persuaded them toward their forms of violence, what social and economic conditions nurture ideologies that sanction terrorism, and what measures might be taken to eliminate not just terrorists but causes of terrorism? Considering such possible causes as poverty, powerlessness, desire for revenge, desperation, and indoctrination does not lead to excusing terrorism. It may lead, however, to a greater understanding of the problem and a greater knowledge on which to base solutions.

Terrorism, however, is merely an example here. The fundamental question is an ethical one applied to knowledge. Do we carry any kind of moral responsibility to gain knowledge, see from different perspectives—even to try to grasp a perspective repugnant to us—and to try to understand the complexities of the world within which we make our decisions and take our actions? This is a huge question, much larger than this particular example, as it concerns what we ought to know. Take this question away with you for further thought.

A perspective on religion, spirituality, and concern for others' well-being

by His Holiness the Dalai Lama

Actually, I believe there is an important distinction to be made between religion and spirituality. Religion I take to be concerned with faith in the claims to salvation of one faith tradition or another, an aspect of which is acceptance of some form of metaphysical or supernatural reality, including perhaps an idea of heaven or nirvana. Connected with this are religious teachings or dogma, ritual, prayer, and so on. Spirituality I take to be concerned with those qualities of the human spirit—such as love and compassion, patience, tolerance, forgiveness, contentment, a sense of responsibility, a sense of harmony—which bring happiness to both self and others. While ritual and prayer, along with the questions of nirvana and salvation, are directly connected to religious faith, these inner qualities need not be, however. There is thus no reason why the individual should not develop them, even to a high degree, without recourse to any religious or metaphysical belief system. This is why I sometimes say that religion is something we can perhaps do without. What we cannot do without are these basic spiritual qualities.

The unifying characteristic of the qualities I have described as "spiritual" may be said to be some level of concern for others' well-being. In Tibetan, we speak of *shen pen kyi sem* meaning "the thought to be of help to others". And when we think about them, we see that each of the qualities noted is defined by an implicit concern for others' well-being. Moreover, the one who is compassionate, loving, patient, tolerant, forgiving, and so on to some extent recognizes the potential impact of their actions on others and orders their conduct accordingly. Thus spiritual practice according to this description involves, on the one hand, acting out of concern for others' well-being. On the other, it entails transforming ourselves so that we become more readily disposed to do so. To speak of spiritual practice in any terms other than these is meaningless.

My call for a spiritual revolution is thus not a call for a religious revolution. Nor is it a reference to a way of life that is somehow otherworldly, still less to something magical or mysterious. Rather, it is a call for a radical reorientation away from our habitual preoccupation with self. It is a call to turn toward the wider community of beings with whom we are connected, and for conduct which recognizes others' interests alongside our own.[60]

How large is your circle of caring?

One of the recurring knowledge claims in ethics is that as human individuals we owe something to others—attitudes of respect, concern, or even love, and actions that promote their welfare along with our own. Ethical systems based on consequences aim for the maximum of human happiness, ethical systems based on principles present doing good for others as an obligation, and ethical systems based on care stress empathy and nurturing relationships. Major religions of the world teach variations on the golden rule—to treat others as you would like to be treated yourself.

As you undertake service as part of your CAS programme, do you believe that helping others is a moral obligation? Do you experience service as something you *ought* to do, or as something you *want* to do? Would you argue against helping others? Think back to your TOK discussions on emotional empathy and CAS in Chapter 2. With the time that has passed since then, have your views changed in any way?

As we conclude this section on ethics, we leave you with another question for further thought. If you are concerned for the welfare of others, how large is your circle of caring? Do you care about your family and friends? Do you extend your concern to others in your society or the world, and try to respond to need? If you want to contribute to a better life for others in your society or your world, what forms might your contribution take?

Questions for reflection

● Do I have any moral responsibility to inform myself about my society and the world?

● Do I have any moral responsibility to act for the good of others?

"Why the suffering? What to do about it?
These are the primary moral questions of our times."

A perspective from an IB graduate

Jean-Marc Mangin,
IB graduate 1983,
Executive Director of CUSO

Jean-Marc Mangin has had
nearly 20 years of international
experience gained in the field and
in headquarters with NGOs, the UN
and the Canadian Government. From August 2003
to July 2006, he was the Canadian International
Development Agency (CIDA) representative in
Nepal. Prior to his current posting, he was the Chief
of Operations at the International Humanitarian
Assistance Programme at CIDA. Before joining the
federal public service in 1998, he led the
Emergency Response Unit at CARE Canada. He has
been involved in humanitarian operations in several
African countries, the Americas, in Asia, and in the
Balkans.

What motivated you to go into relief and development work?

The humanitarian imperative—that I believe is
universal—is and remains my main motivation. What
is the humanitarian imperative? Quite simply it is the
conviction that all possible steps should be taken to
prevent and reduce human suffering caused by war,
disaster, and abject poverty. On a personal level, I
also find it easier to create meaning in my life as the
challenges to be faced are so utterly stark. Although
the dilemma of aid can often be soul wrenching, the
questions to be asked (Why the suffering? What to
do about it?) are very obvious and fascinating. These
are the primary moral questions of our times and,
contrary to previous generations, we have the tools
and knowledge to stop unnecessary suffering among
our fellow beings. Therefore our responsibility to
protect and assist is also greater.

What kind of work do you do? Do you think it makes a difference in the world?

I am currently the Executive Director of CUSO, the
largest and the oldest volunteer-sending international
development NGO based in Canada. The nature of
the volunteer experience has changed a great deal
over the last 50 years but the willingness to care, the
desire to make a difference remains. When all the
elements are in place (needs-driven community
programming; committed southern partner;
mobilizing human and financial resources; linking
local action with national and international advocacy
for social justice), volunteers can help make the
world a better place. My job is to ensure that CUSO
effectively connects the dots (that all the elements
are in place for effective programming and advocacy
for poverty reduction and justice) and helps to create
social capital. Social capital is an abstract concept but
can be summarized as a greater willingness to
connect and cooperate between real people and
communities, even when they do not personally
know each other. The public good can only survive
and grow if social capital is healthy, if people realize
out of their own free will that they have moral
obligations to others.

Do you think that all people have some kind of obligation to help others?

Yes. As a matter of human rights and responsibility
and as a matter of self-interest for our common
survival. I have met poor people across the planet
and across amazingly different cultures. What is
common to all is an innate sense of injustice over
suffering that can easily be prevented. Of course,
opinions on what to do about it vary a great deal.
Nonetheless, one of the outcomes of the human
rights revolution that began less than 300 years ago
and has accelerated since the end of the second
world war is to expand the circle of caring (from the
family to the community, ethnicity, nation, globe). A
huge gap remains between the vision of a fairer and
more just world and the reality of pervasive injustice.
I have little patience with the widespread excuse of
the lack of political will as the key obstacle to action.
We have the politicians that we deserve and, if
issues of global injustice really mobilize a substantial
section of the electorate, the political will and action
will follow. There is no valid ethical reason, no
economic rationale for human beings to die of
hunger in a world of plenty. Yet they do and their
unnecessary death shames us all.

6 Knowledge in the world

The World Bank's World Development Report in 1998–99, entitled *Knowledge for Development*, started with the following words:

> Knowledge is like light. Weightless and intangible, it can easily travel the world, enlightening the lives of people everywhere. Yet billions of people still live in the darkness of poverty—unnecessarily. Knowledge about how to treat such a simple ailment as diarrhea has existed for centuries—but millions of children continue to die from it because their parents do not know how to save them.[1]

This chapter focuses on applying what you've learned about knowing, knowers, and knowledge to concrete issues in the world. How can we better understand, for example, a dispute between two neighbouring cities over a river, an escalating disagreement between two countries over a border, a heated clash about whether or not a particular social group should be allowed certain rights, or an issue such as global warming which affects us all?

The kind of exploration we will map out for you in this chapter is not one many people embark on. With TOK in your knapsack, you are now qualified to do what few even attempt: to achieve a well-rounded and critical understanding of the most crucial issues of our time.

Selected world issues

If you were making a list of world issues yourself, trying to choose the most important ones, what changes would you make to this selection? More importantly, why?

Why world hunger?

In this book we have chosen a case study to demonstrate how to apply critical thinking skills to one world issue, using an approach that can be applied to any other.

Out of all possibilities, we have chosen world hunger. Why? We could give many reasons, but in the end it came down to a choice on the part of your authors. We have selected it out of our own feelings and values.

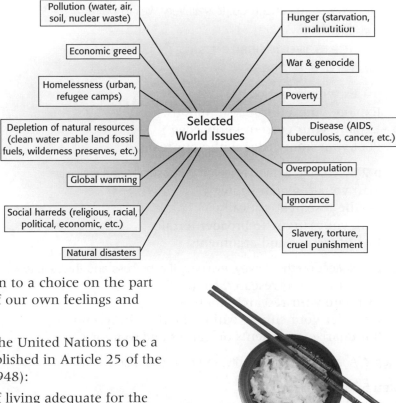

Pollution (water, air, soil, nuclear waste)

Economic greed

Homelessness (urban, refugee camps)

Depletion of natural resources (clean water arable land fossil fuels, wilderness preserves, etc.)

Global warming

Social harreds (religious, racial, political, economic, etc.)

Natural disasters

Selected World Issues

Hunger (starvation, malnutrition

War & genocide

Poverty

Disease (AIDS, tuberculosis, cancer, etc.)

Overpopulation

Ignorance

Slavery, torture, cruel punishment

Food is a universal need and declared by the United Nations to be a universal right. The right to food was established in Article 25 of the Universal Declaration of Human Rights (1948):

- Everyone has the right to a standard of living adequate for the well-being of himself and his family, including food, clothing, housing and medical care and necessary social services, and the right to security in the event of unemployment, sickness, disability, widowhood, old age or other lack of livelihood in circumstances beyond his control.

● Motherhood and childhood are entitled to special care and assistance. All children, whether born in or out of wedlock, shall enjoy the same social protection.

To reduce by half the proportion of people who are undernourished by 2015 is the first of eight Millennium Development Goals (MDGs) affirmed in the United Nations Millennium Declaration in September 2000 by the 189 UN member states. The goals are specific and achievable, and the UN defined indicators to monitor progress. According to the 2005 hunger report published by the Food and Agriculture Organization of the United Nations (FAO), rapid progress in reducing hunger is a pre-requisite for progress toward the other seven MDGs.

Food: a universal need

Prior to any concrete cultural shaping, we are born with human bodies, whose possibilities and vulnerabilities do not as such belong to one culture rather than any other. Any given human being might have belonged to any culture. The experience of the body is culturally influenced; but the body itself, prior to such experience, provides limits and parameters that ensure a great deal of overlap in what is going to be experienced, where hunger, thirst, desire, and the five senses are concerned. It is all very well to point to the cultural component in these experiences. But when one spends time considering issues of hunger and scarcity, and in general of human misery, such differences appear relatively small and refined, and one cannot fail to acknowledge that "there are no known ethnic differences in human physiology with respect to metabolism of nutrients. Africans and Asians do not burn their dietary calories or use their dietary protein any differently from Europeans and Americans. It follows that dietary requirements cannot vary widely as between different races".[2]

Exploring a world issue using TOK skills: steps in the process

Step 1 Explore the explorer(s)
a Explore your ethical assumptions.
b Explore your current knowledge.
c Pool your knowledge with your team.

Step 2 Survey the terrain: research purposefully and critically
a Plan your research strategy.
b Do the research, critically.
c Link your survey to broader terrain.
d Identify issues and arguments.

Step 3 Reflect on the survey: evaluate the process and the results
a Reflect on your research strategy.
b Evaluate your research findings.
c Consider your survey within the broader terrain.
d Summarize arguments on causes and solutions.

Step 4 Analyse the arguments: examine cause and solution

Step 5 Take your own stand
a Develop and support an argument of your own.
b Take an overview of analysing arguments.

Step 6 Explore the explorer(s)
a Return to the self-knowledge of step 1 and evaluate growth.
b Consider implications that knowledge may have for action.

You will get a better feel for the process modelled in this chapter if you keep a journal of your own explorations. We invite you to keep a *TOK World Hunger Journal*, wherein you can

1 write your responses to the proposed exercises and activities,
2 make notes about your encounters with the world issue outside of school (newspapers, movies, conversations with others, websites, emails, CAS), and
3 keep a record of the insights you gain about the world and about yourself during this exploration. If you date your entries, this journal can result in a record of your own evolution as a knower.

In what ways can this case study on world hunger be used?
A list of suggestions is given at the end of the chapter.

Step 1 Explore the explorer(s)
Before you explore any world issue, first start with yourself. Reflect on how you feel about it, what you know about it, and any possible assumptions and biases you may have about it. Take private time with your *TOK World Hunger Journal* to respond to the questions in 1a and 1b.

1a Explore your ethical assumptions
In your *Journal*, respond to the following questions.

1 Do people have an intrinsic right *not* to go hungry and not to be malnourished? Why or why not?
2 Does your answer change if you consider the rights of (a) a child born in a part of the world where there is chronic food scarcity; (b) a child born to an impoverished family in a developed country; (c) an unemployed adult?
3 Should humanity attempt to significantly reduce or eliminate world hunger? Why or why not? If so, who do you believe should be working to solve the problem?

What is within my circle of caring?
The chapter on ethics concluded with the question, "How large is your circle of caring?" In considering the welfare of others or the planet, who or what do we take into account? What do we care most about? Circles of caring vary in diameter: the smaller ones are restricted to one's self and immediate family and the largest ones encompass the entire world and all living and non-living things within it.

In your *TOK World Hunger Journal*, explore your own circle of caring. Draw a large circle. Inside it, quickly write down the people, things, and ideas that you care about.

You may wish to think in terms of

● relationships (Who do I care about?)
● particular issues or values (What do I care about?)

- geography (Where are the people and places that I care about?)
- time (When? Do I care about the past, the present, the future?)
- values. (Why? What makes all these important to me?)

Later, review the information you gained on the following in your discussion of ethics in Chapter 5:

a   Lawrence Kohlberg's stage theory of moral thinking, based on justice

b   Carol Gilligan's moral development theory, based on caring

c   Abraham Maslow's hierarchy of needs.

According to each theory, at which level are you now, and which level would you like to reach in the future?

Describing hunger to the well fed...

Trying to describe hunger to a well-fed person is like trying to describe things other than shadows to the man inside Plato's cave. Or trying to describe the colour blue to a congenitally blind person. Go ahead. Try it.

To begin to get a sense of hunger, you would have to be handcuffed with your hands behind your back, with absolutely no knowledge of when, if ever, the shackles would be removed. Or placed by helicopter onto a rocky cliff or shipwrecked on a small deserted island, with no idea of when, if ever, a rescuer would come.

People starving in parts of Africa today and the Holocaust inmates in the Nazi concentration camps had no expectation of recovery from their agonizing despair. Maintenance of the daily ration meant a slow death. Any reduction in the daily ration meant certain death. This anguish is not within the realm of the well-nourished.

A day of fasting is not a good example of experiencing hunger, particularly when preceded by a feast and followed by another feast wherein you will bemoan your net gain of weight. Nor is skipping a meal every day for a month. You always know where and when your next meal is coming from, and know you could eat if you wanted to. The only thing that starving people can count on is further despair, stomach pains, disease, and witnessing the deaths of those around them. Now would be a good time for you to try to describe the colour "blue" to a congenitally blind person.

Harvey Levy

FRAME 1 *Personal story*

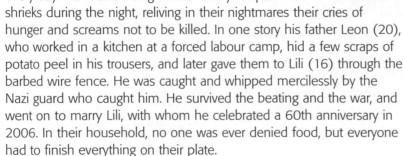

Harvey Levy is the son of Holocaust survivors who met in a concentration camp. He was born in Munich near the Dachau camps, then grew up in Brooklyn, New York, hearing stories of how his parents had to survive on one piece of bread and one cup of weak coffee, while working 12–16 hours every day. He recalls being awakened by his parents' shrieks during the night, reliving in their nightmares their cries of hunger and screams not to be killed. In one story his father Leon (20), who worked in a kitchen at a forced labour camp, hid a few scraps of potato peel in his trousers, and later gave them to Lili (16) through the barbed wire fence. He was caught and whipped mercilessly by the Nazi guard who caught him. He survived the beating and the war, and went on to marry Lili, with whom he celebrated a 60th anniversary in 2006. In their household, no one was ever denied food, but everyone had to finish everything on their plate.

1b Explore your current knowledge

Respond to the following questions in your *Journal*.

1   When and how were you last exposed to this issue? Was it through a news report? personal experience? a film? a novel? a photograph? a conversation?

2   When you hear "world hunger", what other words do you hear in your head? Who said them? What personal memories do the words "world hunger" generate? What do you feel when you hear these words?

3   Do people go hungry where you live? What do they look like? Try to remember a few of their faces.

4   What is the sound and smell of hunger? Take a few minutes to recollect what it is like, or to imagine what it may be like.

5   Think of all the ways in which you enjoy food and drink in the company of other people. Imagine what it would be like not to be able to do that.

6   Can you imagine yourself suffering from chronic hunger, had the conditions in your life been different (if you had different parents, or had been born in a different country, or at a different time)? What emotions do you think you would feel? (If you have trouble imagining, enter "famine" as a search term in Google Images or a search engine of your choice.)

Still in your *Journal*, gather your thoughts as quickly as possible on hunger, using the panoramic brainstorming questions: What? Who? Where? When? Why? How?

- **What** is hunger—its definition, its description, its effect?
- **Who** are the key people and organizations involved—the victims, the problem creators, the problem solvers?
- **Where** does hunger happen?
- **When** does hunger happen?
- **Why** does hunger happen?
- **How** have people tried to end hunger in the past? How can it be ended in the future?

1c Pool your current knowledge with your team

If your class is large, divide yourselves into smaller teams. You will work with your team throughout the exploration of this case study. Appoint a scribe to take notes as you share your background knowledge on the panoramic questions. Use some means whereby all participants can end up with a copy: for example, large flipchart pages to be posted on a wall or handwritten or computer notes to be copied for all of you to include in your *Journals*.

FRAME 2

"Only when we free ourselves from the myth of scarcity can we begin to look for hunger's real causes."[3]

Panoramic questions: WWWWWH?

Things our team knows about hunger

Note things your team as a whole is fairly sure about.

Panoramic questions: WWWWWH?

Our team's questions about hunger

Note things your team is not very sure about or does not agree on, and questions that came out of discussion.

Roughly classify your questions as:

a   *Definitional*: Your group did not agree about the meaning of a certain term. (e.g. Does "hunger" include malnutrition as well as starvation? How is hunger measured?)

b   *Factual*: Your group did not agree about facts relevant to the issue. (e.g. Is hunger mostly due to political reasons such as war, or is it a chronic problem? Does hunger exist in developed countries such as the US?)

c   *Ethical*: Your group did not agree about relevant moral aspects. (e.g. What, if anything, are we obliged to do about world hunger?)

> **"** *The way people think about hunger is the greatest obstacle to ending it.* **"** [4]

World issues, knowledge issues

Any particular world issue is rich with TOK knowledge issues, in which the discussion centres on knowledge itself. A few which emerge from step 1, applied to the particular world issue, include:

- *Classification and definition of knowledge*: What is the difference and the relationship between knowledge through personal experience and knowledge through information?
- *Ways of knowing*: To what extent is it possible to extend personal knowledge by means of emotional empathy and imagination? What areas of knowledge and CAS experiences most contribute to the development of empathy? In what ways? To what extent can such development be measured?
- *Assumptions, prior knowledge and perspectives*: In what ways does what we already know affect, in new situations, what we perceive, what we feel, how we use language, and how we apply our reasoning? To what extent are we attached to the coherence test for truth, dependent on past knowledge, and resistant to accepting conflicting information?
- *Classification*: What is the effect on knowing of classifying questions and statements into definitions, statements of observation or fact, value judgments, and metaphysical statements?
- *Ethics as an area of knowledge*: Does moral judgment apply to emotions and attitudes, or only to actions? Is caring about other people an ethical obligation? Is acting toward others with concern for their welfare an ethical obligation? How would you justify your response?

Step 2 Survey the terrain

Finding answers to these apparently simple panoramic questions may feel overwhelming. World issues are intrinsically complex and multidisciplinary; much research is conducted about them, and there are no easy answers. You will witness minefields of disagreement over the meaning of terms, measuring techniques, historical and current data, interpretations, and opinions. You will encounter many applications of the persuasive devices of Chapter 4 in the service of different interests and agendas.

Your job at this point is merely to survey—which means to examine and report on—the terrain. Imagine that you're a bird flying over a very large territory to find out what it holds. You can't expect to examine everything that's out there or become an expert in every aspect of it. Your intent at this point is merely to become as familiar as you can with what others claim to know about hunger. Later you'll be able to narrow your focus to one tree, while being aware of the entire forest.

Prepare to do the survey purposefully.

> **Panoramic questions: WWWWWWH?**
>
> **What** is hunger—its definition, its description, its effect?
>
> **Who** are the key people and organizations involved—the victims, the problem creators, the problem solvers?
>
> **Where** does hunger happen?
>
> **When** does hunger happen?
>
> **Why** does hunger happen?
>
> **How** have people tried to end hunger in the past? How can it be ended in the future?

In step 2 you will start as a team for planning, then split up to do the research. You will join together again as a team in step 3 to discuss what you have learned.

2a Plan your research strategy

● With your team, *review the questions* you identified earlier, for which you will be seeking answers.

● Together, *list sources of information that are available* to you. Your goal should be to obtain information from different kinds of sources, including (a) books, (b) documentary films, (c) websites, (d) magazines, (e) newspapers, and (f) television. At the end of this chapter you will find some sources your school library may wish to make available.

● Remind yourselves of all the *tips on evaluating sources* you have been given in this book. Review the Source-Statements-Self guide to evaluation at the end of Chapter 3, and tips on evaluating sources in Chapter 4.

● Note in advance *strategies for taking notes*. Planning saves you from potential confusion and much frustration later on.

Plan the time frame. Give the research as much time as you are able to, but be aware that without a pre-set number of hours to contain you, you could be starting an endless journey.

Plan to write down full reference information on the source as you find material, so that you can find your way back to the information later and acknowledge it appropriately if you use it. For a book, note author, title, full publishing information (publishing company, place and date of publication) and page reference. For a website, note its web address and the date you read it.

Plan to evaluate sources as you go. You might even use a scale of 1 (not credible at all) to 7 (extremely credible) to rate each, and note it next to the citation as you take notes.

Plan to keep your notes organized as you go. We suggest that you use your *Journal* to keep track of your ideas and reflections. To take notes, we recommend you use separate sheets of paper or large filing cards. Consider labelling six large cards with each of the six panoramic questions (WWWWWH?). On each, keep track of key terms or words that are relevant to each question, together with their sources. These cards will serve as your personal index, providing a compact overview of the extensive terrain you will encounter. To take notes on the panoramic questions as well as the specific questions your team identified, we suggest you label a separate sheet of paper or large card for each. As you identify new questions, place them on a new sheet of paper or card.

2b Do the research, critically

Working independently or with a partner, research critically for the fullest knowledge you can gain within the limits of the time you have.

● Since what you are doing is an overview survey, do not take detailed notes as you might for the narrowed, focused topic of

What is hunger—its definition, its description, its effect?

How have people tried to end hunger in the past? How can it be ended in the future?

your extended essay. Instead, *catch key ideas by noting the key words* in your sources (with their reference information) on your cards. For example, on your *What is hunger?* card you might note a distinction that a news magazine makes by noting key words "acute hunger", "chronic hunger", and "hidden hunger". On your *Why is hunger?* card you might note key words such as "drought", "exports favoured over feeding locals", or "overpopulation". Allow space around your initial notes so that you can fill in related ideas as you go.

- In addition, *jot down any answers* that you find to the definitional, factual, and ethical questions your team generated in step 1c in the list "Our team's questions about hunger".

Pay close attention to the form of representation in which the information is given, the degree of effectiveness of the communication, and its apparent purpose. Is the information given in the form of generalized information, or particular images or stories? Keep in mind the different strengths of the particular and the general considered as a theme through Chapter 5 on areas of knowledge.

Is the information given through language, metaphors of language, photographs, maps, or statistics? You may wish to refresh your memory on some knowledge issues that these representations raise by looking back to language as a way of knowing in Chapter 2 and persuasive devices using representation in Chapter 4.

As you gather information in its various forms of representation, be aware that you will be sharing your critical assessment with team-mates in step 3, when you will discuss your findings.

Statistics: Find statistics, for whatever years data is available. Note statistics you find particularly informative or striking. Are they consistent with each other?

Maps: In what ways are maps informative or striking? Are they consistent with each other?

Stories: Pay attention to the stories you encounter about real people suffering from hunger. Check out at least one relief organization that uses a "help children like Jorge" campaign to elicit donations. Make a note of a few stories that you find particularly captivating, and try to figure out why they struck a chord in you. Also include in your list any fictional stories involving hunger which you consider memorable.

Images: Reference in your *Journal* at least a couple of images which you find compelling and why you think they struck you as they did.

Language and metaphors: Notice language and metaphors that you consider particularly powerful, and keep track of quotations you find compelling.

> "The metaphors we use to describe the natural world strongly influence the way we approach it, the style and extent of our attempts at control. It makes all the difference in (and to) the world if one conceives of a farm as a factory or a forest as a farm. Now we're about to find out what happens when people begin approaching the genes of our food plants as software."[6]

Idea for presentation: If you have not previously done presentations on the knowledge issues raised by persuasive use of photographs or statistics, for example, you may wish to prepare such a presentation while you research this case study and give it when your team discusses your findings in step 3.

Hoodia, a traditional herbal appetite suppressant used by San Bushmen in the Kalahari desert to reduce their hunger pangs is now being grown in plantations in South Africa with the intent to manufacture a diet product for the overweight. Hoodia has been described as "a metaphor for a divided world".[7]

Tips for researching hunger

Statistics of hunger: Search for statistics, for example, on the following relevant topics:

- number of adults/children that die annually from hunger-related causes
- number of malnourished people
- percentage of food produced locally vs. imported from a distance of more than 100 km
- food crops vs. cash crops
- percentage of farmland area growing genetically modified seeds.

Stories of hunger: Good sources of stories about hunger and food include the Annual Reports published by Bread for the World. Three other sources, narrated in the first person, are the books *Hunger, an Unnatural History*, by S.A. Russell, *Hope's Edge*, by mother and daughter Frances Moore Lappé and Anna Lappé, and Miron Dolot's *The Hidden Holocaust* (about deliberate starvation of Ukrainian farmers in the 1930s).

Images of hunger: The video documentary *Silent Killer: The Unfinished Campaign Against Hunger* has images from several parts of the world. It is also a good source of stories, and of examples of people working effectively toward solutions.

2c Link your survey to broader terrain

Even while you are doing a broad survey of hunger, trying to gain an overview of the entire forest, *keep in mind the even broader survey* that includes many forests (and their surveyors) and the trails between them. In doing your survey, keep in mind what you have discussed in TOK regarding correlation and cause, and about the approaches to knowledge of different disciplines.

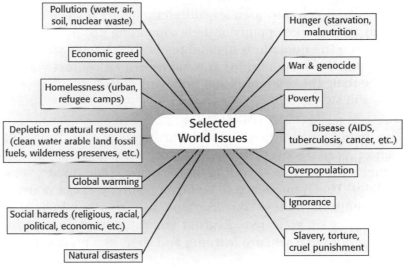

Note links to other world issues: Keep track of links between world hunger and other world issues.

Recognize links to areas of knowledge: Many of the facts—and even some of the arguments—you encounter will be based on the subjects that are part of your Diploma Programme and TOK areas of knowledge treated in Chapter 5. As you conduct your survey, *keep track of knowledge claims and methodologies* pertinent to hunger that are used within the different disciplines.

- How and what can biology tell us about the impact of starvation on the body? How and what can psychology tell us about the impact of starvation on the mind?
- What methods do the natural sciences provide for measuring calories or finding the cause of problems with crops, for example?
- What methods do the human sciences provide for gathering data on the hungry in a major city?
- What questions would you pose for geography, environmental science, history, the arts, politics, or ethics? With careful identification of knowledge issues and a sufficiently narrow focus, you could find effective material for a TOK presentation.

Because nobody can be expected to be an expert in all disciplines, it is crucial when conducting research of this scope that you identify which specialists you may need to consult to help you check for factual accuracy or further explanation.

2d Identify the issues

As you gather information in its various forms in this survey, notice that the material is seldom presented randomly—as bits of factual information without purpose or interpretation. *Note disagreement, inconsistencies, and sustained arguments.*

Note disagreements and inconsistencies. You are likely to note inconsistencies between the different sources. Just as in the questions your group listed in step 1, classify inconsistencies as definitional, factual (loosely defined as "what is"), and ethical (loosely defined as "what ought to be"). Keep track of the disagreements you encounter; you will return to them later when evaluating some of the information and ideas you're identifying here.

Note and summarize arguments. You will encounter different solutions proposed to reduce or end world hunger, and arguments proclaiming that there are more pressing problems we should attend to instead. Keep track of a few different arguments you encounter. Summarize the key points of their supporting justifications as well as you can. (The quotations highlighted in this chapter are all examples of arguments or support for arguments, whose context you can find by checking the references and following links.)

Step 3 Reflect on the survey

The timeframe you specified for your survey is over. Your *TOK World Hunger Journal* is overflowing with your ideas and responses. Now gather with the rest of your team to compare and discuss your findings. This is not a step to be taken lightly: you can potentially learn more from these conversations than from hundreds of hours researching on your own. Register your insights in your *Journal*, both about what you are learning and about the process in which you are engaging.

3a Reflect on your research strategy

- *Compare your research strategy* with that of other team members. What kinds of sources (books, websites, etc.) did you pursue, and why? What would each of you change about your research strategy if you knew at the beginning of the survey what you know now? Compare notes with each other. Which kinds of source (books, websites, etc.) did you find most fruitful? Why?
- *Compare biases you encountered*: Who were the "us" in the "About us" sections of websites, and the authors of the pieces you read? What editorial agendas did you encounter? Which sources did you consider to be the most credible, and why? Which sources did you consider to be the least credible, and why?

" Why is it that everyone plays ostrich and sticks their head in the sand when it comes down to admitting that most of today's food and water problems are only problems because of the rapid growth of the world's human population?" [8]

Panoramic questions: WWWWWH?

What is hunger—its definition, its description, its effect?

Who are the key people and organizations involved—the victims, the problem creators, the problem solvers?

Where does hunger happen?

When does hunger happen?

Why does hunger happen?

How have people tried to end hunger in the past? How can it be ended in the future?

3b Reflect on your research findings

● *Share the key words you noted* to catch the key concepts for each of the panoramic questions, and be prepared to discuss with others in your team any words that are unfamiliar.

For this process, appoint a scribe for the group to take notes as you share your key words. Do this in such a way that you can readily cluster key concepts together as you contribute them and all participants can end up with a copy: for example, large flipchart pages to be posted on a wall, or handwritten or computer notes to be copied for all of you to include in your *Journals*. An example of such a list can be found in Table 1 at the end of this chapter. The degree of detail of such a list will depend on the amount of time you are able to allot to doing research.

Quickly identify, as you go, any problems of overlapping or conflicting classifications with words in your list. Pick out some words that carry strong connotations, or have emotional overtones. Be aware of these in preparation for a later step of examining arguments.

● *Share answers to your team's own questions.* Do you now have answers, or greater uncertainty, regarding the questions you generated in step 1c in the list "Our team's questions about hunger"? If questions remain unanswered, consider both what kind of question it is (definitional, factual, ethical) and why it might remain unanswered. (Is the question too complex? If you had more time to research, would you find an answer?)

● *Share your observations and reflections on different forms of representation.* For each of statistics, maps, stories, images, and language (including metaphor), compare your findings within the group.

Share examples of representations—stories, photographs, statistics— that you feel particularly increased your understanding or struck an emotional chord in you. Try to explain why. As you listen to each other, pay attention to whether the example affects you as deeply as it did the teller. This is a good way to be reminded, yet again, that what pulls one person's heartstrings or rational mind doesn't necessarily affect another.

Identify representations used persuasively, and try to pin down the perspectives of the people or groups who have created them or used them. Picking particularly persuasive representations, consider whether you would call them "subjectively truthful" or "biased", and why. Is emotion always (or in principle) something to be avoided in communication regarding a world issue?

Consider frames 1 to 4 on pages 244–258. What forms of representation are being used for communication? What are the different appeals created by each of these examples? As a critical thinker, try simultaneously to respond, and be aware of your response. Try to be aware of what moves you, how it can persuade you, and whether that purpose is one which you accept—but without becoming unduly suspicious of any emotional appeal.

If you chose to prepare a presentation on knowledge issues raised by statistics, photographs, or other representations you found in your research, be ready to give it now, and invite your classmates to join in follow-up discussion of the knowledge issues you raise.

Imagine that you are a relief worker, doling out rations to people dying painfully of starvation. You ask yourself, "What does it take to make people see? What does it take to make them understand their own part in this? What does it take to make people care?"

FRAME 4

3c Reflect on the place of your survey within the broader terrain
Links to other world issues: Return to the Selected World Issues diagram at the start of this chapter. Based on your research and experiences in the world, do you think that are there any world issues that are not correlated to hunger? Do you agree with the FAO that rapid progress in reducing hunger is a prerequisite for progress toward the other seven Millennium Development Goals (p. 242)?

Links to areas of knowledge: Compare as a group the links you found with different areas of knowledge in your research, both for their claims and for their methodologies. Is there any subject you've studied in school that cannot be applied to obtaining an understanding of world hunger? If you planned a presentation involving any of the links you found, do it now.

3d Summarize arguments on causes and solutions
You are ready now for a final undertaking in this sequence of reflections. You have already noted in step 2d the disagreements, inconsistencies, and arguments you have encountered in your own exploration of world hunger. You have considered whether they concerned definitions and hence understanding of key concepts, or whether they were instead disputes over facts or ethical values. You have also analysed in step 3b the use of representations to communicate not only facts and feelings, but also perspectives and arguments.

Work as a team now to pool the major arguments you have found in your research. Again appoint a scribe to take notes as you identify and group them together as a team. Make sure all team-mates have copies to include in their *TOK World Hunger Journals*.

Since you cannot within a limited time deal with every argument on all aspects of hunger you surveyed, focus specifically on

● arguments for the causes of hunger and
● arguments for the solutions.

As a group, discuss which, at this point, strike you as most convincing.

W?

Why does hunger happen?

Summarize the arguments you have encountered on the causes of hunger.

H?

How have people tried to end hunger in the past? How can it be ended in the future?

Summarize the arguments you have encountered on solutions to hunger.

Step 4 Analyse the arguments

Some common aspects of arguments are illustrated by frame 5. Quickly discuss with your group: What argument is being illustrated by the photos and the legends included in the frame? What causes are being invoked, and what solutions are being suggested? What feelings does the argument elicit? Who stands to gain and who stands to lose if you're convinced by the argument?

Feelings

Intense emotion surrounds most issues that have impact on the people of the world, and none, surely, more than world hunger. Not to feel, it could be argued, is simply not to understand.

Most people would probably say that frame 5 elicited, or was intended to elicit, a guilty conscience, or pity for the people who can't afford even part of a fast food meal with an entire day's earnings.

Is this manipulation, or is it an example of an effective persuasive argument?

Among the tactics of manipulation you learned earlier (Chapter 4) was one called "appeal to pity". Are pity and other emotional responses to be blocked as irrelevant in any serious consideration of argument? Let us ensure that no confusion arises on this point. The appeal to pity, like the appeal to fear or the appeal to a sense of belonging, becomes a fallacy only when it is used to deflect an argument—to distract attention from the facts and persuade toward a conclusion that bypasses careful thought. Persuasion, similarly, becomes dubious only when it is dissociated from concern for truth. In analysing arguments, we expect ultimately to be persuaded—persuaded by the best arguments, those with sound justification and

" *You have your data, I have my data. So why don't we recognize that we're analyzing this from different world views? You have your value system, I have my value system.* " [9]

" *In the 21st century—the age of cell phones and Internet, and all that—for people to die of hunger, it's just abominable, it's wrong.* " [10]

FRAME 5

What argument is given here?

US $7.42

" *Today there's enough food in the world to feed nine billion people. The real problems are poverty and distribution: three billion people live on [US]$2 a day, and people lack access to land to produce the food they need.* " [11]

concern for truth. But we cannot, and should not, turn off our hearts. As we saw in Chapter 2, our reasoning and our emotional faculties are inseparable.

Cui bono?

This is not a reference to Bono Vox, the musician who actively promotes the end of poverty in campaigns such as "Make Poverty History". "Cui bono?" (kwē bō'nō) is a phrase in Latin, quoted by the historian Cicero at the time of Julius Caesar. It is still used today—quite often, actually—and means, "Who does it benefit?" or "Who stands to gain from this?"

You've done extensive surveying of the "Who" question. Consider all the key groups of people you identified. Which of these groups stand to gain if you're persuaded by frame 5? Which stand to lose?

Arguments do not exist in a vacuum. They are made by people with their own perspectives, and often their own interests at stake. If indeed we agree that on the one hand the world produces enough food, and on the other hand that allowing hunger in the 21st century is "abominable and wrong", one might logically ask why humans are allowing this suffering to happen. Several possible answers come to mind. Perhaps people are ignorant, and don't know enough about world hunger to realize that it's a solvable problem. Perhaps they don't care enough about the issue to learn more. Perhaps they're just repeating behaviours and attitudes which they learned from their forebears and have never questioned. Or perhaps they're very consciously benefiting from the status quo, for example by hiring starving people to work literally for peanuts, and are actively resisting the eradication of world hunger in the same way that many slaveholders in the Americas resisted abolition.

This is where the concept of power very explicitly enters any analysis of knowledge at work in the world. Who benefits from maintaining the status quo, or who benefits from a specific proposed change? As critical thinkers, in order to understand what seems illogical we need to be aware of the realities of power in the world. One way to do this is to keep the question "cui bono?" alive in our minds.

As you examine arguments for solutions to world hunger, ask yourself which groups of people (other than the victims of hunger) might benefit from each proposed solution. Consider "interest" or advocacy groups who try to influence government policy or legislation, as well as specific industries and other groups who might benefit economically. Think in ample terms, and consider different kinds of demographic groupings based on race, gender, age, geography, culture, or class. The following, for example, might be relevant to your analysis: people in industrialized nations, people in the developing world, local economies, global economies, agribusinesses, fast food chains, small farmers, proponents of sustainable development, vegetarians, retired people, to name only a few.

Note that identifying a group as a potential beneficiary does not necessarily mean that their members are acting out of self-interest. But, if potential beneficiaries fund studies that consistently conclude that their proposed solutions are better than all others, or if they support political candidates who in return will help them to legalize actions that benefit their agendas, we should at least raise a skeptical eyebrow…or two.

Note also that if one group stands to gain from implementing a proposed solution, other groups often stand to lose. Take this question with you as you examine solutions to world hunger: Who stands to gain, and who stands to lose, if each of the proposed solutions is implemented?

Arguments for causes, arguments for solutions

To what causes, explicit and implicit, does frame 5 attribute hunger? What solutions does it suggest?

Much of an analysis of argument depends on interpretation of cause, which, as you know from previous chapters, is extremely complex. Causal explanation involves numerous knowledge issues (see Chapters 2, 4 and 5). The cause you identify for hunger will affect your proposed solution; your proposed solution implies a particular understanding of the cause.

Have at hand your *TOK World Hunger Journal*, your notes on key words from your research in step 2, and your summary from the end of step 3 of arguments on causes and solutions.

Work as a team, to connect the arguments you have encountered for causes with the arguments you have encountered for solutions. Use the diagram below as a guide to organize your own data. What does your version of "Overview of causes and solutions" look like?

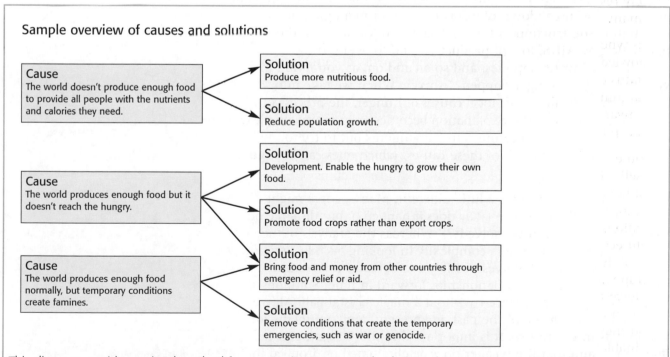

Sample overview of causes and solutions

Cause
The world doesn't produce enough food to provide all people with the nutrients and calories they need.

Solution
Produce more nutritious food.

Solution
Reduce population growth.

Cause
The world produces enough food but it doesn't reach the hungry.

Solution
Development. Enable the hungry to grow their own food.

Solution
Promote food crops rather than export crops.

Cause
The world produces enough food normally, but temporary conditions create famines.

Solution
Bring food and money from other countries through emergency relief or aid.

Solution
Remove conditions that create the temporary emergencies, such as war or genocide.

This diagram provides a visual method for connecting causes and solutions, for you to use as a guide for your own set of arguments. This example is based on Table 1 and Table 2, which you will find at the end of this chapter. Table 1 is a sample of what your research results might look like, using panoramic questions and key word answers. Table 2 gives a sample summary of possible solutions.

Counter-arguments for causes, counter-arguments for solutions

In the debate over world hunger, both causes and solutions can be examined by seeing what might be said *against* them. The process of counter-arguing is a process of thoughtful examination.

First, counter-arguing the cause is an attempt to scrutinize a causal analysis by looking for weaknesses. What are the problems with the methods of research? What are the flaws in the evidence it uses to justify its conclusions? What are the flaws in the reasoning? The methods of the natural sciences, human sciences, and history are immediately relevant in the close examination of conclusions reached about cause. These areas of knowledge provide to an informed debate on not only the findings of their areas but also general methods of questioning evidence and causal arguments. In your own survey of the terrain, the conflicting arguments you encountered are likely to have contained much counter-argument, as someone arguing for one causal explanation may have given considerable attention to refuting arguments for another.

If two causes are actually contradictory, then arguing for one is in effect arguing against the other. The first two causes given in the diagram on the previous page are opposed to each other. Does the world produce enough food—or does it not? Accepting one cause or the other is rather like accepting an axiom: all your further conclusions reasoned from that assumption will be affected.

More frequently, however, arguments for causes are not contradictory and do not refute each other. Far too many causes for hunger can exist simultaneously in a region of the world—conflict of armed groups, breakdown of infrastructure for marketing or distribution, destruction of the seed supply, devastation of the population by AIDS, loss of productive land to overgrazing, contaminated water supplies, and so on and on, as you found in your "Why does hunger happen?" survey. When we take into account the simultaneous, local causes of hunger, the process of counter-arguing a causal explanation becomes even more complex. Its goal becomes not to refute causal arguments but to try to prioritize them. Out of all of these causes, which ones can be argued to be the major ones?

Counter-arguing a solution is a little different. Many people might agree on a particular cause (*Why* does it happen?), but disagree on the solution (*How* can we solve it?). Whereas the analysis of the cause of hunger encounters complexity in looking back in time, the analysis of solutions involves possibly even greater uncertainties: it means projecting causal relationships forward in time. Solutions require an eye to the future—without a magic crystal ball. All we have is the knowledge of the past and present, and arguments for likelihoods in the future. It is important that those arguments be good ones, and that the weaker ones be eliminated or dropped in priority by a process of counter-argument.

Taking one of the causes listed in the sample overview of causes and solutions, counter-argue each of the proposed solutions. As a team, try to complete each counter-argument sentence given on the next page.

What besides sustenance do the hungry miss?

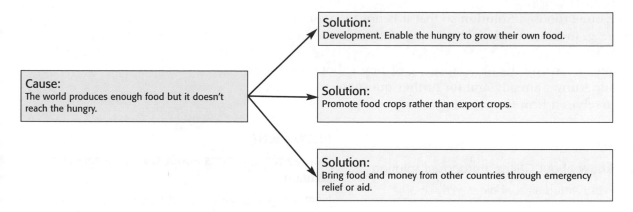

1   Development. Enable the hungry to grow their own food.

    counter-arguments: "We shouldn't do this because _____."

2   Promote food crops rather than export crops.

    counter-arguments: "We shouldn't do this because _____."

3   Bring food and money from other countries through emergency
    relief or aid.

    counter-arguments: "We shouldn't do this because _____."

After this process of counter-arguing, it may be that weaknesses
appear in some solutions: they may be impractical, or create many
further problems, or work only in the short-term, or not work
adequately in the short-term, or so forth. In this kind of process,
some solutions may end up eliminated in serious debate, while
others are ranked according to various criteria—such as urgency,
local applicability, cost, political viability, and many other factors.
Ultimately, there's no rule that says that we can only choose one
solution. Many solutions could be applied at the same time, since
they are rarely mutually exclusive. Consider the positive impact that
all solutions on Table 2 might have, if they were simultaneously
implemented, in different places, according to what would work best
at each place. Thus, a final argument that can generally be made
against any proposed solution is "Yes, but this other solution would
work even better…*here.*"

As you end step 4, make sure that everyone on your team has a
copy of your own version of the overview of causes and solutions.

Step 5 Take your own stand
Already your panoramic survey of hunger has closed in on particular
arguments, and you have moved still closer in starting to counter-
argue certain ones yourself. It is now time to come right to the
ground, to a spot in the forest that you choose.

As a team, you will use your own version of the Overview of causes
and solutions to consider what solutions to world hunger you
genuinely think are the best ones, and why.

1   Choose *one* cause to focus on (e.g. the world does not produce
    enough food).
2   Decide which one of your possible solutions is the best one. Call
    it your Proposed Solution (e.g. increase food yields using
    sophisticated technologies).

257

3 Narrow your Proposed Solution so that it is not too vast to explore (e.g. increase food yields using genetically modified (GM) crops).

4 Now duplicate swiftly the brainstorming of step 1, both for things your group knows already and for further questions to pursue. Give yourselves a firm time limit.

WWWWWH?

Things we know about GM as a proposed solution

Note things your group as a whole is fairly sure about.

WWWWWH?

Our team's questions about GM as a proposed solution

Note things your group is not very sure about or does not agree on, and questions that came out of discussion.

---

5 Do a final round of research to fill in the gaps in your knowledge, again with a firm time limit. Come back as a team to share and evaluate your information in a way now familiar: evaluate the sources and the representations for reliability, and note further arguments that your research has uncovered. Do not expect to become expert but, more modestly, simply to tip the balance on your team's lists from "our team's questions" to "things we know".

6 Ready? Now divide your team in two. One half will work to formulate supporting arguments in favour of your Proposed Solution (e.g. increase food yields using genetically modified crops). The other half will work to formulate counter-arguments to the Proposed Solution.

7 Get your team back together. Take the supporting arguments for the Proposed Solutions one at a time and consider counter-arguments. Consider the counter-arguments as well for how they in turn might be counter-argued. If you wish, you could run this exchange as a debate, but do keep in mind that your purpose is not to win in a contest but to scrutinize the arguments.

8 Finally, reach conclusions about your Proposed Solution. Do you all agree at this point? If you do not, why not? Are the differences in definitions, facts, or values? Do you think that research for further information would resolve the disagreements? If not, why not?

Step 6 Explore the explorer(s)

In step 1 of this exploration you explored the explorer. It's time to do that again, with the hindsight of what you learned. Please answer the following questions as honestly as you can. Share with your team or not, as you wish.

About the proposed solution

1 Where do you personally stand about the proposed solution your team chose to explore? Do you support it or reject it?

2 How did your team's interaction through the process affect the solution proposed, the general conclusion reached as a group, and the degree to which members accepted it as a sound conclusion?

3 Did the arguments you analysed change your opinion about the proposed solution? If so, in what ways?

Analysis of arguments: an overview

Analyse the media used

1 What medium was used to publish each argument?
2 How often are you exposed to arguments like these? Through what media does each kind usually reach you?
3 Who receives each message, and who does not?

Analyse the authors

4 Who authored the arguments? What other works have these authors or organizations produced? What qualifies them to author such arguments?
5 What biases, personal, institutional, or political, might these authors have?
6 Do the authors explicitly state their objectives?

Analyse the interest groups

7 Cui bono? Who might gain and who might lose if the argument prevails? If the counter-argument prevails?
8 Whose voices are heard in these arguments? Whose are not heard?
9 What are the values underlying the arguments?

Analyse how the arguments are presented

10 How does each side present its point of view? What does it use most extensively and most persuasively—images, language, metaphors, statistics, or maps?

11 Do any of the arguments strike you as propaganda?

Analyse the facts used as evidence in the arguments

12 How reliable do you consider the information given by those presenting the arguments?
13 If the evidence given is contradictory, what criteria determine the selection of facts?
14 Who paid for studies on which arguments are based?

Analyse ethical aspects

15 Are there conflicting values explicit or implicit in the arguments?
16 What ethical issues are involved?

Evaluate the quality of the reasoning in each argument

17 Are hidden assumptions or premises used as bases for the arguments?
18 Are the arguments valid?

Evaluate the strength of each argument

19 How strong is each argument? On an IB scale of 1–7 (1 = certainly false, 7 = certainly true), how do you rate the strength of each?
20 Does everybody on your team have same opinion of which argument is most convincing? If not, why not?

4 How certain are you of your position?
5 What further questions would you need answered to feel more certain?
6 What would it take to change your mind about the proposed solution you explored?

About world hunger

7 Revisit your answers in step 1 to questions on your own assumptions and knowledge, which you wrote in your *Journal* before investigating world hunger. If your answer would be the same today as it was then, place a checkmark by your first answer. If your answer has changed, explain how and why in today's *Journal* entry.

About your responsibilities

8 Do you feel that you have any kind of responsibility towards the hungry of the world? If so, do you intend to act on it? How?

The path of knowledge and the path of action

Few people who go through the process you experienced in this chapter will have placed checkmarks next to all the answers in their first *TOK World Hunger Journal* entry to confirm they have not changed. Few people will have remained unscathed, untouched, unmoved, unchanged by this exploration.

For those who were somehow affected by this journey, two interwoven paths open up at this point. The first is the path of knowledge. This experience has given you new eyes: you will start to perceive things which you didn't notice before. You may wish to keep track of these things in your *Journal*, even after this exploration is formally over. What invisible things in the world are now in front of you? What are you aware of in your own environment which you didn't notice before? What have you become aware of in your personal life or in your own community?

You may wish to continue exploring on your own. Perhaps you will continue to read about world hunger in magazines and newspapers, with a deeper understanding of the arguments, and of how complex and interconnected they are with other world issues. Perhaps someday you will return to step 4, choose a different cause or another proposed solution, and analyse more arguments to gain an ever deeper knowledge and understanding of world hunger—or of another world issue.

Or perhaps you will take the path that intertwines with the path of knowledge: the path of action. The final reflective question above was whether you felt you had any kind of responsibility toward the hungry of the world. If you answered "yes", another question follows: do you have any responsibility to act—to work towards a solution for world hunger?

That is a very difficult question. If we look at the IB learner profile for guidance, we conclude that the text isn't quite clear about what is meant by "act": "IB learners strive to be principled. They act with integrity and honesty, with a strong sense of fairness, justice, and respect for the dignity of the individual, groups and communities."[12] Likewise, service is only one of three components of your CAS programme. You are the only one who can answer, with your conscience and a sense of your priorities, talents, and capabilities, whether or not you wish to help eradicate world hunger, or help resolve another global issue which you consider to be even more pressing and critical.

If you choose the path of action—if you wish to make a difference, now or in the future—be aware that there are many different ways to do so. From supporting nonprofit organizations with time or money, to engaging in political action for social change, there are myriad smaller and larger ways in which you can make a difference. Even ways that may seem insignificant—such as choosing to buy (or not buy) certain products, or turning off the lights when you leave a room, or sharing with others the reasons why you're doing these things—are small but effective ways to influence what happens in the world, especially if many people do the same. Remember the butterfly effect!

Focusing on hunger in this chapter has allowed you to transform this issue into a personal question. You know your way a little better in the forest now; at least you have a compass and some sort of map. May your choice be a conscious and purposeful one, whichever it may be.

References

Books

Altieri, M. 2001. *Genetic Engineering in Agriculture*. Oakland, CA, USA. Food First Books.

Balkin, K. (ed.) 2004. *Poverty: Opposing Viewpoints*. Farmington Hills, MI, USA. Greenhaven Press.

Boucher, D.H. (ed.) 1999. *The Paradox of Plenty: Hunger in a Bountiful World*. Oakland, CA, USA. Food First Books.

Dolot, M. 1987. *Execution by Hunger: The Hidden Holocaust*. New York, NY, USA. W.W. Norton and Co.

Ford Runge, C. *et al.* 2003. *Ending Hunger in our Lifetime: Food Security and Globalization*. International Food Policy Research Institute. Baltimore, MD, USA. Johns Hopkins University Press.

Lappé, F.M., Collins, J. and Rosset, P. 1998. *World Hunger: Twelve Myths. Second Edition*. New York, NY, USA. Grove Press.

Lappé F.M. and Lappé, A. 2003. *Hope's Edge: The Next Diet for a Small Planet*. New York, NY, USA. Jeremy P. Tarcher/Putman.

McDonald, B. and Jehl, D. 2003. *Whose Water Is It? The Unquenchable Thirst of a Water-Hungry World*. Washington DC, USA. National Geographic Society.

Pawlick, T.F. 2006. *The End of Food*. Fort Lee, NJ, USA. Barricade Books.

Pollan, M. 2006. *The Omnivore's Dilemma*. New York, NY, USA. Penguin Press.

Russell, S.A. 2005. *Hunger: An Unnatural History*. New York, NY, USA. Basic Books.

Shiva, V. 2000. *Stolen Harvest: The Hijacking of the Global Food Supply*. Cambridge, MA, USA. South End Press.

Sider, R.J. 2005. *Rich Christians in an Age of Hunger: Moving from Affluence to Generosity*. Nashville, TN, USA. W. Publishing Group.

Images

Menzel, P. and D'Aluisio, F. 2005. *Hungry Planet: What The World Eats (A Photographic Study)*. Napa, CA, USA. Material World Books and Ten Speed Press.

Silent Killer: The Unfinished Campaign Against Hunger. Film by Hana Jindrova and John de Graaf. www.silentkillerfilm.org (accessed 4 September 2006).

UN Millennium Development Goals Report 2005. http://unstats.un.org/unsd/mi/pdf/MDG%20Book.pdf (accessed 21 August 2006).

Websites (accessed 21 August 2006)

Bread for The World Annual Hunger Reports: www.bread.org/learn/hunger-reports/

Center for International Earth Science Information Network (CIESIN)'s Poverty Mapping Project: www.ciesin.columbia.edu/povmap/

Food and Agriculture Organization (FAO) Animated Hunger Map (data for several years): www.fao.org/es/ess/faostat/foodsecurity/FSMap/map14.htm.
Food and Agriculture Organization (FAO) The State of Food Insecurity in the World. Yearly reports from 1999 onwards: www.fao.org/SOF/sofi/index_en.htm.
Millennium Development Goals Indicators: http://unstats.un.org/unsd/mdg/default.aspx.
UN Cyberschoolbus Data about Country Groupings: http://cyberschoolbus.un.org/infonation3/menu/advanced.asp.
UN World Food Programme (WFP) interactive real-time world hunger map: www.wfp.org/country_brief/hunger_map/map/hungermap_popup/map_popup.html.

Tables 1 and 2 exemplify possible results from step 3 and supplement your own ideas in preparation for step 4. How detailed your lists are depends in part on the time available.

Table 1 Possible key word list (step 3b)

1a What is hunger?
- Starvation, malnutrition, malnourished, undernutrition, food insecurity, food security, energy requirements, balanced diet
- Acute hunger, chronic hunger, hidden hunger
- Nutrients, protein-energy malnutrition (PEM), micronutrient malnutrition, over-nutrition (empty calories with nutrient deficiencies), ketosis, dehydration, wasting
- Granaries, millet, sorghum, cassava, maize, corn, beans, legumes, food chain
- Anorexia nervosa, bulimia nervosa

1b What are the effects of hunger
- Premature death, disease, infections, malaria, tuberculosis, pneumonia, diarrhoea, measles, HIV/AIDS
- Disabilities, low birthweight, hindered fetal development, pre-term birth, stunted physical growth, stunted intellectual growth, mental retardation, blindness, propensity to illness
- Confusion, slow thinking, sapped energy
- Attention focused on getting food and water; despair, hopelessness, fear

2 Who are the victims of hunger?
- Infants, children, women, homeless, destitute, disadvantaged, rural poor, urban poor, slum dwellers, unemployed, elderly
- Peasants, smallholder farmers, rural landless
- Refugees, displaced persons, socially disadvantaged, victims of racism and other forms of discrimination, migrant populations, civilian victims of conflict

3 Where does hunger happen?
- Countries: Niger, Haiti, Darfur (West Sudan), Afghanistan, Korea (PDR), Colombia, Dem Rep Congo, Mali, Southern Africa, Bolivia, (WFP data)

Panoramic questions: WWWWWH?

What is hunger—its definition, its description, its effect?

Who are the key people and organizations involved—the victims, the problem creators, the problem solvers?

Where does hunger happen?

When does hunger happen?

Why does hunger happen?

How have people tried to end hunger in the past? How can it be ended in the future?

- Regions: Central Africa, East Africa, southern Africa, India, other South Asia, Caribbean, Central America (FAO data)
- India, Mexico, Brazil
- USA and first world countries (malnutrition and overnutrition), anorexia, bulimia, obesity

4 When does hunger happen?

- Temporary: famines, insects (locusts), drought, floods, war, genocides, political crises
- Chronic: for the several reasons listed in "why" and others related to other world issues

5 Why does hunger happen?

- Insects (locusts), erratic weather (drought, floods), global warming/climate change/greenhouse effect, political crises (war)
- Chronic poverty, AIDS, no access to markets, scarcity, hoarding, lack of money to buy available food, lack of money to buy seed, fertilizer/agrochemicals, and tools, lack of know-how, lack of water to use for irrigation/animal husbandry
- Lack of agricultural infrastructure, roads, storage, silos, exports favoured over feeding locals, farmers paid not to plant, waste
- Soil erosion, topsoil loss, mineral depletion, overcropping, desertification, overgrazing, depletion, pollution, deforestation, degradation, illegal logging
- Groundwater, over-pumping, waterlogging, salination, poor drainage, water diversion, groundwater contamination, damming, sewage, global warming, pollution of the oceans (Inuit can no longer subsist on traditional diets)
- Food crops, cash crops, meat consumption, competing uses for grain (livestock feed, ethanol for motor vehicles), competing uses for animal protein including fish (livestock feed and pet food in Europe and North America), land speculation
- Industrialization of farming, globalization, monocultures, monopolies, agricultural subsidies, agribusinesses, large landowners, displacement of small food producers into more fragile lands, urban sprawl, canal irrigation, cattle ranching
- Population density, population growth, fertility rates, overpopulation, family planning
- Yields, cropland per person, scarcity, per capita food supply, FAO undernourishment measure (national food availability, not food actually consumed by people)
- Maldistribution of food, sharecropping, tenant-operated farms

6a How have people created hunger or tried to end it in the past?

- Green Revolution, intensive agriculture, herbicides, petrochemical fertilizers, fossil fuels, pesticides, agrochemicals, insecticides, irrigated agriculture, tubewells, crop agriculture, Blue Revolution, fisheries, fish farms, monoculture, machinery, superfarms, corporations, Livestock Revolution, dairy farms, meat farms, livestock feed, growth hormones, antibiotics, food processors, exporters, shippers

- International Monetary Fund, World Bank, General Agreement on Tariffs and Trade (GATT), World Trade Organization (WTO), privatization, deregulation
- The World Food Summit (WFS, 1996), Millennium Development Goals (MDGs), Rome Declaration on World Food Security, World Food Summit Plan of Action

6b How can it be ended in the future?

- Provide soil, water, seeds, fertilizers, proper tools, infrastructure (roads, electricity), pest management education, credit to small-scale farmers
- The Gene Revolution, GMOs, genetically modified organisms, genetically engineered seeds, biotechnologies, *Bacillus thuringiensis* (Bt), plant biotechnology, genomics and molecular breeding, transgenic crops, patents, biodiversity, seed diversity, drought-tolerant seeds, herbicide tolerance, super weeds, Monsanto
- Potable water, desalination plant
- Agroecological farming, indigenous knowledge, sustainability, diversity, interdependence, synergy, intercropping, crop rotation, mixing of plant and animal production, intentional diversity, compost, manure, permaculture, crop and livestock diversity, educate women, green manures, agroforestry, water management
- Change system of food distribution, subsidies, global vs. local, legal reforms (right to food), land reform
- Food safety, water safety, nutritional quality, fortify foods with micronutrients, vegetarian diet, mariculture, aquaculture
- Food aid, World Food Program (WFP), emergency rations, food banks, soup kitchens, relief organizations, factory canteens, foreign aid
- Community supported agriculture, farmers markets, buying local, political action

Table 2 Some proposed solutions to world hunger (step 3d)

- Increase food yields by using sophisticated technologies (GMOs, aquaculture, mariculture).
- Continue to increase food yields by using the methods of the Green Revolution.
- Increase food yields by using sustainable methods (agroecological farming, water management, intentional diversity).
- Promote land, credit and tax reform to enable small farmers to use land that currently lies fallow.
- Educate the hungry to enable them to escape poverty.
- Provide the hungry with the tools to feed themselves (clean water, seeds, fertilizers, proper tools, roads, electricity, etc.).
- Reverse the tendency to grow food for export rather than to feed the country's hungry (food crops instead of cash crops, grain feeding people instead of livestock).
- Promote globalization, so that more poor people can make more money and buy food.
- Oppose globalization, so that poor people are less exploited and not trapped in poverty.

- Transport food from more fertile areas to less fertile (including emergency relief, charities from individuals).
- Reduce population growth.
- Etc.

World hunger

Knowledge in the world: how to use this chapter

This chapter grows out of the theory of knowledge course, in harmony with its aims, and reinforces the thinking skills of the course. It demonstrates both the flexibility of teaching methods used in TOK, in which no two classrooms will be identical, and the place of TOK in contributing toward the IB learner profile: "The aim of all IB programmes is to develop internationally minded people who, recognizing their common humanity and shared guardianship of the planet, help to create a better and more peaceful world."[13]

In this chapter, we have structured an application of TOK thinking to world issues, choosing world hunger as the case study. Our goals are:

- to give students practice in applying TOK awareness and thinking skills, such as gaining self-awareness, recognizing multiple perspectives, thinking critically about information, making interdisciplinary connections, and considering responsibility for action
- to show students how those skills can be carried far beyond their IB graduation as they become lifelong citizens of the world.

We encourage students and their teachers to adapt the exploration of a chosen world issue to the circumstances of their own school. Different possibilities:

- The case study, followed sequentially, could be the culmination of the TOK course.
- The world issue selected could provide topics for class presentations scattered throughout the course in preparation for the case study's sequence of activities at the end.
- The treatment of the world issue could be done in co-operation with other Diploma Programme courses and CAS activities.
- The research portion of the world issue could provide topics for extended essays in various subjects, while the analysis of specific knowledge issues could provide topics for TOK presentations.
- With *great* care in identifying and emphasizing knowledge issues, the TOK course could be taught with a world issue as its focus.
- This chapter on a world issue could be a resource for reading and discussion. Even reading the chapter may give students a greater sense of the important contribution TOK makes to their total IB education.

From amongst the alternatives on offer in my school at the time, I chose Robotics. I thought it would be a course I would enjoy and I remember being pretty excited about starting. But quickly I felt so frustrated that I tried to change into another class. Although I had been studying a lot and trying quite hard, the assignments and questions on the tests confused me and I could never find a strategy that worked. My marks were pretty bad and I felt that I would never get it right. I just didn't know what the teacher or the course expected from me.

The desolate scene above is imaginary but, in some contexts, could be very real. It is far, however, from what you should be experiencing in your IB Diploma Programme classes. For the IB diploma, every assessment task you are required to complete has been designed to collect information about the extent of your learning in relation to a series of pre-established criteria. Long before an examination is written or the TOK titles for a session are decided, everyone involved, including you the student, knows by what measures (or criteria) your work will be judged (or assessed).

Using criteria to promote TOK learning

As in all your other Diploma Programme subjects, the assessment criteria for TOK do not depend on your school or region, nor on the session or year in which you are entered for the Programme. The criteria do not change over long periods of time—about seven or eight years—and when they do change schools are advised of changes well in advance so that they can have no negative effect on your learning and your results.

The criteria are not only pre-established and stable, they are also public. They are published in the subject guide and should be shared with you. While it is very likely that you have already seen and practised using the criteria for TOK work, if you have not, we strongly suggest you ask your teacher to provide them to you now.

This system of assessment, known as "criterion referencing" or "criterion-based assessment" is one of the pillars of the IBO's educational philosophy and policies. Amongst other reasons, the IBO adopted this system as a result of a conclusion reached through research on teaching and learning: the clearer students are about what is expected in a task, an assignment, or examination, the more likely they are to achieve that expectation. In other words, by having the criteria of assessment on hand, you don't need to guess what you need to do to get good results. You can easily find out by consulting the assessment criteria for each of the assessment tasks in the different subjects in which you are enrolled. In principle, the more fully acquainted you are with the criteria that teachers, examiners, and assessors will use to mark these tasks, whether you produce them under examination conditions or during regular class time, the more effectively you can work towards successful results.

You are probably very familiar with a kind of assessment by which you either *know* or *don't know* something (the capitals of all African nations, the chronological order of the main events of the French revolution), or know or don't know how to do something (multiply three-digit numbers, find the area of a figure). In contrast to this "all or nothing" approach, observe the table below. This is one of the criteria used for assessing the TOK essay. Each criterion is a continuum and the "descriptors", as they are called, portray different levels of achievement along it—from a demonstration of knowledge and skills that is basic and simple to one which is more developed and complex (9–10).

Criterion A Understanding Knowledge Issues
(*TOK Guide, 2006, page 52*)

Achievement level	Descriptor
0	Level 1 is not achieved.
1–2	The essay includes very little treatment of knowledge issues that are relevant to the prescribed title and demonstrates little understanding of them. If present, areas of knowledge and/or ways of knowing are merely mentioned.
3–4	The essay includes some treatment of knowledge issues that are relevant to the prescribed title and demonstrates a rudimentary understanding of them. Some links to areas of knowledge and/or ways of knowing have been attempted but they are largely ineffective.
5–6	For the most part the essay treats knowledge issues that are relevant to the prescribed title, and demonstrates some understanding of them. Some effective links are drawn between areas of knowledge and/or ways of knowing.
7–8	The essay consistently maintains as its focus knowledge issues that are relevant to the prescribed title. Effective links and some comparisons between areas of knowledge and/or ways of knowing are drawn, so that the essay demonstrates a good understanding of the knowledge issues under consideration.
9–10	The essay consistently maintains as its focus knowledge issues that are relevant to the prescribed title. Effective links and comparisons between areas of knowledge and/or ways of knowing are elaborated, so that the essay demonstrates a sophisticated understanding of the knowledge issues under consideration.

You can use descriptors like these to help you judge where you are on the continuum at any time in the course with respect to any piece of work for IB assessment. Although your final goal will be to produce work that fits the top achievement level in every criterion, be realistic and kind to yourself by having lots of intermediate goals or stepping stones as you gain more experience and practice in doing TOK tasks and homework assignments.

The criteria used to assess your work in IB subjects have been written to fit neatly together with the course objectives as formulated in the subject guide and reproduced here. Although the language in which they are written might sound a little formal, try to think of each objective in terms of the activities you have done in the previous chapters. Slowly but surely you have been working towards these objectives since the very start.

To reach your own conclusion about how you are doing in TOK, periodically look at these objectives and ask yourself, "To what extent have I demonstrated this or that TOK objective (in today's classroom discussion, in the assignment I handed in, etc.)?" Aim to move towards the higher achievement levels, bit by bit.

So, Course assessment go hand in hand. Unlike many other systems in which students quite rightly wonder what is going to appear on a test and how their work will be marked, in the IB generally and TOK in particular these are not mysteries that you need to solve.

TOK course objectives

Having followed the TOK course, students should be able to:

1 analyse critically knowledge claims, their underlying assumptions and their implications

2 generate questions, explanations, conjectures, hypotheses, alternative ideas and possible solutions in response to knowledge issues concerning areas of knowledge, ways of knowing and students' own experience as learners

3 demonstrate an understanding of different perspectives on knowledge issues

4 draw links and make effective comparisons between different approaches to knowledge issues that derive from areas of knowledge, ways of knowing, theoretical positions and cultural values

5 demonstrate an ability to give a personal, self-aware response to a knowledge issue

6 formulate and communicate ideas clearly with due regard for accuracy and academic honesty.

from the IBO TOK subject guide[1]

TOK assessment requirements

You will have to complete two assessment tasks to fulfil the Diploma Programme requirements for TOK:

● do a TOK presentation in your own classroom
● write a TOK essay on one of ten titles from a list that the IBO publishes for the session for which you are registered.

Here's some good news: unlike most of your other IB subjects, TOK is not assessed under examination conditions. You will have plenty of time to devote to TOK assessment, if you want to take it.

Presentation

Although you cannot redo the same presentation to try to improve your mark, your teacher will provide students with as many opportunities as time and scheduling permit to do presentations as an integral part of the TOK classroom experience. It is likely that you will have more than one chance to do a presentation.

You can also expect that by witnessing your classmates' presentations and participating in the class discussions they provoke, over time you will form a clearer and more complete picture of what a good TOK presentation is like.

The TOK presentation is "internal assessment". In other words, your own teacher will decide the appropriate mark using the pre-established IB descriptors and submit that mark to the IBO. If you do more than one presentation, your teacher will send in the highest mark achieved.

You will find more advice about presentations later in this chapter.

Essay

You may write as many drafts of your TOK essay as your heart desires (and the school deadlines permit). Your teacher is not allowed to make detailed comments on a draft, but he or she is allowed to give you general guidance. You are also permitted to exchange drafts with your classmates for general advice. Like you, they will be working with the TOK descriptors.

The TOK essay is "external assessment". In other words, your school will send your final essay to an external assessor, who is a TOK teacher or former TOK teacher, or someone such as a university professor familiar with TOK. The assessor will decide the appropriate mark using the very same descriptors that you're using for the essay. Remember as you write that the assessor will not understand references to particular events in your school, or perhaps even your country, so make sure that you include any necessary explanation.

You will find more advice about essays later in this chapter.

Knowledge issues

If you have ever had a cast on your leg or arm, you might remember noticing many other people in the same situation, something it is unlikely you would have done under "normal" circumstances. As a result of any number of personal circumstances—from having a broken leg to recently having dyed your hair blue—ordinary people and things that might have previously been quite invisible to you can be transformed into subjects you register or become particularly interested in.

Some students of TOK have claimed, especially towards the end of the course, that the TOK perspective that they have acquired makes visible to them what in the past would have been invisible, in a similar way. We want to help you to achieve this state. Although the term "knowledge issues" has been used many times throughout this book, owing to its centrality in the assessment of your TOK work, the next few pages offer further support to improve your understanding of "knowledge issues" and some exercises you can undertake to become an expert at pinpointing them with increasing ease and precision.

In your IB courses you have probably come across some course content and assessment tasks framed in terms of "issues". IB economics treats "international issues". Geography tackles "developmental issues" and language B recommends that oral presentations cover "social, cultural, or global issues". For example, in geography students learn about trade, aid, and indebtedness and about environmental quality. These developmental issues have to be treated from not one but two perspectives: that of "richer countries" and that of "poorer countries".

As their name indicates, *knowledge issues* are a specific kind of issue. The main characteristic that knowledge issues share with all other issues is that they elicit discussion or even debate. Many issues may attract a curious mind and invite exploration and argument. *Knowledge issues* direct that questioning approach toward knowledge itself.

Knowledge issues have been part of your experience of TOK through this book from the very first pages. Do you recall your opening profile of yourself as a knower, and the map of the world you drew? The main knowledge issue there was the way that different personal characteristics and experiences affect what people know—a fundamental knowledge issue which has returned again and again as we considered our ways of knowing and areas of knowledge. Every time you asked yourself whether an argument was valid or not, or whether someone's justification for making a claim was sound—as you did in previous chapters—you also raised knowledge issues, in this case about what constitutes a good argument and about what may be better and worse reasons for believing.

Knowledge issues may be easy to identify within this book and your TOK discussions, in retrospect. You can readily look back on exercises and discussions about whether the particular language you speak affects what you know, when evidence is enough evidence for a sound inductive conclusion rather than a hasty generalization or a stereotype, whether photographs pass perfectly the correspondence test for truth, what the difference is between persuasion and propaganda, what the role is of assumptions in everyday interpretation and in areas of knowledge, what sources may be more reliable than others and why, what counts as a good explanation, how metaphors may affect how we think and what we believe, whether knowledge has to be useful to be of value, and so on. Go back to the first paragraph in this section starting with "If you have ever had a cast on your leg…". What knowledge issue do you notice in this paragraph?

Still, for TOK assessment—and for your future as a critical thinker—you will want to be able to pick out knowledge issues not just within this book but also in the world around you. You are well prepared to do so, but will probably benefit from some practice. As a start, read the following example of an imaginary situation in your own town and see how it is rich with knowledge issues.

Situation A: Over the last week or so you have been following the story of a crime committed not far from where you live. Tonight's news coverage includes short interviews with the Chief Inspector of Police, the Mayor, a priest, and the victim.

First, consider what you know about the situation already by asking whichever of the panoramic brainstorming questions apply to this situation. Consider what you might want to check again in the newspaper or on the Internet. Then start to pick out the issues—the *knowledge* issues. Possible results are exemplified below.

Finding the knowledge issues

1 **What** was the crime reported on the news?
A woman was grabbed from behind. A gun was jammed into her back, and a man's voice growled threateningly, "Your money!" When she pulled out her wallet, he snatched it and fled.

Knowledge issue of selection of information: What makes this particular event newsworthy while other events go unreported? More generally: what factors of selection and emphasis influence the knowledge of current events that the public can gain from the media?

2 **Who** was the victim? Who was the robber?
The woman was Mrs Thomas, who was walking home from the bus stop. The robber's identity is not yet known, but police are following clues. Mrs Thomas said that the man "sounded like a Spick".

Knowledge issues of evidence, language as an indicator of bias, stereotypes: What evidence is there that the attacker was Hispanic? What evidence is there that such an identification could be the result of prejudice or local stereotyping? More generally: What is the effect on knowledge of stereotyping?

3 **Who** on the news was giving information?
The reporter, the Mayor, the Police Inspector, a priest, Mrs Thomas.

Knowledge issues of perception and sources: Who is the best source of information and understanding of an event? How do personal characteristics affect what each of the interviewees selects to report and to interpret as the cause? What is the best method for someone seeking the truth amid different perspectives?

4 **Where** did it happen?
The robbery took place on Gerald Street, six blocks from Main. Mrs Thomas lives on the next block.

Knowledge issue of explanation and interpretation of cause: What kinds of cause are given in the news? Human motivation? Ongoing background causes? Immediate trigger causes? How far "out" and "back" is it useful to trace causes for the explanation of a specific event, the robbery? (Why was the new port built? Why did the boss give priority to the client's needs rather than his employee's?) To what extent do decisions on solutions to the problem depend on the analysis of the cause?

5 **When** did it happen?
10:00 pm

Knowledge issue of ethics, responsibility: Does the crime give any particular responsibility to Mrs Thomas, her neighbours, the priest, the Police Inspector, or the Mayor? If so, what and why? Does knowledge of a problem give any responsibility for finding a solution?

6 *Why* did it happen?

Neighbours say that they have been asking the town council to install better streetlights, but have been ignored.

The Police Inspector says that theft has increased with a recent increase in drug trafficking, ever since the new port was opened in a nearby city.

The Mayor says that the problem is insufficient public funding for the police force.

Mrs Thomas says that the man was violent and evil. She also says that she would not have been out there on the dark street at night if it weren't for her boss, who required her to do overtime to get a report ready for a demanding client.

The priest says that many of his parishioners have become anxious recently about their personal security even in their own homes, and deplores violence and the easy availability of guns.

Knowledge issue of ethics, gun control: In what ways is the topic of gun control an ethical issue? How can it be treated appropriately in argument? Should the issue be assessed in terms of principles (right to carry a gun, right to personal safety, rights of individual vs. rights of community) or in terms of consequences? Is there another way of evaluating situations and choices ethically?

7 *What* was the effect?

The police have the crime under investigation, interviewing witnesses who saw a man loitering earlier in the area. The Hispanic community has protested that crime in this town is always blamed on them. Mrs Thomas and her neighbours have again formally requested better street lighting.

Knowledge issue of…: Your turn to add!

Now, using the crime story as a model, choose either situation B or C from below and in small groups check any further information necessary for understanding the situation. Then formulate as many knowledge issues about it as you can.

Hint: If you have difficulty getting started, flip through the section headings and questions of the previous chapters, noticing TOK concepts (classification, authority, sources, sense perception, influence of technology on justification, truth…).

Situation B: You always follow the Tour de France bicycle race, marvelling at the cyclists who face this gruelling test of speed, strength, and nerves. The winner in 2006 tested positive for doping.

Situation C: You heard on the news in August 2006 that there are now eight planets in the solar system, not nine as you learned in school, and as your parents and grandparents learned in school. Members of the International Astronomical Union voted to remove Pluto's planetary status.

Tips for recognizing and formulating knowledge issues for TOK

Knowledge issues are embedded in everyday situations, as in A, B, and C above.

Knowledge issues are present in all your subjects at school.
Every knowledge claim made in every academic course you take is
potentially a source of knowledge issues. Your subject teachers will
sometimes point out to your class explicit connections with TOK.
But do not wait for the teacher to do your job. It is really up to you
to think about how the areas of knowledge or the subjects you are
studying connect to knowledge issues, and how what you are
discussing and thinking about in TOK relates to your other subjects.
What knowledge issues could you raise about the facts, theories, or
ideas you learnt about in school today (or any day)?

When you wish to practise identifying knowledge issues, do the
following exercise. Review the examples below and, with a
classmate, formulate a few knowledge issues that you can see could
emerge from them. Alternatively, you could do this same exercise
starting from things you really have learnt or have been asked to do
in your subject classes.

- In biology, you watched a video about Crick and Watson's
  discovery of the "double helix".
- In computer science you were given the task of writing code that
  will facilitate the IB Diploma Programme coordinator's job: to
  organize and manipulate data regarding students' groups 3, 5,
  and 6 options.
- In mathematics, you worked during a whole hour using the
  symbol ∞ for infinity. You remember reading Rabindranath
  Tagore's poem "On the seashore" and your teacher insisting that
  it was about infinity.
- Your economics (or psychology) teacher told your class that for
  decades students were given a particular textbook to study from.
  It had sold over four million copies, 15 editions were published
  and the text was translated into 41 languages. Your class wasn't
  given this text this year. According to your teacher, it has fallen
  into disrepute.

Lurking in your IB subjects are some good presentation topics and
examples for TOK essays: more about both later on in this chapter.

Knowledge issues are present in moments of your everyday life.
These everyday situations also suggest knowledge issues. Either use
these to practise or try the alternative activity that follows.

- As you walk down a hallway at school, you hear someone
  remark: "There have always been rich and poor in every society.
  It is the way of the world."
- A friend of yours is extremely thin. She exercises for hours every
  day, usually declines any food offered her, or sometimes eats a
  lot and quietly finds a toilet. You have tried to encourage her to
  eat, but she seems convinced that she is overweight.
- Two friends are discussing whether it is fair or not that TOK and
  the extended essay each contribute only 1.5 points to the IB
  diploma. Personally, you think it's unfair that CAS receives no
  point recognition at all.
- Some students in your class want to organize a school event to
  raise consciousness about brand name clothing sweatshops

around the world. They asked you to participate in the steering committee to decide what kind of event would be most effective.

● A friend phones you with the information that your best friend's fiancée, someone you have never trusted, has been seen dancing extremely close to another man on Saturday night and might even have gone home with him, and suggests that you warn your friend that she is unfaithful.

Activity

Every member of your TOK group should take a few minutes in class to recall a situation of the kind given above and then briefly describe it on a piece of paper. Put all the pieces of paper in a hat or bag and have every member of class select one. Everyone should then find knowledge issues implicit in someone else's situation. Then pair up and improve on each other's identifications of the knowledge issues.

Knowledge issues are present in local and international events and in the media which report them.

Complex topics such as AIDS or global warming are rich with knowledge issues, as you have seen in the treatment of world hunger in Chapter 6. So is media coverage of any international conflict, as you have seen repeatedly throughout this book. Spotting knowledge issues in the news is an important part of your TOK education. Be warned, though, that if you want to use a complex topic as material for a TOK presentation or for examples in your TOK essay, you must narrow the topic to something of manageable size. It is to practical advice that we turn next.

The more you can develop your skill at identifying knowledge issues, the better you will do on all TOK assessment. That is a promise.

Developing your voice and perspective

Another important feature of TOK learning concerns a skill that is natural to all of us as human beings. Each one of us has a unique, distinguishable voice, with its particular register, timbre, and tone. TOK learning stimulates the development of your own personal voice and perspective on knowledge issues. Your TOK work will be assessed for the extent to which your voice is sharp and clear and conscious of itself as one amongst many others.

You can help yourself develop a personal voice and perspective in a host of ways, from more simple ones like sharing your opinions and ideas with your classmates, and listening to theirs, to refining your ideas in the light of class discussions, readings, and experiences.

Do not assume that merely using "I believe (or think, or conclude...) that..." when writing your TOK essay will guarantee you a high mark on Criterion B: Knower's Perspective. If you are comfortable doing so you should feel free to write in the first person ("I"). But it is not necessary to do so. It is perfectly possible to convey your voice and perspective writing in the third person ("he, she, it"), that is, using a more formal style. Similarly, do not think that in order to get a high mark, you must share with your audience any personal information about yourself. If you feel comfortable using a personal example that serves to illustrate or highlight an important point in your essay, then include it. Throwing in a story or two about yourself, however, is not sufficient. Assessors will be looking for relevant examples, not just personal ones.

Fix in your mind the qualities that describe Knower's Perspective in the context of the TOK essay and presentation (boxes below). Take note of what assessors will be looking for as marks or symbols of this skill—having your own distinctive knower's perspective.

TOK essay

Criterion B: Knower's perspective[2]

- To what extent have the knowledge issues relevant to the prescribed title been connected to the student's own experience as a learner?

- Does the student show an awareness of his or her own perspective as a knower in relation to other perspectives, such as those that may arise, for example, from academic and philosophical traditions, culture or position in society (gender, age, and so on)?

- Do the examples chosen show an individual approach consciously taken by the student, rather than mere repetition of standard commonplace cases or the impersonal recounting of sources?

TOK presentation

Criterion C: Knower's perspective[3]

- Did the presentation, particularly in the use of arguments and examples, show an individual approach and demonstrate the significance of the topic?

To summarize, shape your essay and your presentation to show a personal, reflective exploration of knowledge issues. Choose your examples from your IB Diploma Programme subjects and from topics that really do concern you, from your own life experience and from the experiences of others in your community. Consider perspectives you have heard in your own class as well as those you have read or heard from other sources.

In this book, people's voices accompanied by their photos have been included in an effort to bring to life many other perspectives. Remember that the quality of your work will improve by taking other experiences and views seriously, and by showing that you are sensitive to the fact that yours is just one voice amongst many, one perspective amongst many others. We invite you to add your own voice to the many you have read about in this book and that surround you wherever you live.

The TOK presentation

The TOK presentation is an opportunity for you to show your skill at identifying and discussing knowledge issues in the context of the relatively comfortable surroundings of your own classroom. Each presentation should have two stages: an introduction briefly describing the real-life/contemporary situation or topic you have chosen; and then a treatment of knowledge issues in this topic. The very broad term "real-life/contemporary situation" was purposefully conceived by the authors of the subject guide to allow all TOK students to find topics of genuine personal concern and interest to them as knowers. Your teacher might provide you with some alternative topics to choose from, or might instead leave you to decide completely on your own. Locate the TOK presentation icon in previous chapters to remind yourself of the kinds of topics that can count as real-life or contemporary situations that are appropriate for assessment purposes.

Putting TOK into the presentation

The scenery or context: real-life/contemporary situation

Time for TOK presentations? Whether you are working on your own or with other members of your class in a small group, start by defining some situations or general topics that concern or interest you. Focus on ones that might pique your classmates' curiosity in order to engage them in a great classroom discussion after your presentation.

Some strategies for finding a topic include the following:

- Collect written material from newspapers and different sorts of magazines. Notice photographs, captions, charts, graphs, and headlines. Be conscious of the kinds of stories that catch your attention. What do they have in common? Read some articles more thoroughly than you may have done at the time of the events or when you first read or heard about them.
- Consider activities you particularly enjoy. What are your hobbies? Special skills? Sports? Do you play in a band? Do you go to art exhibitions or go to every film or play you can? Are you a member of a club, society, or local community?
- Think about your own life experience. Your experience as a best friend or grand-daughter, part-time worker, or immigrant can provide interesting material for reflection.
- Think about your favourite IB subject. Consider the topics or skills within it that interest you most and the reflections that are stirred in your mind.
- Consider your CAS programme, and your most enriching experiences within it.
- Think about any cause, local or global, that you support.

If you are working in a group, share your ideas. Then narrow your choices down to two or three topics. You now have a "short list".

Knowledge issues: the heart

First, to decide which topic on your short list is the winner, ensure that you can formulate the knowledge issue(s) that make it relevant and interesting from a TOK point of view. Discard any topic about which you cannot pose at least one clear question concerning knowledge. Go back to the section on knowledge issues earlier in this chapter if you aren't sure. This is a vital step in this process. If you skip it, or skimp on it, your presentation will not fulfill the essential TOK requirement.

Second, ensure that the topic is a practical and effective choice for the amount of time you have. Be conscious of your time constraints. TOK presentations can be done by a single student or a small group working together, with a maximum of five students per group. You will have approximately 10 minutes per member of the group with a maximum of 30 minutes. In other words if you work on your own, you will be given 10 minutes (not counting the discussion time your presentation provokes); if you work with a classmate, 20 minutes, or if you work with a group of three to five, about 30 minutes. Time management and planning are crucial for ensuring a successful presentation.

Discard, therefore, any topic which requires considerable background information before you can begin to treat the knowledge issue. If you need 20 out of your 30 minutes to present to your class information on a topic about which they know almost nothing (e.g. chaos theory, the details of a cause you support, or the legal requirements for refugee status), it's probably not a good topic. Similarly, if you are contemplating a topic with a lot of detail, such as the conflict between your country and its neighbours, you would be well advised to look elsewhere if you cannot narrow it to the point that most of your time, effort, and creativity are put into developing the knowledge issue(s).

One certain way to guarantee that knowledge issues are the centre of attention in your presentation is to fulfil what is an IB requirement anyway: do a good job on the presentation planning document which your teacher will ask to discuss with you in advance. In it, you will have to state:

- the knowledge issue(s) that will be the focus of your presentation
- a summary in note form of the way you plan to deal with it in your presentation.

The action on stage

Decide on the kind of "action" you are going to stage for your presentation in terms of how best to portray the perspectives on, and convey the depth of, your understanding of knowledge issues applied to the situation you have chosen. Live skits (say of news reporting or interviews to a panel of experts) and dramatized readings are popular ways of getting across to your audience different perspectives on knowledge issues, as are showing video clips or listening to a recording of you and your group doing something out of class as a means to launch into your live analysis. You can use music, costumes, props of all sorts, and any material (visual or otherwise) that you think will work in the service of your prime objective: to demonstrate how much and how well you can apply TOK skills to a real-life/contemporary situation. What takes place "on stage" should help your audience understand the heart of the matter.

Knowledge issues—the heart of your TOK presentation

In this book and in your classroom you have read about and discussed an enormous variety of knowledge issues. Choose one or a few well-defined, related issues that emerge from or are implicit in the real-life/contemporary situation you have chosen. Spend most of your presentation treating them from different perspectives.

Your topic—a real-life/contemporary situation...the context or scenery you choose

Decide from amongst a vast array of possibilities, including:

- your personal life experience as a unique individual or member of a community
- local, national, or regional discussion and affairs of interest to you
- global or international problems, dilemmas, crises that matter
- aspects of interest within areas of knowledge you are studying
- news or news coverage of events: political, scientific, technological amongst others.

Fending off potential disaster

The two scenarios below describe presentation plans that will not lead to good presentations. Can you see why?

1   You and the other members in your group are very motivated to learn about global warming, so you decide to choose it as the topic of your TOK presentation. Since there are three classmates in the group, each chooses a different aspect of global warming to research. You spend a Sunday afternoon explaining your findings to each other, and create a PowerPoint presentation in which you include not just the information you gathered but also graphs and photographs about climate change as complementary visual aids to heighten your classmates' understanding of this phenomenon. You are confident that you will engage the other members of your TOK class so much, that they too will want to find out more about this topic.

2   A few weeks ago you saw a video about birth control in which amongst other things, a fetus was shown to feel acute pain. You decide that the real-life situation for your TOK presentation is abortion. You decide first to answer for your class some basic questions concerning types of abortion, the variety of ways it is possible to induce it and a description of what you have learnt is called "post-abortion syndrome"; then to present some comparative facts about abortion laws in different countries. Since two of the members of your group are strenuously opposed to abortion, while you and one other member think that abortion is a choice that belongs to each woman, the class is guaranteed to hear both sides of the argument. Everyone in the

class will want to participate in the discussion your presentation is sure to provoke.

Review the TOK Presentation Criteria and in particular, the description of the top achievement level for each, given below. In their light, identify the defects in these presentation plans, modify the design, and in the process discover some common problems so that you can avoid them when you do your own presentation.

TOK presentation assessment criteria[4]

A Identification of knowledge issues
Did the presentation identify a relevant knowledge issue involved, implicit, or embedded in a real-life situation?

Achievement level	Descriptor
5	The presentation identified a knowledge issue that was clearly relevant to the real-life situation under consideration

B Treatment of knowledge issues
Did the presentation show a good understanding of knowledge issues, in the context of the real-life situation?

Achievement level	Descriptor
5	The presentation showed a good understanding of knowledge issues

C Knower's perspective
Did the presentation, particularly in the use of arguments and examples, show an individual approach and demonstrate the significance of the topic?

Achievement level	Descriptor
5	The presentation, in its distinctively personal use of arguments and examples or otherwise, showed clear personal involvement and fully demonstrated the significance of the topic.

D Connections
Did the presentation give a balanced account of how the topic could be approached from different perspectives?

Did the presentation show how the positions taken on the knowledge issues would have implications in related areas?

Achievement level	Descriptor
5	The presentation gave a clear account of how the question could be approached from different perspectives and considered their implications in related areas.

Putting the TOK into the presentation: a real-life odyssey

by Manjula Salomon

1 Search link: find a topic

Start with your own questions, your passions, or your concerns.

Collect many newspapers and magazines of different kinds. Flip through them, seeking a topic in which you're highly interested—one which you'd like to deepen your understanding of. (Note that it's easier to choose a topic of wide scope and narrow it down, than to choose a limited topic and stretch it out.)

Or you may hear about an interesting real-life situation in one of your classes, such as geography. For example, you decide to investigate recent natural disasters attributed to global warming.

2 Question link: formulate a question

Go to a reliable website that gives background information on your chosen topic. Once you understand what has happened, you can explore the situation with a focus on knowledge issues.

Think: what knowledge issues offer themselves? In the natural disaster example: prediction, cause–effect, ethical aspects, coverage in the media, others particular to the natural disaster you chose.

Formulate your knowledge issue as a question. For example, could this disaster have been predicted? Was it a consequence of global warming? To what extent is there a moral instinct to help others in the face of disaster? Who has the responsibility to help others?

3 Organizational link: plan the presentation

a Honour the Knowledge Tripod:
  1 a real-life situation leads to
  2 identification of knowledge issues, which are analysed through
  3 different perspectives.

b Be aware of the organizational sequence expected in a TOK presentation. Can you cover all the necessary points in the time allotted? Is your focus on the knowledge issue(s)? Do you feel personally involved with the topic? Are you exploring and analysing it from different perspectives? Do you recognize the implications of these perspectives?

c Decide how you're going to deliver the presentation. If you're working with others, set up the protagonists, the members of your group who will represent sides or perspectives. Use them to bring out your "connections" of different perspectives. Will you present a role play, a re-creation of an event, a talk show, a panel…? Use your imagination to figure out how best to deliver the key elements of your presentation.

4 Performance link: deliver the presentation

Create a common understanding in the first few minutes. Set up the topic with only as much narrative as needed for your audience to understand the issue. Perhaps you need a handout, a news clip, a mini skit. Go for what interested you in the first place—strike gold with your own interest and passion about the topic.

Audience involvement is to your advantage. Perhaps you want to take a poll of their opinion before and after your presentation.

Bon voyage. Use your own approaches. Use your own country. Use distinct cultural viewpoints. Contrast viewpoints. Do not seek to "win" a debate, but to walk a modest mile in the company of your TOK peers. TOK students do not stay on the shore. Begin your odyssey. The sirens of knowledge call.

Final tips on presentations
- Cover one or a few knowledge issues in depth rather than trying to cover a lot in a shallow way. Clearly identify them in the planning document you have to hand in to your teacher.
- When you make a claim, statement, or judgment about your topic, immediately seek out counter-claims by asking yourself what someone who disagrees with you would say, and what reasons he could give.
- Don't forget that yours is one amongst various perspectives on the topic. How might a person from a different culture, or of a different age, generation, class, religion, educational background, or academic discipline think about this issue? Incorporate these perspectives in the format of your presentation, in your decision about what will take place on centre stage.
- It may be easy enough to find fault in other people's positions, and to identify their questionable assumptions, presuppositions, and biases. What are yours? Probably these are harder to spot, but constitute a very important part of TOK learning which, once acknowledged, will earn you points on your presentations. This is an essential life skill.

You will be asked by your teacher to assess your own presentation using the TOK assessment criteria. Your teacher will hope to confirm your self-assessment. If not, though, it will be the teacher's marks that are sent to the IBO. Do your best to get it right, and to earn the highest score you can.

The TOK essay

Myth: Every subject requires a different kind of essay.

Fact: Although there are some surface differences in approach, all Diploma Programme subjects, the extended essay, and theory of knowledge demand some fundamental qualities in a good essay:

- a demonstrated understanding of the topic under discussion

- a demonstrated skill in analytical thinking in the form learned in the particular subject

- a well-organized and clearly written presentation of the ideas, with control of overall argument

- honesty in not plagiarizing, and formalization of this principle by following accepted practice of footnotes and bibliography.

Gaining control of essay writing in any one part of your Diploma Programme helps in all other parts.

Unlike the topics for your class presentations, the questions you will answer for your TOK essay—called "prescribed titles"—come from the IBO. Your teacher will reproduce for you a list of ten titles out of which you will choose one to answer individually, as will all other IB candidates for the session in which you are registered. Two-thirds of your final TOK mark for the IB rests on how well you can demonstrate, through this essay, the breadth and depth of your TOK learning.

The TOK essay can be a great pleasure to write. It is your chance to show your own keen mind at work, truly engaged with significant knowledge issues. It is your chance to demonstrate that you have thought about the huge range of ideas raised in TOK and are ready to speak about them in your own voice, taking your own perspective and being *aware* that you are doing so. These are sophisticated skills, but as you emerge from a TOK course thoughtfully followed, you are ready to demonstrate them. If you can do a fine TOK paper, you will have reason for immense satisfaction as you graduate with your IB diploma.

Think of the essay as a performance. Admittedly, you will not have an audience to give you thunderous applause nor a stadium of fans to cheer as you step onto the winner's podium. But if you can be clear about your goals in performance and meet them *as well as you can*, you will have achieved a private triumph. In the upcoming section, we will give you advice on setting these goals—and we encourage you to aim high. Go for gold!

Six steps to a really good theory of knowledge essay

Step 1 Select a title from the IB prescribed list

Do not instantly seize upon a prescribed title that sounds appealing and plunge into it headlong. Often titles that at first glance seem easy are the most difficult of all, so really read all ten titles on the list. Remember that you may not change the title to something else that you *wish* you had been asked, but must respond exactly to what the IBO has given.

Which three or four titles allow you to demonstrate best your understanding of TOK knowledge issues and your own critical thinking skills? Of those, which ones most catch your personal interest and give you a sense that you have something to say that will show your perspective as a knower? If you are at all unsure about the meaning of "knowledge issues", go back to the earlier parts of this chapter.

What are the key concepts? Which knowledge issues will you treat?

There are some key words you will find in each of the titles, for example, "evidence", "belief", "knowledge", "truth", and "justification". Are you clear about what they mean? Are there multiple possible meanings or ambiguities in their meaning? Think back on class discussions and check class notes. Refresh your memory on chapters in this book that are particularly relevant.

Put the title into your own words to make sure you understand what is being asked, and check your understanding with your teacher.

Identify explicitly what is/are the central knowledge issue(s) of the title. If after having given it some thought you still aren't sure about this, choose a different title, no matter how much time and effort you have expended. Without clarity regarding the knowledge issue(s) involved in the title, you will not be able to write a good TOK essay.

Step 2 Read the instructions and reread the assessment criteria

1   Read the title you have chosen, paying attention to its particular instructions. What exactly are you being told to do?

What are the key words of instruction?

Identify any tasks the title asks you to undertake by paying attention to action words. If you are told to "assess" or "evaluate" a claim, then you are supposed to consider the arguments both for and against it, taking into account any ambiguities in interpreting it. Possible responses include, *for example*:

- that the claim is justified in these ways or up to this point, but not justified in those ways or beyond that point

- that whether or not the claim is justified depends on what is meant by one of its key words or concepts, so that if you understand the key word this way the claim is justified, but if you understand it that way it is not

- that, although some justification can be offered for this point of view, the claim is really an oversimplification of an issue which needs to be understood with awareness of the following complexities…

If you are asked "to what extent" or "in what way" or "how" a statement is justified—or whether a given statement is true—then you are being asked the same thing, but in different words.

Notice that the instructions on making and supporting arguments are not unlike those for all other courses where essays are required.

2 Review the general instructions found at the top of the prescribed title list. These apply to all TOK essays, regardless of what the key words of instructions within them may be. These instructions tell you exactly what you are expected to do in your essay. The instructions will be similar to the following:

Remember to centre your essay on knowledge issues and, where appropriate, refer to other parts of your IB Diploma Programme and to experiences as a knower. Always justify your statements and provide relevant examples to illustrate your arguments, and remember to consider what can be said against them. If you use external sources, cite them according to a recognized convention. Examiners mark essays against the title as set. Respond to the title as given; do not alter it in any way. Your essay must be between 1,200 and 1,600 words in length.

3 Now read over the criteria according to which your essay will be marked. Pay attention to the top descriptor to set in your mind the standard of excellence towards which you are aiming. You have to know what is required to get the gold.

TOK essay assessment criteria[5]

A Understanding knowledge issues

This criterion is concerned with the extent to which the essay focuses on knowledge issues relevant to the prescribed title, and with the depth and breadth of the understanding demonstrated in the essay.

A **relevant** knowledge issue is one that directly relates to the prescribed title undertaken, or one that the essay has shown is important in relation to it.

Depth of understanding is often indicated by drawing distinctions within ways of knowing and areas of knowledge, or by connecting several facets of knowledge issues to these.

Breadth of understanding is often indicated by making comparisons between ways of knowing and areas of knowledge. *Since not all prescribed titles lend themselves to an extensive treatment of an equal range of areas of knowledge or ways of knowing, this element in the descriptors should be applied with concern for the particularity of the title.*

- Does the essay demonstrate understanding of knowledge issues that are relevant to the prescribed title?
- Does the essay demonstrate an awareness of the connections between knowledge issues, areas of knowledge and ways of knowing?

Achievement level	Descriptor
9–10	The essay consistently maintains as its focus knowledge issues that are relevant to the prescribed title. Effective links and comparisons between areas of knowledge and/or ways of knowing are elaborated, so that the essay demonstrates a sophisticated understanding of the knowledge issues under consideration.

B Knower's perspective

- To what extent have the knowledge issues relevant to the prescribed title been connected to the student's own experience as a learner?
- Does the student show an awareness of his or her own perspective as a knower in relation to other perspectives, such as those that may arise, for example, from academic and philosophical traditions, culture, or position in society (gender, age, and so on)?
- Do the examples chosen show an individual approach consciously taken by the student, rather than mere repetition of standard commonplace cases or the impersonal recounting of sources?

Achievement level	Descriptor
9–10	The essay shows much evidence of independent thinking about the knowledge issues related to the prescribed title. The student has shaped the essay in a way that shows both a personal, reflective exploration of the knowledge issues and significant self-awareness as a knower. There is serious consideration of different perspectives. Examples chosen are varied and effectively used.

C Quality of analysis of knowledge issues

- What is the quality of the inquiry into knowledge issues?
- Are the main points in the essay justified? Are the arguments coherent and compelling?

- Have counter-claims been considered?
- Are the implications and underlying assumptions of the essay's argument identified?

This criterion is concerned only with knowledge issues that are relevant to the prescribed title. Analysis of knowledge issues that are not relevant to the prescribed title is not assessed.

Achievement level	Descriptor
9–10	The inquiry explores with a high degree of insight, in considerable depth and/or detail, knowledge issues. All main points are justified and arguments are coherent and compelling. Counter-claims are explored and evaluated. Implications and underlying assumptions of the essay's argument are identified.

D Organization of ideas

- Is the essay well organized and relevant to the prescribed title?
- Does the use of language assist the reader's understanding and avoid confusion? Are central terms explained or developed clearly in a way that assists comprehension?

Note: This task is not a test of "first language" linguistic skills. No account should be taken of minor errors unless they significantly impede communication.

- When factual information is used or presented, is it accurate and, when necessary, referenced? "Factual information" includes generalizations.
- If sources have been used, have they been properly referenced in a way that allows them to be traced? Internet references must include the date on which they were accessed.

Note: See the TOK subject guide for further guidance.

An essay that fails to meet the required limit of 1200–1600 words will not score above level 4 on this criterion.

An essay that has no relevance to the prescribed title will score 0 on this criterion.

Achievement level	Descriptor
9–10	The essay on the prescribed title is very well structured, with an effective overall organization. Concepts are used clearly and, where appropriate, refined by helpful explanations. Factual information used to support arguments is correct. Sources of information and ideas are acknowledged; all referencing permits tracing of sources. The word limit has been met.

Step 3 Gather your ideas

1   Brainstorm. Brainstorm in several sweeps across the ideas. Have paper in front of you, and a pen ready for quickly jotting down your ideas.

First sweep: You've already identified the knowledge issues in the title and your instructions. Now—what comes to your mind? Jot it down! What assumptions might there be within the title? What areas of knowledge and ways of knowing will you talk about in your essay? What kind of comparisons will you make between them? What examples can you think of already? Don't give any attention to sentence structure or beautiful phrasing. Just write quickly until your mind storm, inevitably, passes.

Second sweep: Use circles, arrows, links, or whatever other markings work for you to connect up the main jotted ideas on the page in front of you. Cluster them: group them for similar points. Then focus your mind again on the knowledge issues of the title, and brainstorm again, pushing your thoughts more deliberately now. Are there perspectives on the issues other than the ones you have noted—perspectives from other cultures, other age groups and interest groups, other areas of knowledge than the ones that came to you first? Can you notice any assumptions that you are making yourself? Scribble down your thoughts. If they obviously and instantly belong to your first clusters, add them there, but otherwise just write.

Third sweep: Read over everything you have written and mark new clusters forming. Then focus your mind again on the knowledge issues of the title, and brainstorm again, this time giving much more deliberate attention to what you have gathered so far. Think in reverse. What can be said against the points you are starting to make? What counter-claims might expose their limitations or add a level of complexity? What are the implications of your main points? If you accept them then what else do you end up also accepting? What follows from them, logically? What key words do you find yourself using, and are you clear in your mind what they mean? What areas of knowledge and ways of knowing, from amongst the first ones you noted, would be the best ones to use? Without discarding anything yet, start to highlight the main points toward an essay that will not merely do a superficial tour of ideas and areas of knowledge, but select the most relevant for giving depth and effective treatment to the knowledge issues in the title.

What ways of knowing and areas of knowledge are relevant? Which ones are the best to discuss here?
Think broadly, drawing links and comparisons between ways and areas. Try drawing lines between parts of the TOK diagram and think of connections that your title suggests. Think about different perspectives on the issue that other people may have.

2   Now enrich your immediate ideas by going back over notes from your TOK class to remind yourself of discussions that are relevant to your title. Go back through this book, using chapter

titles and headings—and, of course, memory—to locate relevant
ideas. Gather examples to illustrate your points from notes and
texts from your other Diploma Programme courses, the media,
people you know, your own experience, or any other relevant
sources. But remember that the TOK essay is not a research
paper: you will not find your response to the title in a book or a
website. Books and other sources give you only the *raw material*
from which you, as knower and author, must shape your *own*
response. Review the section "Developing your voice and
perspective" (see page 274).

3   If time allows, live with your ideas floating in your mind for a
week or so at this point, gathering more as thoughts hit you in
class, your CAS activities, or elsewhere. This step of gathering
ideas is often challenging—and extremely enjoyable. It is a
chance to engage your own mind in considering the central TOK
question: "How do I/we know?" If you find it interesting to
consider different ideas, or like to reflect on what beliefs or
knowledge your life experience and education have given you,
you will probably find this stage personally stimulating.
Moreover, as you have seen, you will be given credit in your
essay for pulling together the relevant ideas in a way which
reflects your own thinking and draws illustrations of ideas not
only from public facts and explanations but also from your own
life experience. Find your own connections, and prepare to
speak with your own voice.

Step 4 Organize your ideas in preparation for writing

Now comes probably the greatest challenge—to move from scribbled
notes toward a plan for an essay which lays out a sequence of
arguments that clearly respond to the title. If you find this step
difficult, remember that no one is born already knowing how to
write an essay. It takes concentration and practice to learn to swim,
to tango…or to organize ideas for an essay. Allow yourself only a
few minutes to wail "But I *can't*…!" and then settle down to start
planning.

1   Cluster all your many, many ideas into related groups. At this
point, you should concentrate on identifying your *thesis*—that is,
the central point that you want to make about knowledge issues
in response to the title, the *argument* that emerges from your
thoughts on your rough material. Distil this argument into a
single sentence to write at the top of your plan. Your thesis is the
single most important sentence in your entire essay. *Make sure*
that it responds to the title and focuses on knowledge issues.

Now shuffle your ideas into an order that will work to develop
this argument throughout your essay. Make sure that every
subsection of your essay develops this core idea in some way,
including considering counter-arguments to it. If any ideas you
gathered in step 3 are not actually relevant to your thesis, force
yourself to cut them out of your plan no matter how much you
like them.

2   Refine your general line of argument: will you agree with the
title's assertion (if it makes one) or will you disagree? Some of
the best essays agree (or disagree) *with reservations*. What will

287

these be? There is almost always something to be said for different perspectives and for different sides of an argument. Make sure that you consider opposing views and that you are as critical (or as forgiving) of your own perspective as you are of those that you oppose or contest.

3   There is no formula for a perfect plan. The only thing essential is that the sequence of ideas as you move from subsection to subsection in the body of your essay must develop your thesis, which in turn must respond to the set title. Generally, however, it should be possible to follow the argument of your essay simply by reading your thesis in the introduction, the topic sentence of each of your paragraphs, and again the restated thesis in your conclusion, clinching the argument.

Some basic essay patterns

There is, we repeat, no formula for a perfect essay plan. However, if you are aware of common patterns, you may make your own organizational choices more effectively.

> Will you place your thesis *first*, or your thesis *last*?

In order to decide on an overall strategy for argument it might be useful to consider the following two major patterns of essay development.

Placing the thesis first

In this pattern of development, you place your thesis in your introductory paragraph (usually as its final sentence after an opening stylistic flourish and a sentence or two to establish your topic) so that your central argument hits the reader right at the beginning. Each subsection of the body of the essay then supports and develops the thesis to create a sustained argument.

The overall argument is created by the sequence of main points: the thesis gives the main argument and the topic sentences of paragraphs give the supporting arguments. The conclusion picks up the thesis again, restating it in somewhat different words as an argument which you have, by that point, firmly established.

Note that the thesis will often have the counter-argument built right into it (e.g. "Although X has some justification, Y is more convincing."). You will usually treat counter-arguments at the beginning, in order to lay them aside as you move on to give—in order of climax with the most persuasive at the end—the arguments which you think are best justified.

Placing the thesis last

In this pattern of development, you place in your introduction (usually as its final sentence, just as with the thesis first pattern) a focused question raising for discussion the knowledge issue(s) of your title. Each subsection of the body of the essay then treats aspects of the question or possible answers to it, usually in order of climax with the most convincing answer at the end. The thesis then emerges firmly at the end of the essay as the conclusion of the argument, the answer to the question posed at the beginning. This pattern simulates the process of thinking and reaching a conclusion. Do not be fooled, though, into thinking that you really can just think and write as you go. This pattern demands just as much advance planning as the other; you will need to know before you start exactly what your introductory question will be, exactly what your answer will be at the end, and the sequence of questions that will lead your reader through the simulated reasoning process from beginning to end.

Different school systems or writers favour one pattern or the other. If you are in doubt about which to use or unsure of your writing skills, however, the thesis-first pattern is safer in immediately getting your argument on track and giving a reader confidence in your control of ideas.

How will you handle major structural comparisons?

The essay of comparison

The marking criteria demand "effective links and comparisons" if you are to get the gold. Links are the connections you make in your writing that show that you understand, for example, the relationship of a particular way of knowing to a particular area of knowledge. A link may be elaborated with supporting arguments and examples, but may also be made as a minor argument, using quite a light touch. If you simply mention the term "sense perception" or the term "history" in passing, though, you demonstrate nothing useful to your argument. Even a link with a light touch needs to be developed enough to fit into your argument.

In a comparison, the connection between parts of the course is developed through treatment of similarities and differences—through balancing equivalent elements against each other so that their essential characteristics emerge more clearly. A comparison may balance mathematics, on the one hand, with science on the other. It may balance reasoning as a way of knowing, on the one hand, with sense perception on the other. If you are making comparisons, however, make sure that you are doing so not just to demonstrate your capacity to reproduce class notes or make tidy tables or lists. *Use* that comparison to make a point. Use it to support your argument on knowledge issues.

Like links, comparisons may be made quite lightly in sub-arguments. Often, though, they give structure to an essay. If a comparison is central to your argument, then start by making two parallel columns, for example one for mathematics and one for the natural sciences. Work out what you consider to be the points of similarity and the points of difference, and then try to line them up side by side.

Only then are you ready to consider the fundamental patterns for an essay of comparison—the *alternating pattern* and the *block pattern*. What you are doing in either is essentially classification. You have five main points of comparison, for example, which you are using as arguments to support your thesis, and two areas of knowledge between which you are drawing these comparisons. Will you base the outline of your essay on a five-part structure or a two-part structure?

- In the alternating pattern, you will base your outline on the five-part structure, the sequence of points of similarity or difference. For example, you may open with two features that mathematics and science have in common, treating first mathematics and then science (or vice versa) in a consistent order. You may follow with three features that show their essential differences. (All the points of comparison, whether they are similarities or differences, will, of course, be the ones relevant to your thesis, which in turn is your response to the prescribed title.)

- In the block pattern, you will base your outline on the two-part structure, treating all of one element first (e.g. mathematics) and all of the other element second (e.g. science). It is essential in the block pattern to have your sub-points in parallel between the two blocks; the features of similarity and difference that gave the structure to the alternating pattern become in block pattern the sequence of supporting points within each half of the comparison. If you use the block pattern, make sure that you create a strong comparative bridge between the areas as you move from one to the other, and in your second block make comparative references ("Like X, Y also does...") back to the first, or your essay may seem to fall apart into two unrelated pieces, neither of which successfully makes any argument at all.

- The advantage of the alternating pattern, when the elements being compared line up against each other quite neatly, is that it gives a strong sense of argument. The advantage of the block pattern is that it accommodates imbalance in degree of development a little more easily. It is also more adaptable to three blocks if you want to extend your comparison from two elements to three (e.g. mathematics, sciences, arts).

Remember, though, that your ideas do not serve the pattern; the pattern you choose has to serve your ideas. Adapt it and modify it to your argument.

> How will you introduce counter-arguments without seeming to contradict yourself?

The essay of argument and counter-argument

The marking criteria demand, for a top performance, that "counter-claims are explored and evaluated". How can you argue, though, on both sides, or several sides, of a claim? If you do so clumsily, you will end up contradicting yourself or confusing your reader.

First, make sure that you understand any claim that the title is either making or asking you to consider, and that you have thought about the implications of accepting or rejecting the claim. That is, if you accept the claim, what else logically follows from it that you are also accepting? (If A, then B.) The following examples of *implications* are based on TOK prescribed titles of past years:

- If you accept a certain definition of truth, for example, then what are the logical consequences for how you evaluate truth in science or history? Does that definition include or exclude certain scientific or historical claims, or include or exclude certain methods of testing?
- If you accept that the ultimate test for a scientific theory or a work of art is the test of time, then what follows regarding this year's contributions to those areas of knowledge? How might the implications change if you take a different interpretation of "the test of time"?
- If you accept that we can know something that has not yet been proved true, then what other ideas are you also accepting regarding knowledge and certainty? What further consequences logically follow for the justifications for knowledge in different areas?

Once you have understood the claims and their implications, you are ready to make your own claims, seeing also their implications. You are ready to prepare your arguments to support or to reject the claim, and to consider how best you can justify with good reasons the stand that you are taking.

But pause. After an entire course in TOK, which has explored complexity, will you simply accept or reject a claim without considering what could be said against either too-ready acceptance or too-ready rejection? Unlikely. Take your own conclusions about the claims you are considering, and first examine them. What can be said against them? Imagine yourself placed inside someone else's mind and try to argue against your own point of view.

Remember as you do so that the purpose is not simply to play some sort of word game or to prepare to win some kind of debating contest. The purpose is genuinely to scrutinize from different perspectives knowledge issues embedded in the title and its claims, in order to achieve a fuller understanding of complexity and an outside perspective to frame your own thoughts. When you have thought about the claims and the arguments that support them, you must reach your own conclusion. Get past any temporary paralysis of the mind, and argue for what you genuinely think is the best justified view, the one you find most convincing. Listen to the voices around you, but find your own.

Clarify in your mind your own perspective and your own conclusions. Clarify in your mind your thesis and its supporting sequence of arguments. You have only one difficulty left: what are you going to do with those arguments on the other side?

There are several ways to stay on track with your own argument while still acknowledging counter-claims. The three possibilities below are not the only ones.

1 Using sentence structure

As you write, tuck demonstrations of your awareness of counter-claims into subordinate positions in your sentences and your paragraphs. Include them, but do not let them derail your own argument. (e.g. Although someone from a part of the world with no distinct seasons will have good reason to impose limits on this generalization, the cycles of seasons in the year surely affect our assumptions about patterns of life and the metaphors we build into our languages…)

2 Using dialectic pattern of organization

Structure your essay in dialectic pattern, rather like a debate. In your introductory paragraph, firmly plant your thesis, but include within it some acknowledgment that the generalization you are about to make does not apply to all cases, or that it would be too easy to oversimplify. As you start the body of your essay, then, you want to acknowledge the other side of the argument—and then move on to establish the superior justification of the argument with which you agree.

Acknowledge a counter-argument (counter, that is, to your own), consider it, then show its weaknesses and lay it aside as refuted.

Acknowledge a second counter-argument, one that may be stronger, then lay it aside as being a possible way of looking at things, but not a wholly persuasive one.

Acknowledge a third counter-argument, one which you take much more seriously, consider its weaknesses, and concede that it really does have a point.

Then, at the turning point, accept that your own argument does have its limitations, but assert that it has even more supporting arguments, all of which are well justified (with evidence, reasoning, etc.). Make sure that this organizational pivotal point is clear, probably accompanied by a return of your thesis.

The rest of your essay will be in support of your own argument, the one established in your thesis. Treat your points in order of climax, with the most compelling supporting argument at the end.

Your concluding paragraph brings back your thesis with its acknowledgement of counter-argument, and affirms the point of view that you have now persuasively argued.

3 Using sequence in organization

Balance your essay between two or three perspectives. This pattern considers a sequence of alternatives, along with their limitations, and works toward the most fully supported perspective, if there is one, at the end.

In your introduction, recognize that there are alternative ways of looking at the knowledge issues you are examining, perhaps each based on somewhat different assumptions and leading to somewhat different implications. Identify the alternatives and establish a thesis that either supports all three (or two, or four) as equal possibilities or inclines toward one as most persuasive for a particular reason.

Treat one of the alternatives, giving supporting arguments and justifications for it, but conceding that it does have its limitations, which you present as counter-arguments to it.

Treat a second alternative similarly.

Treat your third alternative similarly if you are equally persuaded by all, but otherwise place the one which most persuades you at the end.

In your conclusion, take the balance that you consider appropriate and unite your essay by some kind of comparison—perhaps of assumptions and implications of different methodologies or worldviews.

It is not necessary to debate and refute points in your essay as long as you have explored counter-claims and their supporting arguments and evaluated them. It is not necessary to reach a conclusion in which one view excludes others if you have given well-supported arguments for including all.

Indeed, it is not essential to take a firm position on a knowledge issue to construct a thoughtful argument. After a course in TOK, you may be the more aware that there are many things that you (and perhaps all human beings) do not know for sure.

As you consider applying any of these three methods of handling counter-argument, again beware. These patterns are not cookie cutters with which to stamp out essays in a particular shape. They are merely argumentative approaches that can help you to sort out your own arguments and handle them with more confidence.

Oh. And one more thing. For all the patterns we have just given you, transitional expressions between sentences are helpful in guiding the reader through your essay by showing the relationship of your ideas.

similarity: similarly, likewise, in like manner, both…and…

difference: in contrast, in sharp contrast, unlike A, B…, however, nevertheless, on the contrary, yet, on the other hand, still

concession: to be sure, no doubt, of course, granted that…, it must be conceded/acknowledged that…

addition: in addition, not only…but also…, moreover, furthermore, besides, for one thing, for another, again

exemplification: for example, for instance, in particular, as a case in point

qualification: perhaps, maybe

emphasis: above all, in fact, indeed, most important, surely, indeed

summary: therefore, thus, consequently, clearly, finally, on the whole, to sum up, in conclusion, all in all

Step 5 Write your draft essay and revise it
The actual writing is only a small part of a good essay. If you have prepared well, however, the writing part should be straightforward—fortunately. After all, you have gone through some elaborate planning up to this point and, with the deadline looming ahead on the horizon, you still have no essay to hand in.

Before you write, use all the advice up to this point to write a clear outline. Know what your thesis is and keep a large copy of it pinned up somewhere so that you can see it at all times as you write. Know where you want to go with your arguments from the introduction right through to the conclusion. To write a golden essay, have a golden plan.

Beware, before you start, of some of the most common pitfalls that assessors of TOK essays can recognize in an instant. Avoid them at all costs.

Common pitfalls

- Avoid sweeping claims (overgeneralization and oversimplification). If you do not intend to show that you are aware you are making a large generalization or to analyse it in some way, stay far away from it or risk losing a lot of marks on criterion C, quality of analysis of knowledge issues. Go back to Chapter 4 if you need to refresh your memory on flawed generalization.

- Avoid caricatures and stereotyping: for example, all historians—willingly or not—are victims of bias; all adherents to religion possess blind, perfect faith in what their religion tells them to believe; because of their professions, scientists rely on reason, artists on emotion, always. Go back to the section on reasoning as a way of knowing for a review of the dangers of the hidden "all", and go back to the section on classification to remind yourself of its possible dangers.

- Avoid an essay composed principally of questions, paragraph upon paragraph of questions: What is truth? Can we ever be certain? How can we know? If you do not try to answer the questions, they will be considered as empty rhetoric and you will be penalized.

- Avoid rent-a-quote essays, in which you have entered key words from the title into the search engine in hopes that it will do the work for you. An essay that merely pastes quotations together can never substitute for one with critical analysis and argument.

- Avoid full-blown preaching from the pulpit. The *absence* of counter-claims, counter-arguments and acknowledgment and consideration of alternative perspectives will undermine the soundness of your own argument.

- Avoid using this book as a substitute for thought. We have written it to stimulate your *own* thinking—to encourage you to consider thoughtfully a multitude of knowledge issues within your own experience as a knower, with a perspective of your own of which you are increasingly aware. Please do not lift entire arguments or key examples from it, even with citations. Have confidence in yourself. After a course in TOK, you are entirely ready to fly on your own.

Now write.

Make your introduction concise. Use it to catch your reader's attention, establish the knowledge claims that you are going to discuss, and give your thesis. The taste for stylistic flourishes and fine writing in an introduction varies from culture to culture, but be warned that the marking criteria do not reward elegance of style, but do count the words in a preamble as part of your maximum allowed.

As you write, try to develop ideas in proportion to their importance in your overall plan. Your essay must be between 1,200 and 1,600 words in length, so control the degree to which you expand on an idea as you go. Doing so is not easy, but it is easier than trying to readjust the whole essay at the end. Beware: if your essay falls short of 1,200 words or goes over 1,600 you will be penalized in criterion D by being eligible for no more than 4 out of 10 marks.

Clarify concepts as you go, defining and/or exemplifying terms if they are key terms necessary to your argument. Do, however, exhibit restraint:

- Do not pad your essay with definitions of terms which are not particularly ambiguous.
- Do not drop into your essay lumps of definition which are not clearly linked to your argument and are ignored thereafter.
- Do not, above all, use a dictionary definition to bypass complexities: no teacher or examiner will be impressed if, after a course in which you discuss possible understandings of "truth" or "knowledge", you resolve this issue of knowledge by plunking down a citation from the dictionary as if you have thereby settled the matter.

Develop and illustrate your arguments with examples that, as the marking criteria demand, are "varied and effectively used". A well-chosen example can bring an argument to life. If you have gained perspective on your own assumptions as you interviewed victims of hunger, or expanded your knowledge in ways that you would argue to be significant as you learned to play the oboe, or realized an important connection between your history course and your literature course that makes you think further about an issue of knowledge, or recognized other cultural perspectives as you lived for a time in a country far from your own—or had innumerable other relevant experiences—then you have insights that could be shaped to provide effective examples within an overall variety.

Do not restrict your examples to personal ones, though, or over-emphasize your own experience at the expense of breadth. Select your examples from a wide variety of sources, traditions, cultures, and areas of knowledge. Draw from the media, books that you have read, protest walks or political rallies you have attended, lectures on special topics that you have heard, documentary films that you have seen. Draw from your other Diploma Programme courses and course textbooks. (Make sure, of course, to note the full reference of the book, newspaper, website or so forth for the purpose of acknowledging your sources later in footnoting.)

Make sure, as you select them, that the examples really do illustrate the points you are making. Anecdotes and descriptions may be very pleasant in themselves, but add nothing whatever to your essay if they are not used to exemplify a point that you are making through your argument. Recall, too, that examples do not prove a point; remember all that you learned about the evidence base necessary for sound inductive conclusions. Instead, they *illustrate* a point; they make a point clearer, clarify a definition, elaborate a comparison, or further a demonstration of your understanding. Note that hypothetical examples, though they may clarify a point, are more limited than real ones: "Suppose the historian from one side of the conflict were to write a history…" is far less effective than, for example, an account of the specific conflict between China and Japan over the history textbooks in Japanese schools.

Be warned that some examples have been used so often that every assessor is aware of their weaknesses. A reference to the Copernican Revolution and Galileo, for example, might illustrate a change in beliefs, but it does not demonstrate an understanding of revolutions in thinking within contemporary science. Notice that science has moved on in the past 400 years, and find another example. Similarly, do not use Inuit words for snow as your example to illustrate *anything* about language—unless you speak Inuktitut yourself. Far too many IB students in the world use this example, often without being clear about exactly what argumentative point the example is exemplifying. The world abounds with languages, with immense varieties of structure and vocabulary. From within the wealth of possible examples, find something else. Settling for trivial or flat examples, moreover, like burning your hand on a hot stove as an illustration of knowledge by experience, will not successfully demonstrate "independent thinking".

As you bring in examples or make generalizations, check your facts. Are your assertions accurate, sufficiently specific and detailed? Do you have a reference that can be traced for all the information that you have included? You will be penalized if you do not. Give the source of any quotation or unusual pieces of information, using accepted conventions of footnotes and bibliography. (If in doubt, it is better to footnote too much than too little.)

Polish the essay as you finish writing. Check for mistakes in sentence structure, grammar, word choice, and spelling. Errors can interfere with the clarity of your communication.

You are almost finished, but there is still an essential step between the draft and your final version: you have to make sure that you have not drifted from the expectations of a top performance that you had in mind as you began. With the marking criteria in hand, go through the essay to confirm that it is as close as you can make it to the description of the top achievement. Read carefully, check, and pick out features of your essay that you may still strengthen and polish. This done, you are ready, triumphantly, for the final step.

Step 6 Hand it in—and celebrate!

A good TOK essay demands that you think deeply about questions about knowledge and truth that thread themselves through all areas of your life. If you have done your best to take a significant issue of knowledge and make it your own, you have achieved a goal central to TOK and your International Baccalaureate diploma—and important in the growth of your own thinking. Congratulations! Regardless of what the mark on the essay may end up being, you have reason for celebration. You have won the gold.

8 References

Photographs, maps, artworks,and interviews are reproduced with permission.

Chapter 2 How do we know?

Sense perception

1 Damasio, A. 2005. *Descartes' Error: Emotion, Reason, and the Human Brain*. New York, USA. G.P. Putnam.

2 An effective search string might be "hearing sight animals".

3 Woolf, V. 1993. *Flush: A Biography*. New York and California. Harvest Books, Harcourt Inc. pp.130–132.

4 Johnston, V.S. 1999. *Why We Feel: The Science of Human Emotions*. Reading, MA, USA. Perseus Books. p.13.

5 Motluck, A. 29 January 2005. "Senses Special: The Art of Seeing Without Sight." *New Scientist*. http://www.newscientist.com/channel/being-human/brain/mg18524841.700 (accessed 20 November 2006).

6 Cohen, B. December 1992. "What Columbus 'Saw' in 1492". *Scientific American*. p.56.

Language

7 Alston, W.P. 1964. "Theories of Meaning" *Philosophy of Language*. Englewood Cliffs, NJ, USA. Prentice-Hall Inc.

8 Eco, U. 2001. *Experiences in Translation*. Trans. A. McEwen. Toronto, Canada. University of Toronto Press. p.17.

9 Sacks, O. 1990. *Seeing Voices*. New York, USA. Picador.

10 *Beyond the Bay: Music of Alumni of Lester B Pearson College of the Pacific*. "Sunlight in the Garden" track, by Simon Thomson. CD sold as a fundraiser for scholarships on the online store linked from http://www.pearsoncollege.ca (assessed 20 November).

11 Woods, K.M. 20 March 2003. *Take back the language: Words tell a story of their own*. http://www.poynter.org/content/content_view.asp?id=25910&sid=2 (accessed 20 November 2006).

12 Kiderra, I. 12 June 2006. *Backs to the future: Aymara language and gesture point to mirror-image view of time*. http://ucsdnews.ucsd.edu/thisweek/2006/june/06_12_backs.asp (accessed 20 November 2006).

13 Roszak, T. 1986. *The Cult of Information: The Folklore of Computers and the True Art of Thinking*. New York, USA. Pantheon Books.

Emotion

14 Nussbaum, M. 2001. *Upheavals of Thought: The Intelligence of Emotions*. Cambridge, UK. Cambridge University Press. p.1.

15 Ruiz Zafón, C. 2004. *The Shadow of the Wind*. Trans. L. Graves. London, UK. Penguin Books. p.35.

16 Gardner, H. *Multiple Intelligences: The Theory in Practice*. New York, USA. Basic Books. p.9. Cited in Goleman, D. 1997. *Emotional Intelligence*. Toronto, Canada. Bantam Books. p.39.

17 Goleman, D. 1995. *Emotional Intelligence*, Bantam, Toronto and New York. Appendix A.

18 Evans, D. 2001. Joy (some say "happiness"), distress (or "sadness"), anger, fear, surprise, and disgust. *Emotions*. Oxford, UK. Oxford University Press. p.7. You may also wish to look into Paul Ekman's research on core emotions.

19 Lancaster, J. 27 February 2006. "Pursuing Happiness". *The New Yorker*.
http://www.newyorker.com/printables/critics/060227crbo_books (accessed 20 November 2006).

20 Matsumoto, D. 1996. "The Diversity of Human Feeling". *Culture and Psychology*. Brooks/Cole, Florence, KY, USA. pp.247–251.

21 Ratey, J.J. 2001. *A User's Guide to the Brain: Perception, Attention, and the Four Theaters of the Brain*. New York, USA. Pantheon Books. p.231.

22 Philips, H. 11 October 2003. "The Pleasure Seekers". *New Scientist*. http://www.wireheading.com/pleasure.html (accessed 20 November 2006).

23 Haidt, J. 2006. *The Happiness Hypothesis*. New York, USA. Basic Books.

24 Ratey, J.J. 2001. *op cit*. p.251.

25 The Dalai Lama and Cutler, H. 1998. *The Art of Happiness: A Handbook for Living*. London, UK. Penguin Group. p.14. Chapter 1, which includes this quotation, may be available online at the Barnes & Noble website (perform a search for the title), http://www.barnesandnoble.com (accessed 20 November 2006).

26 LoTempio, S.M. 20 July 2006. *"From Fear to Storytelling: Covering Disability from Outside Your Comfort Zone."*
http://www.poynter.org/column.asp?id=58&aid=104987 (accessed 20 November 2006).

Reasoning

27 Dubuc, B. *The Evolutionary Layers of the Human Brain*.
http://www.thebrain.mcgill.ca/flash/a/a_05/a_05_cr/a_05_cr_her/a_05_cr_her.htm (accessed 18 June 2006).

28 Cohen, J.D. 2005. "The Vulcanization of the Human Brain: A Neural Perspective on Interactions Between Cognition and Emotion". *Journal of Economic Perspectives*, Vol. 19, No. 4, Fall. pp.3–24.
http://www.csbmb.princeton.edu/ncc/PDFs/Neural%20Economics/Cohen%20(JEP%202005).pdf (accessed 18 July 2006).

29 Markoff, J. 18 July 2006. "Brainy Robots Start Stepping into Daily Life". *New York Times*, 18 July 2006, Section A, Page 1, Column 2. http://www.nytimes.com/2006/07/18/technology/18brain.html (accessed 18 July 2006).

30 | Sunday | Chiara | eloquence |
Monday	Lee	empathy
Tuesday	Paul	athletic prowess
Wednesday	Tim	rationality
Thursday	Maimouna	essay skills
Friday	Christina	understanding self
Saturday	Sally	singing amazingly

31 Birner, B. *Language Acquisition*. Linguistic Society of America. http://www.lsadc.org/info/ling-faqs-lang_acq.cfm (accessed 18 June 2006).

32 Russell, B. 1912. *The Problems of Philosophy*. London, UK. Thornton Butterworth. Chapter VI, "On Induction". http://www.ditext.com/russell/rus6.html (accessed 20 July 2006).

33 Baiamonte, E. 1997. *The 91% Factor: Why Women Initiate 91% of Divorce*. American Political Press.

34 Blogs: IT Facts. 2 March 2006. *91% of emails in India are spam.* http://blogs.zdnet.com/ITFacts/?p=10306 (accessed 14 November 2006).

35 University of Rochester Medical Center. 5 June 2006. *82% of Cancer Patients Report "Chemo Brain" During, After Treatment.* http://www.urmc.rochester.edu/pr/News/story.cfm?id=1141 (accessed 14 November 2006).

36 Blogs: IT Facts. 6 October 2005. *By 2009 74% of all corporate phone lines will be VOIP.* http://blogs.zdnet.com/ITFacts/?p=9133 (accessed 14 November 2006).

37 Blogs: IT Facts. 17 July 2005. *56.2% of software developers use open source components.* http://blogs.zdnet.com/ITFacts/?p=8375 (accessed 14 November 2006).

38 *Personal communication*, Dr. Matthew Hayat. 19 July 2006.

39 British Broadcasting Corporation. *How To Understand Statistics.* 28 July 2003. http://www.bbc.co.uk/dna/h2g2/A1091350 (accessed 14 November 2006).

40 Similar activities: *Dealing with Induction, a game with playing cards* can be found at http://www.philosophersnet.com/games/dealing_with_induction/dws1.php (accessed 26 March 2006). There are many websites programmed to use the hypothetical-deductive method to guess what you are thinking. Also along these lines, the short and fun Animal Game can be found at http://animalgame.com (accessed 20 July 2006) and Mastermind at http://www.netrover.com/~jjrose/deduction/deduction.html (accessed 20 July 2006).

41 de Bono, E. 1975. *The Use of Lateral Thinking*. Markham, Ontario, Canada. Penguin Books. (First published 1967.) pp.22–23.

Classification

42 Uppsala Universitet. *Systema Naturae—an epoch-making book.* http://www.linnaeus.uu.se/online/animal/1_1.html (accessed 14 November 2006).

43 Hunt Institute. *Order from Chaos: Linnaeus Disposes. The search for a natural classification system.* http://huntbot.andrew.cmu.edu/HIBD/Exhibitions/OrderFromChaos/pages/02Linnaeus/search.shtml (accessed 14 November 2006).

44 Miller, G.A. 1956. "The Magical Number Seven, Plus or Minus Two: Some Limits on Our Capacity for Processing Information". *The Psychological Review*. Vol. 63. pp.81–97. http://www.well.com/user/smalin/miller.html (accessed 12 November 2006).

45 Canadian Human Rights Commission. 1928. *Defining "persons" under the BNA act.* http://www.chrc-ccdp.ca/en/timePortals/milestones/30mile.asp (accessed 14 November 2006).

46 Lakoff, G. 1987. *Women, Fire and Dangerous Things*. Chicago, IL, USA. University of Chicago Press. pp.5–6.

47 Grayling, A.C. 2001. *The Meaning of Things*. London, UK. Phoenix. pp.80–82.

48 Gladwell, M. 2005. *Blink*. New York, USA. Little, Brown. pp.84–85.

Chapter 3 Knowledge and the search for truth

1 Kampschror, B. 2006. "Pyramid Scheme". *Archaeology*, Vol. 59, No. 4, July/August. http://www.archaeology.org/0607/abstracts/bosnia.html (accessed 21 November 2006).

2 Rose, M. 2006. "The Bosnia–Atlantis Connection". *Archaeology*, 27 April 2006. http://www.archaeology.org/online/features/osmanagic (accessed 21 November 2006).

3 Markey, S. 2006. "Bosnia 'Pyramid' Is Not Human-Made, UK Expert Says". *National Geographic News*. 13 June 2006. http://news.nationalgeographic.com/news/2006/06/060613-pyramid.html (accessed 22 November 2006).

4 Fagan, G.G. 2003. "Seductions of Pseudoarchaeology: Far Out Television". *Archaeology*, Vol. 56, No. 3, May/June. http://www.archaeology.org/0305/abstracts/tv.html (accessed 22 November 2006).

Chapter 4 Persuasion and propaganda

1 Michael Beeler, IB student. Thanks for posing.

2 Sontag, S. 2001. *On Photography*. USA. Picador. pp.5–6.

3 Hitler, A. 1925. *Mein Kampf*. Boston, USA. Houghton Mifflin. p.176. Cited in: Pratkanis, A. and Aronson, E. 2001 *Age of Propaganda: The Everyday Use and Abuse of Persuasion*. New York, USA. W.H. Freeman and Company. pp.318–319.

4 Bragg, M. and Gardiner, R. 1998. *On Giants' Shoulders: Great Scientists and their Discoveries from Archimedes to DNA*. London, UK. Hodder and Stoughton. Epigraph.

5 Propaganda posters reproduced with permission.

6 Hedges, C. 2002. *War is a Force that Gives Us Meaning*. New York, USA. Public Affairs.

Chapter 5 Areas of knowledge

Mathematics

1 Crease, R.P. 2004. "The greatest equations ever". *Critical Point*. October 2004. http://physicsweb.org/articles/world/17/10/2/ (accessed 22 November 2006).

2 Jet Propulsion Laboratory, California Institute of Technology. 2003. "Spacecraft". *Voyager, The Interstellar Mission*. http://voyager.jpl.nasa.gov/spacecraft (accessed 22 November 2006).

3 Runde, V. 2003. "Why I don't like 'Pure Mathematics'". *π in the Sky*. September 2003. pp.30–31. http://www.pims.math.ca/pi/issue7/page30-31.pdf (accessed 22 November 2006).

4 Jaschke, S. 2002. *10 Theses in the Nature of Mathematics*. http://www.jaschke-net.de/cf-role-of-math.html (accessed 22 November 2006).

5   Runde, *ibid*.

6   "Euclidean geometry". 2006. *Encyclopædia Britannica Library from Encyclopædia Britannica 2005 Ultimate Reference Suite DVD*. Encyclopædia Britannica, Inc.

7   Weisstein, E.W. "Euclid's Postulates". *MathWorld—A Wolfram Web Resource*. http://mathworld.wolfram.com/EuclidsPostulates.html (accessed 22 November 2006).

8   Loy, J. 1998. *Non-Euclidean Geometries*. http://www.jimloy.com/geometry/parallel.htm (accessed 22 November 2006).

9   Lappé, F.M., Collins, J. and Rosset, P. 1998. *World Hunger: Twelve Myths*. 2nd edn. New York, USA. Grove Press. p.3.

10 Notice the point at which you divided by $(A-B) = 0$, because $A = B$.

11 Weisstein, E.W. "Fermat's Last Theorem". *MathWorld—A Wolfram Web Resource*. http://mathworld.wolfram.com/FermatsLastTheorem.html (accessed 22 November 2006).

12 Public Broadcasting Corporation. "Solving Fermat: Andrew Wiles". 2000. Material supplementary to "The Proof", episode of *NOVA*. http://www.pbs.org/wgbh/nova/proof/wiles.html (accessed 22 November 2006).

13 Hesselink, W.H. 2005. *Computer verification of Wiles' proof of Fermat's Last Theorem*. http://www.cs.rug.nl/%7Ewim/fermat/wilesEnglish.html (accessed 22 November 2006).

14 Overbye, D. 15 August 2006. "Elusive Proof, Elusive Prover: A New Mathematical Mystery". *New York Times*. http://www.nytimes.com/2006/08/15/science/15math.html (accessed 17 August 2006).

15 Public Broadcasting Corporation. *Solving Fermat: Andrew Wiles*. *ibid*.

16 Irvine, A.D. 2003. "Principia Mathematica". *Stanford Encylopedia of Philosophy*. http://plato.stanford.edu/entries/principiamathematica (accessed 22 November 2006).

17 S. Banach, quoted. University of Connecticut Department of Mathematics. *Mathematics Quotes*. http://www.math.uconn.edu/miscellaneous/quotes.php (accessed 22 November 2006).

18 Chaitin, G.J. 1975. "Randomness and Mathematical Proof". *Scientific American*, Vol. 232, No. 5, pp.47–52. http://www.cs.auckland.ac.nz/CDMTCS/chaitin/sciamer.html (accessed 22 November 2006).

19 Chaitin, G.J. 2000. *"A Century of Controversy over the Foundations of Mathematics"*. In: Calude, C. and Paun, G. 2000. *Finite versus Infinite*. London, UK. Springer-Verlag. pp.75–100. http://www.umcs.maine.edu/%7Echaitin/lowell.html (accessed 22 November 2006).

The natural sciences

20 *Quotes About Thinking*. http://quotes.zaadz.com/topics/thinking?page=2 (accessed 22 November 2006).

21 "Live Long? Die Young? Answer Isn't Just in Genes". *New York Times*. http://www.nytimes.com/2006/08/31/health/31age.html (accessed 22 November 2006).

22 Public Broadcasting Corporation. "Deep Jungle: New Frontiers". *Episode of Nature*. http://www.pbs.org/wnet/nature/deepjungle/episode1_bios.html (accessed 22 November 2006).

23 Example attributed to George Porter. Llewellyn Smith, C.H. "What is the Use of Basic Science?". *What is CERN?* http://press.web.cern.ch/Public/Content/Chapters/AboutCERN/ WhatIsCERN/BasicScience/BasicScience3/BasicScience3-en.html (accessed 22 November 2006).

24 Derry, G.N. 1999. *What Science Is and How It Works*. Princeton, NJ, USA. Princeton University Press. Chapter 1.

25 McDuffie Jr., T.E. (2001). "Scientists—Geeks & Nerds? Dispelling Teachers' Stereotypes of Scientists". *Science and Children*. May 2001. http://www.nsta.org/main/news/pdf/sc0105_16.pdf (accessed 22 November 2006).

26 Medawar, P. 1982. *Pluto's Republic*. Oxford, UK. Oxford University Press. p.116.

27 Klemke, E.D., Hollinger R. and Kline, A.D. 1980. "Introduction to Part 3, Theory and Observation". *Introductory Readings in the Philosophy of Science*. New York, Prometheus Books, pp.142–143.

28 Polanyi, J. 19 June 2005. *Toronto Star*, p.D1.

29 Packard, N. in Gleick, J. 1987. *Chaos: Making a New Science*. New York, USA. Penguin Books. p.251.

30 Gleick, J. *op cit*. p. 305.

31 Gleick, J. *op cit*. p. 251.

32 Medawar, P. *op cit*. p. 53.

33 Boiling point of water calculator at Big Green Egg. *Boiling Point of Water*. http://www.biggreenegg.com/boilingPoint.htm (accessed 22 November 2006).

34 Park, R.L. 31 January 2003. "The Seven Warning Signs of Bogus Science". *Chronicle Review, The Chronicle of Higher Education*. http://chronicle.com/free/v49/i21/21b02001.htm (accessed 22 November 2006).

The human sciences

35 Avidor, R. *Murphy's Laws Site*. http://www.murphys-laws.com/murphy/murphy-laws.html (accessed 22 November 2006).

36 Ministry of Education, Chile. 2003. "Filosofía y Psciología: Problemas de Conocimiento". Programa de Estudio de Educación Media. pp.129–130. (Translation: "Problems of Knowledge (Philosophy and Psychology)". *Programme of Studies for High School Students*.

37 Craven, J. 1990. *Economics: An Integrated Approach to Fundamental Principles*. Cambridge, UK. Blackwell. p.11. Italics added by author.

38 Geertz, C. quoted in American Anthropological Association. *What is Anthropology?* http://www.aaanet.org/anthbroc.htm (accessed 22 November 2006).

39 Crawford, Carolyn, interviewed in British Broadcasting Corporation. "Galaxies". *In Our Time* (podcast series). 29 June 2006.

History

40 Kirk, T. 2003. *Physics for the IB Diploma (IB Study Guides)*. Oxford, UK. Oxford University Press. p.7.

The ichthyologist

41 Eddington, Sir Arthur E. 1958. *The Philosophy of Physical Science*. Ann Arbor Paperbacks, University of Michigan Press. p.16.

The rainbow

42 Acknowledgment: This article was inspired by Raymond Lee and Alistair Fraser's *The Rainbow Bridge*, Pennsylvania State University Press, 2001, from which most of its examples are taken.

43 Lee, R. and Fraser, A. *op cit.* p.6.

44 Lee, R. and Fraser, A. *op cit.* p.321.

45 Harburg, E. Y. 1939. "Somewhere Over the Rainbow". Lyrics to *The Wizard of Oz* movie theme song. http://thewizardofoz.warnerbros.com/movie/cmp/r-lyrics.html (accessed 27 November 2006).

46 Ciceronis, M.T. 1896. *De Natura Deorum (On the Nature of the Gods)*, Chapter XX, written 45 BC. Trans. Francis Brooks. London. Methuen. http://oll.libertyfund.org/Texts/Cicero0070/NatureOfGods/HTMLs/0040_Pt04_Book3.html (accessed 27 November 2006).

47 Wordsworth, W. 1875. "CCLXXXVI. 'My heart leaps up when I behold'". *The Golden Treasury*. Francis T. Palgrave, ed. http://www.bartelby.com/106/286.html (accessed 27 November 2006).

48 Lee, R. and Fraser, A. *op cit.* p.43.

49 Merriam-Webster. 2003. *Merriam-Webster's Collegiate Dictionary*, 11th edn. Springfield, MA, USA. Merriam-Webster.

50 Keats, J. 1884. "Lamia". *The Poetical Works of John Keats*. http://www.bartleby.com/126/37.html (accessed 27 November 2006).

51 Lee, R. and Fraser, A. *op cit.* pp.22–25.

52 Constable, J. Perhaps 1812. Comment accompanying the oil on canvas "Landscape and Double Rainbow". Victoria and Albert Museum no. 328–1888. http://www.vam.ac.uk/school_stdnts/schools_teach/teachers_resources/constable_resource/biography/index.html (accessed 27 November 2006).

53 Lee, R. and Fraser, A. *op cit.* Chapter 7, "Color the Rainbow to Suit Yourself".

54 Yahweh (God), Genesis 9:13.

55 Lee, R. and Fraser, A. *op cit.* p.27.

The arts

56 The three quotations are from *Album Notes, Beyond the Bay: Music of Alumni of Lester B Pearson College of the Pacific*. Theo and Eileen Dombrowski, (eds.) 2004. www.pearsoncollege.ca online store.

57 *ibid.*

58 *ibid.*

Ethics

59 Kofi Annan on Guernica, November 3, 1998. in van Hensbergen, G. 2004. *Guernica. The Biography of a Twentieth-Century Icon.* London. Bloomsbury. p.1.

60 His Holiness the Dalai Lama. 1999. *Ethics for the New Millennium.* New York. Riverhead. pp.21–24.

Chapter 6 Knowledge in the world

1   The World Bank, Washington DC. 1999. *Summary, World Development Report 1998/1999.* http://www.worldbank.org/wdr/wdr98/overview.pdf (accessed 11 November 2006).

2   Lappé, F.M., Collins, J. and Rosset, p.1998. *World Hunger: Twelve Myths.* 2nd edn. New York, USA. Grove Press. p.12.

3   *ibid.*

4   Nussbaum, M. 1993. "Non-Relative Virtues: An Aristotelian Approach". In M. Nussbaum, and A. Sen, (eds.) *The Quality of Life (Studies in Development Economics).* Oxford, UK. Clarendon Press, p.263.

5   Post, T. 2005. "Strengthening Rural Communities". *Hunger Report 2005 Executive Summary: Bread for the World Institute's 15th Annual Report on the State of World Hunger.* http://www.bread.org/learn/hunger-reports/hunger-report-2005-executive-summary.html (accessed 22 November 2006).

6   Pollan, M. 2001. *The Botany of Desire: A Plant's-Eye View of the World.* New York, USA. Random House. p.191

7   KCTS Television, 2005. *Hoodia. Silent Killer: The Unfinished Campaign Against Hunger.* http://www.silentkillerfilm.org/hoodia.html (accessed 11 November 2006).

8   Tony Marshallsay, commenting on "Viewpoints: The water debate". *BBC News*, 27 November 2004. http://news.bbc.co.uk/1/hi/sci/tech/3752590.stm (accessed 11 November 06).

9   Schoch, R. 2001. "A Conversation with Miguel Altieri". *California Alumni*, June 2001. http://www.alumni.berkeley.edu/Alumni/Cal_Monthly/June_2001/QA-_A_conversation_with_Miguel_Altieri.asp (accessed 11 November 06).

10 KCTS Television, 2005. "Kinyua M'Mbijjewe". *Silent Killer: The Unfinished Campaign Against Hunger.* http://www.silentkillerfilm.org/interview_mmbijjewe.html (accessed 11 November 2006).

11 Schoch, R. *op cit.*

12 International Baccalaureate Organization. 2006. "The IB learner profile". *IB Learner Profile Booklet.* p.6. http://www.ibo.org/programmes/documents/learner_profile_en.pdf (accessed 22 November 2006).

13 *ibid.*

Chapter 7 Course assessment

1 International Baccalaureate Organization. 2006. *Diploma Programme: Theory of Knowledge Guide*. p.5.

2 "Assessment criteria. Part 1, Essay on a prescribed title, B, Knower's perspective". In International Baccalaureate Organization. 2006. *Diploma Programme: Theory of Knowledge Guide*. Cardiff, Wales. p.53.

3 "Assessment criteria. Part 2, Presentation, C, Knower's perspective". In International Baccalaureate Organization. 2006. Diploma *Programme: Theory of Knowledge Guide*. Cardiff, Wales. p.59.

4 "Assessment criteria. Part 2, Presentation". In International Baccalaureate Organization. 2006. *Diploma Programme: Theory of Knowledge Guide*. Cardiff, Wales. pp.57–60.

5 "Assessment Criteria. Part 1, Essay on a prescribed title". In International Baccalaureate Organization. 2006. *Diploma Programme: Theory of Knowledge Guide*. Cardiff, Wales. pp.52–56.

Twenty-one thematic links

The following list of page references is not a conventional index tabulating every person or supporting example mentioned in this book. Instead, its goal is to demonstrate some interconnections and encourage you, the student, to take similar key concepts and consider the TOK course in their light. This list complements the linking terms offered in the TOK subject guide, and offers yet further opportunities for you to knit together central ideas of knowledge.

Such a list can never be complete, however, as concepts of "critical thinking", "truth", and "knowledge" are part of the very weave of this book, this course, and all of your learning. It is for you ultimately to create your own links in your mind as you integrate the ideas of the TOK course into the whole of your knowledge.

Assumptions: 73-5, 55-6, 80, 101, 122-3, 129-30, 145, 166-7, 180, 182-5, 196, 225-8, 232, 242-3, 246, 256, 259, 268, 270, 281, 285-6, 292-5; and culture: 30-1, 43, 62, 67, 88, 123, 172, 178, 216; premises: 71-7, 81-2, 122-3, 129, 138-41, 224-5, 259; axioms: 138-41, 146-7, 166, 173, 195; hypotheses: 42, 81-2, 154, 156-8, 161, 169, 192.

Beliefs: 4, 9, 15-6, 19, 50, 55-6, 63, 88, 99-111, 115, 122-4, 135, 188, 193, 207, 213, 238, 245, 282, 287; and knowledge: 9, 109-111, 150-1, 196-7; justifications for: 58, 73, 104-11, 113-4, 120, 132, 149, 154, 228-234; and culture: 15-6, 29-30, 58, 86-8, 98-9, 120, 128, 204, 235, 237.

Cause and Explanation: 36, 50-3, 55, 64, 107, 127-9, 132-3, 149-51, 153-5, 158-161, 163-4, 170, 173, 176-7, 187-193, 195, 204, 221, 227, 233-4, 237-9, 242, 245, 249, 252-60, 271-2, 280, 291; and description: 17, 19, 23-6, 28-9, 35, 39-40, 43-5, 48, 53-4, 63, 69, 78, 83, 86, 91, 108-9, 134-7, 140-1 153-4, 158-60, 161, 166, 169-75, 188, 19-205, 204, 207, 229, 233, 244-5, 248-9, 275-6, 295; and correlation: 78-9, 98, 127-9, 161, 177, 182, 249; and prediction: 54, 64, 157-8, 161, 163, 165, 167, 178, 182-4, 227, 231, 233-4, 280.

Classification: 53-4, 64, 83-8, 90-5, 105, 108-9, 131, 135-6, 141, 148-9, 153, 159, 171, 187, 196, 205, 246, 250-1, 272, 289, 294; and categories: 33-4, 50, 68, 70-1, 73-5, 83-8, 90-5,

100, 103, 106-11, 131, 150, 156, 172, 183, 205.

Emotion: 4, 49-64, 83, 86-8, 90-3, 96, 107-10, 151, 245-6, 251-4, 294; and creativity and intuition: 4, 62-3, 82, 108-9, 141-3, 156, 164, 192-4, 213, 219-20, 277; and areas of knowledge: 153, 172-6, 179, 189, 193-4, 204-8, 213-4, 217-8, 222-3, 227, 231, 235-6, 239; and culture: 53-4, 60-2; and persuasion: 103-4, 118-121, 129, 237-8.

Generalizations: 12, 54-6, 68-9, 73, 76-82, 85-8, 91, 124-5, 152-3, 165, 167, 190, 194-5, 207, 217, 229, 232-4, 248, 285, 292-6; in the sciences: 27, 65, 154, 157, 160-1, 167-8, 171-6, 183, 204, 229; patterns: 26-7, 52, 54-5, 61, 65, 69, 74, 81-2, 91, 123-4, 134-8, 144, 152-3, 158-64, 173, 190, 195-7, 205, 214, 288-93; stereotypes and prejudice: 57, 62, 85-8, 99-100, 118, 134, 156, 169, 172, 197, 248, 262, 270-1, 294.

Justification and Evidence (see also Belief): 14, 22, 53, 58, 65, 71, 73, 77, 80-1, 86, 101-5, 108-14, 116-7, 119-20, 124-5, 150-1, 256, 259, 270-1, 282-5, 291-2; and counter-justifications: 69, 75-6, 86, 102, 114, 167, 225, 235, 256-9, 281, 285-8, 290-4; and areas of knowledge: 92, 128, 130-3, 141-5, 149, 155, 160-1, 165-8, 173-4, 187, 190-4, 197, 199-201, 208, 222-9, 235, 250, 253-7. See also every page in this book.

Knower(s) and Knowing: 50-1, 92-7, 110-1; You as a Knower: 10, 19-21, 26, 28-9, 35-7, 39, 40-1, 42-4, 46-8, 50-2, 55-67, 69-70, 74, 76, 79, 81-2, 84-5, 87-8, 90-4, 97-102, 104-8, 110-2, 115-8, 120-1, 127-8, 130-1, 134, 136, 138, 141-2, 145, 148-50, 152, 154, 156, 158, 161, 164, 168-70, 172-81, 184-90, 194-5, 197, 199-201, 204, 206, 208, 210-3, 217-8, 220-1, 223-4, 226-8, 230-1, 239, 241-65, 266-96; communities of knowers: 19, 86, 103, 132-3, 142-5 (see also Knowledge Creation Diagram); and certainty: 4, 9, 60, 75-81, 95, 101-4, 113, 146-8, 166-7, 204, 223, 232-5, 251, 256, 259, 291, 294.

Knowledge Creation Diagram: 114, 132-3, 144-8, 155-60, 164-5, 167-70, 182, 211-3, 222-3, 231.

Knowledge: 90-114 (see also Belief); knowledge issues: 6, 133, 170, 172, 188, 190, 201, 204, 246, 248-9, 151,

255, 265, 267-92, 294; knowledge claims: 91, 94, 97-114, 120, 132-3, 145-6, 149-51, 159, 165, 167, 207, 225, 239, 249, 268, 294; knowledge sources: 16-8, 98-9, 108-14, 120-1, 185-90, 194-7, 200, 216, 226-8, 232; knowledge and usefulness: 16, 84-6, 90, 97, 100-3, 110, 130-1, 135-6, 140-1, 144-5, 148, 151-5, 158, 161, 163, 166-7, 182-4, 192, 195, 270; knowledge and power: 13-5, 45, 86, 117-8, 133, 184-5, 197, 207, 216-8, 238, 254-5.

Language: 32-49, 117-8, 137-8; and areas of knowledge: 40-1, 134-5, 137-8, 148, 153, 174-80, 200, 205-7, 214, 216-8, 223, 226, 229, 251; and persuasion: 42, 104, 117-9, 129, 218, 248, 251, 259; and culture: 34, 36-7, 41-2, 46-7.

Maps: 12-6, 48, 78, 90-1, 110, 116; and persuasion: 116, 259.

Metaphors: 40-1, 46-7, 54, 64, 72, 88, 90, 129-30, 133-4, 141, 156-8, 160, 185-7, 195-6, 248-9, 251, 259, 270; and persuasion: 118, 125, 127, 259, 270.

Photographs: 21, 48, 79, 90, 93, 114, 116, 197, 252-3, 256; and persuasion: 116, 121, 248, 251, 253, 259, 270.

Reasoning and Fallacies: 64-86, 108, 115-29; and areas of knowledge: 76-88, 131, 138-44, 146-9, 156, 165-7, 174-6, 191-4, 207, 225-230, 232, 235-7; and persuasion: 104, 108, 115, 121-23, 127-7, 129-132, 150-1, 224-6, 270, 288.

Sense Perception: 21-32; and areas of Knowledge: 31-2, 114, 138, 155-8, 164-7, 173-6, 204, 207, 219, 227, 231; and persuasion: 115-7.

Statistics: 78-80, 125; and persuasion: 125, 127, 181, 248, 251, 253, 259.

Symbolic Representations (see also language, maps, photographs, statistics): 12-6, 32-4, 41-3, 48, 79-80, 84, 90, 114-5, 117, 124, 135-8, 141, 153, 185, 188, 210, 213, 248, 251-2, 258; symbolic systems: 36-7, 41, 48, 135-141, 146-7.

Technology: 24-5, 113, 116, 141, 143, 155-9, 162-3.

Truth and Validity: 70, 74-6, 102-5, 100-10, 114, 139-41, 146-7, 149, 154, 157-8.

World Hunger: 13, 21, 127, 141, 170, 240-65, 274, 295.